JBuilder Essentials

Cary Jensen
Blake Stone
Loy Anderson

Osborne McGraw-Hill

Berkeley New York St. Louis San Francisco
Auckland Bogotá Hamburg London Madrid
Mexico City Milan Montreal New Delhi Panama City
Paris São Paulo Singapore Sydney
Tokyo Toronto

Osborne/**McGraw-Hill**
2600 Tenth Street
Berkeley, California 94710
U.S.A.

For information on translations or book distributors outside the U.S.A., or to arrange bulk purchase discounts for sales promotions, premiums, or fund-raisers, please contact Osborne/**McGraw-Hill** at the above address.

JBuilder Essentials

JBuilder Essentials

1234567890 DOC DOC 901987654321098

ISBN 0-07-882223-8

Publisher
Brandon A. Nordin

Editor-in-Chief
Scott Rogers

Coordinating Editor
Loy Anderson

Acquisitions Editor
Megg Bonar

Project Editor
Mark Karmendy

Editorial Assistant
Stephane Thomas

Technical Editor
Blake Stone

Copy Editor
Dennis Weaver

Proofreader
Pat Mannion

Indexers
Cary Jensen
Loy Anderson

Computer Designer
Sue Albert

Illustrator
Arlette Crosland

Cover Illustration
Mina Reimer

About the Authors...

Cary Jensen, Ph.D., is President of Jensen Data Systems, Inc., a Houston-based company that provides database developers for application development and support. He is an award-winning, best-selling author of 15 books, including *Delphi In Depth* (1996, Osborne/McGraw-Hill) and *Programming Paradox 5 for Windows* (1995, Sybex). Cary is also Contributing Editor of *Delphi Informant Magazine*, where his column, DBNavigator, appears monthly. Over the years he has published more than 150 articles in a wide variety of computer magazines, and has written training material for numerous software training courses. For the past several years he has been an advisory board member for the annual, international Borland Conference, and is one of the world's leading speakers on the software seminar and conference circuit.

Blake Stone has recently become a Senior Software Engineer on Borland's JBuilder R&D team. As the Technical Director for DKW Systems Corporation, a Calgary-based consulting firm specializing in leading-edge software development and integration, Blake was responsible for providing technical insight for numerous application development projects. His familiarity with a wide variety of object-oriented development environments and passionate attitude towards elegant solutions has made him a popular speaker at conferences around the world.

Loy Anderson, Ph.D., is Vice President of Jensen Data Systems, Inc. Loy has teamed with coauthor Cary Jensen as an award-winning, best-selling author of 15 computer books. She also writes courseware for software training that is distributed worldwide, and previously served as Associate Editor of *Paradox Informant Magazine*. Loy has a Ph.D. in Human Factors Psychology specializing in human-computer interaction.

Table of Contents

Acknowledgments

Writing, like programming, tends to be both an intense and a solitary process. The production of a book, however, like a large application development project, requires the input and contributions of many individuals. We would like to take this opportunity to thank those others who participated, both directly and indirectly, in this book. In particular, we wish to thank Scott Rogers, Editor-in-Chief at Osborne/McGraw-Hill, at whose suggestion we undertook this project more than a year and a half ago. (Who knew then that the product wouldn't ship until September 1997?) We also want to thank Megg Bonar, our Acquisitions Editor, for her input and guidance on this project; Mark Karmendy, our Project Editor, for navigating this book smoothly through production; Dennis Weaver, for his excellent copy edit; and the many others at Osborne who worked on the book. Our appreciation also goes to DKW Systems Corporation, for their enormous patience and generosity for donating Blake Stone's time to the writing process—they are to be commended for their insight regarding JBuilder's potential at a very early stage. We want to thank our many good friends at Borland International, Inc., who provided us with assistance and support at various stages in this process, including Nan Borreson, Karen Giles, Christine Ellis, David Intersimone, Michel Gerin, Edwin Desouza, and Charles Calvert. We also want to thank Theresa Lanowitz, JBuilder Group Project Manager, for her kind foreword. And we certainly do not want to forget the members of the JBuilder's R&D team whose insight into the inner workings of the product proved invaluable to this project. In particular, thanks to Jayson Minard, Carl Quinn, Carl Fravel, Steve Shaughnessy, and Joe Nuxoll. Thanks also go to Sejer Johansen of DAPUG and Sejer Johansen Informatik ApS, Neal Ford of the DSW Group Inc., as well as our many other friends at Softbite International, Desktop Associates Ltd, The DSW Group Inc., and Infocan Management Consultants Group Inc., for their motivation and support. And last, but not least, we want to thank Mark Brady, who was intimately involved in the initial stages of the project.

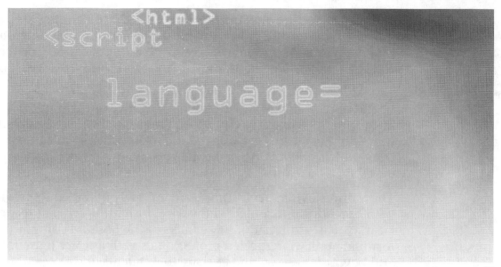

Foreword

Over the years, the name Borland has become synonymous with great technology. Borland has led the technology charge in the name of the developer by delivering creative and innovative products. Borland was the first software company to introduce a compiler for the PC. Borland raised the bar for development tools with Delphi and made "visual programming" truly visual. And now, Borland is leading the way in Java development tools with JBuilder. Borland is a developer's company founded by developers for developers.

When the shot of the Java revolution rang out around the world, Borland was swift to respond with a plan. Borland announced that a truly productive and visual Java IDE tool would be created for developers of the Java language. Because Borland is very much in tune with developers' needs, the rich features of JBuilder 1.0 are viewed as triumphant by Java developers. Java developers want a productive and visual environment in which to work; they need to be able to create, deploy, and share JavaBeans with other developers; and they need to be able to create database applications. JBuilder delivers on all of these requirements to the Java developer.

JBuilder's truly refined architecture provides the developer with significant advantages in this fast paced market. JBuilder is built on the JDK 1.1 from Sun, supports a fully extensible architecture, and supports JavaBeans completely. In fact, Borland was instrumental in defining and creating the specifications for the industry standard JavaBeans component model. Using JBuilder, developers can create real database applications, debug their Java code in a world-class environment, and work with the JavaBeans component model.

In this book, you will experience the elegance of the JBuilder environment, learn to think like a Java developer, understand what true database functionality means, get a firsthand look at what JavaBeans is all about, and truly understand how to make the Java mantra of "write once and run everywhere" a reality.

The authors of *JBuilder Essentials* are uniquely qualified to provide the reader with exceptional technical knowledge, insightful tips and techniques, and clear, concise explanations. Members of the Borland community are indeed fortunate to have respected professionals such as Cary Jensen, Blake Stone, and Loy Anderson willing to share their talents and expertise.

Using JBuilder, developers are able to create 100 percent pure Java applications. Pure Java applications mean that the previously unattainable holy grail of platform independence has been achieved. Platform independence today means any desktop box can run any application...but just imagine the possibilities of what platform independence can deliver in the future! Borland and JBuilder are right there ready to work with Java developers to deliver on the present and the future of computing.

Theresa Lanowitz
JBuilder Group Product Manager
Borland International

Introduction

It seems as though Java has been on the minds of almost every computer professional for several years now. Until recently, however, Java development tools were positively stone age. Early adopters used little more than a simple word processor to write their code, compiling their source using the command-line compiler from Sun Microsystems, Inc. With the introduction of JBuilder, those days are gone forever. JBuilder provides you with a tightly integrated development environment that not only gives you drag-and-drop placement of JavaBeans components, but provides you with an integrated debugger as well. In fact, JBuilder does so much to assist in the development of Java code it is sometimes possible to forget that you are working in Java.

This power, however, comes at a price. While JBuilder is a remarkable piece of software, it requires a lot of RAM (Random Access Memory) in order to run. We want to make this clear right up front—if you do not have enough RAM in your computer, you will not be happy with JBuilder's performance. Although Borland states that 32MB of RAM is a minimum, they point out that 48MB or more is recommended. Even with 48MB of RAM, you might still not be happy. It has been our experience that JBuilder requires at least 64MB of RAM in order to provide the snappy performance you will demand from an application development environment.

If you currently do not have enough memory in your computer, this requirement may sound extreme. Fortunately, RAM has never been cheaper than it is right now. As a result, you can save your sanity and time by upgrading your computer's memory as soon as possible.

If your computer simply does not support enough RAM but utilizes Windows 95, you might want to consider switching to Windows NT 4.0. Some developers have reported that Windows NT, with 48MB RAM, is a workable configuration. We are not actually suggesting that you should upgrade to Windows NT in order to use JBuilder; however, if you have been considering this move anyway, here is one more reason in favor of doing so.

Another thing to keep in mind is that Java is a new programming language, with many future enhancements on the horizon. Anyone who developed in C++ 10 years ago will remember what that was like—lots of promising capabilities, but it took time for them to be fully realized. Clearly, Java is poised to be one of the leading languages as we move into the 21st century. As an early adopter of Java, you should be prepared for changes and additions as this language matures.

About This Book

This book is designed to provide you with a solid foundation for the use of JBuilder to create Java applications and applets. In writing this book, we have made every attempt to capture the spirit of Java development with JBuilder. In order to achieve this, we have gone out of our way to avoid making assumptions about what types of programming experience you have. Specifically, we are not assuming that you are already a seasoned Java developer. Indeed, Java is so young that this designation applies to few individuals anyway. In addition, unlike the vast majority of Java books we have read, we do not assume that you are a C/C++ programmer.

If you are a C developer, you should feel right at home with both JBuilder and this book. However, if you have little or no C experience, we feel that you will find our descriptions to be clear and complete.

This book begins with an introduction to JBuilder, including an overview of both JBuilder and Java. It continues in Chapter 2 with a look at Java's object model, and how JBuilder permits you to easily work with and explore objects. In Chapters 3, 4, and 5, the basic design elements of applications are discussed. Topics covered here include how to control windows, how to define menu and tool bars, and how to use layout managers.

Applets are explored in Chapter 6. Here you will learn how to create and view them within JBuilder.

Chapters 7, 8, and 9 cover database application development in JBuilder. Chapter 7 provides you with an overview of database issues and JBuilder's related components. In Chapter 8 you learn how to create several types of database applications, and in Chapter 9 you learn how to leverage Java to add advanced features to your database applications.

Chapter 10 shows you how to use threads in Java, and describes the support JBuilder provides you for doing this. In Chapter 11 you learn how to use JBuilder's integrated Debugger, and in Chapter 12 the issues surrounding deployment of your applications and applets are discussed.

In Chapter 13 you will find a detailed discussion of JavaBeans, and in Chapter 14 you will learn how to create "Beans" of your own. And finally, Chapter 15 takes a look at the model-view architecture used in many of the JavaBeans provided in JBuilder.

If you are new to Java, or are looking for a concise review of the language, Appendix A and B are for you. These are detailed descriptions, but we decided to have them as appendixes rather than disrupt the focus on JBuilder maintained within the book's chapters. However, we do recommend that if these appendixes are of interest to you, you read them first. Alternatively, read them after reading Chapter 1 but before continuing onto Chapter 2.

Many different applications and applets are created during the course of this book. We encourage you to work through the steps to create the projects described. We have also provided the source code for almost all the projects on the CD-ROM that accompanies this book. (Some projects are so trivial that they do not appear on the CD-ROM.) Appendix C describes the steps you must take if you want to access these projects. Appendix C also includes the URL (Uniform Resource Locator) for a web site that we have set up to support this book.

Who Is This Book for?

This book is for anyone interested JBuilder. If you are a developer or software engineer, you will find sufficient detail to begin developing Java applications and applets using JBuilder. If you are interested in understanding how JBuilder speeds Java application development, you too will find the information here that you need.

About the CD-ROM

This book is accompanied by a CD-ROM. This disk contains two files of particular interest. The first is the JBuilder Professional Publisher's Edition. This is a special version of JBuilder that you can use to evaluate this product.

JBuilder Professional Publisher's Edition is a full version of JBuilder Professional. Once installed, however, you will be able to use it for 90 days, and then it will expire. This should provide you with sufficient time to evaluate this product. We are confident that once you try JBuilder, and see what it can do for your Java development efforts, you will be eager to purchase the full version of JBuilder.

The second file of interest contains the sample projects described in this book. If you intend to work through the steps described in the various chapters of this book, you will not need these projects. However, if you want to sidestep creating the projects manually, see Appendix C for a description of installing these files.

The CD-ROM also contains some additional files of interest. For a complete description of these files, read the file named README.TXT that appears in the root directory of the CD-ROM.

Where to Start

At the beginning? Maybe. As mentioned in a preceding section, we have provided two appendixes that give you an introduction to the Java language. If you have not previously programmed in Java, you will want to start there. Alternatively, you might want to read Chapter 1, "Overview of JBuilder," to provide yourself with a frame of reference before reading these appendixes.

If you are a Java programmer already, start at the beginning. Each chapter builds on the one that precedes it, and you will find yourself building Java applications with JBuilder in no time at all.

CHAPTER 1

Overview of JBuilder

JBuilder is the new Java development environment from Borland International. JBuilder permits you to create Java applications and applets quickly and easily. The applications and applets that you build are pure Java, meaning that they consist of the same byte code that you would produce if you wrote your Java programs manually and compiled them using the Java compiler. JBuilder simplifies this process tremendously, however, by writing much of the required Java code for you, and providing you with support for the code that you must write manually.

The key to JBuilder is its Integrated Development Environment, or IDE. The JBuilder IDE consists of the main JBuilder window, the AppBrowser, and a large number of support dialogs. You use the IDE to create, modify, maintain, debug, and deploy your Java applications and applets.

Because the effective use of JBuilder's IDE is essential, it is the primary focus of this chapter. However, this chapter begins with a brief introduction to the Java language, what it is and why it is important. Because this book focuses on JBuilder, and not on Java in general, this discussion is necessarily brief.

The introduction to the IDE begins with a general overview of its various parts, then continues with a tour of the essential tools that it provides. In order to provide you with a meaningful reference point for this discussion, this chapter walks you through the creation of a simple Java application using JBuilder. At each stage in the process, the JBuilder tools that you use are introduced.

Overview of Java

Java is a true object-oriented language that incorporates some of the most powerful new concepts in computer language design introduced in the last two decades. Java was designed to make programmers more productive by hiding much of the complexity that is visible in other languages. While Java strictly enforces many rules at compile time, it also includes features to allow extremely dynamic code to be written. Java includes native support for multithreaded development, makes use of modern exception handling, and applies sophisticated garbage collection techniques to take care of memory management automatically.

Java is a compiled language, but the object code is not machine specific. Any computer with a Java Virtual Machine (VM) can run the same compiled Java code. A comprehensive collection of standard Java classes gives the Java developer a head start in developing database, network, and graphical applications. All of these features are important, but what is truly unique about Java is the level of industry acceptance that it has received. No other language has seen wide spread support and acceptance this rapidly in the history of the computing industry.

Java programs can take many forms. The most commonly discussed form of a Java program is the applet. An applet is Java code that is automatically downloaded from the Web and runs within a Web browser on the user's desktop. This install-free approach to distributing and running software is extremely attractive for some markets, and Java's built-in security provides assurances that the applet cannot misbehave within its limited environment. Java applets are being used to collect data, display graphical summaries, and provide interactive entertainment over the Web.

1

Java can be used to develop full-fledged applications as well. These applications are installed on an individual system or network in a more traditional manner, and are free of the security restrictions placed on applets, giving them the ability to perform almost any task that programs written in other languages can perform. Java has outstanding multithreading and network connectivity libraries, and applications written entirely in Java can run on a variety of systems without needing recompilation. Java developers are able to take advantage of this highly productive language to develop new kinds of software, including distributed applications and collaborative tools.

Other kinds of Java programs are appearing regularly, including server technologies and operating systems. Java is still maturing, and while it is currently being used most often to solve problems that more mature technologies do not address, it is expected to achieve mainstream acceptance for other tasks as it evolves.

Many of the chapters in this book assume that you have a basic familiarity with Java. In short, they assume that you understand basic Java types, know how to use Java keywords, and can create syntactically correct Java expressions. If you are not familiar with these topics, or are looking for a concise refresher course in Java, you will want to read Appendixes A and B before continuing with Chapter 2. These appendixes are designed to provide you with an understanding of the Java programming language sufficient to work through the topics and examples in this book.

This is not meant to imply that Java is ignored in this book. Indeed, by using JBuilder you are writing Java code. Consequently, additional issues concerning Java are introduced throughout the chapters of this book. For example, Chapter 2 includes an introduction to objects, object-oriented programming, the declaration of classes in Java, and the navigation of objects using JBuilder.

Nonetheless, this book is designed to focus squarely on JBuilder. As a result, there are some Java-related issues that are not explicitly covered. If you are interested in reading additional material concerning Java in particular, refer to JBuilder's online help concerning the Java language or a book devoted exclusively to Java, such as *Java 1.1 Handbook* (Osborne/McGraw-Hill).

Overview of the JBuilder IDE

JBuilder is a visual programming environment. This means that much of the work you do involves interacting with visual elements, such as buttons, labels, frames, and so forth. These elements can be placed, sized, and configured without your needing to write the corresponding Java code manually. The actual process of writing the Java code that defines the location of an object, what size to draw it, and which properties to set is performed by JBuilder. This relieves you of the mundane tasks of Java programming, permitting you to focus instead on the actions that should take place—for instance, to program what happens when a button is clicked by the user.

The primary tools that you work with in JBuilder are provided by the IDE. The IDE consists of a number of windows and dialogs, the most prominent of which are the JBuilder main window and the AppBrowser. Other essential windows that you use include the Inspector, the Object Gallery, the IDE Configuration dialog, and the various wizards provided by JBuilder. A wizard is a small program that assists you with a specific task, such as creating a new project or deploying an application.

This section introduces you to the tools of the IDE and provides you with a basic understanding of their use. In order to demonstrate many of these features, you are shown the steps that you can use to create a JBuilder *project*. A project is the collection of files and settings that are compiled into an application or applet. Technically speaking, the files are compiled into *classes*. These classes provide the basis for an application or applet. If you have access to a computer on which JBuilder is installed (you can use the trial version on this book's CD-ROM), you should use the following steps to create a project. This will give you hands-on experience with the various essential tools of the IDE.

The Main Window

When you load JBuilder, the main window is displayed, along with the last project that you had open. If this is your first time loading JBuilder, a sample project named welcome.jpr is displayed, as shown in Figure 1-1. The window in which a project is displayed is called the AppBrowser, and it is the most versatile tool that JBuilder provides you. (The AppBrowser is described in detail later in this chapter.)

The main window consists of three parts: the main menu, the toolbar, and the Component Palette. Each of these parts is considered next.

The Main Menu

The main menu contains menu items that provide you with access to most of JBuilder's features. The actions of some of the items available from JBuilder's main menu are also available through other parts of JBuilder's interface, such as the toolbar. If you are working at a computer while reading this chapter, you might want to take a moment and drop down each of the menus on JBuilder's main menu to familiarize yourself with the items that appear on these menus.

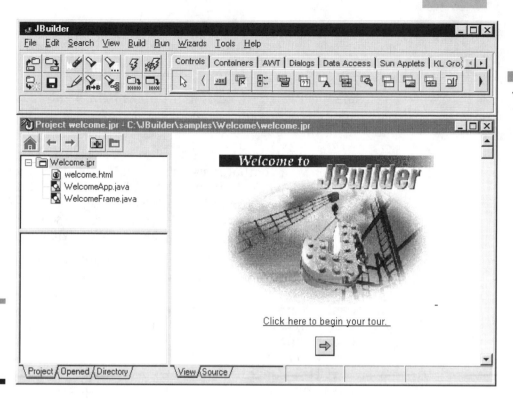

1

JBuilder when
you load it for
the first time
Figure 1-1.

The Toolbar

The toolbar, consisting of a collection of buttons at the upper left-hand side of the main window, provides you with instant access to the features of JBuilder that you are likely to use most often. These buttons permit you to open and close projects, run and debug applications and applets, make or build your code, and search your projects and source files, among other things. Each button on the toolbar displays a bitmap that indicates its purpose. In addition, if you pause with the mouse pointer over one of the toolbar buttons momentarily, the name of the tool button will appear, describing what that button does.

There are two ways to modify the display of the toolbar. First, you can use the splitter control between the toolbar and the panel to its right (called the Component Palette) to adjust how much space in the main window is allocated to each. For example, if you want to see more of the Component Palette and less of the toolbar, reposition the splitter to the left by dragging it with your mouse. Second, you can suppress the toolbar's display altogether by selecting View|Toolbar from JBuilder's main menu. When the View|Toolbar menu item is checked, the toolbar is displayed, and when it is not checked, the toolbar is hidden. To restore the display of the toolbar after hiding it, select View|Toolbar once more.

The Component Palette

The Component Palette appears in the upper right-hand side of the JBuilder main window. You use the Component Palette in order to manually place components into your project.

The Component Palette consists of multiple pages, each identified by a tab. Depending on your computer screen's resolution and the number of different pages of the Component Palette, all of the available tabs may not be displayed simultaneously. When this is the case, a pair of left-right arrows in the upper-right corner of the palette permits you to scroll the palette to the right or left, scrolling formerly hidden pages into view.

Each page of the Component Palette contains a number of component buttons that you use to place components. If you pause the mouse pointer over one of the component buttons momentarily, the name of the component will appear, including the full class name (for example, *borland.jbcl.control.ButtonControl*). When you want to place a component from the Component Palette, you begin by selecting the tab associated with the page on which the component appears. You then click the component button to select it. Once the component is selected, you can place it into your project using the AppBrowser. Placing components using the AppBrowser is described in a later section of this chapter.

When the width of the Component Palette does not permit all of the components on the selected page to be displayed, you can click the arrows at the right and left ends of the page to shift the page to the right and left, scrolling the hidden components into view.

The Object Gallery

The Object Gallery is a dialog that displays wizards and snippets that you can use to speed your development of applications and applets. Wizards are small programs that perform some specialized task. For example, the Project Wizard builds a new project for you, while the Applet Wizard assists you in creating applets.

Most wizards display a dialog, providing you with the chance to define options that customize the task it performs. For example, the Project Wizard permits you to define the title and filename of your new project. Others, such as the HTML Wizard, perform a task without displaying a dialog.

To use a wizard, you typically select it from the New page of the Object Gallery shown in Figure 1-2. (Some wizards, such as the Project Wizard and

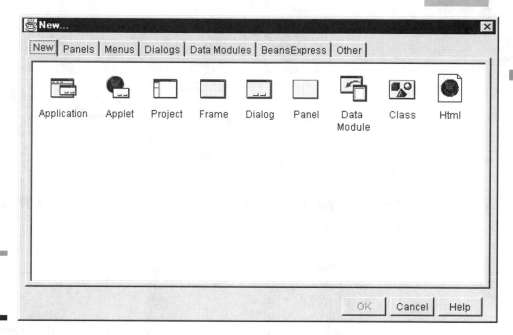

The Object
Gallery
Figure 1-2.

the Deployment Wizard, can be displayed by selecting menu options.) The
Object Gallery is displayed by selecting File|New. The New page of the
Object Gallery displays wizards. Each of the icons on the New page
represents a different wizard. To select a wizard, select an icon and click the
OK button. Alternatively, double-click the icon associated with the wizard to
execute it.

One wizard you will use all the time is the Project Wizard. To display the
Project Wizard, you can select the Project icon from the New page of the
Object Gallery or you can select File|New Project.

The other tabbed pages in the Object Gallery, called Panels, Menus, and so
forth, contain snippet icons. Snippets are stored code samples that provide
you with a quick and convenient way to create and reuse containers (frames,
dialogs, applets, and so forth) in your projects. JBuilder comes with a number of
useful snippets for you to use. You can even add your own snippets to the
Object Gallery, permitting you to reuse them easily in other projects.

To use a snippet, select File|New to display the Object Gallery, then click the
tab of the page that contains the snippet, select the snippet icon, and then
click OK. (Or, just as you can with wizards, double-click the icon associated
with the snippet.) To save a container that you created to the Object Gallery
as a snippet, move to the page in the Object Gallery where you want your
snippet to appear, right-click the page and select Add Snippet, and then
complete the following dialog.

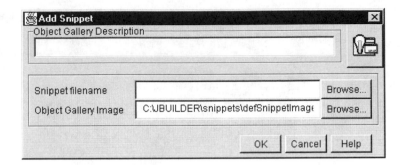

Using the Object Gallery to Create a Simple Project

Some of the features of JBuilder are described in this chapter with respect to a simple project. As mentioned earlier, if you have access to JBuilder while you read this chapter, you will want to follow the steps provided here to create this simple project.

1. If you have any projects currently open, including the Welcome project, close them by selecting File|Close All. (If you are displaying the Object Gallery, you will need to first close it in order to close any open projects.)

2. Display the Object Gallery by selecting File|New.

3. Select the Application icon (the Application Wizard) and then click OK. (Alternatively, you can double-click the Application icon.)

4. Since no projects are currently open to which an application can be added, JBuilder first runs the Project Wizard. The Project Wizard provides a default project name, and defines that this project should be stored under the c:\JBuilder\myprojects directory (assuming that you have installed JBuilder in its default directory). In general, you should always store your projects under the myprojects subdirectory. (Saving projects elsewhere requires that you change your project source path. See the online help for information on changing your source path.) Accept all the default values on the Project Wizard and click the Finish button to complete the creation of the project.

5. Once the Project Wizard has completed the creation of the project, the Application Wizard runs automatically since you first selected the Application icon in the Object Gallery. This wizard consists of two pages. The first page, called Step 1, permits you to define the package and class names for your application. A package is really nothing more than a directory. A class is created from a Java source file in that

directory. Accept the default values and select Next to move to the second page, called Step 2, of the Application Wizard.

6. The Step 2 page of the Application Wizard permits you to set the application title, as well as other options. At the Title field, enter **JBuilder Essentials** and check the checkboxes next to the Generate menu bar, Generate tool bar, Generate about box, and Center frame on screen options. Click Finish to complete the application definition.

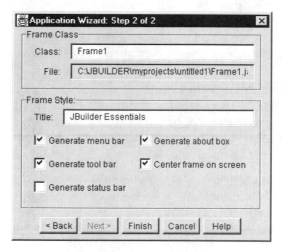

JBuilder generates an application and a frame, and adds them to the new project. The new project is now displayed in the AppBrowser, as shown in Figure 1-3.

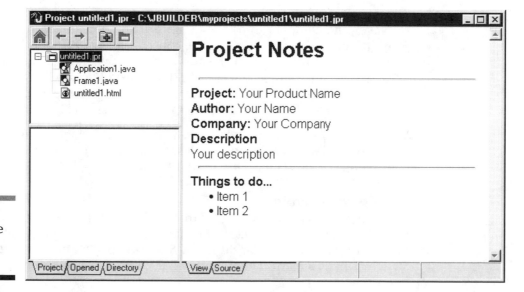

The new project in the AppBrowser
Figure 1-3.

The AppBrowser

The AppBrowser is a powerful project management tool that you use to build, maintain, run, debug, and document your projects. Indeed, the AppBrowser is the primary interface element for a JBuilder project. The AppBrowser also serves to organize the files of your projects, as well as those files that support your project management efforts.

The AppBrowser is divided into three parts, called panes. These are the Navigation pane, the Structure pane, and the Content pane. When one pane is selected, you can easily move to the next pane by pressing ALT-N. Each of these three panes is described in the following sections.

The Navigation Pane

The Navigation pane, the upper-left pane of the AppBrowser, initially displays the files of your project. However, depending on the mode of the AppBrowser, it may display classes, selected reference files, a file browser, or object hierarchies.

You use the Navigation pane to navigate the objects that appear within it. When you are working with a project, you use the Navigation pane to select the file within the project that you want to work with. For example, initially the name of the project is selected in the Navigation pane. If this is the first project you have ever created with JBuilder, that project was given the default name untitled1. To work with one of the other files of the project, such as the file named Frame1.java, click Frame1.java (or the desired file) in the Navigation pane. Once this new file is selected, the Structure pane and the Content pane display information relevant to this file, as shown in Figure 1-4.

The simple project being created here consists of only a few files at first. However, many more can be added, if needed. These initial files include the project file (*.jpr), which defines the contents and settings of the project; two Java source files, one for the application (Application1.java) and one for a frame (Frame1.java); and an HTML (HyperText Markup Language) file (*.html). When the project is selected in the Navigation pane, the contents of its HTML file are displayed in the Content pane.

You can easily add additional files to your project, including additional Java source files, HTML files, graphics files (*.gif, *.jpg, and *.bmp), sound files (*.wav and .au), and compressed ZIP files (.zip).

The Structure Pane

When the project itself is selected in the Navigation pane, the Structure pane is empty. As soon as you select the Frame1.java file in the Navigation pane, however, many objects appear in the Structure pane. The contents of the Structure pane are affected by both what you have selected in the Navigation

Navigation pane   Content pane

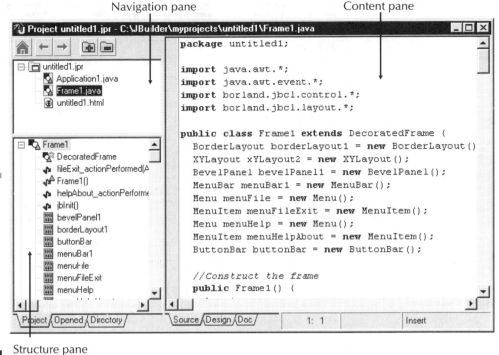

1

The Structure pane and the Content pane display information based on what is selected in the Navigation pane

Figure 1-4.

Structure pane

pane and what tab you have selected in the Content pane (described in the next section).

The Structure pane actually has five different modes that you select by clicking on tabs that appear at the bottom of the Structure pane. The default mode is the project mode, in which the files and related classes of your project can be inspected. There are four additional modes: opened, directory, hierarchy, and search. You access these modes by selecting the Opened, Directory, Hierarchy, or Search tab at the bottom of the Structure pane, respectively. The mode you select in the Structure pane not only affects what it displays, but what is displayed in the Navigation pane as well.

The Project Mode When you select the Frame1.java file in the Navigation pane, the Structure pane displays a tree structure, some of which can be seen in Figure 1-4. This view contains a visual description of the file selected in the Navigation pane. Since the Frame1.java file contains several classes,

including the various instance variables and methods defined for that class, these definitions appear as nodes within the Structure pane.

The contents of the Structure pane also include the interfaces, constructors, and superclass references of the selected file. These are particularly useful when the details of the class that you are working with need to be explored.

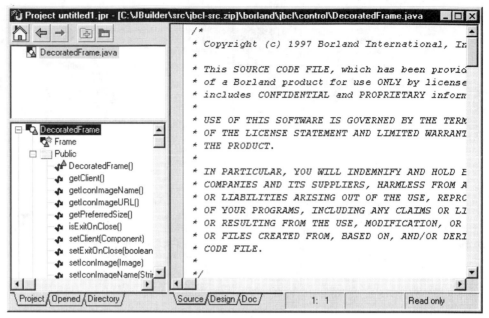

For example, you are viewing the Frame1.java file, which defines a class named *Frame1*. This class descends from the class *DecoratedFrame* (the superclass of *Frame1*). At some point, you might want to know more information about *DecoratedFrame*. You can navigate to the *DecoratedFrame* class information by double-clicking on the node labeled *DecoratedFrame* in the Structure pane. Doing so causes the *DecoratedFrame* class file to be loaded and displayed in the Navigation pane. Furthermore, since the contents of the Navigation pane have changed, so have the contents of the Structure pane. It now displays the various class, instance variable, method, constructor, interface, and superclass definitions of the file displayed in the Navigation pane, as shown in Figure 1-5. This is referred to as *drilling down* into a class. Note that the Source tab of the Content pane must also be selected for this feature to be available.

Double-clicking on a node in the Structure pane can have a significant impact on the definitions that you see. Fortunately, these various definitions can be easily traversed using the buttons that appear immediately above the Navigation pane. For example, when you want to return to the Frame1.java file in the Navigation pane, click the button with the bitmap of the house (this is the button called Home to first in browser history). The Home button always returns you to the first file from which you began your navigation. Alternatively, you can click the Prior and Next buttons to navigate backwards and forwards through the files that you have visited.

1

The Opened Mode   When the Opened tab is selected in the Structure pane, the Navigation pane displays a list of project files that you have modified during your current session with the project. This list permits you to quickly identify and work with these files.

It is also possible to add additional files to the Opened tab. These additional files, which are not necessarily part of the current project, can then be navigated just as easily as those files within your project. This provides you with a convenient way to view, display, and navigate related files without having to explicitly add them to your project. For example, if you need to refer to the *java.awt.Window* class while working on your project, you can add this class to your Opened list.

You add additional files to the Opened tab of the Structure pane by dragging the node representing the file from the Navigation pane and then dropping it onto the Opened tab of the Structure pane. While this can be done while the Structure pane is in any mode, the most common modes used when adding files to the Opened tab are the directory mode, hierarchy mode, and search mode. Dropping a file onto the Opened tab is demonstrated next during the discussion of the directory mode.

The Directory Mode   When you select the Directory tab of the Structure pane, you see a simple browser that permits you to look for files on your disk drives and network. This mode is useful for locating files. For instance, you might use it to browse for a particular class file so that you know what package to import.

The directory mode is also useful for locating files and adding them to your Opened tab of the Structure pane. By adding them to your Opened tab, you can quickly return to that file to inspect and even navigate its contents.

To demonstrate the use of the directory mode and the opened mode, begin by selecting the Directory tab of the Structure pane. Initially, it displays the available drives on your system. Assuming that you installed JBuilder on drive C, double-click the C-drive icon in the Navigation pane (or the drive letter corresponding to where you installed JBuilder). Next, double-click the JBuilder subdirectory under C (or the directory name under which you installed JBuilder on the selected drive). Finally, double-click myprojects. If you have already used JBuilder, this directory may contain projects, other project-related files, subdirectories, or any combination of these. This directory also contains a file named myprojects.txt.

Select the file named myprojects.txt and drag it to the Opened tab of the Structure pane and drop it. You do this by first selecting the myprojects.txt file in the Navigation pane and then holding down the left mouse button. With the mouse button still depressed, move the mouse so that its cursor appears over the Opened tab of the Structure pane. As soon as the mouse cursor appears on the Opened tab, the cursor will change, indicating that this tab is a valid drop zone for the file you are dragging. Release the left mouse button.

To see that the file named myprojects.txt has been added to the Opened tab of the Structure pane, click the Opened tab. The file myprojects.txt now appears in this list. Select this file to view its contents in the Content pane, as shown in Figure 1-6.

The Hierarchy Mode   You use the hierarchy mode to display the class hierarchy for a selected Java source file. This information is particularly important when you need to closely inspect a class in order to better understand its definition and capabilities.

There is no Hierarchy tab on the Structure pane initially, but one will appear as soon as you inspect the hierarchy of a Java file. To demonstrate the hierarchy mode, select the Project tab of the Structure pane to view the current project. In the Navigation pane, right-click Frame1.java and select Class Hierarchy. After a moment, the Hierarchy tab appears and is selected on the Structure pane, and the interfaces and imports of the selected source

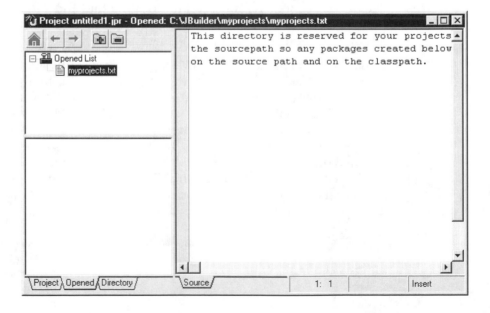

Selecting the Opened tab permits you to easily view files without them necessarily being part of your project

Figure 1-6.

file are displayed. In addition, all related classes, interfaces, and superclasses of the selected file are displayed in the Navigation pane, permitting you to navigate the related definitions of the selected source file quickly and easily. In addition, if you want to be able to quickly view the contents of the source file associated with any of the definitions displayed in the Navigation pane, drag that definition and drop it onto the Opened tab. This adds the associated file to the Opened tab of the Structure pane.

At any time you can drop the Hierarchy tab (or the Directory tab or the Search tab) by right-clicking one of the Structure pane tabs and selecting the option Drop Hierarchy tab (or Drop Directory tab or Drop Search tab, depending on what you have open).

The Search Mode　　You use the search mode to list the classes from the source path in which a particular string appears. The files that are located appear in the Navigation pane, and the structure of those files appears on the Search tab of the Structure pane.

To demonstrate the use of the search mode, select Search|Search Source Path from JBuilder's main menu to display the Search Source Path dialog.

Enter the name of a string to search for in the Search String field. For example, enter the string **OK**. Then, click the OK button to initiate the search.

The files that include the string you are searching for are listed in the Navigation pane, as shown in Figure 1-7. If you want to be able to easily reference the contents of one or more of the located files, drag them, one at a time, from the Navigation pane and drop them into the Opened tab of the Structure pane.

The Content Pane

The Content pane, like the Structure pane, is affected by what you select in the Navigation pane. Initially, when the project file is selected, the HTML file associated with the project (this is the HTML file that has the same name as the project) is displayed in the Content pane. When you click Frame1.java, the Java source file for *Frame1* is displayed.

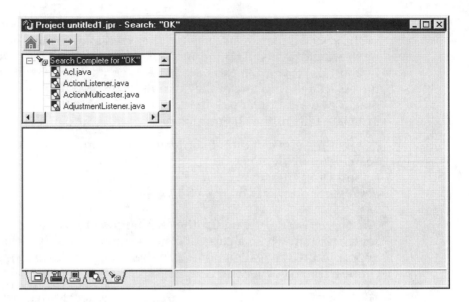

Files located
by a search
are listed in
the Navigation
pane, while
the definitions
from the
selected file
are displayed
in the
Structure pane
Figure 1-7.

The Content pane has four modes: view, doc, source, and design. Similar to
the Structure pane, you access these modes by clicking on the View, Doc,
Source, and Design tabs that appear at the bottom of the Content pane.
Which mode it defaults to depends on the type of file you have selected in
the Navigation pane. For example, when an HTML file is selected in the
Navigation pane, the view mode is the default. By comparison, when a Java
file is selected, the source mode is the default. In addition, the number of
modes available also depends on the type of field you have selected in the
Navigation pane. When you select a Java file in the Navigation pane, the
tabs you will see at the bottom of the Content pane are the Source, Design,
and Doc tabs. When you select an HTML file in the Navigation pane, the tabs
you will see at the bottom of the Content pane are the View and Source tabs.

The View Mode You use the view mode for displaying formatted HTML
or graphics files. When an HTML file is selected, the view mode acts as a
limited browser, displaying the formatted HTML. It is limited in that it does
not recognize all HTML that the most current browsers recognize, nor is it
capable of running applets (that task is left up to the appletviewer that ships
with JBuilder). When a graphics file is selected in the Navigation pane, the
image contained in the graphics file is displayed.

For all other file types, the View tab is not available on the Content pane,
and consequently, this mode is not available.

When a project is selected in the Navigation pane, the HTML file associated
with that file is displayed in the Content pane.

The Doc Mode   You use the doc mode to display documentation for classes that you select in the Navigation pane. This documentation exists for all classes installed by JBuilder. The classes you create will not have this documentation unless you actually create it. You can create this documentation using JavaDoc, which is available in JBuilder's BIN subdirectory. (Using JavaDoc, or Borland's JBDoc utility, which is an enhanced alternative to JavaDoc, is beyond the scope of this book.)

The documentation that exists for the installed classes can be very helpful when you are trying to learn more about a class. Displaying the documentation for a class is described in Chapter 2.

The Source Mode   The source mode is used to display the contents of the selected Java file or text file. You can think of this mode as the source view of the Java file or text file rather than the source mode (and, in fact, we refer to it as the source view in this book). When a Java file is selected, the source mode serves as a powerful code editor—called the Source Code Editor, or Editor, for short. This Editor provides you with a wealth of features, including the following:

♦ Syntax highlighting, which provides visual identification for types of statements. For example, by default, keywords appear in a bold font, comments appear in blue italics, and breakpoints appear in a white font on a red background.

♦ Options for configuring the Editor's behavior. This includes general behavior, such as permitting the Editor to behave similar to several popular code editors, such as Brief and the Windows default editor. In addition, other aspects can be configured, such as how tab characters are represented, the colors used for syntax highlighting, whether undo operations can be performed after saves, and so forth. These features can be configured from the IDE Configuration dialog. To display this dialog, select Tools|IDE Configuration.

♦ Bookmarks can be placed, permitting you to quickly return to a specific line in a file.

♦ Block indenting is supported, permitting you to indent one or more lines simultaneously.

♦ Keystrokes can be recorded, and then played back, permitting you to partially automate repetitive tasks.

♦ Text can be searched. Search and replace options are also available.

♦ The Content pane can be toggled to a "full-window" mode, allowing the Editor to occupy the entire area available to the AppBrowser. You enter this mode from the Editor by pressing ALT-Z, which acts as a toggle. Pressing ALT-Z again returns all panes to their original configuration.

♦ The source file that defines a symbol (class, interface, and so forth) that appears within the Editor can be loaded into the Navigation pane (and, consequently, the Editor as well) by simply right-clicking the symbol in your source code and then selecting Browse Symbol at Cursor from the popup menu. You can return to editing the original file using the navigator buttons that appear above the Navigation pane.

The Editor is synchronized to the Structure pane when a Java file is selected in the Navigation pane. Specifically, when you select a class name, instance variable, method name, or interface, the cursor within the Editor is moved to the line in the Editor where that symbol is declared. This allows you to navigate your code quickly and efficiently, permitting you to treat the Structure pane as an outline of your source code.

For more information on configuring the Editor, creating bookmarks, recording and playing keystrokes, as well as other editing-related topics, refer to JBuilder's online help.

The Source pane is also used to display HTML source files and text files. In this mode, it acts as a simple editor. In these cases it provides only the basic features, such as character entry, search and replace, and block indenting. More advanced features, such as syntax highlighting, are not available for these types of files.

The Design Mode You use the design mode to visually create and manipulate objects defined in a Java file. This mode is where you are most productive in JBuilder. This is because as you use the Designer, JBuilder is busy in the background modifying your Java source code, adding to it the Java statements that produce the effects you are configuring in the Designer.

There are actually two Designers in this version of JBuilder. The most obvious is the UI Designer. The UI Designer is where you visually place and configure the objects on a container, such as a frame, dialog, or applet, for example. The second Designer is the Menu Designer. The Menu Designer permits you to visually define the menu items that make up your menu bars.

Regardless of which Designer you are using, JBuilder automatically keeps the Designer and the underlying Java source file synchronized. This synchronization goes both ways. Specifically, if you place a new button on a frame using the UI Designer, the associated Java file is updated to include the necessary *Button* instance variable and initialization code. Likewise, if you use the Editor to change the Java source code, adding a button manually in code, the next time you open the Designer the button will be represented visually (so long as your code properly declares and initializes the button). Borland calls these features *two-way tools*.

1

Whenever the Designer is active, the Structure pane displays a special view of the associated Java file. This view, called the Component Tree, displays nodes for the various objects that appear in the source file. For example, with Frame1.Java selected in the Navigation pane, select the Design tab of the Content pane to open the UI Designer. When you do, the Component Tree appears in the Structure pane, as shown in Figure 1-8.

Notice in the Component Tree that the top-level node is named *Frame1*. This is the public class defined in the file Frame1.Java. In addition to this class name, the Component Tree contains a hierarchical listing of the objects that appear within this class. These objects appear under one of four nodes. The UI components, such as buttons, field controls, as well as the frame itself, appear under the UI node. If the container uses a menu, a Menu node is present. Data access components, those used to access datasets, appear under the Data Access node. All other components appear under the Other node. The Other node is only visible in the Component Tree when at least one of these *other* components appears in the container. For example, the dialog components available within JBuilder are other components.

One of the key features of the Component Tree is that it permits you to directly select an object whether or not it is visible in the designer. This capability is essential since even those objects that are not UI components, and, consequently, are not visible in the UI Designer, often require special configuration. This configuration is performed using a dialog called the Inspector. Using the Inspector is described in the next section.

The Component Tree is displayed in the Structure pane when the Designer is active

Figure 1-8.

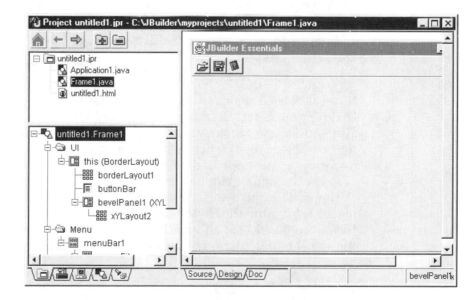

To demonstrate the use of the UI Designer and its relationship with the Component Tree, perform the following steps to add two components to your project:

1. Begin with Frame1.java displayed in the UI Designer. This is the case when Frame1.java is selected in the Navigation pane, the Design tab is selected in the Content pane, and an object under the UI node of the Component Tree is selected. If this is not the case, make the appropriate selections.

2. Click the Controls tab of the Component Palette to display the Controls page and select the component *borland.jbcl.control.ButtonControl.* This component appears as the first button on the left on the Controls page. To select it, click it with your mouse. When selected, its button appears depressed.

TIP: If you ever have a doubt about the name of a given component, pause your mouse pointer over the corresponding Component Palette button momentarily and the full component name is displayed.

3. Click your mouse somewhere near the middle of the UI Designer in the Content pane. In response, JBuilder draws a *ButtonControl* component at the location where you clicked, as shown in Figure 1-9. Notice that in this figure, a new node, labeled *buttonControl1,* appears within the component tree under the UI node.

   While it is not immediately apparent, JBuilder has also responded by adding the following line of code to the *Frame1* declaration in the Frame1.java file:

   ```
   ButtonControl buttonControl1 = new ButtonControl();
   ```

4. Next, click the Dialogs tab of the Component Palette to display the Dialogs page. Select the *borland.jbcl.control.Message* component, and again click approximately in the center of the UI Designer. This time, no new object appears in the UI Designer. Instead, a new node appears under the Other node in the Component Tree. The Message component is a non-UI component, meaning that it does not appear in the UI Designer. The only way to select a non-UI component once it has been placed is by using the Component Tree. UI components, on the other hand, can be selected either using the Component Tree or by selecting the visual representation of the object in the Designer.

1

The new
ButtonControl
component
appears in the
UI Designer as
well as in the
Component
Tree
Figure 1-9.

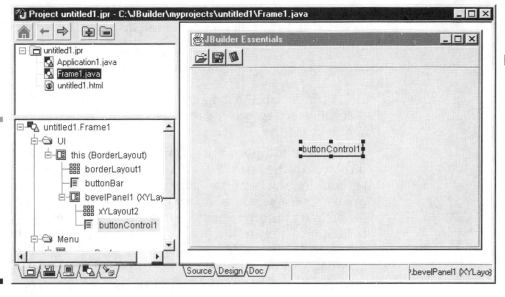

NOTE: When placing a non-UI component, you have the option of
either clicking in the UI Designer, as was done with the Message component,
or clicking in the Component Tree. Both techniques produce the same effect.

In the next section, you will configure these two components using the
Inspector.

The Inspector

The Inspector is a special dialog that permits you to set the properties of, and
define event handlers for, components. *Properties* are values whose settings
influence the appearance and/or the behavior of objects. *Event handlers* are
methods that permit you to add custom Java code that will be executed by
the object. In short, it is through properties and event handlers that you
make an object do exactly what you need.

The Inspector contains two tabbed pages, one labeled Properties and the
other labeled Events. Use the Properties page of the Inspector to set the
properties of the object selected in the Component Tree. (If the component
is a UI component, being selected in the Component Tree is the same as
being selected in the UI Designer.)

Usually, the Inspector is automatically visible when the Design tab of the
Content pane is selected. However, it is possible to close the Inspector, in

which case it is no longer visible. If you have the Design tab of the Content pane selected and you still do not see the Inspector, select View|Inspector to make it visible.

The following steps demonstrate the use of the Inspector:

1. To define the label that appears on the *ButtonControl* you added in the preceding section, select *buttonControl1* in the Component Tree or simply select the visual representation of the button in the UI Designer.

2. The Inspector displays the Properties page by default. If it is not displayed in the Inspector, click the Properties tab. There are two columns on the Properties page: the left column lists the properties you can set for the selected component and the right column contains fields for defining property values. Select the *label* property by clicking in the field immediately to the right of the row named *label*. The property is selected when the field appears with a white background instead of the gray background. When selected, the property is ready to receive input.

3. The text "buttonControl1" already appears in the *label* property. Select this text and erase it, and then enter **Display a Message**. Press ENTER after entering this text to set this property. Once set, the property field will appear in gray again.

   Next, it is necessary to set some properties of the *Message* component, a non-UI component.

4. From the Component Tree, select the node labeled *message1* that appears under the Other node shown here. The Properties page of the Inspector now updates to display the properties of this *Message* component.

5. From the Properties page of the Inspector, set the *frame* property to **this**. You do this by first selecting the *frame* property. Once selected, a down arrow appears in this property field. Click this down arrow to display a drop-down list of items that this property can be set to. Select **this** from the list.

6. Next, select the *title* property. Enter **Message** for the *title* property.

7. Now select the *message* property. Enter **JBuilder creates Java applications and applets** in the message property field.

The properties that you have now set for the *ButtonControl* and the *Message* define how they appear. However, if you want to be able to actually display the message defined for the *Message* component when the *ButtonControl* is clicked, you must add an event handler, and then enter some custom code into the method generated by JBuilder. The following steps show you how to do this:

1. Select *buttonControl1* in the Component Tree or, alternatively, select the visual representation of the button in the UI Designer.

2. Click the Events tab of the Inspector to display its Events page, as shown in Figure 1-10. Just like the Properties page, the Events page contains two columns. The left column lists the events available for the selected component. The fields in the right column are used to define the event handlers.

3. Select the *actionPerformed* event handler. Do this by clicking once in the field to the right of the row labeled *actionPerformed,* and then clicking once again to select it. Once selected, JBuilder automatically enters a method name into this event handler. This method is the one that will be executed when the user clicks on the button from the running application.

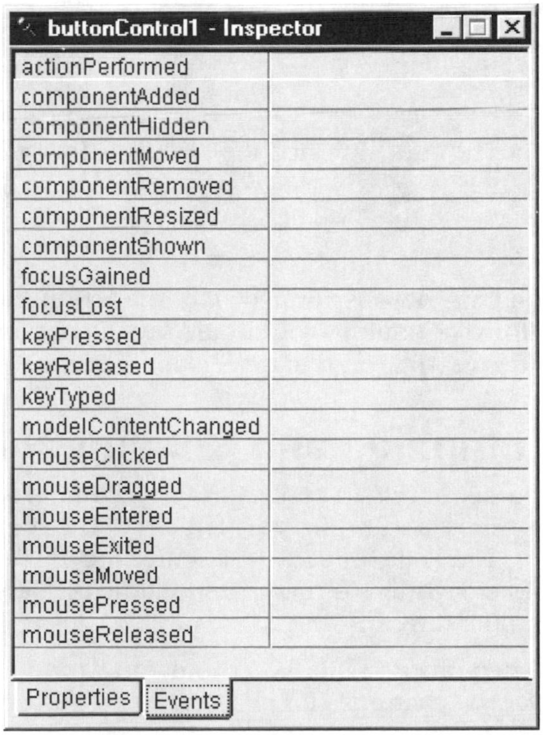

The Events page of the Inspector for a *ButtonControl* component

Figure 1-10.

buttonControl1 - Inspector	
actionPerformed	
componentAdded	
componentHidden	
componentMoved	
componentRemoved	
componentResized	
componentShown	
focusGained	
focusLost	
keyPressed	
keyReleased	
keyTyped	
modelContentChanged	
mouseClicked	
mouseDragged	
mouseEntered	
mouseExited	
mouseMoved	
mousePressed	
mouseReleased	
Properties Events	

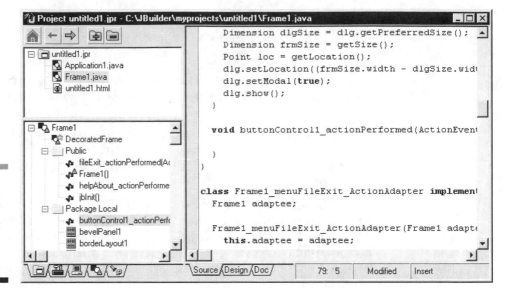

4. With the *actionPerformed* event handler selected, press ENTER. JBuilder will display the Editor and will position the cursor in the newly generated method, as shown in Figure 1-11.

5. Enter the following single line of code into the method generated by JBuilder:

```
message1.show();
```

The entire method looks like the following:

```
void buttonControl1_actionPerformed(ActionEvent e) {
  message1.show();
}
```

You have now performed all of the actions needed to complete a project. Before continuing, you should save all of your work. You do this by selecting File|Save All from JBuilder's main menu.

Compiling and Running the Project

In order to run an application that you have created in JBuilder, it is necessary to compile it. The result of the compilation is the generation of class files, one for each Java source file in your project. By default, these class files are written to the corresponding myclasses subdirectory under the JBuilder directory.

To demonstrate this, you should now run the project that you have created over the course of this chapter. To do this, select Run|Run from JBuilder's

1

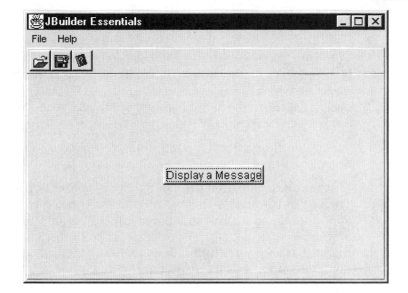

The running
application
Figure 1-12.

main menu. Alternatively, you can either press SHIFT-F9 or click the Run
button on the JBuilder toolbar. After telling JBuilder to run the project, it
will first compile all of the Java files in your application, creating a class file
from each. It will then run the file named Application1.class, which starts
the application, resulting in the display of the frame shown in Figure 1-12.

From this window, click the button labeled Display a Message. In response,
the following Message dialog is displayed:

Click OK to accept the dialog. Select File|Exit from the running application
to close the frame.

While you are working on a JBuilder project, you might have a need to
recompile your project. You can do this by selecting Build|Make Project or
Build|Rebuild Project. Both of these selections recompile any file within your
application that has changed since the last compilation, as well as any
outdated classes that are imported by one of the Java files in the project. This
recompilation of imported classes is recursive, meaning that if a class
imported by one that you import is out of date, it will be recompiled as well.
The primary difference between making and rebuilding is that rebuilding

forces recompilation, whereas making only recompiles files if they are determined to be out of date.

You can also choose to recompile a single Java file currently selected in the Navigation pane. To do this, select Build|Make *filename*, or Build|Rebuild *filename*, where *filename* is the selected Java file in your project. These options perform the same as the project-level versions, except that they only apply to the selected file.

For more information on compiling projects, refer to JBuilder's online documentation.

This concludes the discussion of the sample project presented in this chapter. There is only one task that we have not addressed with respect to this application, and that is the deployment of it. Application deployment involves a number of steps and is beyond the scope of this chapter, which is designed to familiarize you with JBuilder's tools and techniques. For information on deploying applications created in JBuilder, refer to Chapter 12.

Getting Help from JBuilder's Online Help

JBuilder is a feature-rich product that can be used for a wide range of tasks. These include building applications that can run under a wide variety of operating systems, creating applets that run within Web browsers, as well as building servers that provide applications and applets with support, such as supplying them with data from a database. Fortunately, JBuilder ships with a large number of documents online, providing you with a great deal of information on a variety of topics that apply to the use of JBuilder in particular and Java in general.

To access this online help, select Help|Help Topics. This displays the JBuilder Help Viewer, shown in Figure 1-13, which is a Java application itself. Use the Available books field's drop-down list to choose which document (or general category of information) you want to access. For instance, if you want to learn more about the JavaBeans Component Library that ships with JBuilder, select JBCL Reference.

Once you have selected the document that you want to see, a tree control view of the topics within the selected document is displayed in the list beneath the Available books list. Use this control to navigate the topics that are available. To view help on a given topic, select the node in the tree control associated with the desired topic. The JBuilder Help Viewer then loads the HTML document associated with the book (document) you selected and displays the selected contents in the pane on the right-hand side of the Help Viewer.

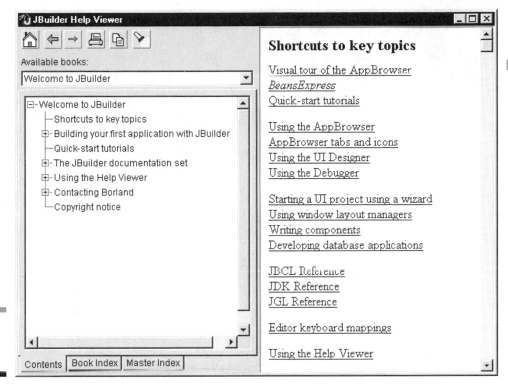

The JBuilder
Help Viewer
Figure 1-13.

The JBuilder Help Viewer includes navigator buttons, similar to those provided for the Navigation pane. As you select links that appear in the selected documents you are viewing, you can use these navigation buttons to revisit help topics that you previously visited or return to the original file from which you began browsing the help files.

CHAPTER 2

Understanding
Objects in JBuilder

Java is an object-oriented language. In fact, you cannot use
JBuilder without using objects. This chapter is designed to
introduce you to object-oriented programming, with
particular attention paid to how objects are declared and
navigated in JBuilder.

If you are already comfortable with object-oriented programming, you will still want to scan through this chapter quickly for information on how JBuilder builds and navigates among objects. If you have never programmed in an object-oriented language, you will want to pay particular attention to the terminology and techniques that are crucial to successful use of objects.

Overview of Objects

Objects are structures that define both data and behavior. The data is generally similar to that which you store in variables, such as integers, floating-point numbers, and object references. The behaviors, often called *methods*, typically perform operations based on that data, as well as report information about the data. While this might sound like a radical idea, it is really just a natural extension of procedure-based, structured programming. However, the characteristics of object-oriented languages go beyond the mere use of objects. In order to be considered object-oriented, a language must also support three basic features. These features are *inheritance*, *encapsulation*, and *polymorphism*.

Another important concept in object-oriented programming is *class* (sometimes referred to as *type*). Every object belongs to a class.

The role of the class is to define the characteristics of an object, and in that respect, a class is very much analogous to the blueprint for a house. The blueprint defines the size and location of each room, the fixtures, building materials, and so forth. You cannot, however, live in a blueprint. Rather, the blueprint is used to construct an instance of a house. The actual house in this analogy is the object. While a given house design may be represented by a single blueprint, many houses can be built based on that blueprint, as shown in Figure 2-1.

The class of an object defines the fields that it has, as well as which methods it contains. In most cases, the class also defines the code for the methods, although some types of classes, referred to as *abstract* classes, declare some methods with no associated code. (You can never have an object that is an instance of an abstract class.) In addition, the class defines which of the fields and methods can be accessed only by an instance of the object created from the class, and which fields and methods can be accessed by any objects. This is defined through the use of visibility modifiers.

Inheritance is the process by which a new class is defined from an existing class. In Java, the new class is said to *extend* the class from which it descends. Furthermore, the class from which the new class descends is said to be the *ancestor* of the descendant class. An ancestor class is often referred to as a *superclass*.

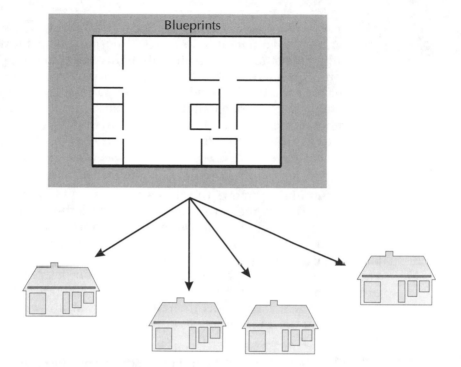

A blueprint describes a house, and many houses can be built using that blueprint
Figure 2-1.

2

Which class a new class descends from is critical. This is because a new class automatically acquires—that is, *inherits*—the fields and methods of the class from which it descends. Consequently, by the simple act of inheritance, a new class is created that is very similar to its superclass (they might even be identical). Of course, simply creating another class that is identical to one that already exists would be of little use, since the new class would be no different than its direct superclass. In practice, a new class is always different from its superclass. For example, a descendant class may add new fields or new methods, and often both. Alternatively, a new class may simply redefine how an existing method works. Methods that work differently in a descendant class are said to *override* the inherited methods. Fields with the same names as fields defined in the ancestor class are said to *hide*, or *shadow*, the corresponding ancestor fields.

NOTE: While overridding (methods) and shadowing (fields) appear to be similar, they are different in one very important characteristic. When overriding a method, you are, for all intents and purposes, replacing the previous implementation and *all* attempts to invoke the method will use the new implementation. When shadowing a variable, you are actually declaring a second instance variable that just happens to have the same name. References in ancestor methods still refer to the first declaration, and methods in the new class or its descendants refer to the second declaration.

As a result of inheritance, the classes that descend from a common superclass share some of the same fields and methods. Indeed, knowing that two objects descend from a common ancestor gives you information about the features of the classes. In addition, objects—that is, instances of a class—can generally be treated as if they were instances of their respective ancestor classes. This capability is known as *polymorphism*. Polymorphism means that related objects share some methods and fields, and in some cases are assignment compatible. Interfaces, discussed later in this chapter, also provide for polymorphism.

The final defining feature of object-oriented languages, *encapsulation*, derives from the fact that the field and methods of one object may be hidden from other objects. This is achieved in Java through the use of *visibility modifiers*. Some visibility modifiers permit you to declare that a field or method may only be accessed from within the class itself (**private**), while others permit you to allow access from any other object (**public**).

Those fields and methods that are declared private permit the class designer to hide the implementation details of the object. What this means is that *how* internal data is represented and manipulated can be entirely hidden from other objects. By hiding certain details of the implementation of an object, the class designer can ensure that the object is used only in intended ways. In other words, a developer using the object can only access those fields and methods designed for such use, and cannot access those fields and methods designed solely for use by the object itself.

The Benefits of Object-Oriented Programming

Object-oriented programming requires a different approach to application development than traditional procedure-based, structured programming. In many cases, this means taking more time analyzing and designing your applications than you would otherwise. As a result, the most common question is, "Why go to the trouble?"

The answer is that objects permit for greater reuse of existing code, and provide a natural mechanism for organizing code. This becomes apparent with a simple example. Imagine that you must write code to control a manufacturing process, such as the control of a reaction vessel. For the sake of simplicity, assume that two chemicals are added to the reaction vessel, and then a specific amount of heat is applied to produce a new compound.

Assuming that you must write a program to control the reaction, there are certain types of information that you need to store. For example, you need to keep track of how much of the two chemicals is added. You will also probably need several functions or procedures. These might include calculating how much new compound will be produced given the heat and the amounts of the two chemicals being added, how long the reaction will last given the heat and chemical amounts, and how much of chemical 1 and chemical 2 is required to create a given amount of the new compound. Also, if the reaction is potentially explosive, you might have a boolean function that indicates if the vessel is safe or not.

2

If you approached this problem using structured programming, you might declare three variables (*heat, chem1, and chem2*). In addition, you might have four subroutines, including ExpectedOutput, TimeLeft, CalcChemicalsRequired, and IsSafe.

While these declarations might work fine so long as you have only one reaction to control, things do get complicated if additional reaction vessels are added in the future. For example, what do you do about the variables? Do you continue to add more variables, calling them *heat1, heat2,* and so forth, for the *heat* variable?

One structured approach would be to declare a record structure, a single variable that permits two or more fields to be associated with a single structure. This could be accomplished in C with **struct**, **record** in Pascal, or **type** in BASIC.

Although the record structure permits the fields to be organized, the functions and procedures are not organized. It is conceivable that the values of two or more vessels might get mixed up in a single subroutine call, producing unwanted or dangerous results.

Wouldn't it be nice if it were possible to associate the functions and procedures with the record structure also? In some respects, that is exactly what an object is, since it permits variables and functions to be organized together. A single class would define the variables and methods. The code would then instantiate—that is, create—one instance of the class for each of the vessels needing to be controlled.

Objects in JBuilder

With the exception of primitive types and keywords, everything else you work with in code is related to objects and interfaces. (Interfaces are similar to class definitions, but they cannot be used to instantiate—that is, create an object. Interfaces are discussed briefly at the end of this chapter.) There are no global variables in Java. Instead, there are class fields (meaning that they must be associated with a particular class). In addition, there are no pure functions or procedures. In Java, all functions and procedures are associated with classes, and are therefore methods. A method is simply that, a function or procedure whose implementation appears within a class declaration.

It is impossible to use JBuilder and not define classes and create objects. Every single project will include at least one frame, applet, or similar object. Furthermore, this object will be defined by a class definition.

To demonstrate this, start by creating a new application. Start by closing any open projects, and then select File|New. Next, select the Application icon (the Application Wizard) from the New page of the Object Gallery. JBuilder will begin by first displaying the Project Wizard. At File, enter **C:\JBuilder\myprojects\osborne\jbe\objects\ch02demo.jpr**, assuming that you installed JBuilder using the default installation directory. If not, enter **osborne\jbe\objects\ch02demo.jpr** after the myprojects subdirectory in the File field. Click the Finish button to complete the Project Wizard.

Next, the Step 1 page of the Application Wizard appears. Leave the Package field set to osborne.jbe.objects and the Class field set to Application1, as shown in Figure 2-2. The contents of this page define the *Application* object that is used to start your application. Now click the Next button to move to the second page of the Application Wizard.

You use the second page of the Application Wizard to define the characteristics of a new *Frame* subclass. A *Frame* is a visible window in which other objects can appear when your application is running. The new *Frame* class will describe the specific characteristics of this window. Leave the Class field set to Frame1 (this is the name of your new class), and enter **JBuilder Demonstration** in the Title field. While still on this page, check the

Use the Step 1
page of the
Application
Wizard to
define the
name of the
Application
object that
starts your
application

Figure 2-2.

Generate status bar option. This dialog should look like that in Figure 2-3.
When you are done, click Finish.

Your project, named ch02demo.jpr, now consists of two Java files,
Application1.java and Frame1.java (these are the Java source files), and one
html file named ch02demo.html. These files appear in JBuilder's Navigation
pane.

Both of the Java files define new classes. Furthermore, they are pure Java.
That is, although JBuilder generated these source files, they are syntactically
correct Java and can be compiled with any Java 1.1 compiler. In order to
better understand the object model in Java, let's begin by considering the
contents of the file Application1.java. To view this file, select
Application1.java in the Navigation pane, and then click the Source tab in

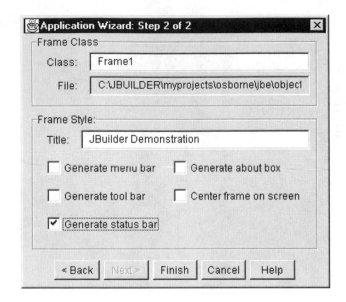

Use the Step 2
page of the
Application
Wizard to
define a basic
Frame that
defines the
main form of
your
application
Figure 2-3.

the Content pane to view the source code in the Editor (the source view).
The following is the code that you will see in the Editor:

```
package osborne.jbe.objects;

public class Application1 {
  boolean packFrame = false;

  //Construct the application
  public Application1() {
    Frame1 frame = new Frame1();
    //Pack frames that have useful preferred size info,
    //e.g. from their layout
//Validate frames that have preset sizes
    if (packFrame)
      frame.pack();
    else
      frame.validate();
    frame.setVisible(true);
  }
```

```
//Main method
static public void main(String[] args) {
    new Application1();
}
}
```

package → directory

In the first statement, the keyword **package** identifies the package in which the *Application1* class is defined. All classes reside in packages, which correspond to directories. In this case, the package name is osborne.jbe.objects, since the Java file that defines *Application1* is stored in the subdirectory osborne\jbe\objects under your myprojects directory.

2

Declaring the Class

Following the package statement is the statement that declares the class. This statement begins with the following line:

```
public class Application1 {
```

The keyword **public** defines this class as a public class, meaning that any object can reference this class. The keyword **class** defines that this declaration is a class declaration, and the word *Application1* specifies the name of the class. Note that class names start with an uppercase letter. Following the class name is a block, defined by a pair of curly braces, { }. These curly braces enclose the entire class definition.

Most class declarations specify an existing class from which this new class descends. This would be done by following the name of the new class declaration with the **extends** keyword, which is then followed by the name of the superclass. When this part of the declaration is omitted, the ancestor class is *java.lang.Object*, by default. *Object* is the highest level object in Java, and the only class that does not have a superclass. *Application1* is a direct descendant of *Object*.

A Variable Declaration

The first line within the class declaration looks like the following:

```
boolean packFrame = false;
```

This statement declares a field, or variable, of the *Application1* class. In this case, the variable name is *packFrame* (by convention, variables begin with a lowercase letter and contain embedded uppercase letters for readability). This variable is declared to be a boolean variable. In this particular case, the declaration of the *packFrame* variable includes an *initializer*. An initializer is a statement that sets the variable to an initial value.

One or more modifiers that influence how the variable can be used sometimes precede variable declarations. These modifiers are **public**, **protected**, **private**, **static**, **transient**, **volatile**, and **final**. Any object can reference public variables, while protected variables are only accessible from descendant classes. By comparison, private variables are only accessible from within the class itself, and are not even inherited by descendant classes.

Static variables are associated with the class itself, as opposed to individual objects. In other words, a static variable is one that is shared by all members of a class. Variables declared static are therefore referred to as *class variables*. By comparison, the values of variables not declared static are associated with instances of the class, and each instance has its own copy of the variable. Variables not declared static are referred to as *instance variables*.

Final variables are constants—that is, their value can never change. Final variable declarations must either include an initializer or be explicitly assigned in the code that immediately follows their declarations.

NOTE: For information on variables declared volatile or transient, see The Java Language Specification, available in JBuilder's online help.

When a variable is not declared either public, protected, or private, the variable is said to have default access. Default access permits the variable to be referred to only by code within the same package.

In the *Application* class, the variable *packFrame* is an instance variable with default access. Because no variables are declared in the *Object* class, the *Application1* class does not inherit any variables. Therefore, *Application1* has only one variable. You could, if you want, declare additional variables for the *Application1* class.

Method Declarations

Following the variable declaration, the class declares one constructor and one method, *Application1()* and *main()*, respectively. *Application1()* is the *constructor*. Although a constructor is not a method, you can think of it as a special method that is called specifically to create an instance of the class. In Java, a constructor always has the same name as the class. Furthermore, a particular class may have more than one constructor, each with the same name. When two methods (or in this case, constructors) appear with the same class using the same name, the method (or constructor) is said to be

2

overloaded. When an overloaded method is called, the compiler identifies which version of the method to invoke by comparing the type of any arguments passed to the method. (Obviously, then, two or more methods having the same name within a given class must be unique with respect to their parameters.)

Not all classes have explicitly declared constructors. A class that does not explicitly declare any constructors has a single implicitly declared constructor that takes no parameters. This constructor's sole action is to invoke the constructor from the parent class that takes no parameters.

The constructor for the *Application1* class is declared public. In most cases, a constructor is declared public so that another object can call the constructor. In rare instances, you might see a class whose constructors are declared private. Such a class cannot be instantiated except by method and variable declarations associated with the class itself.

The *Application1* class also declares a method named *main()*. In order for the Java Virtual Machine to be able to directly execute a class, that class must declare a public, static method named *main()* that takes an array of strings as its sole parameter and has a return type of **void**. Due to the presence of the *main()* method in this class, the *Application1* class can be executed.

 NOTE: The array argument of *main()* holds any command-line parameters that are passed to the application when it is executed.

As you can see from the *main()* method declaration, methods also can be declared using modifiers. For methods, these are **public**, **protected**, **private**, **abstract**, **static**, **final**, **synchronized**, and **native**. The **public**, **protected**, and **private** modifiers control visibility, and have the same effect as those corresponding modifiers used for variables. The **abstract** modifier declares a method that is not implemented in this class, but that will be inherited by a descendant class. A class that includes one or more abstract methods, either by declaring one or more methods to be abstract, or by inheriting but not implementing one or more abstract methods, is referred to as an *abstract class*. An abstract class cannot be instantiated. That is, you cannot create an instance of an abstract class. (When a class includes at least one abstract method, the class itself must be explicitly declared abstract, using the **abstract** modifier.)

A method that is declared to be static is a class method. Class methods, similar to class variables, are associated with the class as a whole, and not individual objects. What this means is that you can call a class method using a class name as the qualifier. By comparison, methods that are not class methods must be called using an instance of the class as the qualifier. The *main()* method is a class method.

When a method is declared final, a descendant object cannot override it. A method is overridden when the descendant object declares a method of the same name and signature (same parameters and same return type). A method cannot be declared both abstract and final, since a descendant object could never implement it.

The **synchronized** modifier identifies methods that are synchronized for the purpose of synchronizing multiple threads. Synchronized methods are discussed in Chapter 10. Native methods—that is, those declared using the modifying **native**—are implemented using code native to a particular platform, such as Windows 95 or UNIX. Native methods should be avoided if you want to produce applications that can run on any platform.

Notice that the declaration of the *main()* method includes the keyword **void**. This specifies the return type of the method. All methods, with the exception of constructors, must declare a return type. The return type may be **void**, in which case no value is returned, or it may be any valid primitive type or reference type.

Viewing the Class Structure

When a Java source file is selected in the Navigation pane and the Source tab is selected in the in the Content pane, the Structure pane displays detailed information about your source file and any classes declared in it. For example, Figure 2-4 displays the Structure pane when the Application1.java file is selected.

Any classes declared in the Java file are displayed as nodes in the Structure pane. Class declarations are identified by the following icon:

When the class node is expanded, the first node beneath the class identifies the ancestor class or superclass. As mentioned previously, the *Application1* class descends from the *Object* class. The ancestor class is identified by the following icon:

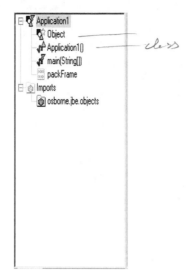

The Structure
pane displays
the
declarations in
the current
Java source file
Figure 2-4.

Methods and constructors of the class also appear in this list. Constructors
are displayed using the following icon:

while methods use an icon similar to this one (runnable and native methods
use a slightly different icon):

If either a constructor or a method is overloaded, its associated node will be
expandable (a small plus sign will appear next to the node). To see the
various versions of that constructor or method, expand the node. Figure 2-5
shows the *Frame* class structure in the Structure pane. The *Frame()* constructor
is overloaded, and the two versions of the constructor appear in the
expanded node.

The Structure pane also displays the variables of a class. There is only one
variable in the *Application1* class, and it is a primitive type (**boolean**).
Primitive types are represented by the following icon. If the variable is a

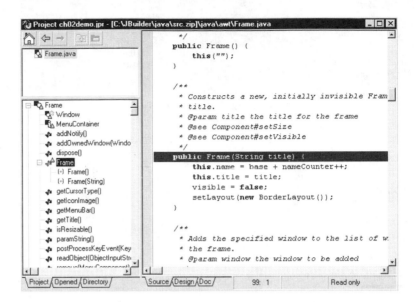

The Structure
pane shows
the
overloaded
Frame
constructor—
the
implemented
constructors
appear in the
Content pane
Figure 2-5.

reference type, the variable is represented with the same bitmap, but with a teal-colored background instead of the white one used by primitive type variables.

Following any class nodes, there is a node for imported packages. This node is labeled Imports. The nodes in the Imports list are the packages used by the Java file. This list always includes the package in which the current Java file resides, as well as any additional packages imported by the source file. The declared package appears first, followed by imported packages in alphabetical order. All the icons for package nodes look like the following, but the icon for the package in which the Java source file resides appears darker than those for imported packages.

The Example Frame Class

The *Application1* class is just one of the two classes defined by the Application Wizard. The *Frame1* class is also defined. To view the *Frame1* class, select the Frame1.java file in the Navigation pane. With the Source tab selected, the following code appears in the Editor:

```
package osborne.jbe.objects;

import java.awt.*;
import java.awt.event.*;          } other packages
import borland.jbcl.control.*;
import borland.jbcl.layout.*;

public class Frame1 extends DecoratedFrame {
  BorderLayout borderLayout1 = new BorderLayout();
  XYLayout xYLayout2 = new XYLayout();
  BevelPanel bevelPanel1 - new BevelPanel();
  StatusBar statusBar = new StatusBar();

  //Construct the frame
  public Frame1() {
    try {
      jbInit();
    }
    catch (Exception e) {
      e.printStackTrace();
    }
  }

  //Component initialization
  public void jbInit() throws Exception{
    this.setLayout(borderLayout1);
    this.setSize(new Dimension(400, 300));
    this.setTitle("Frame Title");
    bevelPanel1.setLayout(xYLayout2);
    this.add(statusBar, BorderLayout.SOUTH);
    this.add(bevelPanel1, BorderLayout.CENTER);
  }
}
```

The *Frame1* class is more complex than the *Application1* class, which is merely used to start the application. The *Frame1* class defines the look and behavior of the window that is displayed when the application executes.

Importing Packages and Classes

The Frame1.java source file begins just like Application1.java, in that it declares the package in which it resides. The next lines, however, were not present in Application1.java. These lines, each of which begins with the keyword **import**, define the packages that will be searched for classes.

The import statement permits classes that reside in other packages to be referenced using their simple class name, rather than having to fully specify the class and package name. For example, imagine that you want a *Button* object to appear on instances of *Frame1*. Since the *Button* class is declared in the java.awt package, your declaration of the instance variable used to refer to the button might look like this:

```
java.awt.Button button1 = new java.awt.Button();
```

While a statement formed this way is always acceptable, it is possible to omit the package name, and refer to the class by its class name alone, by importing the package. The first import statement in Frame1.java does just that. The statement

```
import java.awt.*;
```

instructs the compiler to make all classes from the java.awt package visible to the current file. As a result, the preceding instance variable declaration can be rewritten as follows:

```
Button button1 = new Button();
```

The use of the asterisk character (*) in the import statement has the effect of importing all classes from the specified package. However, single classes can be imported without having to import the entire package. For example, the following import statement also permits a *java.awt.Button* class to be referenced simply as *Button*:

```
import java.awt.Button;
```

As mentioned earlier, a package is really nothing more than a directory. For a package to be imported, the base directory for the package must be set in JBuilder. This can be set by selecting File|Project Properties and then adding the base directory for your packages to the Class Path field of the Properties page. Alternatively, you can select Tools|IDE Options, click the Compiler tab, and then add the base directory for your packages to the Default Class Path field of the Compiler page.

Ref type ?

2

The Frame1 Class

The next set of statements in the source code is the declaration of the *Frame1* class. Like the *Application1* class, *Frame1* is declared public. However, in this case, *Frame1* contains an explicit **extends** statement, which declares that *Frame1* descends from the *borland.jbcl.control.DecoratedFrame* class. Furthermore, while *Application1* declared just one instance variable of the type **boolean**, *Frame1* declares four, all of which are reference-type variables. These reference types all include an initializer. These initializers call a constructor from the corresponding class. For example, the statement

```
BorderLayout borderLayout1 = new BorderLayout();
```

declares a variable named *borderLayout1* of the type *BorderLayout* (declared in the java.awt package). Furthermore, it is initialized with an instance of the *BorderLayout* class using the *BorderLayout()* constructor.

Frame1 also defines a single constructor that takes no arguments. This constructor contains a single **try** ... **catch** statement in it. Within the **try** clause, the *jbInit()* method is called. The method *jbInit()* is created by JBuilder to prepare a *Frame1* instance by setting properties for reference variables associated with the class. In this case, *jbInit()* associates layout managers with containers and places components within the frame. The use of layout managers is discussed in detail in Chapter 5.

There is actually more to the *Frame1()* constructor than meets the eye. Specifically, it is typically the case that the first statement in a constructor will be a call to the constructor for the ancestor class using the keyword **super**. Assuming that the ancestor's constructor takes no arguments, this call would look like the following:

```
super();
```

If the constructor does require an argument list, that would be included between the parentheses that follow the keyword **super**. If the code within the constructor does not make a call to the ancestor's constructor, the compiler automatically adds a call to the superclass constructor that takes no parameters.

As you learned earlier in this chapter, constructors can be overloaded. In some cases, you will find that one constructor contains a call to one of the other constructors. This is generally done when one or more parameters are necessary in order to create an object, but a constructor with fewer than the required number is provided for convenience. Consider, for example, the constructor for the *Frame* class (the one from which *DecoratedFrame* descends). The *Frame* class requires a constructor with one *String* parameter, that parameter being used for the title of the *Frame*. Nonetheless, the *Frame* class also includes a constructor that requires no methods. The code within this constructor calls the constructor that requires one parameter, passing an empty string as the parameter. Another constructor within the same class is called using the keyword **this**. The parameters of the constructor are passed between the parentheses that follow the **this** keyword. This is demonstrated in the following code, which appears in the java.awt.Frame.java source file. Comments have been removed from this code segment in order to simplify it.

```
public Frame() {
        this("");
    }

public Frame(String title) {
    this.name = base + nameCounter++;
    this.title = title;
    visible = false;
    setLayout(new BorderLayout());
    }
```

In this particular case, the compiler adds the call to the constructor of the *Frame* class ancestor in the version of the *Frame(String)* constructor (it requires one *String* argument).

NOTE: When *this()* is used in a constructor, it refers to other constructors in the same class. In other words, it is an implicit call to another constructor in the same class that has the same parameter list as that provided in the () of the *this()* call. However, **this**, when qualifying a method or variable from within a constructor or method, refers to the instance of the object for which the constructor or method is executing. For example, in the preceding code sample the statement `this.title = title;` is used to set the title of the instance of the object being instantiated to the value of the formal parameter of the constructor.

As mentioned earlier, the *jbInit()* method is used to initialize the *Frame1* instance. JBuilder's wizards automatically create this method for you when you create an *Applet*, a *Frame*, a *Dialog*, or other similar container for other components. It also adds a call to *jbInit()* to the class's constructors. If you add additional constructors to the class, it is important that you also add a call to the *jbInit()* method in order to initialize any objects that have been placed on your container.

Local Variables

Local variables are those declared within a method. Their scope extends from their point of declaration within the method, and continues for the remainder of the method. As a result, a local variable cannot be accessed outside of the method (hence, the name *local*). Local variables can be either primitive or reference types, and they are initialized when their declaration is executed within the method and released when the method terminates.

Local variables are always referred to using their simple name, and cannot be referenced using the package and class name notation. Furthermore, local variable declarations never include any modifiers except **final**.

2

You can demonstrate the use of a local variable by adding a new method to the *Frame1* class. To do this, add the following code immediately following the *jbInit()* method, but before the final closing curly brace of the *Frame1* class:

```
void setCaption() {
  String a = "Welcome";
  statusBar.setText(a);
}
```

Since this method is contained within the *Frame1* class, it is customary to indent it two spaces with respect to the left alignment of the *Frame1* declaration. As a result, *setCaption()* will be indented to the same extent as the *jbInit()* method and *Frame1()* constructor. Indenting in this way serves to visually emphasize that these methods are contained within the *Frame1* class.

Within this admittedly pointless method, the variable *a* is declared. This variable does not exist until the *setCaption()* method is called, and is released as soon as the method terminates. If you want to view the effects of *setCaption()*, you can add a call to it as the last statement of *jbInit()*. Figure 2-6 shows how the source view may look if you added this code.

If you now click the Run button on the JBuilder toolbar (or alternatively, press SHIFT-F9), the application runs and the frame is displayed. Since the call to *setCaption()* appears in *jbInit()*, the word Welcome appears in the status bar when the frame is first displayed.

Adding Methods

Java does not support pure functions or procedures. This means that you cannot declare a function or procedure outside of a class declaration—all functions and procedures must be declared as methods of a class.

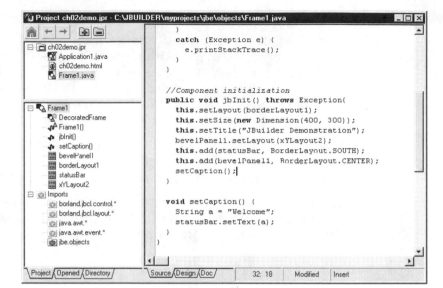

A new method, named *setCaption()*, in the Source view
Figure 2-6.

A method begins with zero, one, or more modifiers, and is then followed by the return type of the method. If the method is a procedure, use the keyword **void**. Otherwise, the return type can be any primitive or reference type.

The name of the method immediately follows the return type. By convention, all methods begin with a lowercase letter, but can include embedded uppercase letters for readability. The method name is then followed by open and close parentheses. If the method requires any arguments, these appear within the parentheses.

What appears next depends on whether the method was declared abstract or not. If the method was declared abstract (using the **abstract** keyword), the parentheses are followed by a semicolon, concluding the method declaration. Otherwise, a code block, indicated by curly braces, follows the parentheses. A semicolon never follows the close curly brace. The code that defines the behavior of the method appears within the code block.

Methods should generally be associated with the object upon which the methods operate. However, when you need to declare two or more related methods, and they really do not apply to a particular object, you should create a class solely for the purpose of declaring and organizing the methods. This can be easily accomplished using the Class Wizard.

Using the Class Wizard

To create a new class, select File|New, and then double-click the Class icon (the Class Wizard) in the New page of the Object Gallery. JBuilder's Class Wizard displays the New Object dialog shown in Figure 2-7. If you want to declare this class in another package, enter the package name at Package. In this case, keep the package name osborne.jbe.objects. In the Class Name field, enter the name for your new class. By default, this class name will be MyClass1, which works fine for this example. Notice that the File Name field contains the fully qualified path name and class name, ending with the .java extension.

The final step is to choose the existing class that your new class will extend. Since this class is simply going to hold a method, leave the Extends field set to java.lang.Object. If there already exists an object that contains field and method declarations that you would like to inherit in this object, enter that fully qualified object name in the Extends field.

Using the checkboxes in the Style section of the New Object dialog, you can select additional options for the code generation that JBuilder will perform for your new class. For this example, leave the Public and the Generate default constructor options checked, and the others unchecked.

Click OK when you are done. JBuilder adds the new class to your package and to your project.

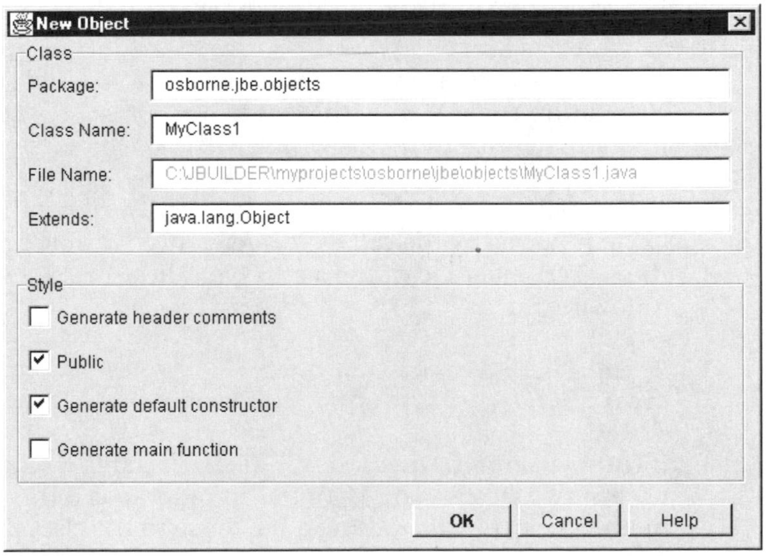

2

The New
Object dialog
is displayed
by the Class
Wizard

Figure 2-7.

At first, your new class will look like the following:

```
package osborne.jbe.objects;
public class MyClass1 {

  public MyClass1() {
  }


}
```

Add a new method immediately below the constructor *MyClass1()*, immediately before the closing curly brace of the class declaration. The following shows how this class will look when you are done.

```
package osborne.jbe.objects;
public class MyClass1 {

  public MyClass1() {
  }

  public String reverseString(String text){
    String temp = "";
    int i;
    for (i = (text.length() - 1);i != -1; --i)
      temp += text.charAt(i);
    return temp;
  }
}
```

Now, you can return to the *Frame1* class by clicking Frame1.java in the Navigation pane. Modify the call to `statusBar.setText` in the *setCaption()* method. Replace the existing line with two lines. The first line should declare a local variable of the type *MyClass1*, and you should initialize it with a call to the *MyClass1()* constructor. The second line should pass the value returned by the call to this reference variable's *reverseString()* method to the *setText()* method of the status bar. These two lines should look like the following:

```
MyClass1 newObject = new MyClass1();
statusBar.setText(newObject.reverseString(a));
```

If the *reverseString()* method was declared static, it would not have been necessary to instantiate *MyClass1* in order to call this method. Static methods can be called using a reference to the class itself. Consequently, if *reverseString()* was static, you could call the method using the following code:

```
statusBar.setText(MyClass1.reverseString(a));
```

As you can see, using *reverseString()* would be simpler if it was declared static. However, this method was not declared static so that the Override Methods Wizard could be used to override it. The following section describes why you might want to override a method, and how to do so.

Overriding Methods

One of the advantages of declaring a class that extends an existing class is that you can override one or more of the methods declared in the ancestor class. An overridden method can simply replace the behavior of the ancestor, or it can extend it. As mentioned earlier in this chapter, the advantage of inheritance is that it permits you to use a common method call for objects descending from a common ancestor. This same method name, however, may behave differently for different classes, providing a behavior that is appropriate to the class for which it is called. Overriding methods provides for this customization of an inherited behavior.

2

If you want to simply replace the behavior of a method inherited from an ancestor, a descendant class only needs to redeclare a method using the same name and parameter types as that which it inherited, and then provide a completely new implementation. If the inherited method is overloaded, you need to declare and implement each of those versions of the inherited method that you want to override.

While replacing an inherited method is the simple case, it is somewhat limited. In many instances, it can be beneficial to leverage the inherited behavior in your descendant object. Specifically, you may want to have the inherited behavior executed, but then add additional operations. By doing so, you can introduce additional behaviors at each level in the object hierarchy without having to duplicate the code that defines the behavior of the ancestor(s). When done properly, the result is smaller classes and easier to maintain code. For example, if it is necessary to make a change to the implementation of a method in an ancestor class, that change is automatically inherited by all descendant classes. If it were necessary to reimplement the entire inherited behavior in each descendant class, a minor change might require you to modify every class that implements that behavior.

Using the Override Methods Wizard

All you need to do to override a method is to redeclare it in a descendant class. However, this operation can be made even easier using JBuilder's Override Methods Wizard. Furthermore, using the Override Methods Wizard helps you avoid two common mistakes when trying to override a method: misspelling the method name and getting the parameter list wrong. Both are perfectly legal, but result in a totally new method declaration rather than a method override.

The following demonstration creates a new class that descends from the *MyClass1* class created in the preceding example. The *reverseString()* method is then overridden using the Override Methods Wizard. Also, the previous behavior of reversing the order of the characters of the string is extended in this example to include converting the string to uppercase. Since the inherited method already reverses the string, the behavior defined by the *MyClass1* class will be leveraged without having to reimplement this behavior in the descendant class.

If you want to follow along with this example, but did not create the *MyClass1* class discussed earlier in this chapter, do so before continuing.

Start by using the Class Wizard from the Object Gallery to have JBuilder automatically create your descendant class. Begin by selecting File|New, then double-click the Class icon. On the New Object dialog, accept the default class name MyClass2, but in the Extends field enter **osborne.jbe.objects.MyClass1**. The form should look like that shown in Figure 2-8. Now, accept these settings by clicking OK.

Once you have accepted the New Class dialog, JBuilder adds a new file, named MyClass2.java to your project. This file contains the following code:

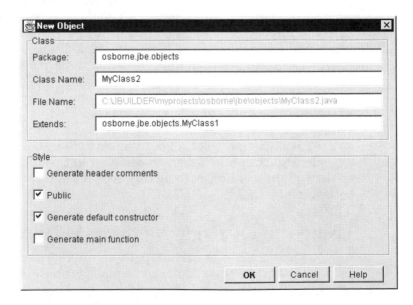

Use the New Object dialog to declare a new class that descends from *MyClass1*

Figure 2-8.

```
package osborne.jbe.objects;

public class MyClass2 extends MyClass1 {

  public MyClass2() {
  }
}
```

You are now ready to override the *reserveString()* method. To do this, select Wizards|Override Methods. The Override Inherited Methods dialog, shown in Figure 2-9, is displayed.

2

Since the selected Java source file, MyClass2.java, declares only one class, that class is automatically displayed at Class Name. If more than one class is declared in the currently selected source file, you need to select for which object you want to override methods in the Class Name drop-down list. The Inherited Methods tree appears below the Class Name. You use this tree to select which methods you want to override.

The Inherited Methods tree is organized by class, with the immediate ancestor appearing as the first node in the tree, and more distant ancestors appearing as later nodes, in order of inheritance. Expand the node associated with each object that declares a method you want to override (click the + sign) and then click the method to highlight it. If you want to override two or more methods at once, hold down the CTRL key while you select the method names.

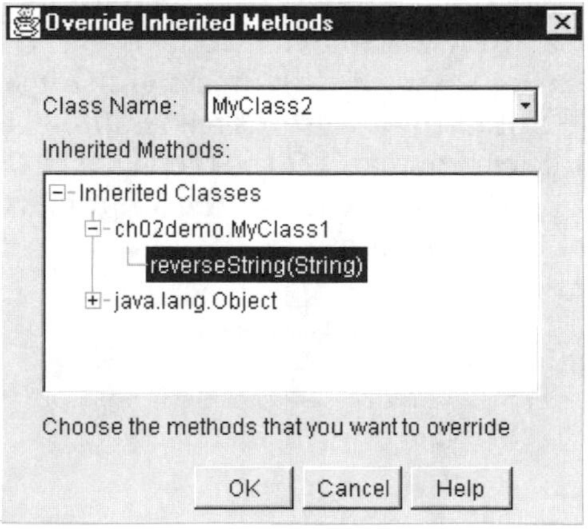

The Override Inherited Methods dialog is displayed by the Override Methods Wizard

Figure 2-9.

For this example, only override the method *reverseString()* declared in
MyClass1. Do this by expanding the *MyClass1* node and selecting
reverseString(). Continue by clicking OK. The Override Methods Wizard
responds by inserting the following method override into your *MyClass2*
class:

```
public String reverseString(String parm1) {
  //TODO: override this ch02demo.MyClass1   method;
  return super.reverseString( parm1);
}
```

If you wanted to completely replace the method *reverseString()* with this new
version, you should remove the **return** statement that includes the call to
`super.reverseString()`. You would then write your new code, making
sure that you return a *String* object (which is required by the method
declaration).

If you want to extend the inherited behavior of an overridden method, you
call the inherited method using the **super** keyword as the qualifier. When
you do so, you are calling the version of the method defined in the
superclass, producing the result defined there. You then add additional code
to the overridden method, thereby adding to the behavior that was
inherited. Whether you place your additional code before the call to the
ancestor method or after (or both before and after) depends on the effect you
are trying to achieve. In this particular instance, it does not matter since we
could just as easily pass an uppercase version of the string to the ancestor as
convert the string returned by the ancestor's *reverseString()* method to
uppercase.

Begin by removing the comment line that the Override Methods Wizard
placed as a reminder that you must modify this code. In its place, declare a
local *String* variable named *temp*. Next, replace the line that includes the
return keyword with an assignment statement where the value returned by
the call to the ancestor's *reverseString()* is assigned to *temp*. Finally, add
another line that returns the value of *temp*, converted to uppercase using the
toUpperCase() method of the *String* class. The overridden method now looks
like the following:

```
public String reverseString(String parm1) {
  String temp;
  temp = super.reverseString( parm1);
  return temp.toUpperCase();
}
```

NOTE: This method was made longer than it needed to be for the sake of readability. Alternatively, rather than using a local variable to convert the value returned by the ancestor's *reverseString()* method to uppercase, the value returned by this method could have been converted to uppercase directly. In that case, the following single line could replace all three lines of the preceding example:

```
return super.reverseString(parm1).toUpperCase();
```

2

You can now demonstrate the execution of this overridden method by changing the local variable declaration in the *setCaption()* method of the *Frame1* class. Specifically, change this declaration to declare a variable of type *MyClass2*, instead of *MyClass1*, and initialize this variable with the *MyClass2* constructor. After this change, the *setCaption()* method will look like the following:

```
void setCaption() {
    String a = "Welcome";
    MyClass2 newObject = new MyClass2();
    statusBar.setText(newObject.reverseString(a));
}
```

If you run the application, the status bar contains the word welcome in uppercase and backwards when the application first loads, as shown in Figure 2-10.

Interfaces

An interface is very similar to a class in that it can include method and constant declarations. However, unlike a class, an interface has no constructors, and its methods are implicitly abstract. That is, the method signatures are defined (including the return values and parameters). However, the code logic that defines the behaviors of the methods is absent. As a result, it is never possible to instantiate an interface.

This section is provided to give you a brief overview of interfaces, so that you will be familiar with the concept when it appears later in this book. However, a complete description of interfaces is beyond the scope of this chapter. If you are interested in additional information about interfaces, refer to the Java Language Specification in JBuilder's online help system.

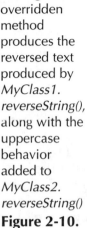

Calling the overridden method produces the reversed text produced by *MyClass1. reverseString(),* along with the uppercase behavior added to *MyClass2. reverseString()*
Figure 2-10.

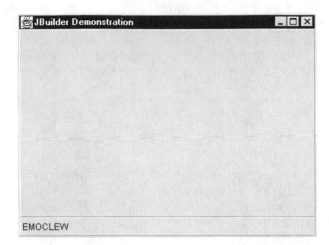

Interface Overview

An interface is used to define methods as well as variables that are public, static, and final (in other words, constants). This definition can then be used as part of a class declaration. Specifically, a class declaration can include the keyword **implements** followed by the name of one or more interfaces (separated by commas). Such a class is said to *implement* the interfaces that are listed. For example, the following is the declaration of the *java.lang.Thread* class, which extends *java.lang.Object* (since no **extends** keyword is used) and implements *Runnable*:

```
public class Thread implements Runnable {
```

When a class implements an interface, it automatically inherits all variables defined by the interface. Furthermore, the class becomes obligated to provide an implementation of every method declared by the interface. Consider the interface *java.lang.Runnable*:

```
public interface Runnable {
/**
 * When an object implementing interface <code>Runnable</code> is used
 * to create a thread, starting the thread causes the object's
 * <code>run</code> method to be called in that separately executing
```

```
 * thread.
 *
 * @see     java.lang.Thread#run()
 * @since   JDK1.0
 */
public abstract void run();
}
```

declare a method that is not implemented in this class.

2

This interface declares one method, *run()*. This method, like all methods declared in an interface, does not include a code block. Method declarations simply define the signatures of the methods, not their behavior.

Because *Thread* is declared to implement this interface, this class is required to declare *run()* and provide the code logic performed by it. Alternatively, if a class that implements an interface inherits one or more methods declared in the interface, this implementation is satisfied. A compiler error is generated if a class is declared to implement an interface, but then fails to include all methods defined by the interface (whether by declaration or inheritance)

The purpose of interfaces is twofold. First, they define methods that a class that implements the interface will support by definition. As a result, interfaces provide a second means by which two or more objects are guaranteed to have the same methods (the first means being inheritance, but this requires that the two or more objects descend from a common ancestor). Second, interfaces provide for assignment compatibility between objects that do not descend from a common ancestor. If you consider these two benefits, you will see that interfaces provide for polymorphism outside of the class hierarchy.

Some languages, C++ for example, permit a new class to extend two or more existing classes. This is known as multiple inheritance. While Java does not provide for multiple inheritance, the support for interfaces provides the same benefits (primarily associated with assignment compatibility between objects), without the problems, such as method name conflicts, that are associated with multiple inheritance.

Even if you are not going to define your own new classes, it is necessary to have a basic understanding of interfaces in JBuilder. This is because a number of methods in Java have as their return type an interface, or require an interface as a parameter. When a method returns an interface type, it is returning a reference to an object that implements the named interface. When a method requires an interface as a parameter, that parameter requires an actual parameter that is an instance of a class that implements the named interface.

Like class definitions, interfaces also exist in a hierarchy. Specifically, an interface can be declared to extend one or more existing interfaces. The interface that is declared to extend an existing interface is referred to as the descendant interface, and the interface being extended is referred to as the superinterface (or ancestor interface). A descendant interface inherits all method declarations defined in the superinterface. Furthermore, a descendant interface is assignment compatible with an object that implements its superinterface. For example, if a method requires a parameter of a particular interface, the actual parameter can be an object that implements that interface or any of its descendant interfaces.

Using the Implement Interface Wizard

JBuilder includes an Implement Interface Wizard that simplifies the process of implementing interfaces. You use this if you are declaring a new class and want it to implement one or more interfaces. Not only does this wizard add the selected interfaces to the class declaration (using the **implements** keyword), but it also inserts method stub code into the class, one method stub for each method declared in the interfaces. A stub is a method declaration with an empty method body. Just add the necessary code to the method body of each method stub to complete the implementation of the interface.

To view the Implement Interface Wizard, select the source file in the Navigation pane that contains the class to which you want to add the interface. Next, select Wizards|Implement Interface to display the Implement Interface dialog, shown in Figure 2-11. If more than one class is declared in the currently selected source file, select for which class you want to implement the interface from the Class Name drop-down list. The Available Interfaces tree appears below the Class Name. This tree includes one node for each of the packages used by the source file, as well as some standard packages that include interfaces that you might want to implement.

To select an interface, expand the node associated with the package that includes the interface declaration. If you want to implement more than one interface at once, hold down the CTRL key while you select the interface names. Click OK when done, and the wizard will add the selected interfaces to the class declaration and create stub methods for all methods defined in the interfaces.

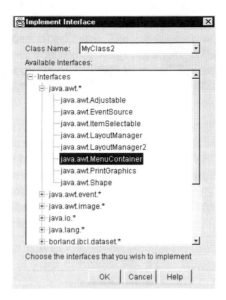

The
Implement
Interface
dialog
Figure 2-11.

CHAPTER 3

Building a User Interface

There are some visual elements that almost every
application will have. These include a main window that is
displayed when the application begins, a menu bar with
that application's choices, a button bar (toolbar) with
buttons for accessing the most frequently used features,
and a status bar for communicating noncritical information
to the user. This chapter details how to add these basic
elements to your user interface, and how to control their
appearance and behavior.

Frames Created by the Application Wizard

When you run the Application Wizard, it creates two classes. One is a new class, whose default name is *Application1*, which is used to display the first window of the application. The second is a *Frame*, which defines the characteristics of this window. The new *Frame* class descends from *borland.jbcl.control.DecoratedFrame*, and the Application Wizard gives you the option to automatically add a *java.awt.MenuBar,* a *borland.jbcl.control.ButtonBar,* and a *borland.jbcl.control.StatusBar* to this frame.

NOTE: There are additional options that are provided in the Application Wizard, such as centering the frame on the screen and generating an About dialog. These topics are covered in the next chapter.

To demonstrate this automatic creation of these elements, start by creating a new application. Begin by first closing any projects that are currently open. Then use the following steps to create the project:

1. Select File|New to display Object Gallery.

2. Double-click the icon for the Application Wizard on the New page in the Object Gallery. Since there is not an open project, JBuilder begins by displaying the Project Wizard.

3. At File, enter **c:\JBuilder\myprojects\osborne\jbe\basicui\basicui.jpr**, then click the Finish button. JBuilder creates the new project and then displays the Application Wizard.

4. Make no changes to the first page of the Application Wizard. Instead, select the Next button to move to the Step 2 page. On this page, check the Generate menu bar, Generate tool bar, and Generate status bar checkboxes. Complete the Application Wizard by clicking Finish. If you select Frame1.java in the Navigation pane and then select the Design tab to display the UI Designer, you will see the basic frame created by the Application Wizard, as shown in Figure 3-1.

While this frame looks simple enough, it is actually more complex than you might imagine. Specifically, in addition to the *MenuBar*, *ButtonBar*, and *StatusBar* components added by the wizard, there is also a *BevelPanel component*. This bevel panel occupies the entire central part of the frame. Furthermore, the Application Wizard assigned two layout managers to the containers on this frame, one for the frame itself and another for the bevel panel. The layout manager assigned to the frame is of the class *BorderLayout*, and it is this layout manager that is responsible for causing the button bar,

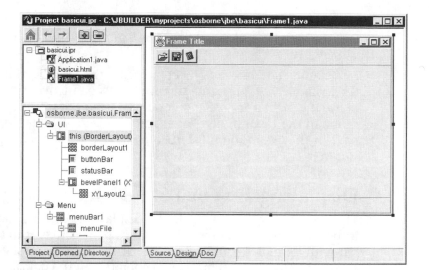

The basic
frame created
by the
Application
Wizard as it
appears in the
UI Designer
Figure 3-1.

The basic
frame created
by the
Application
Wizard as it
appears in the
UI Designer
Figure 3-1.

the status bar, and the bevel panel to be aligned along the top, bottom, and
the center of the frame, respectively. Furthermore, this layout manager
causes the button bar and status bar to remain aligned top and bottom, even
when the size of the frame is changed. Without the *BorderLayout* layout
manager, and the bevel panel to occupy the center of the frame, this
alignment could not be achieved.

The second layout manager is assigned to the *BevelPanel* itself, providing for
the layout of objects that you will place within this container. This layout
manager is of the class *XYLayout*. XYLayout managers are temporary in that
you will generally want to reassign a different layout manager to the bevel
panel before you deliver your application.

NOTE: For more information on using layout managers, refer to Chapter 5.

Now that you have created a basic frame, the next sections take a more
detailed look at three of the objects generated by the Application Wizard: the
StatusBar, the *MenuBar*, and the *ButtonBar*.

Status Bars

As its name suggests, a status bar is used to convey information to the user
about the status of the application. This information may include minor

error messages that do not require a response from the user, whether the preceding operation concluded successfully or not, or the current state of an ongoing process.

By default, the *StatusBar* object created by the Application Wizard is assigned the instance variable name *statusBar*. This name may be different if you manually place a *StatusBar* component from the Component Palette on the frame in the UI Designer. For example, a *StatusBar* placed from the Controls page of the Component Palette may have the instance variable name *statusBar1*.

Displaying Text in a Status Bar

There are two primary vehicles for displaying text in a status bar. The most important, from a database developer's perspective, is to associate a status bar with a *DataSet* component. Once this is done, the status bar automatically displays messages generated by the dataset. The second means of displaying text is the most general—using code.

To see the method and fields associated with the status bar, you need to first select Frame1.java in the Navigation pane. Click the Source tab so that the source view is selected in the Content pane, and a structure tree is displayed in the Structure pane showing a structural analysis of the Java file. Select the node called *statusBar* in the Structure pane (*statusBar* references the *StatusBar* object). Next, double-click the node for *statusBar* in the Structure pane. This is called *drilling down* into a class. For *statusBar*, drilling down brings the *StatusBar* class into view in the Structure pane, as shown in Figure 3-2. The Content pane displays the source code file (the .java file) for the ancestor class *StatusBar*.

 TIP: When you drill down into a class by double-clicking an object node, you can double-click anywhere on that line.

From the *StatusBar* class, you can view the various methods and fields of *StatusBar*. Since the status bar is an object created from the *StatusBar* class, any methods of the *StatusBar* class declared public can be used for the *StatusBar* object.

For additional information, you can also display the documentation file, either a JavaDoc or a JBDoc (JBuilder) file, for the selected class. To do this, select the Doc tab of the Content pane to display the Documentation view which is used to view these HTML (HyperText Markup Language) files. If either a JavaDoc or a JBDoc file associated with the selected class exists, it is

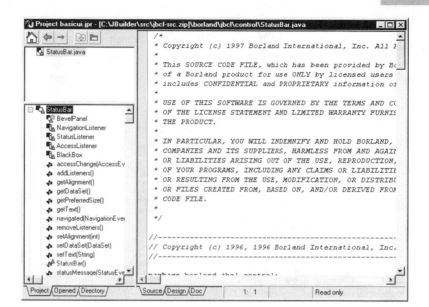

Drilling down into *statusBar* displays the *StatusBar* class source code file

Figure 3-2.

displayed. The JBDoc HTML file associated with *StatusBar* is displayed in Figure 3-3.

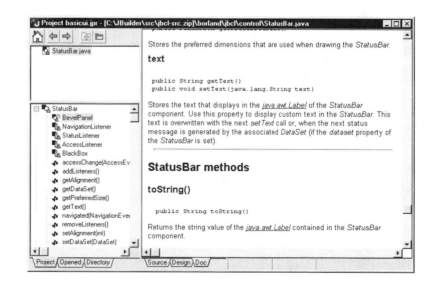

Choosing the Doc tab of the Content pane when a class is displayed in the Structure pane displays a JavaDoc or JBDoc file, if one exists. This figure shows the *text* property of the *StatusBar* class

Figure 3-3.

TIP: You can also drill down into an interface or instance or class reference type. Just double-click the associated node in the Structure pane.

If you examine either the class information in the Structure pane or the HTML file in the Documentation view in the Content pane, you will see that there is a method named *setText()* that you can use to programmatically control the textual contents of a status bar. These two panes display this information differently, however. In the Structure pane, you must scan the list of methods for one whose name suggests the capabilities you are looking for. The method *setText()* certainly implies that it assigns text to a status bar, and in fact it does.

In the Content pane, you will not actually see an entry for *setText()*. Instead, you will see a property named *text*. The JavaBeans model (and all of the components on JBuilder's Component Palette are Beans) makes use of a concept called *property*. Conceptually, a property is information about an object that can be set (if the property is a writable property) and read (if it is a readable property). A property is defined as a name (similar to a variable name, always with an initial lowercase letter) for which there is:

♦   a *get* method (a method whose name begins with *get*, although *is* is used for boolean properties),

♦   a *set* method (a method whose name begins with *set*),

♦   or both a *get* method and a *set* method.

Since the *StatusBar* class defines methods named *getText()* and *setText()*, the *StatusBar* class is said to have a *text* property. The *StatusBar* class also defines a field named *text*, which is used to store the value of the *text* property. According to the JavaBeans specification, this field, if it exists (and there isn't always a field with the name of the property), should never be declared public, and consequently, you as a developer cannot access it directly. You are only permitted to access it using the get and set methods. These methods are sometimes referred to as *accessor methods*, as well as *getter* and *setter* methods.

The bottom line is this: you control the value of the text displayed in a status bar using the *setText()* method. This method has the following syntax:

```
public void setText(String theText);
```

If you wanted to evaluate the current value displayed in a status bar, you would use the *getText()* method. This method has the following syntax:

```
public String getText();
```

It is also possible to control the text that is initially displayed in a status bar when the frame is first created. This can be done using the Inspector. In order to do this, you must first load *Frame1* in the UI Designer. Do so by clicking the Home button above the Navigation pane. Next, select Frame1.java in the Navigation pane, and then display the UI Designer by selecting the Design tab on the Content pane.

Once the UI Designer is displayed, click on the *StatusBar* in the UI Designer. Once selected, the Inspector displays the Properties page with the status bar's available read/write properties (these are properties for which public getter and setter methods exist), as shown in Figure 3-4.

The *text* property permits you to define the value that will be displayed in the status bar when the frame is constructed. Select this property, then click on the field to the right of the *text* property until an insertion point appears, and then type **Welcome to Java** and press ENTER. If you now select the Source tab of the Content pane to display the source view, and then select *jbInit()* in the Structure pane, you will see that JBuilder has added its own call to *setText()* to the *jbInit()* method in order to define the initial value displayed in the status bar, as shown in Figure 3-5.

There are several additional properties that you might want to set at design time for a status bar. These include *alignment* (aligns the text within the status bar), *background* (the background color of the status bar), *font* (the font characteristics for your status bar text), *foreground* (the color of the text in the status bar), and *visible* (whether the status bar is visible or not).

3

The properties for the status bar are displayed on the Properties page in the Inspector
Figure 3-4.

statusBar - Insp...	
<name>	statusBar
alignment	Left
background	Control
bevelInner	Raised
bevelOuter	Flat
constraints	South
dataSet	
enabled	True
font	"Dialog", 0, 12
foreground	Black
margins	0, 2, 0, 2
soft	False
text	
visible	True

Properties | Events

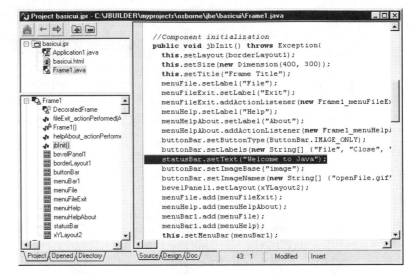

Setting the *text*
property of
statusBar in
the Inspector
produces a
call to
setText()
within *jbInit()*
Figure 3-5.

Customizing Menu Bars

The *MenuBar* component permits you to define a menu bar across the top of your frame. At runtime, when you select one of the labels appearing on this menu bar, either a drop-down menu appears, offering you additional selections, or an event handler is executed if you have also added code to the *actionPerformed* event handler for that item. Most applications provide menu bars that provide the user with access to some or all of the application's features.

Whereas the *StatusBar* class described in the preceding section defines a fairly simple control (it takes almost no setup to use, and is primarily controlled through the use of a single *setText()* method), the *MenuBar* class is more complex. It requires significant setup at design time, and is typically controlled (when control is required) through the use of a number of different methods.

The *MenuBar* itself is actually little more than a container for *Menu* objects. A *Menu*, in turn, is a container for both *MenuItem* objects and other *Menu* objects (a *Menu* object contained within another *Menu* is often called a *submenu*). Figure 3-6 depicts a *MenuBar*. The visible objects contained within this *MenuBar* are labeled to show what type of object they are.

When the Application Wizard generates a menu bar, it creates one with two menus. These menus have the labels File and Help. Both of these menus contain a single menu item. The File menu contains a menu item labeled Exit and the Help menu contains a menu item labeled About.

Menu objects

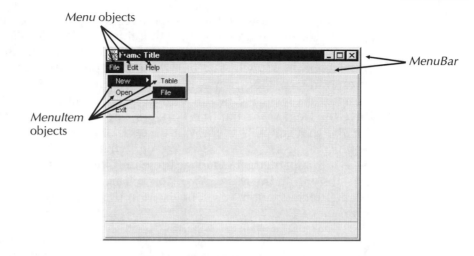

MenuBar

MenuItem
objects

A *MenuBar*
contains
Menu objects.
Menu objects
can contain
both
MenuItem
objects as well
as other *Menu*
objects

Figure 3-6.

3

Like all objects you use in JBuilder, it would be possible to create a menu bar and all of its menus and menu items by adding instance variables to the frame's class declaration, and then initializing these objects when the frame is created. Doing so, however, would be a tedious process. Fortunately, JBuilder makes this process almost effortless by providing you with the Menu Designer.

Using the Menu Designer

You access the Menu Designer through the Component Tree of the Structure pane. The Component Tree is displayed in the Structure pane when the Design tab of the Content pane is selected. Unlike the *StatusBar* and *ButtonBar* components, a *MenuBar* component is not visible in the frame when it is displayed in the UI Designer. Instead, the *MenuBar* component appears under the Menu node within the Component Tree of the Structure pane. To display this node, select the Frame1.java file in the Navigation pane, select the Design tab of the Content pane, and then select the Menu node in the Component Tree. Normally, the Menu node is already expanded. If it is not, expand it now by clicking the + character to the left of the Menu node. The expanded Menu node should look like the following:

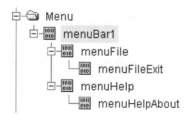

Under the Menu node in the Component Tree, you will see instance variable names like *menuBar* and *menuItem* that refer to each *MenuBar* and *MenuItem* component associated within your Java file. Furthermore, the relative positions of the *Menu* and *MenuItem* nodes representing these items correspond to the locations within the *MenuBar* in which they appear. For example, in the preceding illustration you see that the File *Menu* appears above the Help *Menu*, but that both appear nested within *menuBar1*, the *MenuBar* that contains them. Within each of the *Menu* components, a single *MenuItem* appears. As new *Menu* components and *MenuItem* components are created for a particular *MenuBar*, these new items will take their relative positions within the *Menu* in which they are inserted and their instance variable reference names will be listed in the appropriate positions in the Component Tree.

NOTE: The variable names such as menuFile, menuFileExit, and menuHelpAbout that are displayed in the Component Tree are associated with the Menu and MenuItem components. These are the instance variable names or references that refer to the components.

With the menu bar node displayed in the Component Tree, you activate the Menu Designer by either right-clicking one of the nodes of a menu bar and selecting Activate designer from the displayed popup menu, or double-clicking one of the nodes of a menu bar. In response, the Menu Designer will open in the Content pane. As shown in Figure 3-7, the Menu Designer depicts the *MenuBar* that you are designing. Note that the Menu Designer toolbar appears at the top of the Menu Designer.

There are a number of primary operations that you can perform using the Menu Designer. These include the following:

♦   Adding a new menu to the menu bar

♦   Adding a new menu item to a menu

♦   Adding a menu to a menu

♦   Changing the position of a menu or menu item

♦   Changing a label

♦   Adding separator bars to a menu

♦   Inserting menu items into a menu

♦   Deleting menus and menu items

♦   Enabling and disabling menu items

♦ Creating checked menu items

♦ Adding shortcuts

These operations are described in the following sections.

Adding a New Menu to the Menu Bar

The menus of your menu bar appear across the top of the Menu Designer. When you open the Menu Designer for a new menu bar that you have added to your frame, there will be one empty menu in this list. Move to this item and type the label for the first main menu you want to appear on the menu bar.

If the menu bar already exists, such as when you ask the Application Wizard to create one for you, the empty menu will appear at the end of the list. For example, in Figure 3-7 there is an empty menu to the right of the menu labeled Help. If you want to add your new menu at this last position, move to that position and enter the label. If you want it to appear in any other position, select the existing menu item that appears in the position where you want your new menu to go, and press INSERT or click the Insert Item button on the Menu Designer toolbar. Alternatively, right-click the menu item and select Insert Menu from the popup menu. The Menu Designer will open a new, empty menu in that position and shift the existing menus to the right one position. Now enter the label for the new menu you inserted.

Adding a New Menu Item to a Menu

To add a menu item to a menu, first select the menu to which you want to add the new item. When a menu is selected, any menu items already associated with that menu will appear in a drop-down list.

The *MenuBar* generated by the Application Wizard as it appears in the Menu Designer
Figure 3-7.

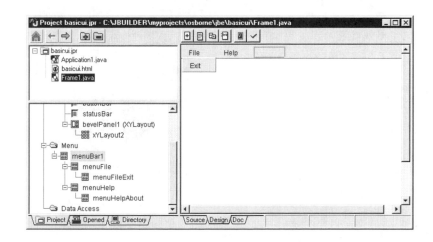

If you select a menu that has no menu items, an empty menu item will appear directly beneath the menu label. Move to this menu item and type a label for it. If there are already menu items in that list, an empty menu item will appear at the end of the displayed drop-down menu. For example, if you select the File menu, an empty menu item appears after Exit in the File menu ready for you to enter a label for this new menu item. (If it is not displayed, click the File menu to show the menu items it contains.) If you want to add a new menu item in this last position, move to this empty menu item and add a label. Once you press ENTER, that menu item now has a label and a new, empty menu item appears beneath it, ready for you to enter a label for another menu item if desired.

If you want to add a new menu item to any other location in the list, select the position where you want the new menu item to appear and press INSERT or click the Insert Item button on the Menu Designer toolbar. Alternatively, right-click that location in the list and select Insert Menu from the popup menu. This causes a new menu item to be inserted in that location, and causes the existing menu item in that position and those in lower positions to each move down one position.

Adding a Menu to a Menu

A menu can be inserted into the drop-down menu for a menu. When you insert a menu into a menu, you can then add one or more menu items (or menus) to this inserted menu. At runtime, if the user selects the inserted menu, its menu items appear in a submenu. Figure 3-8 shows a form that contains a simple menu bar. In this figure, the File drop-down menu contains a menu labeled New. This menu has two menu items, Table and Report.

To insert a menu into a menu, first add a new menu item, as described in the preceding section. Next, right-click the newly inserted menu item and select Insert Submenu as shown here:

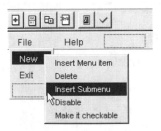

The menu New is added to the File menu in order to provide a submenu. This submenu consists of two menu items, labeled Table and Report

Figure 3-8.

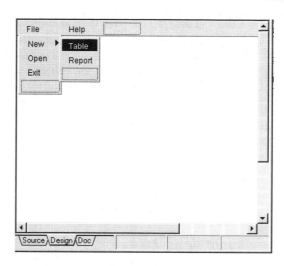

T IP: An alternative way to insert a submenu is to add a new menu item, select it, and then click the Insert Nested Menu button on the Menu Designer toolbar.

Once you insert a submenu into a menu, several things happen. First, the menu item to which you added a submenu is changed into a menu. Second, a small arrow appears to the right of the label of this menu. Third, a new, blank menu item appears to the right of the menu. Move to this new blank menu item and add its label. Add additional menu items to this new submenu, as described in the preceding section.

T IP: There is no limit to the number of levels to which submenus can be nested. For example, a submenu can include one or more menus, and the submenus of these menus can have menus, and so forth. However, for ease of use, it is generally considered bad menu design to create submenus more than three levels deep. That is, the drop-down of a main menu can include submenus, and this first level of submenus can include submenus, but this second level of submenus should not have submenus.

Changing the Position of a Menu or Menu Item

The Menu Designer makes it very easy to change the position of an existing menu or menu item. All you need to do is drag the existing item, and then drop it at the new position. (Drag by pressing and holding the left mouse button over the menu or menu item you want to move. Without releasing the left mouse button, move your mouse to the new position you want for the menu or menu item. Drop by releasing the left mouse button.)

This drag-and-drop technique is extremely flexible. Not only can you drag a menu to another position within the menu bar, or a menu item to a new position within the same menu, but you can also drag a menu to a menu, and you can drag a menu item to the menu bar. If you are dragging a menu to a new location, all of its menu items and submenus are moved with it.

Changing a Label

There are two ways to change the label of a menu or a menu item from within the Menu Designer. You can select the menu or menu item and then change the *label* property in the Properties page of the Inspector, or you can double-click the text of the label in the Menu Designer and edit the text directly.

Adding Separator Bars to a Menu

Separator bars are used to visually separate the menu items or menus of a given menu. Only menus can include separator bars. That is, separator bars cannot be used in the main menu bar. However, a given menu can include as many separator bars as you need. For example, the File menu, shown next, includes two separator bars: one separating the New and Open menus from the Printer and Printer Setup menu items, and another separating the printing-related menu items from the Exit menu item.

To add a separator bar, move to the position in the menu above which you want the separator bar to appear and then either click the Menu Designer's Insert Separator button or right-click the position and select Insert Separator from the popup menu.

Deleting Menus, Menu Items, and Separator Bars

To delete a menu, a menu item or a separator bar, begin by clicking the object you want to delete. A small rectangle will appear around the selected object. Next, either press DELETE or right-click the object and select Delete.

Enabling and Disabling Menus or Menu Items at Design Time

Menus and menu items can be either enabled or disabled. When enabled, the menu or menu item appears in a normal, black font, and the user can select it. If disabled, the menu or menu item appears in a light gray font, and the user cannot select it.

By default, all menus and menu items are enabled. There are three ways to disable a menu or menu item. First, you can select it in the Menu Designer, and then set the *enabled* property in the Properties page of the Inspector to False. (To re-enable a menu or menu item previously disabled, select it in the Menu Designer, and then use the Properties page of the Inspector to set its *enabled* property to True.) The second way is to select the menu or menu item and then click the Enable/Disable Item button in the Menu Designer toolbar to toggle it as either enabled or disabled. The third way is to right-click the menu or menu item and select Disable from the popup menu to disable it and Enable to enable it.

Creating Checked Menu Items

The MenuItem class does not support checkmarks. However, being able to display a checkmark next to a menu item can be a useful user interface feature, permitting you to signal a special state such as an option the user can enable or disable. Fortunately, Java provides an alternative type of menu item that does support checkmarks. The *java.awt.CheckboxMenuItem* class defines a menu item that is very similar to the *MenuItem* class, except that it also supports a checkmark.

The Menu Designer permits you to easily convert a *MenuItem* object into a *CheckboxMenuItem* object. To do this, select the *MenuItem* in the Menu Designer, and then select the Menu Designer's Checkable/Un-Checkable Item button. Alternatively, you can right-click the item and select Make it checkable. The *MenuItem* will be deleted, and a *CheckboxMenuItem* will appear in its place, using the label previously defined for the *MenuItem*. To restore a *MenuItem* to its original state, click the Menu Designer's Checkable/Un-Checkable Item button again, or right-click the item and select Make it un-checkable. The *CheckboxMenuItem* will be deleted and a *MenuItem* will be created in its place, again using the label of the previous *CheckboxMenuItem*.

The *state* property of the *CheckboxMenuItem* component defines whether a checkmark appears next to a *CheckboxMenuItem*. Furthermore, unless you attach an event handler to change the default behavior, when a user selects a *CheckboxMenuItem,* its check state toggles from checked to unchecked, or unchecked to checked. Writing event handlers to respond to the selection of a menu item is described later in this chapter.

Adding Shortcuts

A shortcut is a keypress combination that the user can press to automatically select a menu item without having to interact with the menu bar. For example, if you assign the shortcut CTRL-A to the Help|About menu item, the user can select this item by pressing CTRL-A, without having to drop down the Help menu.

To add a shortcut to a menu item, select it in the Menu Designer, and then set the *shortcut* property in the Inspector. At runtime, the shortcut key combination will appear to the right of the label in the menu item. Note however, that you will not be able to see the shortcut key combination displayed with the menu item in the Menu Designer.

NOTE: Although JBuilder appears to let you assign a shortcut to a menu, doing so does not make sense, and you should avoid attempting to do so.

Menu Item Event Handlers

Menu bars provide users with access to the features of your application. These features are provided by the code that you add to the *actionPerformed* events of your menu items. Unlike a status bar that can be associated with a dataset to provide messages without additional code, menu bars have no default behavior other than displaying menu items and permitting users to select them.

Typically, you will only create event handlers for menu items, which serve as the terminal; that is, the last selectable item on any given branch of a menu bar. If the Application Wizard created the menu, it added at least one event handler. This event handler, associated with the menu item labeled Exit under the File Menu, has the following code:

```
public void fileExit_actionPerformed(ActionEvent e) {
    System.exit(0);
}
```

This event handler has the effect of closing the Java interpreter, which terminates your application.

If you also had the Application Wizard create an About dialog for you, an event handler is also added to the menu item labeled About. This event handler creates an instance of the About dialog, defines its location on the screen, makes it a modal dialog (requiring the user to close it before returning to the frame), and then makes it visible:

```
public void helpAbout_actionPerformed(ActionEvent e) {
  Frame2_AboutBox dlg = new Frame2_AboutBox(this);
  Dimension dlgSize = dlg.getPreferredSize();
  Dimension frmSize = getSize();
  Point loc = getLocation();
  dlg.setLocation((frmSize.width - dlgSize.width) / 2 + loc.x,
    (frmSize.height - dlgSize.height) / 2 + loc.y);
  dlg.setModal(true);
  dlg.show();
}
```

3

Adding an Event Handler

To add an event handler to a menu item, begin by selecting that menu item in the Menu Designer. Next, click the Events tab of the Inspector to view the Events page. Events are listed in the left column of the Events page. The fields in the right-hand column are for creating and naming methods associated with the corresponding events. To create an event handler using JBuilder's default naming, click twice in the field associated with the *actionPerformed* event to have JBuilder select and assign a name to this field. To create an event handler using a name you define, enter the name of your event handler in the field associated with *actionPerformed*. Once the name has been assigned, press ENTER to move to the newly created method.

TIP: When you create an event handler using JBuilder's default naming, you click twice in the field associated with the event, once to select it and once to generate the name. Alternatively, you can click once in the field to select it, and then press F2 to have JBuilder assign the name. Once a name appears in the field, you can either press ENTER or double-click this name to move to the newly created method.

In reality, when you create a new event handler, JBuilder performs the following three tasks:

1. It creates a new method for your *Frame* class. This method contains the code that you want to be executed when the menu item is clicked. This method has the name that appears in the *actionPerformed* field of the

Events page of the Inspector, and is the one your cursor is moved to in the source view when you press ENTER while in this field.

2. It creates a new class that defines the *adapter* (some people refer to the object defined by this class as the *listener*). The adapter class contains a constructor using the default visibility (meaning that this class is visible only within this package) as well as a public method. The constructor takes a single argument, which identifies the *adaptee*. The adaptee is the object that contains the method that provides the response to the event. JBuilder always sets the highest-level container as the adaptee, and that is the *Frame* in this case (this is described in step 3). The public method has the same name as the event, which is *actionPerformed()* in this example. Within the *actionPerformed()* method there is a call to the method of the adaptee that JBuilder generated in step 1.

3. It adds code to *jbInit()*, where it adds a new instance of the adapter created in step 2 to the menu item. This registers the menu item as a potential source of the event. It is because **this** is passed as the parameter to the adapter's constructor that the frame is defined as the adaptee.

NOTE: When you are adding a new event handler to an object, and a related event handler for that object has already been created, a new adapter class is not defined. Instead, the existing adapter class is modified, adding an additional public method. This additional public method, in turn, calls the new adaptee method created in step 1. For example, if you first add a *mouseEntered* event handler, and then add a *mouseExited* event handler for the same object, the adapter created for the *mouseEntered* event is modified to include a public *mouseExited()* method.

You can demonstrate this by adding a new menu item to the Help menu. Enter **Say Hello** for the label of this menu item. With this menu item selected, click the Events tab to move to the Events page of the Inspector. Click twice in the field to the right of the *actionPerformed* event to have JBuilder generate a method name and list it in this field. Then press ENTER. JBuilder generates a method named *menuItem1_actionPerformed()*, and assigns this method to the *actionPerformed* event in the Inspector. The following is the empty *Frame* method created by JBuilder:

```
void menuItem1_actionPerformed(ActionEvent e) {

}
```

This method is called by the adapter, which is named *Frame1_menuItem1_actionAdapter* in this case. The following code is the adapter generated by JBuilder:

```
class Frame1_menuItem1_actionAdapter
    implements java.awt.event.ActionListener {
  Frame1 adaptee;

  Frame1_menuItem1_actionAdapter(Frame1 adaptee) {
    this.adaptee = adaptee;
  }

  public void actionPerformed(ActionEvent e) {
    adaptee.menuItem1_actionPerformed(e);
  }
}
```

Finally, JBuilder adds the following code to *jbInit()*.

```
menuItem1.addActionListener(new
  Frame1_menuItem1_actionAdapter(this));
```

While all of this code may be distracting, you really need to concern yourself with only the one method added to the Frame class. This method, named *menuItem1_actionPerformed()* in this example, is called when you select the menu item labeled Say Hello. To demonstrate this, add the statement statusBar.setText("Hello"); to the method *menuItem1_actionPerformed()*. When you are done, this method should look like the following:

```
void menuItem1_actionPerformed(ActionEvent e) {
  statusBar.setText("Hello");
}
```

Run the application by clicking the Run button on the JBuilder toolbar, selecting Run|Run, or by pressing SHIFT-F9. Once the form is displayed, select Help|Say Hello. In response, the text "Hello" appears in the status bar as shown in Figure 3-9.

Sharing Event Handlers

Normally, every adapter will be associated with a different method of your frame (the adaptee). However, if the response you want to produce from two different menu items is nearly identical, it might make sense for the adapters for two or more menu items to call the same method of the adaptee. To do

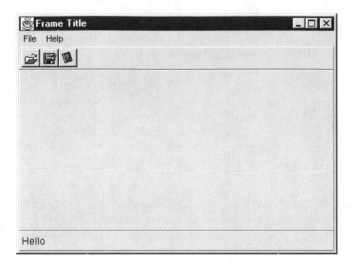

The message
"Hello"
appears in the
status bar in
response to
the
actionPerformed
event handler
assigned to
the Help|Say
Hello
MenuItem
Figure 3-9.

this, assign the same method name in the field to the right of the *actionPerformed* event in the Inspector for the two or more menu items.

The only complexity you introduce when calling the same method from two different adapters is identifying which object produced the event. For example, if the adapters for two different menu items call *menuItem1_actionPerformed()*, how can you tell from within this method which one of the two menu items is requesting a response?

The answer is found in the single parameter passed to the listener, which in turn passes it to the adaptee. This parameter, *e*, is of the class *ActionEvent* in this case, but depending on the event, it could be an object of another class. Although there are many different methods of the *ActionEvent* class, the two that are most appropriate for discerning which object generated the event are *getActionCommand()* and *getSource()*. The method *getActionCommand()* returns a *String* containing the label of the menu item that generated the event, while *getSource()* returns a reference to the object that generated the event.

If all menu items that can generate the event have different labels, you can use either of these methods. However, *getSource()* is typically a better choice, since there is nothing preventing you from giving the same label to two different menu items. By comparison, two different objects always have a different reference.

Use the following steps to demonstrate calling the same listener method from two different menu items. Begin by adding a new menu item to the Help menu. Enter **Another Hello** for its label. With this new menu item selected, display the Events page of the Inspector and type

menuItem1_actionPerformed in the *actionPerformed* event field. Now, press ENTER to move to the *menuItem1_actionPerformed()* method in the Editor. Modify this code to look like the following:

```
void menuItem1_actionPerformed(ActionEvent e) {
  if (e.getSource() == menuItem1)
    statusBar.setText("Hello - "+e.getActionCommand());
  else if (e.getSource() == menuItem2)
    statusBar.setText("Hello - "+e.getActionCommand());
  }
```

Run this application and then select Help|Say Hello, followed by Help|Another Hello. When you select Help|Say Hello, the status bar displays the message "Hello - Say Hello", and when you select Help|Another Hello, the status bar displays "Hello - Another Hello."

It should be noted that the variable names *menuItem1* and *menuItem2* that appear in the *menuItem1_actionPerformed()* method are associated with the two *MenuItem* objects labeled Say Hello and Another Hello, respectively. They are reference types, and the comparison being made is a reference comparison operation. Specifically, the statement e.getSource() == menuItem1 asks if the object being referred to by *e.getSource()* is the same object being referred to by *menuItem1*. If for some reason the *MenuItem* objects that you add are assigned to instance variables with different names, you should use those names in this method.

Popup Menus

Popup menus are menus that are displayed in response to a user's right-clicking the mouse button. They are particularly useful for providing convenient access to frequently needed options. Furthermore, popup menus are typically associated with components on a frame, rather than the frame itself. Moreover, you can have different popup menus for each item on a frame, although most applications have popup menus associated with only some objects (if any at all).

Adding a Popup Menu

To add a popup menu, start by displaying the UI Designer in the Content pane. You add a popup menu to a frame by selecting the *java.awt.PopupMenu* object from the AWT page of the Component Palette. You then drop it either into the Component Tree, or into the UI Designer. Like menu bars, popup menus appear under the Menu node in the Component Tree when the Designer is active.

TIP: To switch to the UI Designer from the Menu Designer in order to drop a *PopupMenu* component in your design, click the **this** node in the Component Tree.

You design a popup menu using the same techniques that you use for menu bars. Begin by selecting the popup menu that you want to design in the Component Tree and double-clicking it to load the Menu Designer.

A *PopupMenu* component is like a single *Menu* component (in fact, *PopupMenu* descends from *Menu*). Within the popup menu, you can place one or more menu items and menus (for submenus). With the exception of there being only one main menu in a popup menu, and shortcuts not being appropriate for popup menus, all other aspects of popup menu design match those for the design of menus. For additional details, refer to the descriptions of menu designing earlier in this chapter. Even the addition of code to produce the features of a popup menus is the same for both popup menus and menu bars. That is, you select the menu item for which you want to create an event handler, view the Events page of the Inspector, and then select the *actionPerformed* event. Press ENTER to create the adapter, listener method, and related *jbInit()* call to *addActionListener()*.

Displaying a Popup Menu

In order to use a popup menu, you need to add the popup menu to the component for which it will pop up using that component's *add()* method, and then display the menu using the popup menu's *show()* method. In some cases, the *add()* method can be called within the *jbInit()* method. However, doing so assumes that the popup menu will be used for that component only. Consequently, it is more common to add the popup menu within the event handler that displays the menu.

Since popup menus are traditionally displayed by right-clicking a component, you will normally use the *mouseClick* event handler to display a menu.

The following steps demonstrate how to create a popup menu and display it:

1. Begin by dropping a *PopupMenu* from the AWT page of the Component Palette into the Component Tree of the Structure pane.

2. Double-click the *PopupMenu* node (*popupMenu1*) in the Component Tree to display the Menu Designer. Select the popup menu in the Menu Designer and then add four items whose labels are **One**, **Two**, **Three**, and **Four**, respectively. (Use the same techniques

described previously for menus to add the menu items and labels to the popupmenu.)

3. Double-click *bevelPanel1* in the Component Tree to display the *Frame* in the UI Designer. Select this bevel panel within either the UI Designer or the Component Tree, and then click the Events tab of the Inspector to display the Events page. Click the *mouseClick* event field twice to have JBuilder assign a method name to it, and then press ENTER to go to that method in the source code.

Add the following code to the event handler:

```
void bevelPanel1_mouseClicked(MouseEvent e) {
  bevelPanel1.add(popupMenu1);
  if (e.getModifiers() == Event.META_MASK)
    popupMenu1.show(bevelPanel1,e.getX(),e.getY());
}
```

The first line of this code adds the popup menu named *popupMenu1* to the bevel panel named *bevelPanel1* in this example. Doing this sets the *parent* property of the *PopupMenu object*. Next, the *getModifiers()* method of the *MouseEvent* parameter is compared with the *Event* constant META_MASK. When this test returns **true**, the user has right-clicked the bevel panel, in which case the *show()* method of the *PopupMenu* object is called.

You pass three parameters to *show()*. The first is the object for which the *PopupMenu* object is being displayed. The second and third are the coordinates of the top-left corner of the popup menu which should correspond to the current mouse location, hence the use of the *e.getX()* and *e.getY()* methods.

Now run this application. When you right-click in the central part of the frame, the popup menu shown in Figure 3-10 is displayed.

Popup Menu Event Handlers

As mentioned previously, event handlers can be created for popup menus using the same technique that you use for menu bars. Specifically, you can assign *actionPerformed* event handlers to the individual menu items. There is, however, an additional option when working with popup menus. Since the options that appear on a single popup menu are often related, it is reasonable to create a single *actionPerformed* event handler for the popup menu as a whole, and then use the *getActionCommand()* method of the *ActionEvent* parameter to determine which menu item was selected. As described earlier in this chapter, the *getActionCommand()* method returns a *String* based on the *label* property of the menu item. Since it is rare for a

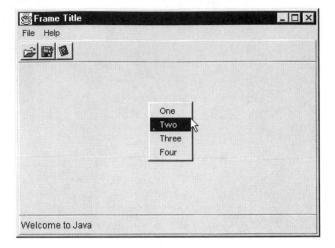

The bevel panel executes its *mouseClick* event handler, displaying the popup menu **Figure 3-10.**

popup menu to contain two or more menu items with the same label, the *getActionCommand()* method permits your code to easily distinguish which menu item was selected, and provide the appropriate response.

To demonstrate this technique, from the UI Designer select the popup menu in the Component Tree of the Structure pane, and double-click it to open the Menu Designer. With the popup menu still selected, create an *actionPerformed* event handler by clicking twice in the *actionPerformed* event field in the Events page of the Inspector and pressing ENTER. Enter the following code in the created event handler:

```
void popupMenu1_actionPerformed(ActionEvent e) {
  String message = "You selected ";
  if (e.getActionCommand() == "One")
    message += "1";
  else if (e.getActionCommand() == "Two")
    message += "2";
  else if (e.getActionCommand() == "Three")
    message += "3";
  else if (e.getActionCommand() == "Four")
    message += "4";
  statusBar.setText(message);
}
```

Now run this project. Right-click the bevel panel and select the menu item labeled Two from the popup menu. In response, the message "You selected 2" appears in the status bar.

Button Bars

Button bars are containers that display buttons that provide users with easy access to the most frequently used functions available from your frame. Button bars are sometimes called toolbars. This section describes how to define your buttons, how to assign graphical images to each button, and how to respond to a user's clicking a button.

Creating Buttons

Although the buttons of a button bar can be defined at runtime using any number of methods, including *addImageButton()*, *addTextButton()*, *setLabels()*, and *setButtonImages()*, the easiest way to control the contents of a button bar is to use the Inspector during design mode. If you want or need to define buttons at runtime, drill down into a button bar to view the *ButtonBar* class information.

To demonstrate creating buttons, click the Design tab to display the UI Designer in the Content pane. Next, select the button bar and move to the Properties page of the Inspector. Click the *labels* property field and then click the "..." (ellipsis) button at the far right of the field to display the *labels* property editor dialog:

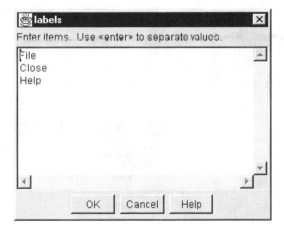

You use the *labels* property editor dialog to define one label for each button. If your button bar is created by the Application Wizard, it is created with three labels: File, Close, and Help. You can modify these labels, delete one or more of them, and/or add additional labels.

Choosing Button Styles

There are three button styles available for the button bar. These are TextOnly, ImageOnly, and TextAndImage. To change the style of button, change the *buttonType* property for the button bar by clicking twice on the

Setting
buttonType to
TextAndImage
displays both
text and an
image on the
buttons
Figure 3-11.

field in the Properties page of the Inspector and selecting the new style from
the drop-down list. For example, Figure 3-11 shows how the button bar
created by the Application Wizard looks when you set its *buttonType* to
TextAndImage.

Selecting Button Images

To display an image on your buttons, you assign the name of GIF files to the
imageNames property of the button bar, one GIF file for each button. This
can be done using the *imageNames* property editor dialog:

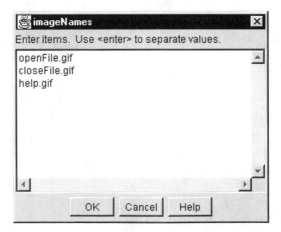

The first filename listed in the *imageNames* property editor dialog is associated
with the first button, the second filename is associated with the second button,

and so on. The file names that you add to the *imageNames* property must have a one-to-one correspondence with files stored in a single directory.

You specify the directory in which the image files are stored using the *imageBase* property. You can assign one of three values to this property: a URL (Uniform Resource Locator), an absolute path, or a relative path. A relative path, when used, refers to a subdirectory of the package in which the class that declares the *imageBase* property resides.

The button bar created by the Application Wizard has its *imageBase* property set to image. This is a relative path and refers to a subdirectory named image, which is located under borland.jbcl.controls, the package in which the *ButtonBar* class is located. You can use the images in this directory, or you define your own directory and place your images in it. The following are the 14 GIF files available in the borland.jbcl.controls.image directory:

cancel.gif	first.gif	next.gif	prior.gif
closeFile.gif	help.gif	openFile.gif	refresh.gif
delete.gif	insert.gif	post.gif	save.gif
ditto.gif	last.gif		

3

Enabling and Disabling Buttons

Normally, buttons are enabled in a button bar. The user can click an enabled button. Occasionally, it is convenient to disable buttons that you do not want the user to click. When a button is disabled, its image is dimmed and the button cannot be clicked.

You cannot disable a button at design time. Instead, you use the *setButtonEnabled()* method at runtime to control individual buttons. The method *setButtonEnabled()* is an overloaded method, meaning that there is more than one version (two, in this case). The following is the syntax of both versions of this method:

```
public void setButtonEnabled(int index, boolean enabled);
public void setButtonEnabled(String label, boolean enabled);
```

The first version is passed an integer to identify the button that you want to enable or disable. Use the number 0 to enable or disable the leftmost button, 1 to enable or disable the second button from the left, and so on. The second version refers to a button using its *label* property to identify it. For example, to disable the button whose label is Close on the button bar created by the Application Wizard, use the following code:

```
buttonBar.setButtonEnabled("Close",false);
```

Button Bar Event Handlers

Unlike menu items, where you can attach code to individual menu items of a menu bar, you cannot attach code to individual buttons in a button bar. This is because, unlike menu items, which are represented by legitimate objects, the buttons of a button bar are not objects. Instead, you attach a single event handler to the *actionPerformed* event of the entire button bar. From within this event handler, you can call the *getActionCommand()* method of the *ActionEvent* passed to the method. The method *getActionCommand()* returns the label of the button that is clicked.

The following simple example demonstrates how you can provide responses to the buttons of a button bar. Begin by selecting the *ButtonBar* object in the UI Designer. Next, display the Events page of the Inspector and click twice in the field for the *actionPerformed* event. Once JBuilder has assigned a method name to the *actionPerformed* event, press ENTER to move to that method in the Editor. Enter the following event handler:

```
void buttonBar_actionPerformed(ActionEvent e) {
  String whichButton = e.getActionCommand();
  if (whichButton == "File")
    statusBar.setText("You clicked File");
  else if (whichButton == "Close")
    statusBar.setText("You clicked Close");
  else if (whichButton == "Help")
    statusBar.setText("You clicked Help");
}
```

NOTE:　This code example is designed to demonstrate providing a different response for each button click. However, the same result could have been produced if the entire implementation of the preceding method had been replaced by the following single line of code:

```
statusBar.setText("You clicked "+ e.getActionCommand());
```

Manually Placing Button Bars and Status Bars

This chapter has described how to control the *StatusBar*, *MenuBar*, and *ButtonBar* objects created by the Application Wizard. You would use these same techniques even if you had placed these objects on a frame manually, although some features, such as the menus File and About and the button bar's button images, would be absent. Being able to place these objects manually is important since, unlike the frame created by the Application Wizard, the Frame Wizard creates a blank frame.

3

As pointed out in the first part of this chapter, the placement of these controls is made more complex by the need to use a *BorderLayout* layout manager to produce the alignment of the button bar, status bar, and bevel panel. This section demonstrates how you can create your own button bar and status bar components, and align them properly. It also describes how to place a menu bar and associate it with the frame.

This example assumes that you already have a project open. If you do not, either open an existing project, or use the Project Wizard to create a new one.

Once you are ready, begin by adding a new frame to your project. Do this by selecting File|New. Select the Frame icon (Frame Wizard) from the New page of the Object Gallery to display the New Frame dialog. Since this is only a demonstration, keep the default names displayed on this dialog. Click OK to continue.

The new frame created by the wizard is empty. You will now want to begin your design by adding three components to this frame: a *ButtonBar* and a *StatusBar* from the Controls page of the Component Palette, and a container (preferably a *BevelPanel*) from the Containers page or a *Panel* from the AWT page. Adjust the position of these components so that the button bar is near the top of the frame, the container is located in the middle, and the status bar is at the bottom. Precise placement of these components is not critical, only their relative positions are important. At this point, your frame may look like that shown in Figure 3-12.

Notice that none of the components are automatically aligned at this time. Even if you were to size all three components so that they appear aligned,

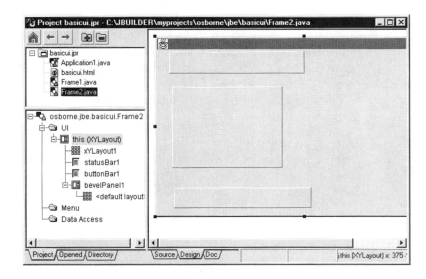

ButtonBar, *BevelPanel*, and *StatusBar* components placed on a new *Frame* component

Figure 3-12.

any changes to the size of the frame would reveal that they are not actually aligned.

In order to align these components, it is necessary to define a layout manager for the frame. But not just any layout manager will do (there are a number of different types). Alignment of these controls requires a *BorderLayout* layout manager. To apply a *BorderLayout* to the frame, select **this** in the Component Tree of the Structure pane. The **this** object refers to the frame itself, and it appears under the UI node in the Component Tree of the Structure pane when the Designer is active. Now move to the Properties page of the Inspector and display the *layout* property drop-down list. Set *layout* to BorderLayout, as shown here:

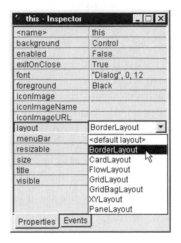

Immediately, the button bar aligns to North (top), the bevel panel aligns to Center, and the status bar aligns to South (bottom). This automatic alignment was based on the relative position of the objects in the frame when the layout manager was selected. If your objects did not get aligned properly, you can select them individually and set their *constraints* item to North, Center, and South for the *ButtonBar*, *BevelPanel*, and *StatusBar*, respectively, using the *constraints* item on the Properties page of the Inspector.

NOTE: Technically, the *constraints* item is not a true property. It appears on the Properties page of the Inspector where you can easily set its values. See Chapter 5 for more information on constraints.

If you do not want to include either a button bar or a status bar, you should still use the technique described here. The *constraints* item of the *BevelPanel* object (or other container you used) will still be set to Center. If you only include a *ButtonBar* object, its *constraints* item will be set to North. Alternatively, if you only include a *StatusBar* object, its *constraints* item will be set to South.

Adding a menu bar manually is somewhat simpler, in that there are only three necessary steps. First, you add a *MenuBar* object from the AWT page of the Component Palette to either the UI Designer or to the Component Tree. Second, select the frame in the UI Designer, and using the *menuBar* property on the Properties page of the Inspector, select the added *MenuBar* object from the frame's *menuBar* property drop-down list. Finally, design the menu bar, as described earlier in this chapter.

As you will learn later in this book, layout managers play an essential role in the satisfactory display of your controls. For more information on layout managers, see Chapter 5.

CHAPTER 4

Controlling Frames and Dialogs

Window is a container class in which the visible objects of the user interface appear. In JBuilder, you do not actually use an instance of the *Window* class, but instead rely upon two classes that descend from *Window*. These are the *Frame* class and the *Dialog* class.

A frame is a window that has a title bar. If at least one window is displayed by your application, it will probably be a frame. When additional windows need to be displayed, these will either be other frames or dialogs. Frames support the use of menu bars and dialogs do not. On the other hand, dialogs can be displayed modally (meaning that the user must close the dialog before returning to the window from which the dialog was opened). Frames can only be displayed nonmodally (although a technique is presented later in this chapter that demonstrates how you can make a frame appear to be modal).

NOTE: Throughout this chapter, the term "window" will be used to refer generically to both frames and dialogs. This is semantically correct since all frames and dialogs are represented by objects that descend from the *Window* class.

This chapter provides you with an overview of the basic techniques for using frames and dialogs. It begins with a discussion of the *Frame* class, with special attention to the frame-controlling code generated by the Application Wizard. You will then learn how to add additional frames to your applications and how to manage them.

Next, this chapter turns its attention to dialogs. The first to be considered is the About dialog generated by the Application Wizard. Then the dialogs that appear on the Dialog page of the Component Palette are examined. At the end of this chapter, you see how to create and use custom dialogs.

This chapter demonstrates the various techniques described here by walking you through the process of creating an application with multiple frames and multiple dialogs A completed version of this application, including all code demonstrated here, is included on the book's CD-ROM.

CD-ROM: The example project frameanddialog.jpr for this chapter can be found in the osborne\jbdcd\frameanddialog subdirectory. See Appendix C for information on installing and using the files on the CD-ROM that accompanies this book.

Using Frames

Frames are used as the top-level window in all Java applications. All frames possess a title bar that displays an icon. Depending on the platform in which the frame is running, it will also have additional features. For example, if you run your application under Microsoft's Windows 95 or Windows NT, the frame will have a Control menu; Minimize, Resize/Maximize, and Exit icons; be resizable, and so on.

To follow along with the examples demonstrated in this chapter, it is necessary to create a new application.

1. Begin by first closing any projects that are currently open, and then select File|New to display the New page of the Object Gallery.

2. Double-click the Application icon. JBuilder begins by displaying the Project Wizard. Set the File field to **C:\JBuilder\myprojects\ osborne\jbe\frameanddialog\frameanddialog.jpr**. Click the Finish button to continue.

3. After creating the project, JBuilder executes the Application Wizard. Do not modify the fields on the Step 1 page of the Application Wizard. Instead, click Next to move to Step 2. On the Step 2 page, enter **Frame and Dialog Demonstration** in the Title field, and enable (check) the following options: Generate menu bar, Generate tool bar, Generate status bar, Generate about box, and Center frame on screen. Click the Finish button. JBuilder creates the basic project shown in Figure 4-1.

Of particular interest is the source code generated by the Application Wizard that centers the frame onscreen at runtime. If you subsequently add additional frames to your application, you may want to duplicate the frame-centering code for the new frame.

4

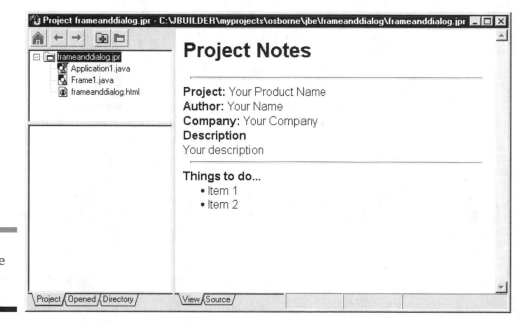

A basic project in the AppBrowser

Figure 4-1.

The following is the frame-centering code generated by the Application Wizard when you check the Center frame on screen checkbox on Step 2 page of the Application Wizard dialog:

```
Dimension screenSize = Toolkit.getDefaultToolkit().getScreen-
Size();
    Dimension frameSize = frame.getSize();
    if (frameSize.height > screenSize.height)
      frameSize.height = screenSize.height;
    if (frameSize.width > screenSize.width)
      frameSize.width = screenSize.width;
    frame.setLocation((screenSize.width - frameSize.width) / 2,
      (screenSize.height - frameSize.height) / 2);
```

It begins by declaring two *Dimension* variables named *screenSize* and *frameSize*, and initializes these variables with the screen and frame dimensions, respectively. These two variables, along with the frame's width and height, are then used to calculate the position for the upper-left corner of the frame. This code is located in the *Application1* class, and is executed immediately prior to making the first frame visible. (To view this code segment, select Application1.java in the Navigation pane and click the Source tab.)

The use of frames is not limited to just the top-level window in an application. Any time that you want to display an additional window in your application, and that window needs to contain a menu bar, you will use a frame.

Adding an Additional Frame to an Existing Application

You add a frame to an existing application in JBuilder using the Frame Wizard. To demonstrate its use, with your frameanddialog.jpr open, select File|New to display the New page of the Object Gallery, and then double-click the Frame icon. Accept the default values displayed in the New Frame dialog shown in Figure 4-2, and click OK to complete the addition.

NOTE: As an alternative, it is possible to add a new frame to an application by typing a new class declaration that extends *Frame*, and then adding code to your main frame to create and display an instance of this class. Doing so, however, would be hard work. It is easier to simply use the Frame Wizard.

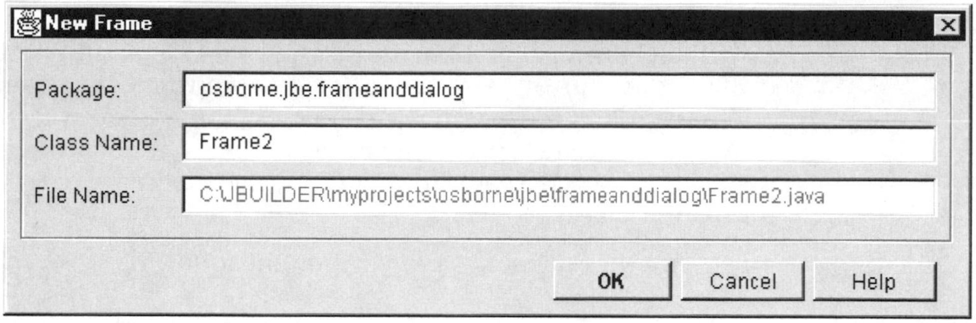

The Frame
Wizard
displays the
New Frame
dialog
Figure 4-2.

The frame created by the Frame Wizard is a subclass of
*borland.jbcl.control.DecoratedFrame (*a class that extends *java.awt.Frame*). To
begin with, the frame is empty. That is, it contains no components, and has
a layout manager as the only instance variable created by default.
Furthermore, it contains a single constructor, which in turn calls *jbInit()*. The
following is an example of a class declaration created by the Frame Wizard:

```
public class Frame2 extends DecoratedFrame {
  XYLayout xYLayout1 = new XYLayout();

  public Frame2() {
    try {
      jbInit();
    }
    catch (Exception e) {
      e.printStackTrace();
    }
  }

  void jbInit() throws Exception{
    xYLayout1.setWidth(335);
    xYLayout1.setHeight(215);
    this.setLayout(xYLayout1);
  }
}
```

4

Controlling a Frame

Once you have created a new frame, there are a number of things that you
might want to do in order to use it in your application. These include
preventing the frame from closing the application, displaying the frame from
code, modifying the frame to behave as if it were modal, and managing child
windows from the frame. These topics are covered in the following sections.

Preventing a Frame from Closing the Application

By default, when a *DecoratedFrame* instance is closed, the entire application exits. This is controlled by the *exitOnClose* property of the frame. If *exitOnClose* is set to true (the default), closing the frame will shut down the Java Virtual Machine (VM), and in the process, the application. In most applications, it is desirable to shut down the application only when the first (or main) frame is closed.

To change the *exitOnClose* property, do the following:

1. Select the Frame2.java file in the Navigation pane, and then display the UI Designer by clicking the Design tab of the Content pane. The frame is already selected in the UI Designer.

2. Move to the Inspector's Properties page and select False for the *exitOnClose* property. Setting the *exitOnClose* property to false, however, has the side effect of preventing the frame from closing when its Close icon is clicked. In order to restore this behavior, it is necessary to add code to the frame.

3. With *Frame2* still in the UI Designer, click the Events tab of the Inspector. Select the *windowClosing* event field (that is, click twice in the field associated with the *windowClosing* event), and then press ENTER to generate the event handler. Within this event handler, add the following call to the frame's *dispose()* method. When you are done, the generated method should look like this:

```
void this_windowClosing(WindowEvent e) {
  this.dispose();
}
```

The method *dispose()* sets the frame's *visible* property to **false**, thereby hiding the frame. Furthermore, it permits the frame to release its resources. What *dispose()* does not do, however, is destroy the frame. That will happen to the frame automatically via Java's garbage collection, sometime after the last reference to the frame is released.

 NOTE: In remaining discussions of adding an event handler, the selecting process (clicking twice on the event field to select the field and generate a name and pressing ENTER to display the source code) is referred to as selecting the field next to the event's name and pressing ENTER, or more simply as adding an event handler or creating an event handler, for brevity.

Displaying the Frame

In order to show the added frame to the user, it is necessary to add code to your first frame. This code should be associated with some user interaction, such as a menu item selection or button click, that signals the user's desire to display the second frame.

The following steps demonstrate this technique:

1. Select Frame1.java in the Navigation pane. Activate the UI Designer by selecting the Design tab on the Content pane, and then double-click *menuBar1* in the Component Tree in the Structure pane to load the Menu Designer.

2. To add one new menu item to the top of the File menu, select File in the menu bar in the Menu Designer to display the File menu, and then select Exit to choose the first position. Press INSERT to insert a blank menu item (and move the menu item labeled Exit down one position). Enter **Open** as the label of this new menu item and press ENTER.

3. Select this new Open menu item (if it is not selected), and move to the Events page of the Inspector. Select the *actionPerformed* event and press ENTER to generate the new event handler.

4

Within this event handler you need to add code that will declare a local variable of the class *Frame2*, call its constructor, and then make it visible. This code might look something like this:

```
Frame2 frame = new Frame2();
frame.setVisible(true);
```

In the preceding code, when the frame first appears it will appear as a window that has no width or height. In order to display a frame using a specific size, you need to specifically call the frame's *setSize()* method. If you manually define a new size for the frame at design time, this call is added to the *jbInit()* method of the frame for you. Alternatively, you can call the *setSize()* method from the same code that creates the frame.

The method *setSize()* is overloaded, taking either a single parameter of type *Dimension,* or two integer parameters. If you use a *Dimension*, the Width and Height fields of the *Dimension* define the width and height of the frame, in pixels. With the second version of this method, on the other hand, the first parameter defines the width of the frame in pixels, and the second the height, also in pixels.

Instead of calling *setSize()*, you usually want to call *pack()* instead. The method *pack()* calculates the preferred size of the components on the frame, and then sizes the frame to be the smallest it can be within limits imposed by the contained components. In the example here, the frame is empty. As a result, *pack()*, if used, would still produce a frame with no width and no height. Note also that the effects of *pack()* are greatly influenced by the particular layout managers used on the frame.

Often, setting the dimensions of the frame is not enough. Specifically, once the dimensions of the frame have been set, it is necessary to ask the layout managers associated with the frame to adjust the size and position of the various objects with respect to their containers. To do this, you call the method *validate()*. The method *validate()* forces the layout manager to scan components and make sure they're in the right place for the container's current size. If you size a frame by calling *pack()*, calling *validate()* is unnecessary.

For example, if you changed your *actionPerformed* event handler as follows, an instance of *Frame2* would be created, and then it would be set to 300 by 200 pixels in size before being displayed. Finally, the call to *validate()* would make any necessary adjustments to the positions of object on the frame (of which there are none in this example).

```
void menuItem1_actionPerformed(ActionEvent e) {
  Frame2 frame = new Frame2();
  frame.setSize(300,200);
  frame.validate();
  frame.setVisible(true);
}
```

NOTE: In practice, you should use *pack()*, as opposed to *setSize()*. The method *setSize()* was used here only because the default size of the empty frame would otherwise be too small.

Even with the preceding code added, the frame will appear in the upper left-hand corner of the screen, by default. If you want to place it in any other location, you will need to add additional code. Of course, one solution would be to copy and modify the frame-centering code generated by the Application Wizard. For example, the following updated event handler will display the instance of *Frame2* centered on the screen. Notice that the call to *setSize()* is executed prior to calculating the frame's location.

```
void menuItem1_actionPerformed(ActionEvent e) {
  Frame2 frame = new Frame2();
  frame.setSize(200,300);
  Dimension screenSize =
    Toolkit.getDefaultToolkit().getScreenSize();
```

```
        Dimension frameSize = frame.getSize();
        if (frameSize.height > screenSize.height)
          frameSize.height = screenSize.height;
        if (frameSize.width > screenSize.width)
          frameSize.width = screenSize.width;
        frame.setLocation((screenSize.width - frameSize.width) / 2,
          (screenSize.height - frameSize.height) / 2);
        frame.setVisible(true);
}
```

If you have been following along with the example so far, modify the menu item's *actionPerformed* event handler to match the immediately preceding code listing.

1. Now run the application by selecting Run|Run, pressing SHIFT-F9, or clicking the Run button in JBuilder's toolbar.

2. Once the initial frame appears, select File|Open to display the new frame. An example of how this might look is shown in Figure 4-3. The sample application now has two frames. The first frame is displayed automatically when the application runs. The second frame is displayed from an event handler added to the first frame when the user selects File|Open.

4

Creating a Pseudo-Modal Frame

By definition, a frame is nonmodal. What this means is that when one frame displays another, the user is free to move back and forth between the two

The second frame in the sample application is displayed when File|Open is selected

Figure 4-3.

frames. There are times, however, when it is preferable to display a second frame, and not permit the user to return to the first frame until they have finished with some task.

Dialogs, unlike frames, can be modal. However, dialogs (whether they are modal or not) do not support menu bars. Consequently, if you want to create a modal window that supports a menu bar, you will need to find some way of mimicking the effects of modality with a frame. One way to do this is to hide the first frame before displaying the second. Since a user cannot select a hidden frame, the basic benefits of modality are preserved.

Before describing this technique further, a couple of points need to be made. The first is that the frame is not really modal. In Java, a modal dialog does not hide the window that opened it. Second, windows that are modal in Java do not have menu bars. Consequently, while this technique is somewhat unorthodox, it represents a feature that you might find useful in your JBuilder applications. Just be aware that in some environments, such as the Macintosh, the presence of a modal-like window that possesses a menu bar will be unexpected.

The technique for hiding a frame requires the following steps:

1. The frame that will be hidden must declare a class variable (one declared both public and static) of the type *Frame* (or *DecoratedFrame*); then, initialize this variable to refer to itself. This variable is used to restore visibility to this frame, as described in step 3.

2. Immediately before displaying the second frame, the first frame hides itself using a call to its *setVisible()* method.

3. When the second frame is closed, it makes the first frame visible again with a call to the first frame's *setVisible()* method. This call makes use of the class variable declared in step 1.

NOTE: This is just one technique for permitting a second frame to reopen the hidden frame that opened it. Another technique would be to have the first frame call a method you create for the second frame, passing to the second frame a reference to the first as a parameter. This approach has the advantage that two or more instances of the first frame can open a second frame modally, with respect to themselves, at the same time. The steps outlined here permit only one instance of the first frame to be opened at a time, since the variable used to hold a reference to the opening frame is a static variable, and hence shared by all instances of the first frame's class.

To demonstrate this technique, it is necessary to first create a new frame using the Frame Wizard before following the preceding steps. Do so by following these steps:

1. Select File|New and double-click the Frame icon on the New page of the Object Gallery to use the Frame Wizard.

2. On the New Frame dialog, accept all defaults and select OK to generate a *Frame* class named *Frame3*.

3. Select *Frame3* in the UI Designer, move to the Inspector, and set its *exitOnClose* property to False.

4. Move to the Events page of the Inspector, select the *windowClosing* event, and press ENTER to create an event handler.

5. Add the following line of code to this event handler:

   ```
   this.dispose();
   ```

   Frame3 is ready. It is now possible to follow the three steps given previously to make *Frame3* modal with respect to *Frame1*.

Step 1 is to declare and initialize a public static *Frame* variable. Select Frame1.java in the Navigation pane. With the Source tab selected in the Content pane, select the top-level node, named *Frame1*, in the Structure pane. Add the following line to the class declaration:

```
public static Frame mainFrame;
```

Move now to the *jbInit()* method for the *Frame1* class, and add the following line of code:

```
mainFrame = this;
```

Step 2 requires that you create an event handler from which to display *Frame3* modally. As in an earlier example in this chapter in the section "Displaying the Frame," you need to add a new menu item to the menu bar of *Frame1*. Select *Frame1*'s menu bar in the Menu Designer and add one new menu item to the File menu. Enter **Open Frame3** for the label of this menu item. Select this new menu item, move to the Events page of the Inspector and create an *actionPerformed* event handler. Add the following code to the event handler:

```
void menuItem2_actionPerformed(ActionEvent e) {
  Frame3 frame = new Frame3();
  frame.setSize(200,300);
  this.setVisible(false);
```

4

```
frame.setVisible(true);
}
```

NOTE: As was done in the preceding example, you could modify this event handler to place *Frame3* in the center of the screen.

The final step is to restore visibility to *Frame1* when the user closes *Frame3*. This requires you to attach code to the *windowClosed* event handler of *Frame3*. Begin by selecting *Frame3* in the UI Designer. Move to the Events page of the Inspector and add a *windowClosed* event handler. Enter the second line of code into the method generated by JBuilder as shown here:

```
void this_windowClosed(WindowEvent e) {
    Frame1.mainFrame.setVisible(true);
}
```

If you now run the application and select File|Open Frame3, *Frame1* disappears just as *Frame3* becomes visible. Closing *Frame3* causes *Frame1* to become visible again.

It should be noted that this project now makes use of one frame *(Frame2)* that is displayed nonmodally, and one that is displayed pseudo-modally. Normally, you would not include both types of frames to be displayed by the main frame. In most cases, all frames displayed from the main frame are displayed either modally or pseudo-modally. Otherwise, you can easily get into a situation where a nonmodal frame is displayed, and then a pseudo-modal frame is displayed (which then causes the main frame to disappear). While this does not necessarily pose a problem, it is awkward to say the least.

Controlling Child Windows

A *child window* is a special frame that is opened by another frame, sometimes referred to as the *parent window*. A child window is special in that it conceptually belongs to the parent window that opens it. Furthermore, a child window is nonmodal. This allows a parent window to open more than one child window at a time.

A good example of an application type that benefits from the use of child windows is a database application that permits a user to view one or more customer accounts simultaneously. In such an application, the parent window would likely display a master list of customer accounts. Furthermore, this frame would offer a button bar, menu item, button, or any combination of these controls that permits the user to open a frame (the child window) in order to display detailed data about an account selected in the parent window. The user could return to the parent window and open additional child windows, permitting many different single account records to be viewed at the same time.

A general rule of parent/child windows is that when the user closes the parent window, all currently opened child windows should be closed automatically. If the parent window is the application's main frame, this effect can be achieved easily by leaving the main window's *exitOnClose* property set to **true** (the default). This technique cannot be used, however, if the parent window is not the main window. This is because if *exitOnClose* is set to **true** for a nonmain parent window, the entire application will close, not just the parent and its children, when the parent is closed.

It is possible to manage child windows from a *DecoratedFrame* instance, but you need to add code. Child windows are managed using the following steps:

1. In the parent window class, declare and initialize a *java.util.Vector* whose purpose will be to hold a reference to each window opened by the parent.
2. Each time you open a child window, use the *addElement()* method of the *Vector* to add a reference to the newly opened window.
3. From the parent window's *windowClosed()* method, copy the contents of the *Vector* into an array of *Window*s, and then iterate through the array, disposing of any reference that is not equal to null.

4

The following example demonstrates how to correctly manage child windows from a parent window.

Controlling Child Windows Example

In this example, a new frame, named *Frame4,* will be created to act as the child window. *Frame3*, which was created in the preceding example, will serve as the parent window.

Begin by adding the new frame to your existing application.

1. Select File|New to display the New page of the Object Gallery, and double-click the Frame icon. In the Frame Wizard, click OK to accept the default values for this new frame.
2. With *Frame4* selected in the UI Designer, move to the Inspector's Properties page and select False for the *exitOnClose* property. With *Frame4* still selected, display the Events page of the Inspector and create

a *windowClosing* event handler. Add a call to the frame's *dispose()* method from this event handler, as shown here:

```
void this_windowClosing(WindowEvent e) {
  this.dispose();
}
```

With *Frame4* now set up to be a child, let's go back to *Frame3* to add the code that will manage the child windows.

3. Select *Frame3* in the Navigation pane and then select the Source tab of the Content pane to move to the source view. Now select the top-level node (named *Frame3*) in the Structure pane to display the *Frame3* class declaration. Add the following line as the first line of the class declaration:

```
java.util.Vector childWindows = new java.util.Vector();
```

4. Now select the Design tab to display *Frame3* in the UI Designer. Click the AWT tab on the Component Palette. Select the *java.awt.Button* from the AWT page of the Component Palette and add a *Button* to *Frame3*. When you are done, the declaration part of the *Frame3* class declaration will look something like this:

```
public class Frame3 extends DecoratedFrame {
  java.util.Vector childWindows = new java.util.Vector();
  XYLayout xYLayout1 = new XYLayout();
  Button button1 = new Button();
```

5. With the button still selected in the UI Designer, move to the Inspector's Properties page and change the button's *label* property to **Show Child Window**. Next, move to the Events page of the Inspector and add an *actionPerformed* event handler to the button. Enter the following code to this event handler. This code creates an instance of the *Frame4* class, adds a reference to it to the vector, sizes and positions the new frame, and then makes it visible:

```
void button1_actionPerformed(ActionEvent e) {
  Frame4 frame = new Frame4();
  childWindows.addElement(frame);
  frame.setSize(100,100);
  frame.setLocation(200,200);
  frame.setVisible(true);
}
```

The final step is to provide for disposing of any instances of *Frame4* when *Frame3* is closing. This requires the following modification to the *windowClosed* event handler for *Frame3*.

6. With *Frame3* in the UI Designer, move to the Events page of the Inspector, select the *windowClosed* event, and press ENTER. Change the event handler that you added in the last example to the following:

```
void this_windowClosed(WindowEvent e) {
  try {
    Window childWindowCopy[] = new
      Window[childWindows.size()];
    childWindows.copyInto(childWindowCopy);
    for (int i = 0; i < childWindowCopy.length ; i++)
      if (childWindowCopy[i] != null)
        childWindowCopy[i].dispose();
  }
  finally {
    Frame1.mainFrame.setVisible(true);
  }
}
```

Instead of simply setting the main frame to be visible again, this code first disposes of any existing child windows. It begins by instantiating an array of windows, setting this array to the size of the vector. It then transfers the references in the vector to the array using the vector's *copyInto()* method. Finally, it iterates through the array and disposes of any window not already **null**. This entire operation is performed in the **try** block of a **try** … **finally** to ensure that the main frame is made visible again, even if an exception occurs during child window disposal.

7. Run this application and then select File|Open Frame3. Now click the button on *Frame3* a couple of times.

Since *Frame4* is not modal with respect to *Frame3,* you can easily move between the various displayed frames. You can even resize some or all of them, and close one or more, as shown in Figure 4-4. When you finally close *Frame3*, any copy of *Frame4* still open will be closed.

Using Dialogs

Dialogs are similar to frames, but they do not support menu bars. While this limits their usefulness, they do have one important property not found in the *Frame* class: *modal*. When *modal* is set to **true** and the dialog is displayed, the user is prevented from interacting with the window from which the dialog was opened until the dialog is closed, even if other windows of the application are visible. Being able to restrict a user in this way is ideal when you need input from the user or the user's acknowledgment of a critical error message.

Both the *Dialog* and the *Frame* classes extend *Window*. Consequently, these two classes have many methods in common. However, when you want to display a dialog modally, it is necessary to call its *show()* method, rather than call

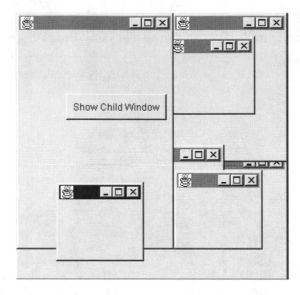

No matter
how many
copies of
Frame4 are
opened,
closing
Frame3 will
close them all

Figure 4-4.

setVisible(true). When you call *show()*, the dialog intercepts all user input to the parent (the frame required in the constructor), which prevents the parent from being accessed until the user closes the dialog (or your code calls either the *hide()* or the *dispose()* method of the dialog). The method *setVisible()* makes the dialog visible, but does not invoke the necessary code to make it modal.

JBuilder provides you with a number of options when it comes to using dialogs. For starters, the Application Wizard can create the code that defines a simple About dialog for displaying information about your application. It also provides four components on the Dialogs page of the Component Palette:

> *borland.jbcl.control.Filer*
> *borland.jbcl.control.ColorChooser*
> *borland.jbcl.control.FontChooser*
> *borland.jbcl.control.Message*

These components are non-UI components (components with no visual representation) that encapsulate standard dialogs, including a load/save file dialog, a color selection dialog, a font selection dialog, and a simple message dialog, respectively.

JBuilder also provides you with several additional dialogs on the Dialogs page of the Object Gallery. These include About Box, Standard Dialog1, Standard Dialog2, and Password Dialog. Finally, you can easily create your own dialog using the Dialog Wizard available on the New page of the Object Gallery. The remainder of this chapter describes how to use these various dialog snippets.

Before continuing, it is important to note that the *Dialog* class differs from many of the other classes that you will work in with JBuilder in that the *Dialog* class does not have a zero parameter constructor—that is, a constructor that takes no parameters. Having a constructor that takes no parameters is a requirement for a JavaBean, and consequently, instances of the *Dialog* class are not true JavaBeans. The component's on JBuilder's Dialogs page of the Component Palette *are* JavaBeans. They are not *Dialogs* themselves, but simply encapsulate calls to a *Dialog* class. However, in order to use these JavaBeans on the Dialogs page, you must first set their *frame* property to a valid frame. Then, when you call the zero-parameter constructor of one of these JavaBeans, it in turn calls the constructor of the *Dialog* that it encapsulates, passing the *frame* property, among other values, as parameters.

The About Dialog

If you check the Generate about box option on the Step 2 page of the Application Wizard, two additional class definitions are added to the Java file for the generated frame. One of these is a class that extends *Dialog*, and another is a class that extends *Panel*. This *Panel* class is used by the dialog.

Because the *Dialog* class declared in this Java file does not have the same name as the Java file itself and its class is not declared public, you cannot use the UI Designer to customize this About dialog. Instead, if you want to modify this dialog, you do so by modifying the source code that appears in the class declaration and its associated *jbInit()* method. For example, consider the following segment of code, which represents the first part of the class declaration:

4

```
class Frame1_AboutBox extends Dialog implements ActionListener {
  Panel panel1 = new Panel();
  BevelPanel bevelPanel1 = new BevelPanel();
  Frame1_InsetsPanel insetsPanel1 = new Frame1_InsetsPanel();
  Frame1_InsetsPanel insetsPanel2 = new Frame1_InsetsPanel();
  Frame1_InsetsPanel insetsPanel3 = new Frame1_InsetsPanel();
  Button button1 = new Button();
  ImageControl imageControl1 = new ImageControl();
  Label label1 = new Label();
  Label label2 = new Label();
  Label label3 = new Label();
  Label label4 = new Label();
  BorderLayout borderLayout1 = new BorderLayout();
  BorderLayout borderLayout2 = new BorderLayout();
  FlowLayout flowLayout1 = new FlowLayout();
  GridLayout gridLayout1 = new GridLayout();
  String product = "Your Product Name";
  String version = "";
```

```
String copyright = "Copyright (c) 1997";
String comments = "Your description";
```

The last four lines of this code segment declare and initialize four strings. You can modify the initializers of these strings, adding customized text specific to your application.

Now consider the About dialog's *jbInit()* method, shown here:

```
void jbInit() throws Exception{
    this.setTitle("About");
    setResizable(false);
    panel1.setLayout(borderLayout1);
    bevelPanel1.setLayout(borderLayout2);
    insetsPanel2.setLayout(flowLayout1);
    insetsPanel2.setInsets(new Insets(10, 10, 10, 10));
    gridLayout1.setRows(4);
    gridLayout1.setColumns(1);
    label1.setText(product);
    label2.setText(version);
    label3.setText(copyright);
    label4.setText(comments);
    insetsPanel3.setLayout(gridLayout1);
    insetsPanel3.setInsets(new Insets(10, 60, 10, 10));
    button1.setLabel("OK");
    button1.addActionListener(this);
    imageControl1.setImageName("");
    insetsPanel2.add(imageControl1, null);
    bevelPanel1.add(insetsPanel2, BorderLayout.WEST);
    this.add(panel1, null);
    insetsPanel3.add(label1, null);
    insetsPanel3.add(label2, null);
    insetsPanel3.add(label3, null);
    insetsPanel3.add(label4, null);
    bevelPanel1.add(insetsPanel3, BorderLayout.CENTER);
    insetsPanel1.add(button1, null);
    panel1.add(insetsPanel1, BorderLayout.SOUTH);
    panel1.add(bevelPanel1, BorderLayout.NORTH);
    pack();
}
```

Modifying this code permits you to customize the look of the About dialog. However, in most cases, you will want to restrict your modifications to only two lines. These are the call to the *setLabel()* method for the OK button and the *setImageName()* method for the *ImageControl* component. You use the button's *setLabel()* method to control the text that appears on the button.

You use the *ImageControl* component's *setImageName()* method to specify a GIF to display on the About dialog.

Because you cannot load the About dialog into the UI Designer, if you are unhappy with the default About dialog you may want to consider creating your own custom dialog for use as an About dialog. There is an About dialog available on the Dialogs page of the Object Gallery that is ideally suited for this purpose.

Dialogs from the Component Palette

The Dialogs page of the Component Palette includes four components. These are *borland.jbcl.control.Filer*, *borland.jbcl.control.ColorChooser*, *borland.jbcl.control.FontChooser*, and *borland.jbcl.control.Message*. Each of these components encapsulates a common dialog with an easy-to-use interface.

While each of these dialog components is different, they do share several properties in common. The most important of these is the *frame* property. This property specifies the parent frame of the dialog. You must set the *frame* property; if you do not, the dialog will not be displayed. Another property they share is *title*, which defines the title that appears in the dialog's title bar.

4

To demonstrate the use of these dialog components, begin by selecting Frame1.java in the Navigation pane and then opening the UI Designer. Next, select the Dialogs page of the Component Palette. Finally, add one of each of these four components to the UI Designer.

As you drop each dialog component into the UI Designer, a new node will be created under the Other node in the Component Tree—dialog components are non-UI components, so they will never be displayed in the UI Designer themselves.

TIP: Rather than dropping these dialog components into the UI Designer, you can drop them directly into the Component Tree. Either way, dialog components always appear under the Other node in the Component Tree.

Next, select each of these dialog components, one at a time, in the Component Tree. As you select each one, move to the Inspector's Properties page and set the *frame* property to **this**. If you wish, you can also set the *title* property. Be sure to set *title* to a value that makes sense for the given dialog. For example, you may want to set the *Message* component's *title* property to **Message**, while you might set the *FontChooser* component *title* property to **Select a new Font**.

Finally, all of these dialogs share the method *show()*. This method displays the corresponding dialog and waits until the user has closed it. Furthermore, each of these dialogs is modal, meaning that the user cannot return to the frame that is showing the dialog until the user has closed the dialog.

From this point on, the use of each of these dialogs is somewhat different. The use of each dialog is described in the following sections.

Using the Message Dialog

The *Message* dialog is the simplest of these components. You use the methods *setTitle()* and *setMessage()* to define the dialog's title and contents, respectively. Alternatively, you can set the title and message properties at design time from the Inspector. (Your message, however, is often not known until runtime, making *setMessage()* a somewhat more important method.) Finally, you call the *show()* method to display the dialog.

To demonstrate the use of the *Message* dialog, add a *Button* and a *TextField* component from the AWT page of the Component Palette onto *Frame1* in the UI Designer. Using the Inspector's Properties page, set the button's *label* property to **Display Message**. Next, double-click the button in the UI Designer to add an *actionPerformed* event handler to it. Add the following code to this generated event handler:

```
void button1_actionPerformed(ActionEvent e) {
  message1.setMessage(textField1.getText());
  message1.show();
}
```

Run the application. Once the main frame is displayed, enter some text into the *TextField* component and then click the button labeled Display Message. The *Message* dialog is displayed with its message consisting of the text you entered into the *TextField* object. This effect is shown in Figure 4-5.

Using the Filer Dialog

You use the *Filer* dialog to display a file browser to the user. This dialog has two modes, Load and Save. When its *mode* property is set to Load, it acts as a load file (open) dialog, in which case the user must select an existing

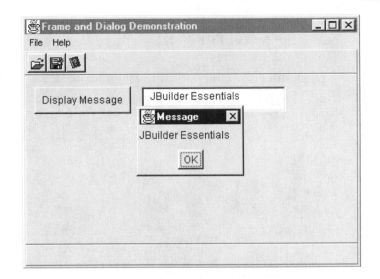

An event handler sets the *Message* dialog with text entered into a *TextField* and displays it in a dialog

Figure 4-5.

4

filename. When its *mode* is set to Save, the user can either select an existing file or enter the name of a file that does not yet exist.

You can set the *Filer* dialog's mode at design time, using the Inspector. Alternatively, you can set it in code using the *setMode()* method. This method takes one argument, which can be either *java.awt.FileDialog.LOAD* or *java.awt.FileDialog.SAVE*.

NOTE: The *Filer* dialog only returns a filename. The actual loading or saving is something that must be performed by the code you add to your application.

Other properties that you may want to use with *Filer* include *directory* (the initial directory that is displayed when *Filer* is displayed), *file* (the initial file selected), and *fileFilter* (a *FileFilter* object that controls which files can be selected).

You call the *show()* method for *Filer* to display this dialog. Your code determines whether the user selected a file or canceled the dialog by calling the *getFile()* method. If this method returns the value **null**, the user closed the dialog without selecting a file. Otherwise, *getFile()* returns the full name of the file the user selected.

To demonstrate the use of *Filer*, follow these steps:

1. Add another button onto *Frame1* in the UI Designer.

2. Enter **Select File** for this button's *label* property on the Properties page of the Inspector.

3. Double-click the button to generate an *actionPerformed* event handler for it.

4. Add the following code to this event handler:

```
void button2_actionPerformed(ActionEvent e) {
    filer1.show();
    if (filer1.getFile() != null) {
        message1.setMessage(filer1.getFile());
        message1.show();
    } else {
        message1.setMessage("Canceled");
        message1.show();
    }
}
```

5. Run this project. When you click the button labeled Select File, your screen will look something like the one shown in Figure 4-6.

Using the ColorChooser Dialog

The *ColorChooser* dialog displays a dialog that the user can use to mix red, blue, and green colors (or hue, saturation, and brightness values) to select a color. The key property of *ColorChooser* is *value*, which is a *java.awt.Color* type. If you set the *value* property before showing a *ColorChooser,* it will be initialized with this color when it is first displayed. If the user clicks the dialog's OK button, the *value* property contains the selected color.

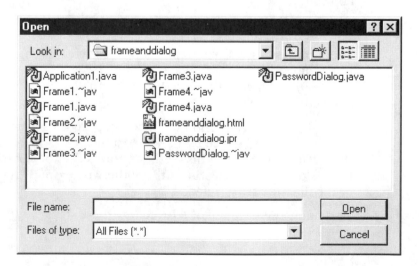

Use the *Filer* dialog to select a file to load or save
Figure 4-6.

Unlike *Filer*, you use *ColorChooser's result* property to determine if the user accepted the dialog or not. The property *result* is an **int** value that is equal to the constant *borland.jbcl.control.Message.OK* if the user accepted the dialog.

To demonstrate the use of *ColorChooser*, follow these steps:

1. Add another button to *Frame1* in the UI Designer.
2. Using the Properties page of the Inspector, enter **Choose Color** for the *label* property of this button.
3. Double-click the button and add the following *actionPerformed* event handler:

```
void button3_actionPerformed(ActionEvent e) {
  colorChooser1.setValue(bevelPanel1.getBackground());
  colorChooser1.show();
  if (colorChooser1.getResult() == Message.OK)
    bevelPanel1.setBackground(colorChooser1.getValue());
}
```

If you now run this application and click the button labeled Choose Color, the dialog shown in Figure 4-7 is displayed. Selecting a color from this dialog changes the background color of the bevel panel.

4

Using the FontChooser Dialog

You use the *FontChooser* dialog to display a dialog with a list of the available fonts and font styles. Using *FontChooser* is almost identical to using *ColorChooser*. The only difference is that the *value* property of the *FontChooser* is a *java.awt.Font* rather than a *java.awt.Color*.

ColorChooser displays a dialog that permits users to select a color

Figure 4-7.

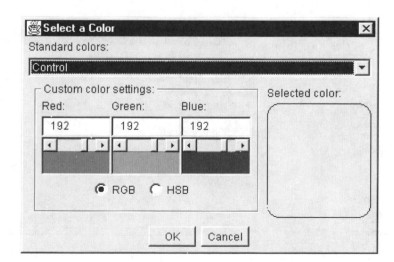

To demonstrate the use of the *FontChooser* dialog, follow these steps:

1. Add one more button to *Frame1*.

2. Set this button's *label* property to **Choose Font** and then add the following event handler to the button:

```
void button4_actionPerformed(ActionEvent e) {
  fontChooser1.setValue(textField1.getFont());
  fontChooser1.show();
  if (fontChooser1.getResult() == Message.OK)
    textField1.setFont(fontChooser1.getValue());
}
```

When you run this application and click the Choose Font button, the dialog shown in Figure 4-8 is displayed. If you choose a font, or change the font size or style, clicking OK applies those changes to the text field on the frame.

Using the Object Gallery Dialogs

The Dialogs page of the Object Gallery shown in Figure 4-9 contains a number of dialog snippets that you can use in your own code. These include an About dialog and a Password dialog, as well as two dialogs called Standard that contain OK and Cancel buttons—one with these dialogs with the buttons placed at the bottom of the dialog, and the other with the buttons placed on the right-hand side.

The About dialog is simple, and it is not necessary to add any additional code to use this dialog. All you need to do is modify the properties of the various *Labels* components and the *ImageControl* component, and it is ready for display (using its *show()* method).

The *FontChooser* dialog permits the user to select fonts and font styles

Figure 4-8.

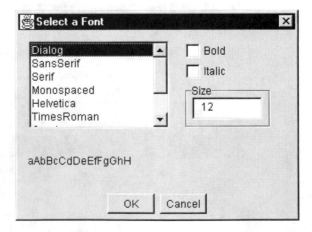

NOTE: For simplicity's sake, you should pass three parameters when calling a dialog's constructor. These are **this** (the container on whose behalf the dialog is displaying), a *String* for use as a title for the dialog, and a boolean true to make the dialog modal. Alternatively, you can call any of its other constructors, but then you must call *setModal(true)* prior to showing the dialog, in order to make it a modal dialog.

The other three dialogs on the Dialogs page of the Object Gallery are not ready for use in their default forms. To start, you must modify the properties of the objects that appear on the dialogs, just as you do for the About dialog (and in the case of the Standard two-button dialogs, add additional objects). Unlike the About dialog, you must also add two class variables, one instance variable, and two additional methods. Furthermore, you need to add some code to three of the existing methods.

Without these additions it is not possible for your code to determine which of the two buttons on these dialogs the user pressed. In most cases, such as when a user is using the Password dialog, your code needs to know which button was pressed in order to execute properly. If the user clicks the OK button on a Password dialog, you must verify the password. If the user clicks the Cancel button, your code must do something else, such as deny access to a restricted feature.

4

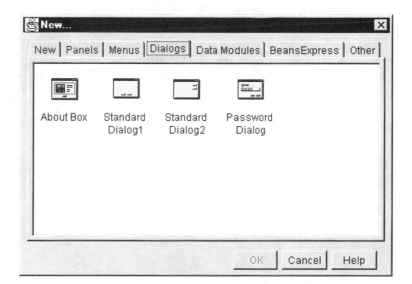

The Dialogs
page of the
Object Gallery
Figure 4-9.

The modifications that you perform to these dialogs are outlined in the following steps:

1. Declare two integer constants (static final variables), one representing the user's selection of the OK button and the other representing the user's selection of the Cancel button. By convention, these constants should be named OK and CANCEL.

2. Declare an integer instance variable named *result*. Initialize it to the value of the CANCEL constant.

3. In the event handler associated with the OK button's *actionPerformed* event, set *result* to OK (prior to calling *dispose()*), and in the Cancel button's *actionPerformed* event hander, set *result* to CANCEL.

4. Write public getter and setter methods for *result*. The getter method should return the integer value of *result*. The setter method should assign an integer parameter to *result*.

For example, the constant declarations can look like the following:

```
public static final int OK =
  borland.jbcl.control.ButtonDialog.OK;
public static final int CANCEL =
  borland.jbcl.control.ButtonDialog.CANCEL;
```

NOTE: It would be acceptable to use any integer, but the integers assigned to OK and CANCEL in the *ButtonDialog* class are used elsewhere in JBuilder, and therefore make an appropriate standard to follow.

The instance variable declaration and initialization, which must appear after the constant declarations, may look like the following:

```
int result = CANCEL;
```

Step 3 requires that you set *result* to the appropriate constant within the event handlers for both buttons. The following is how this modification looks:

```
//OK
  void button1_actionPerformed(ActionEvent e) {
    result = OK;
    dispose();
  }

  //Cancel
```

```
void button2_actionPerformed(ActionEvent e) {
  result = CANCEL;
  dispose();
}
```

5. Finally, you must write public *getResult()* and *setResult()* methods. The following are examples of these methods:

```
public int getResult(){
  return result;
}

public void setResult(int i){
  result = i;
}
```

Assuming that you have made these changes to the Password dialog from the Dialogs page of the Object Gallery, you can place a new button on a frame and add the following code to its *actionPerformed* event handler to use the dialog:

```
void button5_actionPerformed(ActionEvent e) {
  PasswordDialog getPassword =
    new PasswordDialog(this,"Enter your password",true);
  getPassword.show();
  if (getPassword.getResult() ==
    borland.jbcl.control.ButtonDialog.OK) {
    //User accepted the Dialog
    message1.setMessage(getPassword.textField1.getText());
    message1.show();
  } else {
    //The user did not accept the Dialog.
    message1.setMessage("User canceled the Dialog");
    message1.show();
  }
}
```

4

Figure 4-10 displays the completed project, frameanddialog.jpr, which includes a Password dialog (customized as described in the preceding section) and a button that includes the code given in the preceding listing.

Creating Custom Dialogs

In most cases, if you want to create a custom dialog, you will use one of the Standard two-button dialogs from the Dialogs page of the Object Gallery.

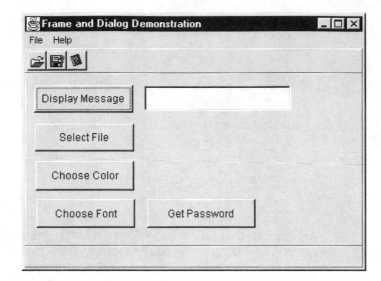

The Frame
project with
buttons for
displaying five
different types
of *Dialog*
Figure 4-10.

However, if you really want to build a completely unique dialog, you will do
the following:

1. Select File|New, and double-click the Dialog icon on the New page of
the Object Gallery.

2. On the New Dialog page, enter the package and class names for the
dialog.

3. Place any desired user interface elements of the dialog. Make sure to
place at least one button (most dialogs have at least one button that will
close a dialog).

4. Create an *actionPerformed* event handler for each button on the dialog.
At a minimum, each event handler should call `this.dispose()`.

5. Add a *windowClosing* event handler to the dialog. Call *dispose()* from this
event handler.

6. If the dialog has more than one button, follow the steps outlined in the
preceding section. Specifically, declare constants for each button, as
well as an instance variable to hold the value of the constant associated
with the clicked button. Initialize the instance variable with a default
value and then set a value for this variable from within each button's
actionPerformed event handler. Finally, write public getter and setter
methods for the instance variable so that a calling frame can determine
which of the buttons is selected by a user.

CHAPTER 5

Visual Design Using Layout Managers

Designing a sophisticated user interface that looks attractive, adjusts correctly when resized, and looks as good on a Macintosh as it does under Windows is a complex problem. The designers of Java understood just how difficult the task was and developed a very flexible solution.

Rather than positioning components using absolute coordinates, a set of rules embodied in a *layout manager* determine the correct position of each component at runtime. The layout manager can consider the size a component needs to be in order to look good on whatever platform is running the application or applet. It can also determine new positions for components whenever the window is resized. Clearly, these layout rules must be very flexible to allow a developer to design any conceivable user interface.

Instead of creating a single set of rules for the task, every Java container can apply a different set of rules by selecting an appropriate layout manager. There are several standard layout managers—some of which are simple, some of which are very sophisticated.

JBuilder was designed to embrace Java standards throughout, and provides elegant tools for managing the standard layout managers. There are also additional layout managers in JBuilder that address needs not met by the standard ones, and each of these additions is pure Java, deployable to any platform that supports Java 1.1.

The basic concepts behind controlling a container's layout with JBuilder are introduced first in this chapter, followed by details on each of the available layout managers. Advanced layout manager topics are covered towards the end, including nesting containers, adding components at runtime, and converting from one layout manager to another. Finally, a complex user interface example is constructed, step by step, at the end of the chapter.

 CD-ROM: The example project LayoutSamples.jpr for this chapter can be found in the osborne\jbecd\layout subdirectory. See Appendix C for information on installing and using the files on the CD-ROM that accompanies this book.

Layouts and Constraints

Two key factors are involved in positioning a component within a container. The container specifies a single policy that is applied to all components within it, referred to as its *layout*, which must be an instance of one of the layout manager classes. This single policy is applied to each and every component, but its actions may be influenced by a set of *constraints* applied to individual components.

For example, consider the frame shown in Figure 5-1. To achieve the desired configuration, the frame uses an instance of *java.awt.BorderLayout* as its layout manager. *BorderLayout* places each component either along one of the four edges, or in the remaining area in the center. The status bar is added with a constraint of *BorderLayout.SOUTH*, a constant that indicates that it should be placed at the bottom. The text area is added with a constraint of *BorderLayout.CENTER*, another constant that allows the component to occupy the remaining space within the frame after reserving the bottom for the status bar.

The resulting frame can be resized, and both components will automatically be placed in the correct positions. Similarly, when the code is run on another platform, the height of the status bar will be determined based on the size of the font available for use within it. All of this happens automatically, requiring no effort from the developer—except initially choosing the right layout manager and applying it correctly.

All containers, including the *java.awt* package's *Frame*, *Dialog*, and *Panel* classes as well as *java.applet.Applet*, have a *layout* property that allows the layout to be specified using the *setLayout()* method or retrieved using the *getLayout()* method. A layout must be an instance of a class that implements the *java.awt.LayoutManager* interface.

Constraints provide additional information to assist a layout manager in positioning a component. Since the constraints are not specified until the component is added to a container, they are not implemented as true component properties. The value is specified when a component is added to a container using one of the container's *add()* methods.

When using the UI Designer to place components within a container, a single line of code is generated that invokes the container's *add(Component,*

5

A frame using *BorderLayout* to position a status bar and a text area
Figure 5-1.

Object) method. This method accepts two parameters: the component to be added and an object that describes its layout constraints. JBuilder typically associates a unique constraints object with each component. Even though constraints aren't actually properties since they don't employ get and set methods, a *constraints* item appears on the Properties page of the Inspector, where you can easily view and modify the constraints for the selected component.

Selecting a Layout Manager

You select a layout manager for a container using its *layout* property, which appears on the Properties page of the Inspector when a container is selected in design mode. Figure 5-2 shows the drop-down list of the available types of layout managers for the *layout* property. The initial value for *layout* when a container is created is <default layout>. When this option is selected, no code is generated to set a layout for the container, and it is assumed that there will be a layout assigned by the container itself when it is created. Subclasses of *java.awt.Container* typically create a layout manager that is used until it is replaced by an explicit call to *setLayout()*. This default value is rarely used since JBuilder does not provide the ability to alter the default layout manger's properties.

Selecting another value for the *layout* property automatically generates two lines of code: one to create an instance of the appropriate layout manager class and another to associate the layout manager with the container. The first line stores a reference to the layout manager in an instance variable, appearing with the definition of all instance variables for the top-level

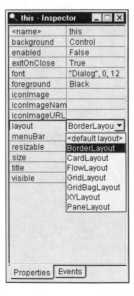

The Inspector's drop-down list of layout managers
Figure 5-2.

container displayed in the UI Designer. In the example shown in Figure 5-1, this declaration belongs to the *Frame* subclass and reads as follows:

```
BorderLayout borderLayout1 = new BorderLayout();
```

The second line sets the *layout* property for the appropriate container, the *Frame* subclass in this example. Like all other property changes, it appears in the *jbInit()* method of the same class:

```
this.setLayout(borderLayout1);
```

Configuring a Layout

When the UI Designer is active, the layout object is represented within the Component Tree in the Structure pane immediately below the container it belongs to. In Figure 5-3 for example, to select the frame's *BorderLayout* object you select the node labeled *borderLayout1* in the Component Tree. When you select the layout using the Component Tree, you can view and modify its properties and events using the Inspector, just as you can for any other selected component.

Layout manager classes do not normally define events, but many of them have properties that affect the way all components within the container are arranged. The properties for each type of layout manager are discussed in the appropriate sections later in this chapter.

5

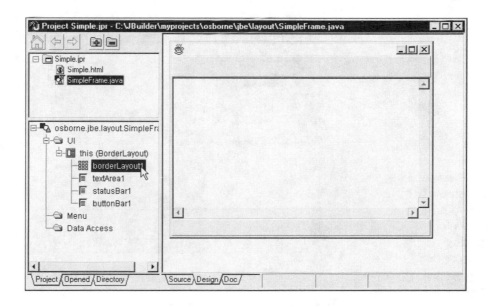

Select *borderLayout1* in the Component Tree. This is the frame's *BorderLayout*
Figure 5-3.

Placing Components

When the UI Designer is displayed, JBuilder assists in placing components by displaying information about the container under the cursor, its layout manager, and the constraint appropriate for the cursor's location. The information is displayed in the lower right of the status bar and is continuously updated as you move the mouse cursor in the UI Designer. Just before clicking to place a component in the UI Designer, pay careful attention to the right side of the status bar for hints about the intended placement. In Figure 5-4, the message in the status bar is

this(BorderLayout): North

It names **this** as the object's intended parent. Since the UI Designer is working on a frame, the frame will be the parent. The class of the parent's layout, in this case *BorderLayout*, is shown in parentheses following the parent's name. Finally, the constraint that will be applied, the value North in this example, is shown following a colon after the layout name.

You can greatly reduce the time required to create a user interface by using these hints to make sure that you are adding the new component to the correct container, and in the correct location. If you are clicking and dragging to place and size a component, always position the cursor in the correct location to get the desired hint, then click and drag down and to the right to specify the component's preferred size. The hint is only displayed

The status bar provides hints just before placing components

Figure 5-4.

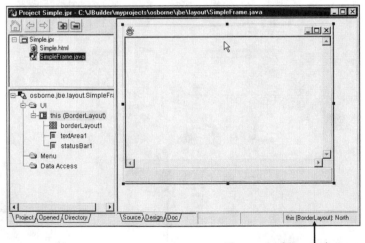

Placement hint on the status bar

based on the cursor position before the initial mouse click, but the component's actual placement is based on the upper left-hand corner of the drag rectangle. Dragging down and right allows the initial click to define this critical corner, ensuring that the component's placement is predictable.

Should a component be placed in the wrong position, you can change the constraints that define its position in a number of ways. Direct editing of the constraints value, dragging and dropping components to new locations, and using layout manager-specific popup menus for components are all discussed in later sections.

Placing Components Using the Component Tree

Sometimes it can be very difficult to position a component within a small or obscured container using the UI Designer. In these situations, you will want to place the component using the Component Tree, which is displayed in the Structure Pane when the Design tab is selected. The Component Tree shows the visual hierarchy of all components, including containers. To place a component directly in the Component Tree, select the desired component from the Component Palette, and then click the desired container in the Component Tree. A new component of the selected type will be added to the container with a default constraints value. The constraints value assigned by JBuilder can always be changed as described later in "Editing Constraints" if this default does not suit your needs.

Changing Component Placement   5

You can move a component in the UI Designer simply by dragging the component to a new position, changing both the constraint and, if required, the parent container with a single action. Once again, the UI Designer's status bar displays a hint about the placement of the component if it is released in its current location. The parent and constraint are based on the upper left-hand corner of the component's drag rectangle, not the center, which seems counterintuitive at first, but actually provides for very precise placement.

Pay close attention when dragging components the first few times, placing the upper lefthand corner in the center of the desired location and watching the status bar's hint for confirmation, and the technique will soon be second nature. Figure 5-5 shows the correct position to drop a component in order to set a constraint of Center for a *BorderLayout*, while Figure 5-6 shows a common mistake in placement, one that actually winds up putting the component in the North position.

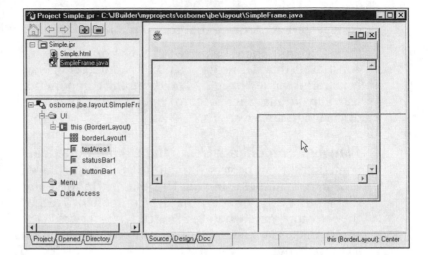

The correct
placement for
centering a
component in
a frame
Figure 5-5.

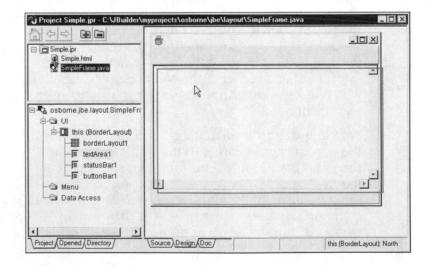

The wrong
placement for
centering a
component in
a frame
Figure 5-6.

Editing Constraints

Each component within a container has a unique constraints value that is
displayed on the Properties page in the Inspector when that component is
selected in design mode. The *constraints* item is not actually a JavaBeans
property, but JBuilder displays and edits constraints in exactly the same way
by simulating a property named *constraints*.

The constraint type, available values, and editing technique differs from one
layout manager to another. A *Button* placed in a frame that uses a
BorderLayout will include a *constraints* pseudoproperty. When you click twice
in this field on the Properties page of the Inspector, you will see a drop-down
list containing the values North, South, East, West, and Center. The same
Button, when placed on a frame that uses an *XYLayout*, would instead display
a set of four coordinate values separated by commas for its constraints value.

This constraints value can be manipulated in at least three distinct ways:

◆ Dragging and dropping the component automatically adjusts the
  constraints value as needed, as described in the last section "Changing
  Component Placement."

◆ The constraints can be edited directly using the *constraints* field on the
  Properties page of the Inspector. Depending on the layout manager used
  by the component's container, you modify the component's constraints
  by either typing in a new value, dropping down a list of acceptable
  values, or bringing up a dialog to manipulate a complex constraint.

5

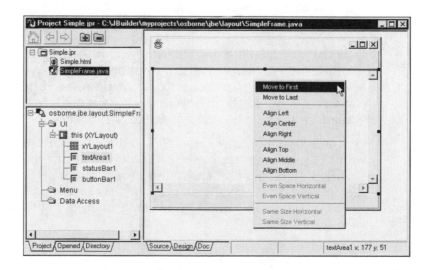

Popup menu
options for a
component
managed by
an *XYLayout*
Figure 5-7.

♦ Right-clicking on a component in the UI Designer will display a popup menu of options appropriate to the layout manager used by the component's container. For example, Figure 5-7 shows the popup menu options for a *TextArea* component managed by an *XYLayout*.

The constraint editing process and popup menus associated with each of the available layout managers are discussed later in this chapter.

Component Sizing Hints for Layouts

Some layout managers impose arbitrary rules to determine the size of the components they manage, but the more sophisticated ones try to consider the needs of the component in question. What is its preferred size? Is it usable below a certain size? The following three methods are introduced by the class *java.awt.Component* and may be used by a layout manager to determine the correct size for a component:

♦ A component's *getPreferredSize()* method reports the size a component would like to be under ideal circumstances. The *BorderLayout*, *FlowLayout*, and *GridBagLayout* classes all attempt to respect this requested size, space permitting.

♦ The *getMinimumSize()* method reports the smallest rectangle the component could appear in and still be usable. The *GridBagLayout* will use this value if there isn't enough room for the components it is managing to use their preferred sizes.

♦ Of dubious value, the *getMaximumSize()* method allows a component to report the largest usable size for the component. Neither the standard layout managers nor Borland's layout managers use this value, but future layout managers may take advantage of the information.

Normally, you do not need to worry about these methods because they are defined for you by the standard components, and layout managers automatically query them as necessary. However, it never hurts to understand a little about how the results are achieved, especially in situations where it becomes desirable to influence the process.

Some components have properties designed specifically to alter their minimum or preferred sizes. The *java.awt.TextArea* class includes *rows* and *columns* properties that are in turn used to compute these sizes. The *borland.jbcl.control.GridControl* actually has a *preferredSize* property that can be explicitly set to control how layouts manage individual grids.

Containers and Sizing Hints

Containers also need to compute their preferred and minimum sizes, but this process works a little differently from other components. The size a container should be depends on the components it contains and the layout manager it uses. As a result, containers defer the task of computing the size of their contents to the layout manager in use, and then pad that size as necessary to include the visual appearance of the container's border, if there is one.

The descriptions of the individual layout managers later in this chapter include a discussion of the technique used to compute the preferred and minimum sizes for the container. This computed size is used in several situations:

♦ Containers are often used as components nested within other containers. In order for the layout manager of the outer container to function, it needs to be able to determine a reasonable preferred or minimum size for the container nested within it.

♦ The *Frame* class has a *pack()* method designed to resize the frame to its preferred size based on its contents. The Application Wizard uses this method by default to determine a reasonable initial size for its frame.

Sample: Creating a Basic Interface

This example uses the techniques described so far to create a frame with an empty text area, a button bar, and a status bar, as shown in Figure 5-8. To create the basic interface, follow these steps:

1. Select File|New Project to display the Project Wizard. In the File field, enter the name **c:\JBuilder\myprojects\osborne\jbe\layout\Simple.jpr** and click Finish.

2. Select File|New and double-click the Frame icon on the New tab in the Object Gallery. On the New Frame dialog, enter **SimpleFrame** for the Class Name, and click OK.

3. Make sure that SimpleFrame.java is selected in the Navigation pane, and click the Design tab to change to design mode.

4. Check that the selection in the Component Tree is on *this*, indicating that *SimpleFrame* is selected. Move to the Properties page of the Inspector and select BorderLayout for its *layout* property.

5. Select the AWT tab on the Component Palette and select the *java.awt.TextArea* component.

5

The finished
basic interface
Figure 5-8.

6. Place the cursor in the middle of the frame and verify that the message displayed in the right side of the status bar indicates that the constraint Center will be used to place the component. Click once to place the text area.

7. Click the Controls tab on the Component Palette, and select the *borland.jbcl.control.StatusBar* component.

8. Move the cursor over the frame and use the message displayed in the status area to find a position that will set the constraint to South. Click once to place the *StatusBar* component.

9. Now make a deliberate mistake in placing the button bar. Select *borland.jbcl.control.ButtonBar* on the Controls page of the Component Palette and place it where the status bar indicates it will receive an East constraint.

10. The component *buttonBar1* should be selected in the Component Tree, and the Inspector should display a *constraints* value of East. Use the Inspector to drop down the list of valid constraints and select the value North.

11. In order to run this as an application, the class needs a *main()* method. Click the Source tab to change to the source view and add the following method to the *SimpleFrame* class:

```
public static void main(String args[]) {
  Frame frame = new SimpleFrame();
  frame.pack();
  frame.show();
}
```

This method creates an instance of *SimpleFrame*, sets it to its preferred size with the *pack()* method, and displays it. To see it in action, select Run|Run, press SHIFT-F9, or click the Run button on JBuilder's toolbar. Resize the frame at runtime to see how it behaves.

The Standard Java Layout Managers

Java defines a number of standard layout managers as a part of the *java.awt* package. Most of these are very simple and perform a single task well, while *GridBagLayout* is very complex and extremely flexible, performing a variety of different tasks. Choosing the right layout manager for a situation is extremely important. Each has its strengths and weaknesses, and it is easy to waste time and effort trying to force a layout manager to perform a task it simply cannot do. It is equally easy to waste time configuring a complicated layout manager to emulate a simpler one. It's a good idea to familiarize yourself with each of the layout managers to avoid these common pitfalls.

The most commonly used layout managers are *BorderLayout*, *FlowLayout*, and *GridBagLayout*. Both *CardLayout* and *GridLayout* have their uses, but are not used as frequently. Each of the standard layout managers is described in depth in the following sections.

Each section provides an overview of the layout manager and its intended use, the properties that can be set on the layout manager itself, appropriate *constraints* values, and additional topics specific to a particular type of layout manager.

5

BorderLayout

A very commonly used layout manager, *BorderLayout* arranges components around the outside of a container. An example of a *BorderLayout* is shown in Figure 5-9. This layout manager provides an ideal mechanism for controlling status bars, button bars, or anything else that remains anchored to the edge of a container. The remaining space in the center of the container may be occupied by a component that resizes both horizontally and vertically as the container is resized.

 CD-ROM: The application shown in Figure 5-9 is in the file BorderLayoutSample.java in the project LayoutSamples.jpr under the osborne\jbecd\layout subdirectory.

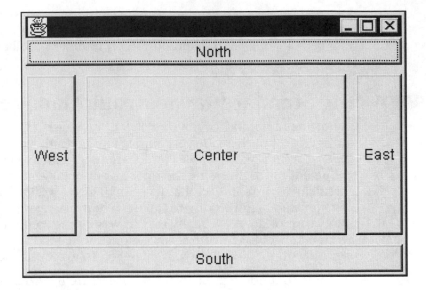

A
BorderLayout
with
horizontal and
vertical gaps,
and all five
constraint
values in use
Figure 5-9.

BorderLayout Properties

The size of the horizontal gap between components can be adjusted with the *hgap* property. The size of the vertical gap is controlled with the *vgap* property. Both values are measured in pixels and default to zero. The *BorderLayout* used in Figure 5-9 has horizontal and vertical gaps of eight pixels.

BorderLayout Constraints

There are five possible positions for components managed by *BorderLayout*, as illustrated earlier. The North and South positions occupy the entire width of the space available in the container, while the height of these components is determined from their *preferredSize()* method. The East and West positions occupy the remainder of the height, with an optional gap, while their width is determined from their *preferredSize()* method. The Center position occupies whatever space remains, less the size of the optional gap between components. Any or all of these positions may be eliminated if no component is assigned to it.

NOTE: No two components should occupy the same position, as *BorderLayout* will overlap them rather than placing them beside one another.

Components managed by a *BorderLayout* have constraints whose values are instances of *String* to indicate which of the positions a component will occupy. The valid values are the strings "North", "South", "East", "West", and "Center". For convenience, the *BorderLayout* class defines the constant values

BorderLayout.NORTH, BorderLayout.SOUTH, BorderLayout.EAST, BorderLayout.WEST, and *BorderLayout.CENTER* that are equivalent to these string values. JBuilder uses these values when generating code on your behalf.

TIP: The UI Designer generates code that uses the longer constant names both for runtime efficiency and compile-time error checking. Code that explicitly declares a string may include misspellings and will still compile. Code that refers to a constant value defined by another class will not compile if the name of the constant is misspelled.

BorderLayout Popup Menu Options

Right-clicking on a *BorderLayout* managed component displays a popup menu with two options:

◆ The Move to First option adds the selected component to its parent container before all other components. This makes the component the first in the tab sequence within the container.

◆ The Move to Last option adds the selected component to its parent container after all other components. This places the component at the end of the tab sequence.

Container Sizing with BorderLayout

The preferred size of a container using a *BorderLayout* is determined as follows:

◆ The preferred width is equal to the preferred width of the West, Center, and East components, plus the size of the horizontal gaps between them.

◆ The preferred height is equal to the preferred height of the North, Center, and South components, plus the size of the vertical gaps between them.

The minimum size of the container is similarly computed from the minimum sizes of components within the container.

NOTE: Sizing a container that uses *BorderLayout* to its minimum size may result in the component in the center being compressed below its minimum size. Although the computed minimum size would seem to make sense, it causes problems because the container always uses the preferred size when placing components along the borders.

5

CardLayout

CardLayout is an unusual and infrequently used layout manager that displays only one of the components it manages at a time, and hides all others. *CardLayout* is most frequently used to emulate the tabbed dialog appearance commonly seen in Windows applications, though JBuilder developers will often opt to use the *TabsetPanel* component, which hides many of the implementation details discussed here.

The conceptual image is that of a stack of cards, all the same size, only one visible at a time. *CardLayout* ignores the preferred and minimum sizes of a component. The visible component always occupies the entire available area inside its container, less an adjustable gap above, below, and to the left and right of the component.

The example in Figure 5-10 uses a *CardLayout* for the top portion of the frame, displaying one of three possible components at a time. The three buttons below are managed by a different layout manager, but serve to change which of *CardLayout*'s components are displayed.

CD-ROM: The application in Figure 5-10 is in the file CardAndFlowLayoutSample.java in the project LayoutSamples.jpr under the osborne\jbecd\layout subdirectory.

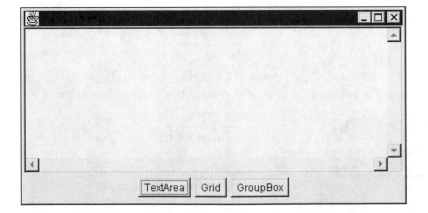

One of three components in a *CardLayout* (top) and three buttons in a *FlowLayout* (bottom)

Figure 5-10.

CardLayout Properties

The gap above and below the visible component can be set by adjusting the *vgap* property, which measures the size of the gap in pixels and defaults to zero. Similarly, the gap to the left and right of the visible component is specified with the *hgap* property, which also defaults to zero.

CardLayout Constraints

Components managed by a *CardLayout* have constraints whose values are instances of *String*. The *show()* method described in the following section, "CardLayout Methods," can be used to display a component by providing a matching string.

NOTE: All components managed by a single *CardLayout* should have a unique constraints value. Since all components occupy the same position, there is no way to have more than one visible at a time.

CardLayout Popup Menu Options

Right-clicking on a *CardLayout* managed component displays a popup menu with two options:

♦ The Move to First option adds the selected component to its parent container before all other components. This makes it the component displayed by default inside the container.

♦ The Move to Last option adds the selected component to its parent container after all other components. The order of components is important for some of *CardLayout*'s methods.

CardLayout Methods

The *show(Container, String)* method is used to display a specific component inside the specified container. The component displayed is the one whose constraints value matches the string parameter.

The *first(Container), last(Container), next(Container),* and *previous(Container)* methods select a component in the specified container without needing a constraints value. The order in which components are added to the container determines which will be displayed. The *first()* and *last()* methods display the first and last components added, respectively. The *next()* method displays the component added after the currently displayed component, or the first component added if the last one is currently displayed. The *previous()* method displays the component added before the currently displayed component, or the last component added if the first one is currently displayed.

5

NOTE: Some layout manager methods require a parameter that specifies a particular container to operate on. This may seem redundant since JBuilder automatically creates a separate layout manager for every container, but it is possible through code to associate more than one container with a single layout manager.

Container Sizing with CardLayout

The preferred size of a container using a *CardLayout* is determined as follows:

♦ The preferred width is equal to the preferred width of the widest component in the container.

♦ The preferred height is equal to the preferred height of the tallest component in the container.

The minimum size of the container is similarly computed from the minimum sizes of components within the container.

FlowLayout

Often used for simpler aspects of a user interface, *FlowLayout* arranges components from left to right until it runs out of space, at which point it starts another row of components below the previous row. The rows of components can be centered within the container, left-justified, or right-justified. There are adjustable gaps between components and rows. The example in Figure 5-10 uses a *FlowLayout* for the bottom portion of the frame, centering three buttons horizontally within a panel.

FlowLayout Properties

The *alignment* property controls the justification of components within a row. This integer value may be set to 0 for left-justification, 1 for centering, or 2 for right-justification. In code, the preferred technique is to use the constants *FlowLayout.LEFT*, *FlowLayout.CENTER*, and *FlowLayout.RIGHT*. The default justification is centered.

The *hgap* property controls the spacing between components on a row. The space is measured in pixels and defaults to 5. The *vgap* property controls the spacing between rows and also defaults to 5.

FlowLayout Constraints

No constraint values have any meaning for components within a *FlowLayout*. The position of components is determined by the order in which they are added to the container.

FlowLayout Popup Menu Options

Right-clicking on a *FlowLayout* managed component displays a popup menu with two options:

♦ The Move to First option adds the selected component to its parent container before all other components. This makes it the first component on the first row.

♦ The Move to Last option adds the selected component to its parent container after all other components. This makes it the last component on the last row.

Container Sizing with FlowLayout

The preferred size of a container using a *FlowLayout* is determined as follows:

♦ The preferred width is equal to the sum of the preferred widths of all components in the container, plus horizontal gaps between components, plus padding equal to the size of a horizontal gap on either side of the row.

♦ The preferred height is equal to the preferred height of the tallest component in the container, plus padding equal to a vertical gap above and below the row.

The minimum size of the container is similarly computed from the minimum sizes of components within the container.

5

NOTE: As you can see from the previous description, the preferred and minimum sizes of the container are computed assuming that the components will be displayed in a single row.

NOTE: Sizing a container that uses *FlowLayout* to its minimum size may result in some components disappearing. Although the computed minimum size would seem to make sense, it causes problems because the container always uses the preferred width when laying out a row, and the final component may not fit. This will result in the component being displayed on the next row, but as mentioned in the preceding note, the size is computed for displaying a single row.

GridLayout

The *GridLayout* is a seldom-used layout manager that arranges components into a rectangular grid in which each component is exactly the same size, as shown in Figure 5-11. Component sizes are determined without regard for their preferred or minimum sizes. Adjustable gaps can be added between rows and columns of components.

CD-ROM: The application in Figure 5-11 is in the file GridLayoutSample.java in the project LayoutSamples.jpr under the osborne\jbecd\layout subdirectory.

NOTE: Since all components are set to the same size, a container whose width does not divide evenly by the number of columns will have wasted space along its right edge. Similarly, containers whose height does not divide evenly by the number of rows will contain wasted space along the bottom.

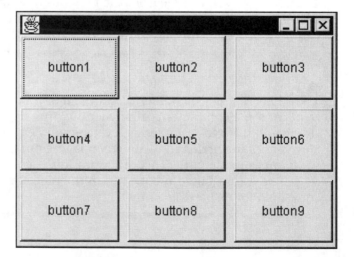

A three-by-three *GridLayout* containing nine buttons

Figure 5-11.

GridLayout Properties

The *hgap* property specifies the width in pixels of gaps between columns of components. The *vgap* property specifies the height in pixels of gaps between rows.

The *rows* property controls the number of rows the grid is divided into. When the value of *rows* is greater than zero, the *columns* property is ignored and the number of columns is computed by dividing the number of components in the container by the number of rows, and rounding upward.

When the *rows* property is set to zero, the *columns* property specifies the number of columns the grid is divided into. The number of rows is then computed by dividing the number of components in the container by the number of columns, rounding upward.

GridLayout Constraints

No constraint values have any meaning for components within a GridLayout. The position of components is determined by the order in which they are added to the container.

GridLayout Popup Menu Options

Right-clicking on a *GridLayout* managed component displays a popup menu with two options:

♦ The Move to First option adds the selected component to its parent container before all other components. This makes it the first component on the first row.

♦ The Move to Last option adds the selected component to its parent container after all other components. This makes it the last component on the last row.

Container Sizing with GridLayout

The preferred size of a container using a *GridLayout* is determined as follows:

♦ The preferred width is equal to the preferred width of the widest component times the number of columns, plus the width of horizontal gaps between columns.

♦ The preferred height is equal to the preferred height of the tallest component times the number of rows, plus the height of vertical gaps between rows.

The minimum size of the container is similarly computed from the minimum sizes of components within the container.

5

GridBagLayout

The most sophisticated layout manager is without question the *GridBagLayout*. No other layout manager can deal with as wide a variety of situations as flexibly. There's a lot of depth, coupled as always with a lot of options, but all of them come in handy in one situation or another and are well worth learning. A single *GridBagLayout* is capable of managing an interface with a variety of components that move and size in different ways, as demonstrated in Figures 5-12 and 5-13.

CD-ROM: The application shown in Figure 5-12 is in the file GridBagLayoutSample.java in the project LayoutSamples.jpr under the osborne\jbecd\layout subdirectory.

The example depicted in Figures 5-12 and 5-13 showcases only a subset of what *GridBagLayout* is capable of, but it's a good introduction to the kinds of capabilities you can look forward to reading about. You may want to refer to these figures to see the following features:

♦ A button's preferred size is based on the length of its label. However, buttons of different sizes in a vertical column do not make a good visual impression. With a *GridBagLayout*, you can make components in a

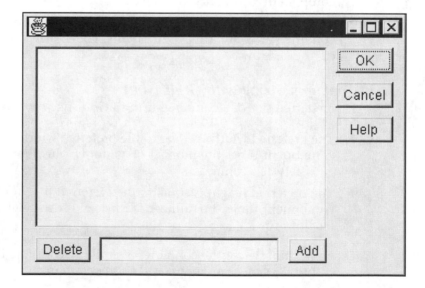

One frame, one *GridBagLayout*, and seven other components
Figure 5-12.

The same
frame after
resizing
Figure 5-13.

vertical column the same width even though they may have different
label lengths. The OK, Cancel, and Help buttons in this interface all have
the same width despite different lengths of labels.

♦ The list box adjusts in size both horizontally and vertically as the frame
  is resized.

♦ The text field between the Delete and Add buttons resizes horizontally,
  but not vertically.

♦ The Add button's right edge is always aligned with the right edge of the
  list box above it.

♦ All components retain nice even gaps between one another, even when
  the frame is resized.

♦ Everything will automatically adjust to a Macintosh, Windows, or UNIX
  interface style.

What follows is a brief discussion of how *GridBagLayout* decides where to
place components. These basic concepts will help make the constraint
information associated with the *GridBagLayout* a lot more comprehensible.

GridBagLayout Concepts

As the name implies, *GridBagLayout* does start with a conceptual grid, but it
bears almost no resemblance to *GridLayout*. The following steps are a rough
approximation of what goes on when a *GridBagLayout* determines how to
position and size components.

1. Determine the size of the grid, and decide which components occupy which cells.

    The constraint for each component carries information about the row and column it begins in, and the number of rows and columns it spans. The layout manager scans all of the components to determine the size of the grid necessary. Figure 5-14 depicts the resulting conceptual grid for the example introduced in Figures 5-12 and 5-13. The grid has four columns and five rows, as indicated by the dotted grid lines. The three buttons along the right side occupy a single column and each button occupies a single row. The text field and the two buttons along the bottom occupy a single row and each occupies a single column. The list box occupies four rows and three columns.

2. Determine which rows and columns resize when the container is resized.

    The constraint for each component describes whether or not it can be resized by specifying a resizing *weight* for the horizontal direction, and another weight for the vertical direction. Weights are floating-point values whose relative values determine how rows and columns are resized. A weight of zero means that a component prefers not to be resized along the specified axis. Any nonzero value is measured relative to other weighting values to determine how much a row or column should grow or shrink. A value of 1.0 is typically used by JBuilder to indicate that a component can be resized along an axis.

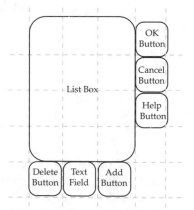

The basic
conceptual
grid
Figure 5-14.

The *GridBagLayout* scans through all components, starting with the ones that occupy the fewest rows, to see which rows are resizable. Continuing our example from Figure 5-14, it starts with the buttons and the text field since they occupy only one row vertically. Since these one-row components have a vertical weight of zero, nothing happens until attention passes to the next taller component, the list box, which occupies four rows. The list box has a vertical weight of 1.0. Since none of the rows that the list box occupies have been assigned weights, the default behavior is to apply the weight to the bottommost row that the list occupies. The fourth row is marked as resizable, with a weight of 1.0.

The *GridBagLayout* repeats the process for columns, starting again with the components that occupy the fewest columns. Of the six components that only take up one column in Figure 5-14, only the text field has a horizontal weight greater than zero. The column it is in records its weight of 1.0. The process continues to wider components and discovers that the list box is also horizontally resizable, with a weight of 1.0. Since one of the columns it spans has already been marked with an equal or greater weight, the *GridBagLayout* leaves the second column as the only resizable column. The resulting information about resizable rows and columns is shown in Figure 5-15.

3. Determine the preferred row and column sizes.

The *GridBagLayout* determines the preferred size of each row by determining the tallest cell in the row. The height of each cell is computed as the sum of the following:

5

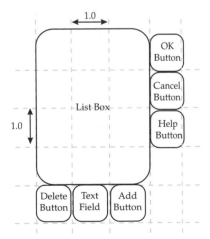

The grid with row and column sizing weights

Figure 5-15.

♦ The preferred height of the component.

♦ The inset specified above and below the component as a part of the component's constraints. This is the gap between it and the cell above and below.

♦ The padding specified for the height of the component as a part of the component's constraints. This can be a positive or negative value to make the component taller or shorter than its normal preferred height.

Once again, the process begins with the components that occupy the fewest rows. If a component spans more than one row and it is taller than the two rows put together, its excess height is distributed among the resizable rows according to their weights. If none of the rows are resizable, *GridBagLayout* just puts the extra height in the bottommost row.

The same process is repeated for columns, using widths rather than heights. When this is done, the grid now knows what size it would like each row and column to be, as shown in Figure 5-16.

4. Adjust row and column sizes to fit the actual container size.

Some rows and columns will need to be adjusted if the container isn't actually at its preferred size. Consider a situation in which the frame is resized so that it is wider and shorter, as previously demonstrated in Figure 5-13. Some column or columns need to be expanded, and some row or rows need to be reduced.

The grid with weights and preferred row and column sizes

Figure 5-16.

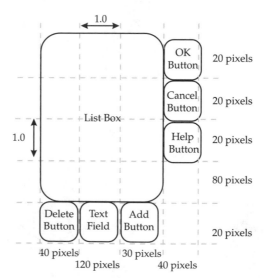

Whether adding or removing space, the *GridBagLayout* only adjusts rows or columns that are marked as resizable. The necessary space is divided among all of the resizable rows or columns according to their weights. For example, a row with double the weighting of another row will always be adjusted by twice as much within the limits of integer rounding.

NOTE: If the size of a container is reduced and no rows or columns are adjustable, or if all of them have been reduced to zero and more space is needed, *GridBagLayout* will not reduce the size of nonadjustable rows or columns. Some components will simply not fit in the container in these situations.

Assuming a target size of 300×90 pixels, the situation conceptually now looks like the one shown in Figure 5-17.

5. Check for success.

    If *GridBagLayout* was unable to make the resulting grid small enough to fit in the container, there's one more trick it will try: it can repeat steps 3 and 4 using the component's minimum size rather than the preferred size. In this example, it isn't necessary.

5

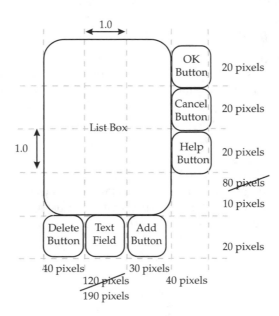

The grid adjusted for the container's actual size

Figure 5-17.

6. Size and place the components.

    Finally, the components are placed in their cells, a process that can be controlled in a number of ways. The component's size is determined as follows:

- ◆ A component is normally displayed in its preferred size, plus any horizontal or vertical *padding* as described in step 3.

- ◆ The component's size will be reduced, if necessary, to fit inside the cell. A component cannot necessarily occupy the entire cell, as space is always reserved for the *inset* spacing that provides gaps between components.

- ◆ The component's constraints may specify a *fill* value of none, horizontal, vertical, or both horizontal and vertical. The component's size will be adjusted to fill the cell in the specified orientations, minus the space for the *inset* spacing.

In the example followed throughout, the buttons along the right all have a horizontal *fill* specified, so that they are all the same width. The text field also has a horizontal *fill*, so that it can be as wide as possible while still retaining the appropriate height. The list box is instructed to *fill* both axes, maximizing its use of the space available.

Once the size of a component is determined, it is then placed inside the correct cell. The position within these cells is determined by its constraint's *anchor* value. The component may be anchored to the center, any side, or any corner of its cell. Regardless of the anchor position, the component is always offset from the actual edge of the cell by the *inset* value described in step 3. This *inset* provides a way to keep components neatly spaced. All components in this example have a center *anchor*.

While *GridBagLayout* can be intimidating at first, JBuilder makes all of these features very accessible, and shows you the result of every change as you make it. The remainder of this section discusses the facilities available for manipulating the constraints value discussed earlier. The sample interface presented at the end of this chapter uses *GridBagLayout* to give you a chance to experience the process of building an interface with this powerful tool.

GridBagLayout Properties
There are no properties associated with *GridBagLayout* instances. Everything is controlled through the constraints associated with each of the components within the container.

GridBagLayout Constraints

The constraints value must be an instance of the class *GridBagConstraints*. This class has the following instance variables, the effects of which are discussed in the earlier section "GridBagLayout Concepts":

♦ The row and column position of the component within the grid is specified through *gridx*, *gridy*, *gridwidth*, and *gridheight* integer instance variables. Like most indexes in Java, the leftmost column and topmost row are given an index of 0.

♦ The resizing weight of the component is recorded in *weightx* and *weighty* floating point instance variables.

♦ The component size padding in pixels is given in the *ipadx* and *ipady* integer instance variables.

♦ The inset values in pixels for all four sides are recorded in an instance variable called *insets*, which must refer to an instance of *juvu.uwt.Insets*. This object in turn has four integer instance variables: *left*, *right*, *top*, and *bottom*.

♦ The *anchor* integer instance variable can be set to one of nine constants: *GridBagConstraints.CENTER*, and the various compass points *GridBagConstraints.NORTH*, *GridBagConstraints.NORTHEAST*, *GridBagConstraints.EAST*, etc.

♦ The *fill* integer instance variable may be set to *GridBagConstraints.NONE*, *GridBagConstraints.HORIZONTAL*, *GridBagConstraints.VERTICAL*, or *GridBagConstraints.BOTH*.

5

When editing the constraints for a component in a *GridBagLayout*, JBuilder presents an editor dialog with the graphical interface shown in Figure 5-18 so that you can focus on the appropriate values and let JBuilder write the necessary code to implement your wishes.

JBuilder's two-way tools generate and expect to find code that creates an instance of *borland.jbcl.layout.GridBagConstraints2* as part of the invocation of the container's *add()* method in *jbInit()*. This class is a subclass of *GridBagConstraints* with one critical difference: it has a constructor that accepts all of the needed values, rather than requiring line after line after line of code to set the appropriate instance variables. The code adding the list box described throughout this section looks like this:

```
this.add(list1, new GridBagConstraints2(0, 0, 3, 4, 1.0, 1.0,
  GridBagConstraints.CENTER, GridBagConstraints.BOTH,
  new Insets(8, 8, 8, 8), 50, 100));
```

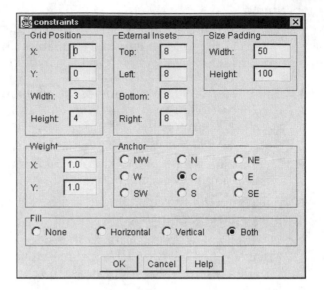

The dialog for
editing
*GridBag-
Constraints*
Figure 5-18.

NOTE: Since JBuilder always uses this JBCL (JavaBeans Component Library) class when defining a *GridBagLayout,* applications and applets designed visually using this layout with JBuilder will always need to be deployed with this *GridBagConstraints2* helper class. See Chapter 12 for details.

GridBagLayout Popup Menu Options

As shown in Figure 5-19, right-clicking a *GridBagLayout* managed component displays a popup menu with numerous options for quick and convenient editing of this complex constraint. Starting at the top, these options perform the following tasks:

◆   The Remove Padding option sets the *ipadx* and *ipady* constraint values to zero.

◆   The Constraints option displays the dialog shown in Figure 5-18 to edit the selected components' constraints values.

◆   Fill Horizontal and Fill Vertical alter the *fill* constraint value to include the appropriate axis. Remove Fill sets *fill* to *GridBagConstraints.NONE.*

◆   Weight Horizontal and Weight Vertical set *weightx* and *weighty* to 1.0, respectively. Remove Weights sets both values to 0.0.

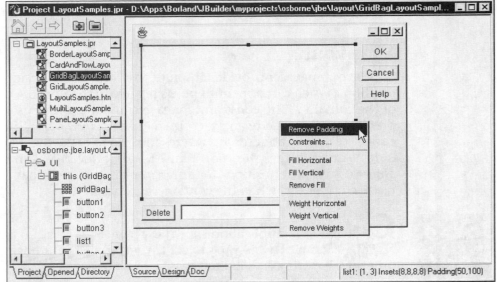

The popup menu options for components managed by *GridBagLayout*
Figure 5-19.

TIP: The popup menu's Constraints option works on multiple selections and is the only way to set *GridBagConstraints* values for more than one component at a time. This can save an amazing amount of time during user interface design. Fields whose values differ among the selected items are left blank in the initial display, but can be changed to affect all selected components.

5

Container Sizing with GridBagLayout

The process described previously in the section "GridBagLayout Concepts" is used to determine the preferred and minimum sizes for containers. Follow steps 1 through 3 to get a feel for what the preferred layout would be. Follow the same steps, adjusting step 3 to use the minimum component size for the minimum layout.

Borland's Additional Layout Managers

The JavaBeans Component Library (JBCL) included with JBuilder defines two layout managers in the *borland.jbcl.layout* package: *XYLayout* and *PaneLayout*. Since both layout managers are written in Java, code that uses either of these layout managers will run on any platform that supports Java 1.1. Consult Chapter 12 for details on deploying JBCL classes with your application or applet. The following sections describe these two layout managers using the same format used earlier.

XYLayout

This layout manager provides absolute positioning by measuring the location of each component in pixels relative to the upper left-hand corner of the container. The constraint for each component may use a component's preferred size or specify an exact size in pixels. These capabilities make it easy to place components anywhere, and also to make them any size very quickly and easily, as shown in Figure 5-20. However, *XYLayout* does not adjust component positions for different platforms, nor does it move or resize components when the container is resized.

CD-ROM: The application shown in Figure 5-20 is in the file XYLayoutSample.java in the project LayoutSamples.jpr under the osborne\jbecd\layout subdirectory.

Typically, developers only use *XYLayout* for prototyping purposes. It is convenient to be able to drag any component to any position before the interface is complete, but once the final arrangement of components has been determined you will typically want to change the container to an appropriate layout manager. This process is described later in the section "Converting Between Layouts."

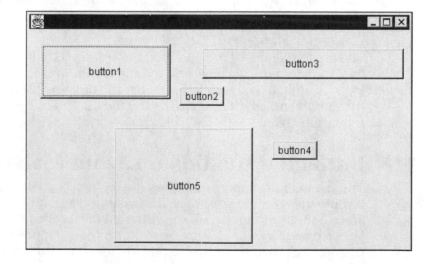

Use *XYLayout* to freely place and size components
Figure 5-20.

XYLayout Properties

The *width* property, when set to a value greater than zero, specifies a fixed preferred and minimum width for the container that uses the layout. The *height* property, when set to a value greater than zero, specifies a fixed preferred and minimum height for the container that uses the layout.

XYLayout Constraints

The constraints value must be an instance of the class *XYConstraints*, which has *x*, *y*, *width*, and *height* integer properties. The *x* and *y* properties are used to determine the position of the component. The width of the component is equal to *width* unless that property contains a value less than zero, in which case it uses the preferred width of the component. Similarly, the height of the component is equal to *height* unless that property contains a value less than zero, in which case it uses the preferred height of the component.

When a component is placed in the UI Designer with a single click, both *width* and *height* values default to -1 to maintain the component's preferred size. Resizing the component replaces one or both of these values with an absolute value in pixels.

The constraints value can be edited in the Inspector as a string, a series of four numbers separated by commas, as shown in Figure 5-21.

JBuilder's two-way tools generate and expect to find code that creates an instance of *XYConstraints* as part of the invocation of the container's *add()* method in *jbInit()*. For example, a *Button* instance that is placed 200 pixels from the left edge and 100 pixels from the top of a container while keeping its preferred size would generate the following line of code:

```
this.add(button1, new XYConstraints(200, 100, -1, -1));
```

XYLayout Popup Menu Options

As shown in Figure 5-22, right-clicking on an *XYLayout* managed component displays a popup menu with numerous options. The options are discussed briefly under the headings that follow, starting with the first items on the popup menu and proceeding downward. While in most products these capabilities would deserve a more detailed description, it is rare that a Java developer would want to make extensive use of *XYLayout* in any capacity other than as a rough prototyping tool.

Tab Order Options   The Move to First and Move to Last options put components at the beginning or end of the tab order by changing the order in which they are added to their container.

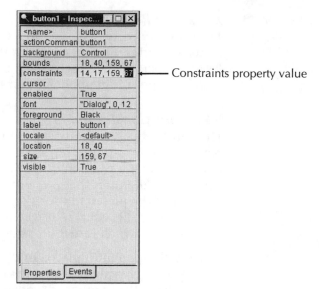

Constraints property value

Horizontal and Vertical Alignment   Align Left, Center, Right, Top, Middle, and Bottom options behave differently depending on the number of components selected. With a single component selected, they act on that component relative to its container. When more than one component is selected, they act on all selected components relative to the first component selected.

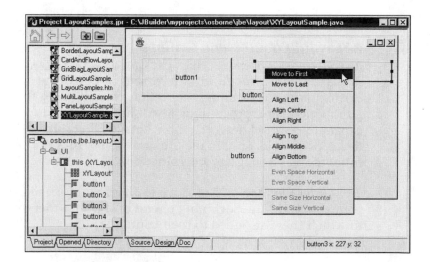

The popup
menu options
for
components
managed by
XYLayout
Figure 5-22.

, Top, and Bottom align the appropriate edge of a single
its container, or align the edges of more than one
the first component selected.

l horizontally center a single component in its
gn the horizontal centers of more than one component
nponent selected.

l vertically center a single component in its container,
cal centers of more than one component with the first
ted.

The Even Space Horizontal and Even Space Vertical
lable when three or more components are selected.
ie first and last component selected in place, and move
nponents to create an evenly spaced row or column. To
tions, place the first and last components in the desired
lect all of the components to be spaced, in order from
bottom, and select the corresponding option:

ontal places components in the order in which they
venly spaced horizontal locations between the first
ted and the last. The spacing automatically accounts for
widths of the components.

cal places components in the order they were selected at
tical locations between the first component selected
and the last. The spacing automatically accounts for differences in the
heights of the components.

Component Sizing The Same Size Horizontal and Same Size Vertical
options operate when more than one component is selected:

♦ Same Size Horizontal changes the width of all components to match the
width of the first component selected.

♦ Same Size Vertical changes the height of all components to match the
height of the first component selected.

Container Sizing with XYLayout

The preferred size of a container using an *XYLayout* is determined as follows:

♦ The preferred width is equal to the value of the *width* property unless
that value is zero. If *width* is zero, the preferred width is computed to be
just wide enough to encompass all components at their specified
positions and widths.

♦ The preferred height is equal to the value of the *height* property unless that value is zero. If *height* is zero, the preferred height is computed to be just tall enough to encompass all components at their specified positions and widths.

The minimum size of the container is similarly computed from the minimum sizes of components within the container.

PaneLayout

This layout manager represents a rectangular region that is proportionally subdivided into individual panes, similar to JBuilder's AppBrowser, as shown in Figure 5-23. Unlike the AppBrowser, when the container is resized, these panes retain their relative proportions. *PaneLayout* is seldom used within any container other than JBCL's *SplitPanel*, which provides the user the ability to resize these panes at runtime.

CD-ROM: The application shown in Figure 5-23 is in the file PaneLayoutSample.java in the project LayoutSamples.jpr under the osborne\jbecd\layout subdirectory.

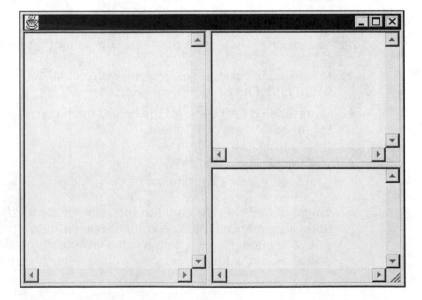

PaneLayout managing three text areas

Figure 5-23.

PaneLayout Properties

The *gap* integer property controls the space, measured in pixels, between panes.

PaneLayout Constraints

The constraints value must be an instance of the class *PaneConstraints*. These constraints describe the pane's position relative to other panes by identifying an existing pane whose space will be subdivided. This process is controlled with the following instance variables:

♦ The *name* string instance variable is used internally by the *PaneLayout* so that panes can identify one another by *splitComponentName*.

♦ The *splitComponentName* string instance variable identifies which pane should be subdivided to create space for this pane. The root pane specifies its own name for *splitComponentName*.

♦ The *position* integer instance variable describes what part of a subdivided pane becomes this pane's territory. The constant values *PaneConstraints.BOTTOM*, *PaneConstraints.LEFT*, *PaneConstraints.RIGHT*, and *PaneConstraints.TOP* are used for all panes but the root. The root pane uses a value of *PaneConstraints.ROOT*.

♦ The *proportion* floating-point instance variable describes how much of the subdivided pane becomes this pane's territory. The value must be between 0 and 1.

When the constraint is modified through the Inspector, a specialized dialog is presented for editing the *position* and *proportion*, as shown in Figure 5-24. The *name* is automatically assigned, and the *splitComponentName* is determined when the component is initially placed. These values can only be edited manually in code.

JBuilder's two-way tools generate and expect to find code that creates an instance of *PaneConstraints* as part of the invocation of the container's *add()* method in *jbInit()*. For example, a *TextArea* that subdivides another *TextArea* by taking over the top half of its space would generate the following line of code:

```
splitPanel1.add(textArea2, new PaneConstraints("textArea2",
  "textArea1", PaneConstraints.TOP, 0.5f));
```

PaneLayout Popup Menu Options

There is no popup menu for components in a container managed by *PaneLayout*.

5

Container Sizing with PaneLayout

The preferred size for a container that uses *PaneLayout* is the smallest size
that, when proportionally subdivided, provides panes large enough to
accommodate the preferred size of each component. The minimum size
reported is always the same as the preferred size.

Advanced Layout Concepts

The previous sections in this chapter introduced the standard layout
managers and how JBuilder allows you to construct a user interface with
them. These techniques alone are enough to create some very sophisticated
applications and applets, but there is always more to learn. The three topics
introduced in this section are all extremely important concepts that build on
the layout manager basics.

At the end of this chapter, in "Sample: Creating a Complex Interface," all of
these techniques will be used to create a single sample application.

Multiple Layouts with Nested Containers

Different layout managers are good at different tasks, so it is only natural
that there will be situations where one part of the user interface would be
best handled by one layout manager, whereas another part would be better
handled by another layout manager. Since each container in a visual design
can be assigned a different layout manager, this is easily implemented.

The frame shown in Figure 5-25 uses *BorderLayout* to arrange three panels. The panel in the Center position uses *XYLayout* to arbitrarily place the three large buttons in the upper left. The panel in the East position uses *GridBagLayout* to create a vertical column of buttons with identical widths. The panel in the South position centers a group of three buttons horizontally using *FlowLayout*.

Adding Components to a Container at Runtime

JBuilder automatically generates all of the code for components created at design time, making the process of creating and managing user interface code very straightforward. Sometimes, though, it is desirable to actually create components at runtime.

Adding Components to a Container

For each component added to the UI Designer, JBuilder writes at least two lines of code: an instance variable declaration and a call to a container's *add()* method to place the component with the necessary constraints. Additional lines of code may be generated to set any number of properties, but the first two lines capture the essence of component creation.

5

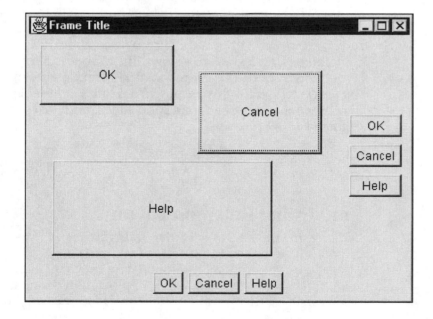

Multiple
layout
managers in a
single frame
Figure 5-25.

The variable declaration seems simple enough. For example, a button is declared with a variable of type *Button*, and an initializer that invokes the default constructor for the *Button* class:

```
Button button1 = new Button();
```

The exact syntax of the call to the *add()* method depends on the layout manager used by the container the component is added to. The type and value of the constraint passed must be appropriate to the layout manager in question. *FlowLayout* doesn't require any constraint, so the call to add the button described above to a panel using *FlowLayout* is very simple:

```
panel1.add(button1, null);
```

If keeping a reference to the button object isn't important, these two lines of code can be condensed into a single line, this time using a *Button* constructor that accepts a label:

```
panel1.add(new Button("New Button"), null);
```

This line of code, when added to *jbInit()*, performs exactly as expected. A button with the label New Button would appear when the code is executed.

Adding Components to a Visible Container

If the exact same line of code just shown is added to an event handler for another component, though, the new button fails to appear. This is because the container is already visible, and has already decided where to display each component within it. When a new component is added after the container is already visible, a single line of code is necessary to update the layout and paint the new component. Every container implements the *validate()* method for this purpose. To create a component at runtime, then, the component must be created and added, and the container must be validated:

```
panel1.add(new Button("New Button"), null);
panel1.validate();
```

Converting Between Layouts

In discussing the *XYLayout* earlier in this chapter, it was introduced as a prototyping tool. You can do all of your initial design in *XYLayout*, where it is easy to move components around, and then move them to an appropriate layout manager once the design is in place. JBuilder makes it remarkably easy to manage the transition from one layout manager to another, which is actually a very complicated process. Not only must the layout manager for a container be replaced, so must the constraints on every single component inside the container! JBuilder does this automatically, approximating the initial layout with the new layout as closely as possible.

To change a layout manager: select the desired container and change its *layout* property to the desired layout manager. Everything else is automatic, although not always entirely predictable. For some kinds of changes, such as changing an *XYLayout* into a *GridBagLayout*, there may be a significant amount of manual cleanup necessary to achieve the desired effect. The majority of the work is done, but there will usually be some rough edges you will need to clean up.

CAUTION: The conversion process happens in a single step, and there is no way to undo the changes made. Always save your file immediately before changing layouts, creating a backup to return to if the change does not work well.

Sample: Creating a Complex Interface

This example uses many of the techniques described to create a frame with nested containers, four different layout managers, and the ability to add components to the user interface at runtime. This final user interface appears in Figure 5-26.

The example begins by creating a basic project and application framework that will be extended through the addition of several components:

1. Select File|New Project to display the Project Wizard. In the File field, enter the name **c:\JBuilder\myprojects\osborne\jbe\layout\Complex.jpr** and click the Finish button.

2. Select File|New, and double-click the Application icon on the New page in the Object Gallery.

3. On the Step 1 page of the Application Wizard, enter **ComplexApplication** in the Class field and click the Next button. On the Step 2 page, enter **ComplexFrame** in the Class field for the Frame Class and click Finish.

4. Select the ComplexFrame.java file in the Navigation pane and click the Design tab.

    Look at the Component Tree and note the frame is using *BorderLayout* and the bevel panel inside it is using *XYLayout*. The next step

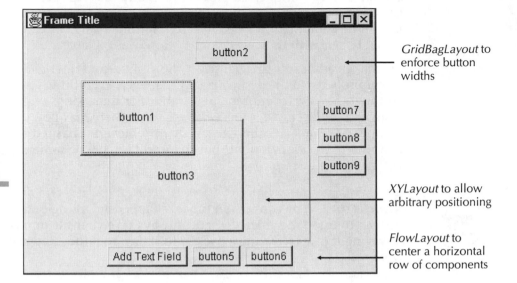

GridBagLayout to
enforce button
widths

XYLayout to allow
arbitrary positioning

FlowLayout to
center a horizontal
row of components

A complex
user interface
with multiple
layout
managers
Figure 5-26.

demonstrates that the *XYLayout* allows arbitrary placement of
components within it.

5. Click the AWT tab of the Component Palette to change to the AWT
   page, and place three instances of *Button* inside the bevel panel using
   random sizes and locations.

   The following steps add a new panel at the bottom of the frame. The
   panel uses *FlowLayout* to arrange another three buttons.

6. Select *Panel* from the Component Palette and click on **this** in the
   Component Tree to add it to the frame. Adding the component to the
   Component Tree is the best technique in this situation. Dropping it
   within the UI Designer would be possible but difficult since most of the
   area of the frame is covered by the bevel panel, and dropping the new
   panel inside the bevel panel would not achieve the desired result.

7. The newly created *panel1* component will still be selected and can be
   manipulated with the Inspector. Using the Properties page of the
   Inspector, change its *layout* property to *FlowLayout* and its *constraints*
   value to South.

8. Place three buttons on *panel1* by dropping them in either the UI
   Designer or by clicking on **this** in the Component Tree to add each one
   to the frame.

9. Select the leftmost button and use the Inspector to edit its *label* property to **Add Text Field**.

    The next set of steps creates another panel on the right side of the frame, scts its layout manager to

    4YLayout for prototyping purposes, and arranges three buttons in a vertical line.

10. Select *Panel* from the Component Palette and click on **this** in the Component Tree to add it to the frame. Using the Properties page of the Inspector, change its *layout* property to *XYLayout* and its *constraints* value to East.

11. Without any contents, a panel using *XYLayout* is invisibly thin. To change this in order to provide prototyping space, select *xyLayout1* beneath *panel2* in the Component Tree. Next, change its *width* property to 100 using the Inspector.

12. Place three buttons in a vertical row inside the newly formed panel on the right edge of the component, clicking to place them rather than dragging and dropping them so that they retain their preferred sizes. See Figure 5-26 for an approximation of the button placement.

    To convert the prototype into a functional design, the following steps change the layout manager for the most recently added panel to *GridBagLayout*. This new layout is then used to arrange the buttons in a neat column and equalize their widths.

13. Select *panel2* in the Component Tree and use the Inspector to change its *layout* property to *GridBagLayout*. The new layout may not be exactly like the original placement, but the appearance will be corrected shortly.

14. Click on the topmost button in the vertical row to select it, and hold the SHIFT key while clicking on the remaining two buttons to select them as well. Verify that *button7*, *button8*, and *button9* are the only components selected by looking at the Component Tree.

15. Right-click one of the buttons to display the *GridBagLayout* popup menu and select Constraints to display the dialog shown in Figure 5-27. Change the settings to match those shown in Figure 5-27 and click OK. The Grid Position values ensure that all three buttons wind up in the same column. The External Insets space the buttons evenly. The absence of Size Padding leaves all buttons at the preferred size. The lack of Weight indicates that nothing resizes. The Anchor places all buttons in the center of their cells. Lastly, the Fill value stretches all buttons to

5

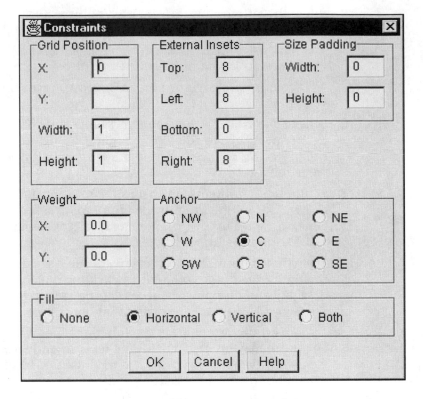

Initial
GridBag-
Constraints
values for the
vertical row of
buttons
Figure 5-27.

the width of their column, which will match the preferred width of the
widest button.

The *GridBagLayout* is now centering the column of buttons in their
container. Normally, this kind of interface appears with all of the
buttons at the top of the column. To accomplish this, the bottom cell
needs to be resizable, and the button in it needs to be at the top of the
cell. The following steps make this change.

16. Select only the bottommost button in the vertical column. Since it is
    already selected as a part of a multiple-selection, the easiest way to do
    this is to click on the appropriate button name in the Component Tree.
    Once selected, right-click it and select Constraints from the popup
    menu to display the dialog for editing constraints.

17. Change the Weight value for the Y-axis to 1.0, and the Anchor to
    North. Click OK to see the results of these changes.

The last step is to create a handler for the Add Text Field button that actually creates and adds a *TextField* component to the panel at the bottom of the frame.

18. Double-click the Add Text Field button to create an *actionEvent* event handler for it. Type the following code into the event-handling method:

```
panel1.add(new Button("New Button"), null);
  panel1.validate();
```

TIP: Double-clicking the component in the UI Designer to create an event handler is a shortcut for selecting the component and using the Inspector to create an event handler.

Test the final application by selecting Run|Run, pressing SHIFT-F9, or clicking on the Run button on the JBuilder toolbar. Experiment with resizing the frame, and test the Add Text Field button.

5

CHAPTER 6

Building and Testing Applets

An applet is a special way of packaging Java code to run within a host application, typically a Web browser. While many people associate Java exclusively with applets, they are actually a limited subset of what can be written using the language. This chapter discusses applets in general, how to package Java code as an applet, how to incorporate the applets in a Web page, the JBuilder Applet Wizard, and special restrictions and features for applets. Finally, techniques for writing Java code that can be used either as an applet or as a stand-alone Java application are introduced.

CD-ROM: The example projects for this chapter can be found in the osborne\jbecd\applet subdirectory. See Appendix C for information on installing and using the files on the CD-ROM that accompanies this book.

The Purpose of Applets

Java introduced applets as a new way of distributing code to the desktop. Unlike a traditional application, which must be installed before use, an applet can be downloaded and executed automatically when a user visits a Web page with a standard Java-enabled Web browser. This allows designers of an Internet site to provide interactive experiences including customizable graphs, real-time stock market data, and much more convenient order-entry capabilities over the Internet. The same technology can be used on corporate intranets to deploy custom applications to tens of thousands of desktops while reducing the administrative burden required to keep these desktops up to date.

Applets play to the strengths of the Java language in a number of ways. The Web browser needs to be able to dynamically load new classes in order to execute applets, and Java is well suited to this task. The code must work on a variety of platforms, so users in multiple operating systems can take advantage of the downloaded code. Java's platform-independent byte code solves this problem neatly. The code that is downloaded must not be able to adversely affect the user's computer. Ideally, it should be impossible to write a virus or Trojan horse in Java, and the design of the language and class libraries restricts applets in a number of critical ways to achieve this goal.

The section near the end of this chapter, "Making the Choice: Application or Applet," discusses the trade-offs made in choosing to deploy Java code as an applet. If none of an applet's advantages sound appealing, you may not need to investigate applet development any further. You may read through this chapter out of curiosity, or skip it altogether as none of the material introduced in this chapter is critical to understanding the rest of JBuilder. If, on the other hand, applets are of interest, then read on to find out more about the process of creating applets with JBuilder.

JBuilder as an Applet Development Tool

Borland has designed JBuilder primarily as a sophisticated Java application development tool. The tools designed specifically for applet development are limited to the Applet Wizard, described in this chapter, and some features of the Deployment Wizard that are described in Chapter 12. JBuilder also recognizes the HTML (HyperText Markup Language) file type for inclusion in projects, and provides debugger support for applets.

This isn't to say that you should not use JBuilder for applet development. Many of the technologies created for application developers, including the UI Designer, happen to work very well with applet code, and offer a compelling reason to do all your Java development in JBuilder. You simply need to be aware that these tools make it very easy to call upon a wide variety of JavaBeans components that will need to be downloaded with your applet. For this reason, an applet designer should be cautious about using JBCL (JavaBeans Component Library) components because of the impact they will have on the download time for the applet. You must also realize that neither JBuilder nor any other Java development tool can do anything to change the applet security system. You must be aware of the restrictions of the applet security model, and ensure that applet code does not violate any of these rules.

The remainder of this chapter provides a tour of JBuilder as an applet development environment. None of the examples explicitly illustrate the use of tools such as the UI Designer in conjunction with applets, but these tools function just as they do when you are developing Java applications in JBuilder.

The Parts of an Applet

An applet consists of two parts: a body of Java code that describes the actual behavior of the applet, and an HTML file that describes a Web page the applet should be displayed on.

NOTE: A basic understanding of HTML is necessary for this chapter. For an introduction to HTML, consult one of the many available HTML guides.

6

The Java portion of an applet is a subclass of *java.lang.Applet*. The subclass defines the behavior unique to that particular applet through methods and instance variables just like any other Java class. When the applet is needed, a Web browser will download the class, create an instance of the class, and communicate with that applet instance to allow it to display itself and respond to user input. If, in turn, the applet calls upon additional classes, images, or sounds, they will also be downloaded from the Web server. For added efficiency, multiple classes and resources, such as images and sounds, may be bundled together in a single download in JAR (Java Archive) file format.

The HTML file provides a context for the applet and information about the location, size, and optional parameters passed to the applet. This information is described using an <APPLET> tag and special attributes. More than one <APPLET> tag can be used in a single HTML file, allowing for any number of applets on a single page.

The process of creating an *Applet* subclass and an HTML container for the applet is covered in the next two sections. A simple applet, written the hard way using JBuilder's Editor, will be used to illustrate the concepts through these sections before introducing JBuilder's Applet Wizard. The Applet Wizard will then be used to create a more sophisticated version of the same applet.

The Applet Class

An applet is always an instance of a class that extends *java.applet.Applet* and adds its own unique behavior by overriding some of *Applet*'s methods. The *Applet* class is a container, inheriting from *java.awt.Panel*, and like all containers, is itself a customizable component.

Because *Applet* is a subclass of *java.awt.Container*, any number of components may be contained within an applet, and their arrangement can be controlled with any of the standard layout managers. JBuilder's UI Designer works well with subclasses of *Applet*, providing the same design functionality that is available for *Frame* subclasses. This technique is well suited to developing traditional user interfaces, using the applet itself solely as a container for more interesting components.

Simple applets that do not need to present a typical user interface can instead opt to customize their own appearance and behavior by overriding methods inherited from *java.awt.Component*.

Overriding Applet Methods

An applet can be designed without overriding a single *Applet* method, but typically one or more of these methods will be overridden so that the applet can take advantage of information about the context it is displayed within.

The browser notifies an applet that it has been created and configured by invoking its *init()* method. Applets should typically override this method to perform initialization actions rather than placing initialization code in their constructor. If the UI Designer is used to create a user interface to an applet, the *init()* method should invoke *jbInit()*. The Applet Wizard described later in this chapter takes care of this task automatically. An applet's *destroy()* method is called just before the applet is discarded. This method is rarely overridden since garbage collection will typically take care of the necessary cleanup.

When the applet is actually displayed, its *start()* method is invoked so an applet can override this method to perform any actions related to being displayed. This is typically when an applet would begin any animation or periodic task that is important while it is visible. If the *start()* method is overridden, the corresponding *stop()* method should also be overridden to cease this activity when the browser moves on to another page. A single applet instance may be started and stopped several times before being discarded.

The methods *getAppletInfo()* and *getParameterInfo()* provide additional information about the applet, but do not directly affect its behavior. The method *getAppletInfo()* returns a string suitable for display that describes the applet and should always be overridden to provide meaningful information. The method *getParameterInfo()* describes the parameters the applet accepts, and should be overridden for any applet that accepts parameters. Applet parameters are described later in this chapter.

Overriding Component Methods

Of the methods inherited from *java.awt.Component*, the most frequently overridden is the *paint()* method, which describes the applet's appearance. The *paint()* method inherited from the *javaapplet.Applet* class paints any components contained inside the applet on the screen. Typically, an applet that contains user interface objects will not override this method, but any applet can further customize its appearance by overriding this method. The sample code presented next defines an applet that uses *paint()* to create its appearance.

Creating a Simple Applet

The applet created here can be used to put a nifty shadowed text rendition of the string "Cool Stuff" on any Web page.

CD-ROM: An example of the complete project Applet.jpr can be found in the osborne\jbecd\applet subdirectory.

6

1. Select File|New Project to display the Project Wizard. In the File field, enter **c:\JBuilder\myprojects\osborne\jbe\applet\Applet.jpr**. Click the Finish button.

2. Select File|New, and select Class from the Object Gallery. On the New Object dialog, enter **osborne.jbe.applet** at Package, enter **SimpleApplet** at Class Name, and enter **java.applet.Applet** at Extends. Disable the option Generate default constructor. Click OK.

3. Display the SimpleApplet.java file in the source view and edit the code to match the following:

```
package osborne.jbe.applet;

import java.applet.*;
import java.awt.*;

public class SimpleApplet extends Applet {
  String text = "Cool Stuff";
  int    size = 24, offset = 2;
  Font   font = new Font("Dialog", Font.BOLD, size);

  public void paint(Graphics g) {
    g.setFont(font);
    g.setColor(Color.black);
    g.drawString(text, offset, size+offset);
    g.setColor(Color.white);
    g.drawString(text, 0, size);
    super.paint(g);
  }
}
```

Save the file by selecting File|Save or by pressing CTRL-S. You now have a complete *Applet* subclass, but no way to actually display it. A look at the code reveals that *SimpleApplet* draws the string "Cool Stuff" in black using a 24-point font, and then draws the same string in white two pixels up and to the left, giving an interesting shadowed appearance. The font, font size, shadow offset, and string are all contained in variables, but no means are provided yet to alter these values.

The next section demonstrates how to create a Web page that contains this applet so you can see it in action.

The HTML <APPLET> Tag

Web browsers attempt to display applets wherever the <APPLET> tag is encountered in the HTML that describes a Web page. The <APPLET> tag reserves a rectangular area within the page for the applet's use, and tells the browser how to load and start the applet class. The <APPLET> tag's syntax is as follows:

```
The browser <APPLET
  CODE = fully-qualified-path.CLASS
  WIDTH = width-in-pixels
  HEIGHT = height-in-pixels
  [ OBJECT = serialized-applet-url ]
  [ ARCHIVE = jar-file-list ]
  [ CODEBASE = class-path-root-url ]
  [ ALT = no-applets-alternate-text ]
```

```
  [ NAME = applet-name ]
  [ ALIGN = alignment ]
  [ VSPACE = vertical-spacing-in-pixels ]
  [ HSPACE = horizontal-spacing-in-pixels ]
>
  alternate-text
  [ <PARAM NAME = parameter-name VALUE = parameter-value> ]
  [ <PARAM NAME = parameter-name VALUE = parameter-value> ]
  ...
</APPLET>
```

The portions of the syntax shown in square brackets are optional. The *no-applets-alternate-text* specified in the *alt* attribute is only displayed by Java-aware browsers that have applets disabled, while the *alternate-text* contained between the <APPLET> and </APPLET> tags is displayed by browsers that are not Java-aware.

Examining the syntax closely reveals that the simplest form of the <APPLET> tag has only three required attributes: *width*, *height*, and *code*. The following HTML is an example of a simple applet container that includes these three attributes, one optional attribute, and a message displayed by browsers that do not understand the <APPLET> tag:

```
<APPLET WIDTH=400 HEIGHT=300
  CODE="osborne.jbe.applet.SimpleApplet.class"
  CODEBASE="/javacode">
  Your browser is not Java-aware.
</APPLET>
```

The most frequently used <APPLET> attributes are described next. The <PARAM> tag is described later in the section "Applet Parameters."

NOTE: Consult a complete HTML guide for a list of attributes supported by different browsers currently on the market.

6

The Width and Height Attributes

An <APPLET> tag must include both of these attributes. The Web page will reserve a rectangular area with a width in pixels equal to the *width* attribute and a height in pixels equal to the *height* attribute. The applet can determine the size of the area reserved for it, but it cannot change the initial values specified in the HTML container. The preceding example reserves a space that is 400 pixels wide by 300 pixels high in which an applet will be displayed.

The Code Attribute

The required *code* attribute specifies the class to be loaded as an applet. The value specified must include the ".class" extension for the class file stored on the Web server, and use the Java dot notation for specifying the package name for the class. The path on the Web server from which code will be requested is adapted from this description. In the previous example, the class described by the relative URL (Uniform Resource Locator) "osborne/jbe/applet/SimpleApplet.class" would be requested from the Web server and loaded as an applet.

The Codebase Attribute

The optional *codebase* attribute can be used to change the way the Web browser requests Java code from a Web server. Normally, the Web browser will request an applet's class files from a URL relative to the HTML file that contains the <APPLET> tag. If the class *osborne.jbe.applet.TestApplet* is referenced by the hypothetical URL http://www.bogus.com/test/TestApplet.html, then the browser will normally attempt to load http://www.bogus.com/test/osborne/jbe/applet /TestApplet.class to find the class definition.

The attribute *codebase* can change the root path used to search for the class file. It is specified relative to the location of the HTML file. Consequently, the *osborne.jbe.applet.TestApplet* class could be loaded from http://www.bogus.com/javacode/osborne/jbe/applet/TestApplet.class with the same HTML example shown previously. This technique would work regardless of the location of the HTML on the www.bogus.com server.

The Archive Attribute

Similar to *codebase*, the *archive* attribute changes the way the Web browser requests Java code from a Web server. When using the default loading mechanism or the *codebase* attribute, classes are loaded one at a time from the Web server, which can be extremely inefficient. The *archive* attribute specifies a compressed JAR archive file on the server that will be searched for the class in question.

NOTE: The Java Developer's Kit (JDK) included with JBuilder has a command-line JAR utility that can be used to create JAR files. The JBuilder Deployment Wizard automates this task and is described in Chapter 12.

The following example would download the URL http://www.bogus.com/javacode/SimpleApplet.jar and look inside it for "osborne/jbe/applet/SimpleApplet.class." When searching for additional classes, the browser will search the archive that has already been downloaded and placed in the browser's cache, thus reducing the time required to load and run an applet from a remote Web server.

```
<APPLET WIDTH=400 HEIGHT=300
  CODE="osborne.jbe.applet.SimpleApplet.class"
  ARCHIVE="/javacode/SimpleApplet.jar">
  You're missing out on a Java applet!
</APPLET>
```

The AppBrowser and HTML Files

HTML files can be added to a JBuilder project by several means, just like any other file type. To create an empty HTML file, select File|Open Open / Create, to display the Open / Create dialog, and then type in a filename with an ".htm" or ".html" extension. Check the Add to Project checkbox and click the Open button. Alternatively, select File|New and select the HTML icon from the New page of the Object Gallery.

 TIP: If you accidentally open a file and forget to check the Add to Project checkbox on the Open/Create dialog, the file will appear on the Opened tab of the AppBrowser rather than on the Project tab. Instead of repeating the create process, just drag the file icon from the Navigation pane to the Project tab and drop it. JBuilder will automatically add the file to your project.

The AppBrowser recognizes HTML files based on their extension and provides special support through two views in the Content pane accessed by the Source and View tabs, as shown in Figure 6-1. The source view displays the file as ASCII text to allow direct editing of the HTML codes. The View tab presents a simple read-only HTML viewer that displays the file as it would be displayed within a Web browser. The Editor and viewer built into JBuilder aren't designed as competition for commercial browsers or editors; they are conveniences that allow basic editing and previewing within JBuilder.

The HTML viewer ignores the <APPLET> tag, previewing Web pages without displaying the applets embedded inside them. While it might seem convenient to be able to view a running applet directly inside the JBuilder environment, this is impractical because the standard Java run time cannot load the same class twice. A host environment must be exited and restarted to view changes to an applet class, which would be inconvenient if the host were JBuilder itself.

6

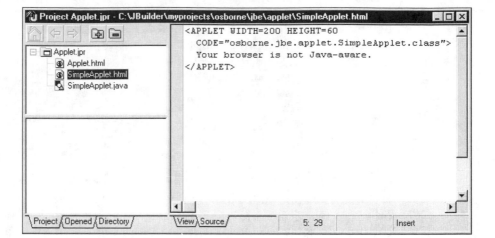

The
AppBrowser
displaying an
HTML file
Figure 6-1.

Creating a Simple HTML Container

Before the *SimpleApplet* class created in "Creating a Simple Applet" can be displayed, it needs to be referenced from an HTML container. The following steps create a new HTML file for this purpose:

1. Select the AppBrowser for the project Applet.jpr that was created in the section "Creating a Simple Applet." If the AppBrowser is not open, select File|Open / Create, enter the filename **Applet.jpr** and click the Open button.

2. Select File|New and double-click the HTML icon on the New page of the Object Gallery. An untitled HTML file is added to your project.

3. Select the file untitled1.html in the Navigation pane and click the Source tab. Replace the current contents of the file with the following:

    ```
    <APPLET WIDTH=200 HEIGHT=60
      CODE="osborne.jbe.applet.SimpleApplet.class">
      Your browser is not Java-aware.
    </APPLET>
    ```

4. Select File|Save As to save the HTML file, and save it in the c:\JBuilder\myprojects\osborne\jbe\applet directory with the name **SimpleApplet.html**.

Running an Applet

Since the HTML viewer built into JBuilder will not display an applet, you need to explicitly run an applet. JBuilder assumes that an applet is being executed whenever you ask to run or debug an HTML file, and takes appropriate actions to provide a host environment.

Running an applet in JBuilder can be done in one of four ways:

♦ Select Run|Run Applet.

♦ Click the Run button on JBuilder's toolbar.

♦ Press SHIFT-F9.

♦ Right-click on a file in the Navigation pane and select Run from the pop-up menu.

If an HTML file is selected in the Navigation pane, it is assumed that it contains an <APPLET> tag and is used to start the applet. If a Java source file is selected, and that file contains a class with a *main()* method, JBuilder attempts to start that class as an application, not an applet. If neither of the above is true, such as when the project file or a Java source file not containing a *main()* method is selected, the *default runnable file* will be used as a starting point as if it were selected in the Navigation pane.

You can change the default runnable file by selecting Run|Parameters to display the Run/Debug page of the project's Properties dialog. Specify the desired file in the Default Runnable File field. The most recent selection is saved with the project file. If the default file selected is an HTML file, JBuilder will launch the applet described by that file, as described previously.

TIP: If JBuilder reports that it is unable to debug an applet, check to see if your Applet subclass has an init() method. JBuilder is only able to debug applets that override this method, though it does not require that the method contain any code.

6

NOTE: Always save changes to the HTML file before attempting to run or debug an applet. JBuilder uses the last version of the HTML that was saved to run an applet; it does not use the version displayed in the Editor.

Testing the Simple Applet

To test the simple applet created earlier in this chapter, you must have already followed the steps in the sections "Creating a Simple Applet" and "Creating a Simple HTML Container." To start the applet, do the following:

1. Select the AppBrowser for the project Applet.jpr that was created in the section "Creating a Simple Applet." If the AppBrowser is not open, select File|Open / Create and open the project file.

2. Select the file SimpleApplet.html in the Navigation pane.

3. Select Run|Run Applet, press SHIFT-F9, or click the Run icon on JBuilder's toolbar.

A console window appears, followed shortly by a window containing a functional applet as shown in Figure 6-2. This applet provides only a static image, a role that a GIF file would serve just as well. The true power of applets is in dynamic or configurable behavior, as is illustrated later in the more sophisticated example in "A Sample Applet Wizard Applet" that builds on the concepts introduced with this simple applet.

The AppletViewer Program

When asked to run or debug an applet, JBuilder uses the *appletviewer* program included as a part of the Java Developer's Kit (JDK). This minimal applet host environment runs inside its own Java Virtual Machine, and creates a simple frame with a status line for display purposes. The appletviewer does enforce applet security and provides a realistic test environment for most purposes, but it cannot be used as a guarantee that an applet will behave properly in other Web browsers.

The
SimpleApplet
in action
Figure 6-2.

NOTE: The appletviewer provides extremely limited feedback about error conditions. The JBuilder execution log can be used to capture and view errors reported if the appletviewer fails to display an applet as expected. See Chapter 11 for details on configuring and viewing the execution log.

Web Browsers That Support JBuilder Applets

A JBuilder applet that displays correctly in the appletviewer may fail to load or display correctly within other Web browsers for a variety of reasons. The most common difficulty encountered is due to the fact that JBuilder is designed primarily as a JDK 1.1 development environment. At the time of this writing, there are very few Web browsers that fully support this version of the Java run time. Sun's own HotJava browser provides full Java 1.1 support, Netscape Navigator 4.02 does not, and Internet Explorer 3.02 does not.

Internet Explorer 4.0 and a forthcoming version of Netscape Navigator are expected to provide Java 1.1 support. At the time of this writing, final versions of these products were not available for testing with JBuilder.

TIP: Java applets should always be tested on the browsers most likely to be used when the applet is deployed. Refer also to Chapter 12 for more information on deploying Java applets.

Applet Parameters

Java provides additional flexibility for applets in the form of input parameters passed from the Web page that acts as a container for the applet. Parameters are named values that are contained inside the <APPLET> tag in HTML that the *Applet* subclass can read. These parameters can customize or configure a single applet to behave differently on different pages, or can allow small adjustments to the behavior of an applet without needing to change and recompile the Java code. In addition to all these benefits, reusing a single applet reduces the download time necessary to move from page to page on a Web site.

6

Defining Parameters from HTML

Any number of <PARAM> tags may be defined between the opening and closing <APPLET> tags. Each <PARAM> tag defines a single parameter that can be read by the applet in question. The HTML that invokes an applet with three parameters looks like this:

```
<APPLET WIDTH=400 HEIGHT=300
  CODE="osborne.jbe.applet.ParamApplet.class">
  <PARAM NAME="Text" VALUE="JBuilder is Essential">
  <PARAM NAME="Size" VALUE=24>
  <PARAM NAME="Offset" VALUE=4>
  Your browser is not Java-aware.
  You're missing out on a parameterized Java applet!
</APPLET>
```

The Name and Value Attributes

Both the *name* and *value* attributes are required, and are the only attributes of the <PARAM> tag. The name of a parameter must be unique, as it is used by an applet to retrieve the parameter's value.

Reading Parameter Values

The parameters are defined in HTML, but need to be read by the Java applet. All applets inherit a *getParameter()* method from the *Applet* class for this purpose. The method takes a single parameter, a string naming the parameter whose value is to be read. The name of the parameter is not case-sensitive. The *getParameter()* method returns a string containing the value defined for the parameter in the HTML container for the applet, or returns **null** if there is no such parameter. Since the *getParameter()* method always returns a string, parameters representing other types of data must be read as strings and converted to the correct data type before use.

CAUTION: A call to *getParameter()* during the applet's constructor will throw a *NullPointerException*. Parameters cannot be read until the applet's *init()* method is invoked as discussed in the following sections.

Describing Parameters

The *Applet* class includes a method, *getParameterInfo()*, designed to describe the parameters recognized by an applet. Overriding this method isn't required for parameter passing to work. However, overriding it is recommended so tools that want to examine the applet can determine the available parameters and describe them to a user.

The method implementation must return an array of string arrays. Each string array must contain three strings, describing the name of the parameter, its type, and the parameter's purpose. An implementation for an applet with three parameters looks like this:

```
public String[][] getParameterInfo() {
  return new String[][] {
    {"Text", "String", "The text to be displayed"},
    {"Size", "int", "The size of the font to be used"},
    {"Offset", "int", "The shadow's offset in pixels"}};
}
```

The Applet Wizard

Creating an HTML container, defining parameters, doing type conversion while reading parameters, and writing the *getParameterInfo()* method are all tedious, repetitive tasks. JBuilder's Applet Wizard takes care of these details automatically.

To use the Applet Wizard, you select File|New to display the New page in the Object Gallery, and then select the icon for the Applet Wizard. The Applet Wizard has three pages in which you define information about the applet class, its parameters, and the automatically generated HTML page.

Step 1: The Applet Class

The Step 1 page in the Applet Wizard shown in Figure 6-3 specifies the package the new class belongs to, and the name of the class. You use this page to supply general information about the *Applet* subclass that the wizard will generate. The parent class is always assumed to be *java.applet.Applet*. The resulting class is always public, and includes the following characteristics:

♦ An empty constructor is automatically defined.

♦ The overridden *init()* method invokes *jbInit()*, allowing the applet's appearance to be modified using JBuilder's visual designers. The default *jbInit()* implementation sets an *XYLayout* as its layout manager.

♦ The *getAppletInfo()* is implemented and returns the string "Applet Information" when called. As the applet's author, you should modify this to provide a more descriptive string.

♦ An implementation for *getParameterInfo()* is provided as described in the second step.

♦ A boolean instance variable, *isStandalone*, is declared with an initial value of **false**.

♦ If you check the option Can run standalone, a *main()* method is declared that automatically sets *isStandalone* to **true**, creates a frame containing an instance of the applet, and calls the applet's *init()* and *start()* methods.

♦ If you check the option Generate standard methods, empty implementations of *start()*, *stop()*, and *destroy()* are provided.

6

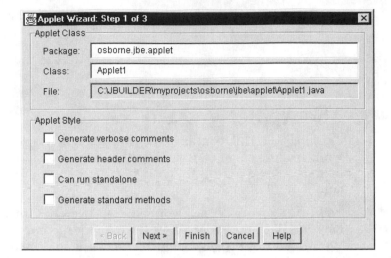

Step 2: The Applet Parameters

The Step 2 page of the Applet Wizard allows any number of parameters to be defined for the new applet. This page describes parameters that the new applet should read. Figure 6-4 shows the five fields that must be filled in for each parameter, each of which is described next. The Add Parameter button defines an additional parameter and the Remove Parameter button removes the selected parameter.

◆ The Name field is used as the *name* attribute of the corresponding HTML <PARAM> tag.

◆ The Type field is used to specify the data type expected in the parameter as one of the commonly used primitive types or the *String* class.

◆ The Desc field is used to provide a complete description of the purpose of the parameter.

◆ The Variable field is used to specify the name of an instance variable that will hold the parameter once it has been read.

◆ The Default field is used to specify the value that the variable will contain if no corresponding HTML <PARAM> tag specifies another value.

JBuilder uses these details to automatically configure the new applet class to read and convert parameters as necessary. The following effects on the new applet class are evident:

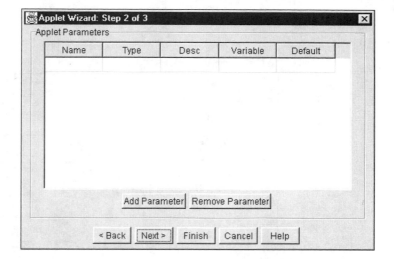

The Applet
Wizard's
second step
Figure 6-4.

◆ The *getParameterInfo()* method returns the correct array of string arrays including the name, type, and description entered for each parameter.

◆ The *init()* method includes code to automatically read each of the parameters, convert it to the appropriate type, and set the corresponding variable. Each call is made using the overloaded *getParameter()* described next and includes the default specified for the parameter.

◆ So long as one or more parameters are specified, *getParameter()* is overloaded with a new version that takes two parameters: the parameter name and its default value. This implementation of *getParameter()* returns the default specified if no such parameter is declared, and uses an alternate mechanism to read parameters if the applet is running as a stand-alone application.

Step 3: The HTML Page

You use the Step 3 page in the Applet Wizard, shown in Figure 6-5, to control an automatically generated HTML document. This page describes the characteristics of the HTML page that will be generated. The generated HTML page can be disabled, and several characteristics can be set. The Title of the page is used in the <TITLE> tag, and the remaining fields specify attributes of the <APPLET> tag.

6

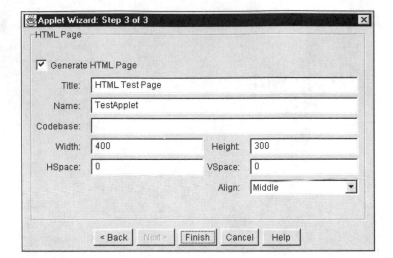

The Applet
Wizard's final
step
Figure 6-5.

NOTE: The Name field specifies the value of the <APPLET> tag's *name* attribute, not the name of the HTML file. The HTML file has the same name as the project file.

A Sample Applet Wizard Applet

The Applet Wizard can generate most of a more sophisticated, parameterized version of the simple applet created earlier in this chapter. All of the code for reading and initializing parameter values is automatically generated, leaving only a few steps to implement the actual functionality of the applet.

CD-ROM: An example of WizardApplet.jpr can be found in the osborne\jbecd\applet subdirectory.

The following steps demonstrate creating an applet using the Applet Wizard:

1. Select File|New Project to display the Project Wizard. At File, enter the project filename **c:\JBuilder\myprojects\osborne\jbe\applet\ WizardApplet.jpr**. Click Finish.
2. Select File|New and double-click on the Applet icon on the New page of the Object Gallery. The Applet Wizard is displayed.

3. On the Step 1 page (shown in Figure 6-3), enter **osborne.jbe.applet** in the Package field, and **ParamApplet** in the Class field. Press the Next button.

4. Fill in the parameter information as shown in Figure 6-6 and click the Next button.

5. None of the settings on the Step 3 page (shown in Figure 6-5) need to be changed for this example. Click the Finish button to allow the wizard to create the ParamApplet.java and ParamApplet.html files.

6. In the source view, add one method to ParamApplet.java:

```
public void paint(Graphics g) {
  g.setFont(font);
  g.setColor(Color.black);
  g.drawString(text, offset, size+offset);
  g.setColor(Color.white);
  g.drawString(text, 0, size);
  super.paint(g);
}
```

7. Next, add a single instance variable below the declaration of *isStandalone*:

```
Font font;
```

8. Finally, add one line to the end of the *init()* method:

```
font = new Font("Dialog", Font.BOLD, size);
```

6

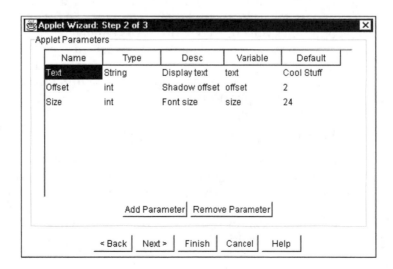

Parameter settings for ParamApplet
Figure 6-6.

9. Select File|Save All to save the resulting code. To test the applet, select the ParamApplet.html file in the Navigation pane and select Run|Run Applet. At this point, the applet displayed will look like the one shown previously in Figure 6-2.

10. Display ParamApplet.html in the source view, try changing the parameters defined by the <PARAM> tags, and run the applet again. Remember to save the HTML file after each change, or you will not see the results.

This newly created applet is similar in many ways to the simple applet introduced earlier, but the characteristics that control the image may now be influenced by the <APPLET> tag's parameters in HTML. The same applet code can be used again and again to produce a wide variety of images with only a single download. The applet is now a much more flexible alternative to creating and downloading a new GIF image each time a graphical heading is needed in a page.

Making the Choice: Application or Applet

Java applications and applets share the same language, the same standard packages, and differ only slightly in their entry points. The choice between the two types of Java programs is usually answered by a single question—Do you want code automatically delivered from a Web server into a browser environment? If so, an applet is the way to go. If not, an application is the right stand-alone solution. Simple, right?

Unfortunately, the decision isn't as simple as it seems. There are some pretty significant restrictions placed on applets by default, and some capabilities that are available to applets aren't supported for applications. Worse yet, sometimes the same code needs to be delivered both as an applet and an application, and consequently, both sets of restrictions become an issue. Some of the major differences between applications and applets are described next, as are techniques for designing hybrid applets that can also function as applications.

Applet Security Restrictions

Applets are typically subject to a wide range of security restrictions designed to prevent them from performing undesirable actions when downloaded from a Web server. The following restrictions are enforced by default:

♦ Applets cannot access the local file system to read and write, nor can they determine the existence or status of a file.

◆ Networking is severely restricted, effectively preventing networking connections to any machine other than the Web server that originally supplied the applet.

◆ Clipboard and printing support are inaccessible.

◆ Frame and Dialog instances created by applets include a visible warning that the window has been created by untrusted code.

◆ Java facilities for starting applications, inquiring about the system and user, and stopping the Java interpreter, for example, are not available.

Attempting to perform any of these or other security-violating actions will result in a *java.lang.SecurityException* being thrown. Typically, it is better to design code to avoid these situations than to rely on extensive exception handling to deal with them.

Starting with Java 1.1, the notion of a *signed* or *trusted* applet was introduced. A JAR file can include a digital signature that a browser may be configured to accept as proof that some or all of these security restrictions should be lifted. How this is configured at the browser level depends on the browser in question. JBuilder does not provide any direct support for creating a signed JAR file, but the full documentation for the necessary command-line tools is included as a part of the JDK included with JBuilder. This is not a trivial process, and should only be undertaken with plenty of spare time to learn the intricacies of the process.

Applet Methods

The *Applet* class includes a variety of convenience methods that turn out to be less than convenient when the applet instance is not created and managed by a Web browser. Each of the methods described here is relayed to a special object provided by the browser that implements the *java.applet.AppletStub* interface. This object, which is referred to as the *applet stub*, is created by the browser and passed to the applet through its *setStub()* method before the *init()* and *start()* methods are invoked. The applet stub provides functionality for controlling the Web browser and loading resources such as images and sounds from the Web browser's cache or a Web server.

An applet attempting to use any of these methods in its constructor will trigger a *java.lang.NullPointerException* since no applet stub has been provided yet. Applets should perform initialization by overriding the inherited *init()* method. A stand-alone application will not have an applet stub provided, and therefore cannot normally use any of these methods.

6

♦ An applet can determine whether or not it is currently being displayed with the *isActive()* method.

♦ The browser that contains the applet can be controlled through an object that implements the *java.applet.AppletContext* interface. This object is returned by the *getAppletContext()* method.

♦ The *getDocumentBase()* method returns a URL for the directory containing the HTML that referenced the applet.

♦ The *getCodeBase()* method returns a URL for the directory containing the applet's class file.

♦ Parameters included within the <APPLET> tag can be read with calls to the *getParameter()* method.

♦ The *resize()* method can be used to request a different size for the applet, although many browsers ignore the request.

AppletContent Methods

The *java.applet.AppletContext* interface describes methods that are used to interact with the Web browser host that is displaying the applet. The *Applet* class itself has a *getAppletContext()* method that returns a reference to an object implementing this interface. Since *getAppletContext()* requires an applet stub as described in the last section, the same restrictions apply to these methods:

♦ *getApplet()* and *getApplets()* can be used to get a reference to another applet object currently displayed by the browser. Using this mechanism, multiple applets can interact with one another on the same page since all are running within the same Java Virtual Machine. In a stand-alone environment, each applet will be running in a different virtual machine and cannot typically interact with other applets through simple references.

♦ *getAudioClip()* can be used to retrieve a sound file that will be played by the browser. Oddly, the Java 1.1 standard provides no way for applications to play sound, only applets.

♦ *getImage()* is a convenient way to start downloading an image in a background thread. JBuilder provides convenience classes to perform the same action as an applet or application.

♦ *showDocument()* directs the Web browser containing the applet to display another Web page. In a stand-alone environment, there may not be a Web browser present to display Web pages.

♦ *showStatus()* replaces the current status line displayed by the browser with the specified text. In an application, this has no meaning since there is no dedicated status display.

Hybrid Applets

In Java, applets and applications are not mutually exclusive categories of development. A single class can fulfill the requirements for being an applet and being an application, and can consequently be used in either role. This kind of development is sometimes referred to as a *hybrid* applet. A hybrid applet must belong to a class that extends *java.applet.Applet*, and must include a *main()* method.

JBuilder provides a basic framework for this kind of development through the Applet Wizard. The first step of the wizard includes a Can run standalone checkbox that adds the following declaration to the *main()* method when this option checked:

```
// Main method
static public void main(String[] args) {
  Applet1 applet = new Applet1();
  applet.isStandalone = true;
  DecoratedFrame frame = new DecoratedFrame();
  frame.setTitle("Applet Frame");
  frame.add(applet, BorderLayout.CENTER);
  applet.init();
  applet.start();
  frame.pack();
  Dimension d = Toolkit.getDefaultToolkit().getScreenSize();
  frame.setLocation((d.width - frame.getSize().width) / 2,
    (d.height - frame.getSize().height) / 2);
  frame.setVisible(true);
}
```

This simple *main()* method creates a *DecoratedFrame* instance as a container for the applet, fills the frame with the applet instance, and invokes the applet's *init()* and *start()* methods. The frame is compressed with the *pack()* method to the smallest size that can contain the applet, and is centered on the screen.

The *isStandalone* variable can be tested to determine whether the code is being run as an application or an applet. This may be necessary because the environments provided for applets and applications are not identical, as discussed earlier.

6

A Hybrid Applet Framework

The fundamental problem with using many of the *java.applet.Applet* methods in a hybrid applet is that the applet stub object normally provided by the browser does not exist. Why can't we simply instantiate an applet stub of our own and use it instead? The standard packages do not include any classes that implement the necessary methods. However, it is possible to create a custom class to provide the necessary functionality.

The source code for StandaloneStub.java presented in this section is a stub class designed to work as a replacement for all of the interfaces provided by a browser. To use this class, the following line must be added to a hybrid applet's *main()* method just before a call to the applet's *init()* method:

```
applet.setStub(new osborne.jbecd.applet.StandaloneStub(applet));
```

This one line of code creates an instance of the *StandaloneStub* class, passing a reference to the applet it will cooperate with to the constructor. This step is critical, because the new applet stub must have a reference to the applet for some of its methods to function correctly. The applet stub is then passed to the applet via *setStub()* to use for all of the delegated functionality.

It isn't necessary to understand the *StandaloneStub* class to use it, but the implementation is fairly straightforward. One instance of the class acts in many roles: as *AppletStub* and *AppletContext* to replace the missing objects normally provided by the browser, as an *Enumeration* to respond properly to the *getApplets()* method, and as an *AudioClip()* to silently ignore audio playback requests.

Wherever possible, the *StandaloneStub* attempts to provide a reasonable facsimile for behavior that can be emulated, but some methods must simply be ignored because they have no corresponding behavior in an application environment. Following is the source code for StandaloneStub.java.

CD-ROM: If you installed the example files from this book's CD-ROM (see Appendix C), you can find this file in C:\JBuilder\myprojects\osborne\jbecd\applet\StandaloneStub.java.

```
package osborne.jbecd.applet;

import java.applet.*;
import java.awt.Image;
import java.net.URL;
import java.util.Enumeration;
```

```
public class StandaloneStub implements AppletStub,
  AppletContext, Enumeration, AudioClip {
  Applet applet;

  public StandaloneStub(Applet applet) {
    this.applet = applet;
  }

  // AppletStub methods

  public void appletResize(int width, int height) {
    applet.setSize(width, height);
  }

  public URL getCodeBase() {
    try {
      return new URL("bogus://localhost/");
    }
    catch(java.net.MalformedURLException ex) {
      return null;
    }
  }

  public String getParameter(String name) {
    return System.getProperty(name, null);
  }

  public URL getDocumentBase() { return getCodeBase(); }
  public boolean isActive() { return true; }
  public AppletContext getAppletContext() { return this; }

  // AppletContext methods

  public Image getImage(URL url) {
    if (url.getProtocol().equals("bogus")) {
      url = applet.getClass().getResource(url.getFile());
    }
    if (url == null) return null;
    return applet.getToolkit().getImage(url);
  }

  public Applet getApplet(String name) { return null; }
  public Enumeration getApplets() { return this; }
  public AudioClip getAudioClip(URL url) { return this; }
  public void showDocument(URL url) { }
  public void showDocument(URL url, String target) { }
  public void showStatus(String status) { }
```

```java
    // Enumeration methods

    public boolean hasMoreElements() { return false; }
    public Object nextElement() { return null; }

    // AudioClip methods

    public void play() { }
    public void loop() { }
    public void stop() { }
}
```

CHAPTER 7

Database Basics

A database is a file, or collection of files, used to store information in a structured format. A database may be located on the same machine as a JBuilder application or applet, in a directory shared by many different users on a local area network (LAN), or on another machine on a network to which the machine running your Java application is attached.

This chapter is designed to provide you with an overview of database development in JBuilder. It begins with a discussion of the various terms used to describe databases. This is followed by an overview of JDBC (JavaSoft Database Connectivity), the underlying technology that provides for data access in JBuilder. Next, the discussion turns to an overview of the components that you use to build your JBuilder database applications. These components, however, cannot be used without the necessary software and configuration. Performing this installation and the accompanying configuration are covered in a section later in this chapter. Finally, this chapter concludes with a step-by-step demonstration of building a simple database application using JBuilder.

If you are new to database development, you will want to read this chapter thoroughly. If you are a seasoned database developer but new to JBuilder, you can skip the first section "Understanding Databases," and continue on to the section entitled "Overview of JDBC."

This chapter is intended as an overview in that it does not go into detail about configuring and using the various database-related components. That information is covered in Chapter 8. Chapter 9 takes this discussion further by demonstrating how to provide additional functionality to your JBuilder application using Java code that you add to event handlers.

Understanding Databases

If you are new to working with database applications, many of the terms and concepts may be unfamiliar to you. This section is designed to give you a brief introduction to the terms and concepts used throughout these database-related chapters. If you are already comfortable with building databases, you will want to scan this section quickly, moving instead to the following section.

Databases and Tables

The term *database* means different things to different people, and this is largely influenced by the terminology used for the various database products. For example, in InterBase, a database is a single file with the extension .GDB. In dBASE, by comparison, a database is considered to be a group of conceptually related data files. In Microsoft Access, to use another example, a database consists of a single file that contains data as well as the forms, queries, macros, and other objects used to manipulate the data. In this book, database will be used to mean the related data of an application, whether it is stored in a single file, as in InterBase and Access, or in multiple files, as in dBASE.

A database consists of one or more *tables*, a table being a structure capable of handling various types of data, including textual information, numbers, dates, binary data, and so on. Some applications use the term *file* instead of *table*. The concept, however, is the same in that both contain structured information. Since the contents of the table may appear in either a single file or separate files, this book uses the more generic term *table*.

Each table in a database is designed to hold data related to a particular object, concept, or relationship. For example, a given database may include one table to hold all of the information about customers. This information may include the customers' account numbers, names, mailing addresses, available credit limits, and so forth. Another table may be designed to hold information about employees, including their salaries, birth dates, number of dependents, and so on. Yet another table may hold information about invoices. Examples of information that this table may contain include the invoice numbers, dates of sales, customers to whom the sales were made, and employees responsible for the sales. The invoice table in this preceding example can be considered to hold a relationship, or association, between a customer and an employee.

Tables are organized by *rows* and *columns*. (These are sometimes referred to as *records* and *fields*, respectively. The terms row and column are used in this book.) A table contains one column for each type of information stored in that table. For example, one column stores the customers' account numbers, and another column stores the customers' credit limits. In addition, each column has a particular data type, which is similar to the concept of Java primitive types. However, unlike Java primitive types, which are defined by the Java language, the data type of a column is limited to those types available for the particular table type. InterBase tables, for example, supports columns of the type Array, while dBASE tables do not. All table types, however, support certain common column types, including text, integers, floating point numbers, dates, and so forth. The number and type of columns contained within a given table is referred to as that table's *structure*.

A given table can contain zero, one, or more rows. A table consists of one row for each item or relationship being stored in the table. For example, if your table contains information about 1,000 customers, your customer table will contain 1,000 rows. A table with zero rows is referred to as an *empty* table.

It is not at all uncommon for the number of rows that a table has to fluctuate. Furthermore, tables can potentially store a very large amount of data. Tables with millions of rows of data are not rare. The number of columns a table has, by comparison, is more or less fixed. (Changing the number of columns is something that is typically done only by the database administrator.) Furthermore, the maximum number of columns is rather

7

low, generally being less than 1,000 columns, and frequently far fewer (this depends on the type of the table). In most cases, tables have only a few columns, rarely exceeding several dozen or so.

Another critical concept associated with a table is an *index*. An index is a support structure (sometimes a separate file) that provides for row ordering, improved database searches, and guaranteed row uniqueness. Many database types require at least one index, which is referred to as the *primary* index. Some databases permit indexes to order records in ascending order, and others permit either ascending or descending indexes.

Indexes that enforce uniqueness are important to prevent two or more records from sharing the same critical identifier. For instance, since it is unacceptable to give two customers the same account number, a customer table would include an index that requires the values in the account number column to be unique for each customer.

While indexes are an important feature for a database, a table's index or indexes are not used directly in JBuilder applications. When JBuilder fetches data from a database, it creates its own indexes on the fly, as needed. Consequently, even when you are reading data from a database that does not include indexes, you get the sorting and speed benefits of an index. JBuilder indexes, however, do not enforce unique rows. That enforcement will only occur when you resolve changes to your data back to the database.

If you are interested in additional information about tables, you should refer to reference materials concerning the specific type of table you are using. For example, if you are working with SQL (Structured Query Language) tables such as MS SQL tables, refer to the MS SQL Server documentation or a book on this subject.

The tables used in the examples presented in this book are InterBase tables. For more information on these tables, refer to the InterBase help files, which are installed when you install InterBase. The Local InterBase Server product comes with JBuilder, but you install InterBase separately—it is not automatically installed when you install JBuilder. Installing InterBase is discussed later in this chapter. Assuming that you installed InterBase in the default directory, the main InterBase help file is located in c:\Program Files\Borland\IntrBase\Bin\ib32.hlp.

Creating Tables

When you install InterBase, it installs a sample database. However, when creating a new database application, you will need to create new tables designed to hold data specific to your needs.

In many cases, you will also have access to a database application, such as Oracle, MS SQL Server, dBASE, Paradox for Windows, or some other similar application. InterBase Windows ISQL (Interactive SQL) is the tool provided by the Local InterBase Server. Most developers use these tools to define the structure of their tables and to create the indexes and other definitions required by their application.

An alternative to using a database application to create your databases is to use the DDL (Data Definition Language) statements of SQL (Structured Query Language) to create and change your tables. For example, you can use the CREATE TABLE SQL statement to create a new table, CREATE INDEX to create a new index, ALTER TABLE to modify a table's structure, and so forth. For more information on using SQL, you will want to refer to a book on the subject.

It should be noted that the proper design of the tables and indexes of your database is very important and is sometimes a time-consuming process. If you are unfamiliar with database design, and relational database design in particular (since all of the databases mentioned here are relational databases), you should consult a book on the design and analysis of databases prior to creating your tables.

NOTE: A relational database is one where related data is stored in related, yet separate, tables. For example, that information unique to a customer is stored in a customer table, all information about an individual employee is stored in an employee table, and the sales made by employees to customers are stored in yet another table.

Overview of JDBC

JBuilder provides access to databases using JavaSoft's JDBC (JavaSoft Database Connectivity) API (Application Programming Interface). The calls to this API, however, are encapsulated in some of the components of the JBCL (JavaBeans Component Library) that ships with JBuilder. As a result, most of the complexities of data access are hidden from you, permitting your application to focus on tasks such as creating database files, inserting records, and updating data rather than the mechanics of these operations.

7

This section provides you with an overview of the JDBC technology. It begins with a discussion of the drivers that you can use to access your data. Next, you will learn about the two-stage method of data access employed by the JDBC—providing and resolving.

NOTE: In order to write database applications using the JDBC, your application must have access to the java.sql package. This package is just one of those installed as part of the JBuilder environment.

JDBC Drivers

The JDBC provides three primary methods for accessing data, all of which require a Java driver class that translates JDBC requests into specific actions for a particular database. The first type of driver is a pure Java driver that communicates directly with the native database. A pure Java driver, by virtue of being written entirely in Java, is platform independent. As a result, Java applications written using the pure Java drivers can run on any operating system supported by a Java VM (Virtual Machine). By using the database's native communication protocol, this driver eliminates the need for special software on the server to support Java clients. This approach places the burden of translating JDBC requests to a native protocol on the driver itself, often necessitating very large driver classes.

A second means of accessing data makes use of a pure Java driver that communicates over a network using a lightweight protocol specific to the Java driver. A special Java-specific server process, in turn, takes responsibility for communications between the Java application and a database. As a pure Java driver, the code can be distributed to any client with a Java application or applet, as it is entirely platform independent. The use of a lightweight protocol designed for use with JDBC keeps the driver as small as possible. Specialized software must be installed on a server to redirect JDBC requests to the final database, but the benefits of a smaller driver are generally worth the additional server-side installation requirement.

Two examples of such lightweight pure Java drivers are Borland's InterClient and Borland's DataGateway for Java. InterClient is a driver for Borland's InterBase. This driver, which is available for free from the InterBase Web site at www.interbase.com, permits Java developers to access InterBase servers using JDBC as long as the necessary middle-ware is installed.

DataGateway for Java provides a pure Java client, written using JDBC classes, that communicates over a TCP/IP (Transmission Control Protocol/Internet Protocol) network with a DataGateway for Java server running on Windows 95 or NT. This server converts these JDBC calls into calls to the Borland Database Engine (BDE), itself a Windows 95 or NT application.

The BDE is a set of 32-bit Windows DLLs (Dynamic Link Library) that can access data from a wide variety of sources, including the following:

♦ Paradox, dBASE, FoxPro, and MS Access

♦ Any database supported by 32-bit ODBC (Open Database Connectivity) drivers

♦ Oracle, Sybase, Microsoft SQL Server, DB/2, and Informix using Borland's SQL Links (native language SQL drivers).

When the Java application is running a Windows-based platform, the server is not necessary, permitting the client to communicate directly with the BDE. Since the client itself is platform independent, DataGateway for Java provides a much better solution to data connectivity than the platform-dependent JDBC-ODBC bridge described next.

DataGateway for Java is included in the Client/Server version of JBuilder. It is also available as a standalone product for use by JBuilder and Java developers.

The final means of accessing data is through a Java driver that uses a platform-dependent intermediate layer of software. An example of this is the driver *sun.jdbc.odbc.JdbcOdbcDriver,* which in turn invokes a native implementation of a driver such as JDBCODBC.DLL, which is a 32-bit Windows (Windows 95 and NT) DLL. The native layer accepts JDBC calls and directs them to a specified ODBC driver. ODBC is a Microsoft standard for communicating with SQL databases. This intermediate layer is referred to as a *bridge*, and consequently, the *JdbcOdbcDriver* class is generally called the JDBC-ODBC bridge.

The JDBC-ODBC bridge driver has several distinct drawbacks, notably that it must be installed and configured on every client machine and that it cannot be used by untrusted applets as it is considered a potential security problem.

The database examples described in this book use the JDBC-ODBC bridge to connect to the Local InterBase Server. While this approach is the least desirable of those described here, it is the only one that can be implemented with the software that ships with the initial version of JBuilder. Consequently, this use of the JDBC-ODBC bridge should not be taken as an endorsement of this approach, but should be recognized as the interim solution that it is intended to be. As JDBC and Java develop further, a number of much more acceptable, cross-platform solutions, such DataGateway, are sure to emerge.

In order to use the JDBC-ODBC bridge, it is necessary to configure the InterBase ODBC driver before it can be used for the first time. Configuring the ODBC driver for the InterBase product that ships with JBuilder for use with the JDBC-ODBC bridge is described later in this chapter.

7

The Provide-Resolve Model of Data Access: DataExpress

JDBC uses a provide-resolve model of data access, which Borland calls DataExpress. This model consists of two distinct steps. In the first step, called *providing*, data is requested from and provided by a database. This data is held locally by a component within the application. While stored in the application, this data can then be viewed, edited, navigated, sorted, and so forth. The provided data may include all of the data in an underlying table, only some of it, or even only a table's metadata. (Metadata refers to information about the data, such as the column names, data types, precision, and so forth.)

In the second step, *resolving*, any changes made to the table by the user or your code are resolved back to the database that provided the data. If for some reason one or more rows cannot be applied to the underlying table, those rows are returned to your Java application, which can ignore the data, discard it, or attempt to update it and resolve it again.

This approach to data access provides a number of important features. These include the following:

1. Database overhead is reduced. Specifically, providing and resolving are done in separate and independent steps. No persisting locks or restrictions are placed on the database tables or rows between these two steps. This reduces potential conflicts for resources between two or more users.

2. The data held locally in the Java application is in a consistent and common format. In other words, regardless of the type of database from which the data was retrieved, the data always appears the same to the application's users and the application's code. This makes the application highly portable, permitting you to change from one database type (say, Oracle) to another (such as InterBase) without requiring other changes to the application.

3. Because providing and resolving are separate steps, there is no limit to the amount of time that passes between the providing and resolving steps.

4. Since the provided data is stored locally in a common, database-independent format, JBuilder can apply its own sort order, and even intertable links, without requiring corresponding indexes on the tables from which the data was provided. Likewise, features such as forward and backward navigation are possible with the provided data, even when the providing tables do not support such features. (Many servers prohibit bidirectional row navigation.)

5. It is possible to permit the user to modify the provided records, and then to discard some or even all changes without ever having affected the underlying table.

6. The provide-resolve model of data access can be used with any database architecture. These include the following:

♦ *Single-user applications* in which one copy of the application has exclusive access to the data

♦ *Multiuser applications* in which the data is shared by two or more users, or two or more applications

♦ *Client/server applications* in which the shared data resides on a database server, which is capable of providing for security, data integrity, transaction processing, and significant data manipulation

♦ *Multitier applications* in which two or more servers on a network provide the application with services, such as security, data integrity, data manipulation, and so on

The components that you use in JBuilder to build database applications can be configured to automatically request data when needed, as well as permit the user to manually request that the data be resolved back to the table from which it was provided. Furthermore, these components offer you methods that you can use to programmatically control the providing and resolving process. These features are discussed briefly later in this chapter, and to a much greater extent in the two following chapters.

JBuilder's Database Components

There are two general categories of components that you use in order to build database applications with JBuilder. These are data access components, and data aware components. Data access components provide for the reading, writing, and manipulation of data. This data may reside in simple ASCII files, database files such as dBASE (.DBF) or MS Access databases (.MDB), or be provided by a JDBC database driver.

Data aware components are used for the user interface. Specifically, they are used to display data to the user, permit the user to enter data, and provide for end-user navigation of the data. An application that manipulates data, but does not provide a user interface, needs only data access components, and not data aware components.

7

There is a third type of object that you will sometimes use with your JBuilder application. It is called a data module. A data module is a container for data access components.

The following sections describe various database components provided in JBuilder. Included is a brief discussion of data modules, although this topic is covered in greater detail in the following chapter.

Data Access Components

Data access components are responsible for connecting to a database, retrieving data from the database, sorting and filtering the data, permitting record insertions and deletions, providing access to individual columns, and resolving edited data back to the original database. These components are non-UI components, meaning that they do not have a visual presence on the container (frame, dialog, applet, and so forth). When you place them into the UI Designer, they appear under the Data Access node of the Component Tree, rather than in the UI Designer itself. Instead of dropping them into the UI Designer, you can drop them directly into the Component Tree.

NOTE: If two or more frames need to use the same data access components, you will want to place them into a data module rather than a frame. Using data modules is described in Chapter 8.

From the developer's perspective, these components encapsulate almost all of the complexity of the database operations. In fact, it is possible to use these components to provide users with access to data without having to write any custom code. However, in most cases, the additional features that you will want to add to a particular database application will require some programming.

The data access components that you work with at design time appear on the Data Access page of the Component Palette. These components, along with a brief description of what functionality they provide, are listed in Table 7-1. Depending on the version of JBuilder that you install, there may be more components on this page. The components listed here are the basic components that are considered in this book and that are available in the JBuilder Professional version.

In addition to the components on the Data Access page, there are a number of additional classes that play an important role in database applications.

Component	Description
borland.jbcl.dataset.Database	Provides for the connection to a database. Your application will typically have at least one Database component for each database your application connects to.
borland.jbcl.dataset.TableDataSet	A component for holding row and column data retrieved from a text file. Data from a query can be stored in a *TableDataSet*, permitting the query to be closed and the connection to the database dropped without losing the data.
borland.jbcl.dataset.TextDataFile	A component for reading and writing structured data stored in an ASCII text file.
borland.jbcl.dataset.QueryDataSet	A component that defines a SQL query. If the query performs a SELECT statement, the data returned by the query is stored in the *QueryDataSet*.
borland.jbcl.dataset.QueryResolver	A default component for providing programmatic control over the resolve process.
borland.jbcl.dataset.DataSetView	A component that permits you to present varying views of the data stored in a *QueryDataSet* or *TableDataSet*, without actually affecting that data. For example, a *DataSetView* can display alternative sort orders, filters, and so on.

The Basic
Data Access
Components
Table 7-1.

7

These include row-related classes such as *borland.jbcl.dataset.ReadRow*, *borland.jbcl.dataset.ReadWriteRow*, *borland.jbcl.dataset.DataRow*, and *borland.jbcl.dataset.ParameterRow*. Other classes that you will encounter are *borland.jbcl.dataset.DataSet* and *borland.jbcl.dataset.StorateDataSet*. You never work with these classes at design time. Instead, you are likely to encounter them as you start working with database-related event handlers to provide additional runtime functionality. Finally, there is the *borland.jbcl.dataset.Column* class. This class permits you to define the properties of individual columns of the database, including display mask, calculation type, alignment, precision, and minimum and maximum values. Datasets serve as containers for columns. (These additional classes are discussed briefly in the following sections.)

NOTE: The components used for data access are found in the borland.jbcl.dataset package in JBuilder 1.0. At the time of this writing, there was some discussion at Borland concerning the possibility of renaming this package in a future JBuilder version. If you are working with a version of JBuilder later than version 1.0, note that the components used for data access may be found in a different package. If this is the case, all of the database-related projects on the CD-ROM for this book will presumably not work. In order to make these projects work it will be necessary to import the new package or packages in which the components used for data access are stored.

Because so much of the functionality that your database applications need descends from these classes, you should become as familiar as possible with the methods that they introduce. For example, the *StorageDataSet* class introduces methods that permit you to save changes made by either your code or the user back to the database from which the data was provided. Therefore, when you need to call methods to save your data, you will want to look at the *StorageDataSet* class to find the available methods. You can do this easily from the Structure pane when the Source tab is selected. Select the dataset object whose changes you want to save and double-click it to drill down into the class (as described in Chapter 3). This will take you to the definition of the appropriate *StorageDataSet* subclass. The methods introduced in *StorageDataSet* that save data will then appear in the Structure pane and the description of *StorageDataSet* will appear in the Content pane.

Row-Related Classes

The four row-related classes permit you to work with a single row of data from a database. These classes are actually related. Specifically, *ReadRow* is the immediate superclass of *ReadWriteRow*. *ReadRow* provides for the reading of the columns in a row. *ReadWriteRow*, as the name suggests, is similar to *ReadRow*, but it adds the functionality required to change the contents of a row.

DataRow extends *ReadWriteRow*. It provides almost no functionality apart from what it inherits. However, it is often used to define the search criteria, such as moving the cursor to a particular record (locate) or retrieving data from a particular record (lookup). A *DataRow* object can also be used as a parameter or return type for those methods that accept or return either a *ReadRow* or a *ReadWriteRow*.

A data row does not necessarily have the same number of columns as the table that it is used with. For example, when used to locate a record, the data row may only have columns that correspond to those that are being searched on.

Another class, which is closely related to *DataRow*, is *ParameterRow*. *ParameterRow* is explicitly used for storing data for use by a *parameterized query*. Parameterized queries are those that include variables, called *parameters*. You assign the values to the parameters of a query at runtime using a parameter row. Parameter rows differ from data rows in that values for a particular column may appear more than once in a parameter row. This is necessary to accommodate the special needs of a parameterized query.

The DataSet Class

The *DataSet* class descends from *ReadWriteRow* and adds significant functionality, permitting it to manage multiple rows of data. This is an abstract class, and it defines the interface for all classes that can manage multiple rows. The *DataSetView* class descends directly from *DataSet*.

The StorageDataSet Class

The *StorageDataSet* class extends *DataSet* and implements most of the functionality necessary to store data. Like the *DataSet* class, *StorageDataSet* is also an abstract class. The interface provided for by *StorageDataSet* permits the resolution of changes to the underlying table that provides the data. Both the *QueryDataSet* class and *TableDataSet* class extend *StorageDataSet*.

Figure 7-1 depicts the hierarchical relationship between all of the data aware components. Notice that the *Database* class and the *TextDataFile* class are unrelated to the other data aware classes, with the exception of descending from the common *java.lang.Object* class. This means that *Database* and *TextDataFile* introduce their own behaviors, none of which is shared with the other data aware classes.

Any database application that gets its data from a database table will use at least one *Database* component in addition to at least one *StorageDataSet* descendant. Usually there will be one *Database* for each logical database (collection of related data files or tables) and one *StorageDataSet* for each table. If the data is stored in an ASCII file, no database component is necessary since no connection to a database needs to be defined. Instead, a *TextDataFile* instance will provide for the data access and a *TableDataSet* instance will hold the provided rows.

7

The Column Class

The *DataSet* class acts as a container for *Column* class objects. Columns are used to store information about the columns of the dataset, including data

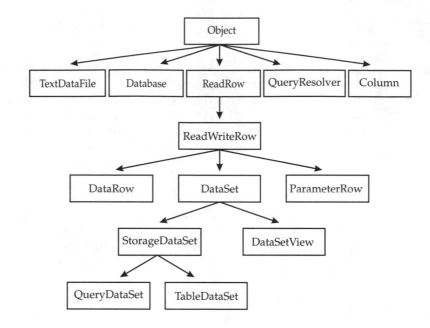

The hierarchy showing JBuilder's data access components
Figure 7-1.

type, precision, display format, and so forth. They also surface event handlers for managing column-level events.

Normally, column objects are created automatically each time data is provided to a dataset. The values of the column properties are defined by the metadata of the table. It is possible, however, to define column properties at design time. When you do so, JBuilder explicitly creates a column object to hold these properties. Such a column is referred to as a persistent column, since its property values persist from one provide operation to another.

You can display the individual columns for a particular dataset by expanding that dataset's node in the Data Access node of the Component Tree. It is when you select one of these columns and set one of its properties that a persistent column is created. When data is provided, the nonpersisting columns are removed from the dataset, leaving only the persistent columns. New, nonpersisting columns are then added, one for each column in the dataset not already represented by a persistent column.

In addition to defining individual column properties, persistent columns are useful for defining calculated fields. Calculated fields are described in detail in Chapter 9.

NOTE: Throughout these database-related chapters, the terms dataset and storage dataset will be used to refer generically to the components related to these two classes. In addition, read row will be used to refer to row-related data access components. The actual class name will only be used when explicit reference to the class, or an instance of the class, is intended.

Data Aware Components

Data aware components, unlike the data access components, are UI components that a user sees and interacts with at both design time and runtime. All of these components appear on the Controls page of the Component Palette. However, several of the components on that page are not data aware. These components are *ButtonControl*, *ButtonBar*, *TabSetControl*, and *TreeControl*.

The remaining components on the Controls page are used to either display data or permit some interaction with it. Of these, most provide access to individual columns of a table. These components include *CheckboxControl*, *ChoiceControl*, *FieldControl*, *ImageControl*, *LabelControl*, *ListControl*, *LocatorControl*, *TextAreaControl*, and *TextfieldControl*. The remaining three components apply to a dataset in general. These include *GridControl*, *NavigatorControl*, and *StatusBar*.

It is important to note that the use of components on the Controls page is not limited to those applications for which a dataset exists. Every one of them can be used in nondatabase applications. (Although it would not make much sense to use a navigator control when there is no underlying data.) However, it is when one or more datasets appear on a frame that the data aware controls can be made to automatically provide data access. In these cases, these controls provide a tremendous advantage over the use of the AWT (Abstract Windows Toolkit) controls, which are not data aware.

7

All of the data aware controls have one property in common—*dataSet*. You assign to this property a reference to the dataset (*TableDataSet*, *QueryDataSet*, *ProcedureDataSet*) that contains the data that is used by the control. For the components that operate on a dataset as a whole (such as the navigator control), that is the only property that you set. For the remaining data aware components, there is an additional property—*columnName*. This is the name of a specific column in the dataset with which you want to associate the control.

Once you specify that a data aware control uses a particular dataset and then enter a column name associated with that dataset, the control automatically takes responsibility for reading the data and updating its display. What actually gets displayed in one of these controls depends on the control type. For example, a *CheckboxControl* is used for boolean data; it is checked when the field contains a boolean true, and unchecked otherwise. A *TextFieldControl*, on the other hand, displays textual data, although it can also be used for the display and entry of numbers and dates since it provides full masking abilities, and will deal with conversion to other data types.

Data Modules

One additional issue that you might need to consider, as far as the data-related controls are concerned, is that of the data module. A data module is an object that is used to contain data access components. While you can generally add your data access controls to the frame that contains the data aware controls, there are times when you want to use the same data access components from two or more frames. When this need arises, you add a data module to your project, and then add a single line of code to each of the frames that requires access to those components. The use of data modules is covered in Chapter 8.

Preparing JBuilder for Database Access

All of the examples used in this book make use of Borland's Local InterBase Server (sometimes referred to as LIBS), a special version of this ANSI 92-compliant SQL server, along with the JDBC-ODBC bridge. If you intend to follow along with these examples, it is necessary for you to first install InterBase from the JBuilder CD-ROM, along with the sample InterBase code examples. In addition, you must configure the InterBase 4.x ODBC driver from Visigenic using the 32-bit ODBC configuration utility. This ODBC driver is added to your machine when you install InterBase. These steps are described in the following sections.

Installing InterBase

Installing the Local InterBase Server itself is fairly simple. Begin by running the installation program on the JBuilder CD-ROM. From the JBuilder installation screen, shown in Figure 7-2, click the Local InterBase button and follow the prompts. (If you are installing InterBase from this book's CD-ROM, you need to run SETUP.EXE in the SETUP\LIBS\DISK1 folder instead.) When the installation routine displays the Select Local InterBase Components dialog, it provides you with the option to install all components. These will occupy less than 10MB of disk space. If you must

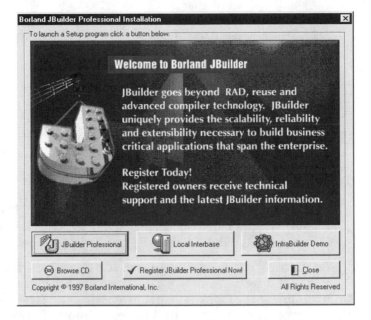

The JBuilder
installation
screen
Figure 7-2.

install only a subset of the components, make sure that you install the
program files, InterBase Windows tools, InterBase example database, and
InterBase ODBC drivers, at the very minimum.

As you near the end of the installation process, the installation routine will
give you the opportunity to configure the ODBC driver. Although you are
free to do so at this point, InterBase is not actually running yet (since you
have only just installed it), so it is not yet possible to test the ODBC driver.
The following description assumes that you will not configure the ODBC
driver at this point. Instead, complete the installation without configuring
this driver.

Also, at some point in the installation you might also be asked if you want to
modify your TCP/IP services file. If this happens, click OK.

By default, JBuilder will install InterBase in the directory c:\Program
Files\Borland\IntrBase. In addition, the installation program will install
several sample databases. The examples used in this book make use of the
employee.gdb database, which is stored by default in the directory named
c:\Program Files\Borland\IntrBase\Examples. The database employee.gdb
contains a number of different tables, including CUSTOMER, EMPLOYEE,
SALES, and so forth, making it well suited for creating the sample database
applications described in this book.

Once you have completed the installation of InterBase, you should exit all
programs and restart you computer. This will ensure that all settings defined
during the InterBase installation take effect. It also ensures that the InterBase

7

server loads properly. If you are running Windows 95 or later, or Windows NT 4.0, after restarting your computer the InterBase server will appear in the taskbar as a small server icon with a green ball behind it.

Configuring the InterBase ODBC Driver

As the last step of the InterBase installation the opportunity is presented to configure the Visigenic ODBC driver. It does this by displaying the ODBC Data Source Administrator dialog as shown in Figure 7-3. If you skipped configuring the ODBC during InterBase installation, you will need to return to the ODBC Data Source Administrator to perform the necessary installation.

Assuming that you did not install the InterBase ODBC driver, you need to install it now using the ODBC Data Source Administrator. To do this, begin by opening the Control Panel by clicking the Start button in the taskbar, followed by Settings|Control Panel. From the Control Panel, double-click the icon labeled 32-bit ODBC. The dialog shown in Figure 7-3 is displayed.

The InterBase ODBC driver from Visigenic will be absent from the User Data Source list (unless you had previously installed it). If it is not listed there, begin by adding it. Click the Add button to display the Create New Data Source dialog shown in Figure 7-4.

You use the ODBC Data Source Administrator dialog to configure the InterBase ODBC driver from Visigenic

Figure 7-3.

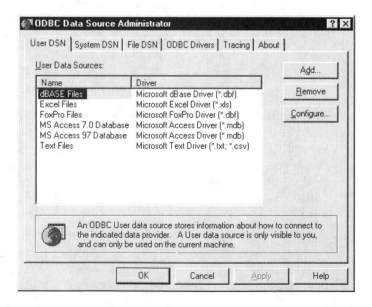

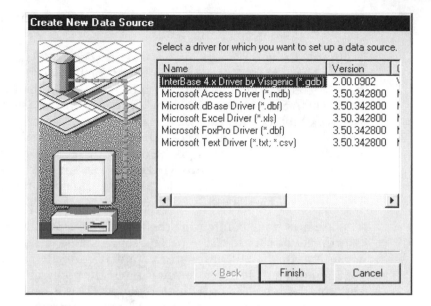

Use the Create
New Data
Source dialog
to add the
InterBase
driver
Figure 7-4.

Select the driver and click the Finish button to add the new ODBC driver.
Doing so takes you to the InterBase ODBC Configuration dialog, shown
in Figure 7-5.

If the InterBase ODBC driver was already installed when you first opened the
ODBC Data Source Administrator dialog (it already appeared listed in the
User Data Sources list box in Figure 7-3), you simply need to select it and the
click the Configure button. Doing so also takes you to the InterBase ODBC
Configuration dialog shown in Figure 7-5. (For the purposes of this example,

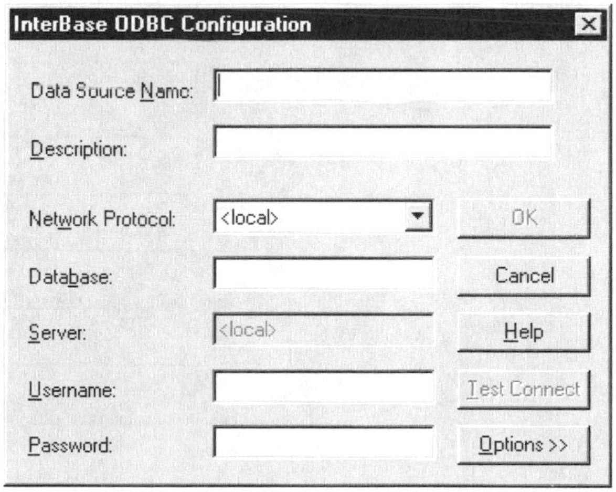

Use the
InterBase
ODBC
Configuration
dialog to
define the
Data Source
Name and
other
parameters of
the InterBase
ODBC driver
Figure 7-5.

7

however, it is better to add a new data source than overwrite an existing data source that has been configured.)

From the dialog shown in Figure 7-5, enter **dataset tutorial** in the Data Source Name field. This is the name that the JBuilder documentation will have you enter to follow along with its tutorials. In the Description field, enter **Data Source for the employee.gdb database**. Do not change Network Protocol; instead, leave it to the default <local>. You must set Database to the fully qualified path of the employee.gdb database. If you installed InterBase using all of the default paths, set Database to **c:\Program Files\Borland\IntrBase\Examples\employee.gdb**. Finally, in the Username field enter **SYSDBA**. Do not bother to enter a password yet. When you are done, this screen will look like that shown in Figure 7-6.

You are now done configuring the InterBase ODBC driver. Before you continue, you should test your data source name (DSN). This permits you to make sure that you have entered your data correctly on the InterBase ODBC Configuration dialog. Before you can test the connection, you must accept the InterBase ODBC Configuration dialog. (This is necessary due to the inability of the ODBC Data Source Administrator to test the connection of a newly configured DSN.) This returns you to the ODBC Data Source Administrator dialog. Then, with the dataset tutorial DSN still selected, click the Configure button again.

Once you return to the InterBase ODBC Configuration dialog, enter the password **masterkey** (all lowercase characters, and no spaces) in the Password field, then click the Test Connect button. You then see a dialog

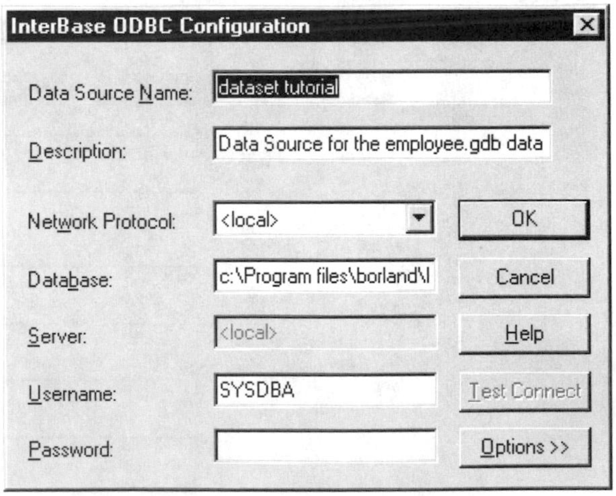

The completed InterBase ODBC Configuration dialog
Figure 7-6.

that warns you that testing the connection will save the current DSN information. Accept this dialog. If you have configured the driver correctly, you will see the following dialog. If not, go back and correct the parameters on the InterBase ODBC Configuration dialog.

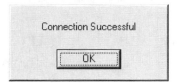

NOTE: If you are installing InterBase for the first time and have not yet restarted your computer, the Test Connect button will fail since the InterBase server will not be running. If this is the case, continue with your installation without testing the connection. After completing your installation, restart Windows. Upon restarting, the InterBase server will be automatically loaded. Then, open the Control Panel and run the ODBC Data Source Name Administrator again. Select the Visigenic InterBase ODBC driver and click the Configure button. Enter the password and then click the Test Connect button to test your connection.

Once you have created and successfully tested your ODBC driver, click OK to close the InterBase ODBC Configuration dialog. Click OK once more to save your changes and close the ODBC Data Source Administrator dialog.

Building a Simple Database Application

Once you have installed InterBase and configured its ODBC drivers, you are ready to build your first database application using JBuilder. This section walks you through the steps of creating an application that will give your users access to the CUSTOMER table in the employee.gdb database installed with InterBase.

7

This application will be somewhat limited in that the user will be responsible for making sure that any changes made to the data are resolved. In most cases, you would add code to the application to test whether unresolved data is present when the user tries to close the application and prompt the user to resolve those changes if some are detected. However, by omitting this code, this example serves to demonstrate just how easy it is to build a JDBC database application using JBuilder.

CD-ROM: The project simpledb.jpr can be found in the osborne\jbecd\simpledb subdirectory. See Appendix C for information on installing and using the files on this book's CD-ROM.

Defining the User Interface

Before you start, close any open projects. Then use the following steps:

1. Select File|New to display the New page of the Object Gallery.

2. Double-click the Application icon (Application Wizard). JBuilder begins by running the Project Wizard. At File, enter **C:\JBuilder\myprojects\osborne\jbe\simpledb\simpledb.jpr**. Click the Finish button to continue to the Application Wizard.

3. Do not make any changes to the Application Wizard. Click Finish to accept all defaults on the Application Wizard and complete the creation of the basic project.

4. Select Frame1.java in the Navigation pane, and then click the Design tab to activate the UI Designer. JBuilder will present a blank frame.

5. Next, click the Controls tab of the Component Palette and place a *StatusBar,* a *NavigatorControl,* and a *GridControl* from the Controls page onto the blank frame in the UI Designer. The *StatusBar* should be placed near the bottom of the frame, the *GridControl* near the center, and the *NavigatorControl* near the top. Exact placement is not important since a *BorderLayout* will be used to position these components.

6. To apply the *BorderLayout,* select the bevel panel in the UI Designer. Using the Properties page of the Inspector, set the bevel panel's *layout* property to BorderLayout.

7. Use the Properties page of the Inspector again to set the *constraints* of the navigator control, grid control, and status bar to North, Center, and South, respectively. Depending on the relative placement of your components, these objects may or may not have the correct constraints. If not, change the *constraints* for each component as necessary. When you are done, your frame should look like that shown in Figure 7-7.

Adding and Configuring the Data Access Components

Now that the user interface is in place, it is necessary to add at least two data access components to the form. In this case, these will be a *Database* and a

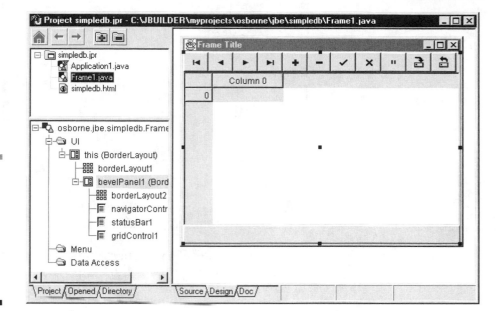

A navigator control, a grid control, and a status bar have been added to the frame

Figure 7-7.

QueryDataSet. These components then need to be configured to access data. This is described in the following steps:

1. Click the Data Access tab of the Component Palette and add one *Database* and one *QueryDataSet* component from the Data Access page. You can do this by either dropping one of each onto the frame in the UI Designer or you can drop them into the Component Tree. These components are non-UI components, so they will not appear on the frame. Instead, they will appear beneath the Data Access node of the Component Tree.

2. Select *database1* in the Component Tree.

7

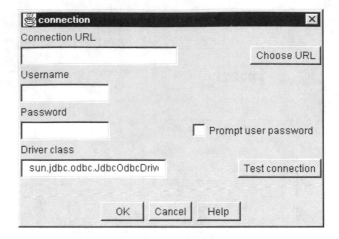

Use the
Connection
dialog to
define the
database
connection.
Figure 7-8.

3. Move to the Properties page of the Inspector and click in the *connection* property field until a button with an ellipses appears (…). Click this ellipsis to display the Connection dialog shown in Figure 7-8.

NOTE: The name of the property that appears in the Inspector, *connection,* is a property name whose accessor is *setConnection()*. However, the type of the *connection* property is *connectionDescriptor.Use the Connection dialog to define the database connection*

4. Click the Choose URL button on the Connection dialog to display the Choose a Connection URL dialog shown in Figure 7-9.

5. The list control on this dialog lists the connection URLs that have been used recently. If you have never created a connection, this list will be empty. If this list is empty, or you want to select a driver that is not displayed, click the Show data sources button to display all available ODBC data sources. Select the **jdbc:odbc:dataSet Tutorial** data source from this dialog, and then click OK to return to the Connection dialog.

6. Next, you must enter the username and password for the selected database. At Username, enter **SYSDBA**, and at Password enter **masterkey** (in all lowercase letters).

7. Before closing the Connection dialog, you should test the connection to the database. To do this, click the Test connection button. If the test failed, the word "Failed" appears beneath the Test connection button. If you are able to establish a connection, the word "Success" appears. If you fail to establish a connection, verify your data. Once you successfully make the connection, click the OK button.

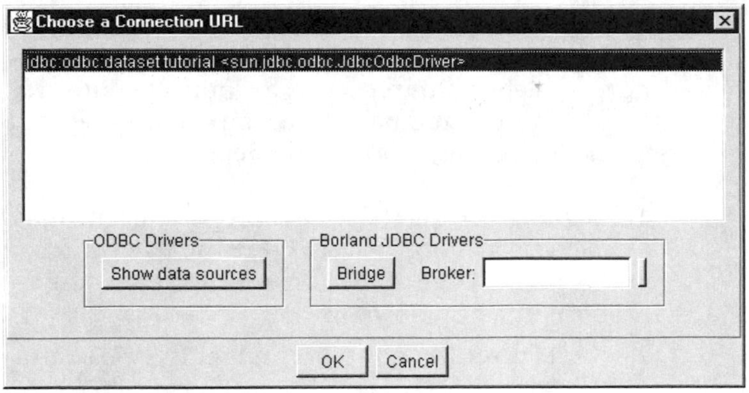

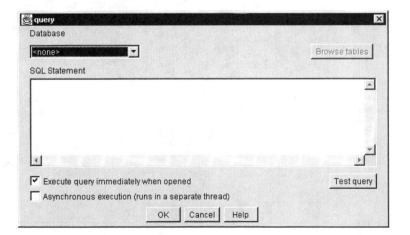

Use the
Choose a
Connection
URL dialog to
select a driver
Figure 7-9.

8. Now select *queryDataSet1* in the Component Tree. In the Inspector, select the *query* property field until it is active and then click the ellipsis button to display the *query* property editor shown in Figure 7-10.

9. Begin by associating this query with the database. To do this, set the Database drop-down list to database1.

10. Next, enter the following SQL statement in the SQL Statement box in the center of the *query* property editor dialog:

```
SELECT  *  FROM  CUSTOMER
```

11. Now, test the query by clicking the Test query button. If the query runs successfully, the word "Success" appears beneath the Test query button. If the query fails, check you SQL statement and click the Test query button again. Once the query succeeds, click OK to close the *query* property editor.

The
query property
editor
Figure 7-10.

Connecting Data Aware Components to the Dataset

The final step in this process is to connect your three data aware components to the data access components prepared in the preceding section. To do this, follow these steps:

1. Begin by setting the _dataSet_ property of the navigator control to _queryDataSet1_ by first selecting the navigator control and then using the Properties page of the Inspector to select _queryDataSet1_ from the _dataSet_ property drop-down list.

2. Next, select the status bar and set its _dataSet_ property to _queryDataSet1_.

3. Finally, select the grid control and set its _dataSet_ property to _queryDataSet1_. When you finish this last setting, the data from the query associated with the query dataset is displayed in the grid control, as shown in Figure 7-11.

Using the Database Application

Before running this application, select File|Save All. Next, click the Run button from JBuilder's toolbar. JBuilder compiles the application and then runs it. The running application should look something like that shown in Figure 7-12.

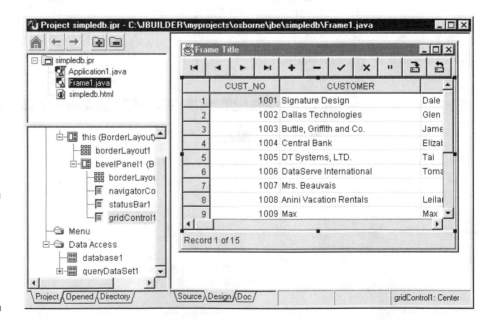

Data displayed in a grid control in the UI Designer
Figure 7-11.

Begin by clicking the Next button (the third button from the left) on the application's navigator control a couple of times to move down several rows. Next, click the First button (the leftmost button) in the navigator to return to the first row. To move to the last row in the query dataset, click the Last button (the fourth button from the left).

The grid control permits you to easily sort the data in the table based on the values in a single column. For example, click on the column label for the CUSTOMER column (the column label appears at the top of the grid above the column's data). The first time you click the column label the values in the table are sorted based on the contents of the column in ascending order. Click the CUSTOMER column label once more. This time the table is sorted by customer name in descending order. To restore the original sort order (sorted by CUST_NO), click the column label for the CUST_NO column.

To change a record, click on the column you want to change once to highlight it, and a second time to begin editing it. For example, click the CUSTOMER column for the last row, the one where the customer name GeoTech Inc. appears. Edit this record, changing GeoTech Inc. to GeoTech Incorporated. Press ENTER to accept this change. (Pressing ESC would have canceled the change.)

Now try resolving the change you made to the last row. Do this by clicking the Save button (the second to last button from the right) in the navigator control. After a moment, your changes are posted, and the message "Posted row" appears in the status bar. Now refresh your view of the data by clicking the Refresh button (the rightmost button in the navigator control). This requests that the database provide a new set of records.

Run the simple database application by clicking the Run button on JBuilder's toolbar **Figure 7-12.**

7

Now restore the customer name for the record you changed. Drag the vertical scroll bar until row 15 is visible again. Click on the CUSTOMER column for this row twice and change GeoTech Incorporated back to GeoTech Inc. Click the Save button again. This not only accepts the change to this column, but also resolves the change back to the database.

Conclude this exercise by closing the application.

CHAPTER 8

Using Database Components

JBuilder comes with a number of components that you can use in your database applications. UI components, such as the *GridControl, StatusBar, NavigatorControl,* and so on, appear in the UI Designer at design time, and have a visual representation at runtime. Other data-related components are non-UI components. These components, such as *QueryDataSet, DataRow,* and *ParameterRow,* only appear in the Component Tree, never in the UI Designer. Furthermore, these components do not have a visual runtime presence. While they provide you with valuable features, a user cannot see them, and cannot interact with them directly.

This chapter provides you with an introduction to the use of the database components. It is assumed that you have read Chapter 7, and have installed and configured the Local InterBase Server and its associated ODBC (Open Database Connectivity) driver. These are necessary since the examples used here make use of the Local InterBase Server, and the example employee.gdb database installed with it.

NOTE: If you have installed DataGateway for Java, InterClient, or some other Java-compatible JDBC (JavaSoft Database Connectivity) driver for the Local InterBase Server, you can use that driver instead of the JDBC-ODBC bridge. However, in order to use that alternative driver, you must select it when establishing your database connection, rather than the JDBC-ODBC driver described in the examples in this chapter.

This chapter introduces topics that can be implemented with little or no coding on your part. These topics include using data modules, designing master-detail views, working with *DataSetView* components, creating persistent columns, and using the *LocatorControl* component. In the next chapter, features that require the addition of a significant amount of custom Java code are discussed.

CD-ROM: The project files and package names for the projects in this chapter are listed at the beginning of each new example. However, the jbecd subdirectory is used in the CD-ROM files in place of the example project's jbe subdirectory. See Appendix C for information on installing and using the files on this book's CD-ROM.

Using a Data Module

While you can add your data access controls to a frame or dialog directly, in most cases you will want to add them to a data module instead. A data module is a non-UI component, and as such is never displayed to the user.

The advantage of using a data module for containing data access components over using a frame or a dialog is that the data access components that you place in a data module can be accessed by one or more frames. By comparison, when you add data access components to a frame or dialog, other frames or dialogs cannot easily access those components. In other words, the data access components on a data module can be easily shared, even at design time.

One of the components that it is particularly important to share is a *Database*. In JDBC, each database represents a separate connection to your server. Most servers, and the InterBase Server is included in this list, have a limited number of connections. (The Local InterBase Server permits a maximum of two connections.) If you place your database and dataset components on individual frames, and are using the Local InterBase Server, you will be able to have no more than two of these data accessing frames open simultaneously. Attempting to open a third frame on which a database appears will throw an exception.

It is possible to add additional connections for most servers. (The Local InterBase Server is one of the exceptions, since it is intended for testing purposes only.) However, most companies pay for database servers by the connection, and depending on the database, each additional connection can be expensive. Consequently, it is best when a single user makes use of no more connections than necessary.

With respect to data modules, two frames (or dialogs) can share either the same instance of a data module or multiple instances of the same data module. When two frames share the same instance of a data module, it is possible for them to use the same database and dataset simultaneously. By doing so, both frames are automatically synchronized to the same row, and use only one connection.

Rather than sharing a single instance of a data module, it is possible for two or more frames to share different instances of the same data module. At a minimum, providing a separate instance of the data module for each frame permits each to have a separate cursor to the data. Another way of saying this is that each frame can have a different current row. Furthermore, if the data access components on the data module include data-validating code or property settings, all frames using the common data module automatically make use of the restrictions placed on the data.

The drawback to using multiple instances of a single data module, as already mentioned, is that each instance uses a separate database and therefore requires a separate connection. A solution to this problem is covered later in this chapter.

8

NOTE: Some databases, in particular, local databases such as Paradox and dBASE, do not limit the number of connections. Consequently, if you are using a driver to access one of these databases, such as Borland's DataGateway for Java, the issue of multiple databases is far less critical. In addition, some databases require a separate connection for each query, making the multiple database issue less relevant. This second issue is revisited later in this chapter.

The following sections demonstrate how to create both types of data modules. The first section demonstrates how to create two frames that stay synchronized through the use of a shared data module. The second section shows you how to create a single data module containing data-validating code, and how separate frames can share that code.

The basic operations demonstrated in this first example are very similar to those that are used in many of the remaining examples. Consequently, each of these operations is presented first in explicit detail with step-by-step instructions. Later examples in this chapter will refer back to these steps, rather than repeat the individual steps. This approach is used to avoid in later examples the unnecessary repetition of steps that are common to each example.

Sharing a Data Module

A shared data module permits two frames to share a single cursor. One of the more common reasons for doing this is to provide two separate, yet synchronized views of the same data. For example, you might have two frames, one that displays a tabular view of your data using a *GridControl*, and another displaying a single-row view using a *FieldControl*. Through the use of a single instance of a data module used by both frames, both views are necessarily synchronized to one another. That is, as you navigate the tabular view, the single-row view always displays the currently displayed row in the *GridControl*. Likewise, if you navigate using the single-row view, the *GridControl* updates to reflect this navigation.

Creating the Initial Project

Use the following steps to create the initial project:

1. Begin by closing all projects.
2. Select File|New to display the New Page of the Object Gallery and double-click the Application icon (Application Wizard).

3. JBuilder first displays the Project Wizard dialog. On this dialog, set the File field to **C:\JBuilder\myprojects\osborne\jbe\shareddm\shareddm.jpr**, then click the Finish button to display the Application Wizard.

4. In the Application Wizard, click the Next button to move to the Step 2 page. On this page, set the Title field to **Data Module Demonstration**. Then enable the Generate menu bar, Generate status bar, and Center frame on screen checkboxes. Click the Finish button to complete the Application Wizard.

Your next step is to add the data module.

Adding the Data Module

To add a data module to this application, use the following steps:

1. Select File|New to display the New Page of the Object Gallery and double-click the Data Module icon (Data Module Wizard) to display the New DataModule dialog shown in Figure 8-1.

2. On the New DataModule dialog, accept the defaults and click the OK button to complete the Data Module Wizard.

After adding the data module, your Navigation pane will look like the following:

```
□ 🗀 shareddm.jpr
        📰 Application1.java
        📄 DataModule1.java
        📄 Frame1.java
        🔷 shareddm.html
```

Use the Data Module Wizard to add a data module to your application
Figure 8-1.

8

The Java source file for the data module, DataModule1.java, is actually quite simple, as shown in the following code:

```java
package osborne.jbe;

import java.awt.*;
import java.awt.event.*;
import borland.jbcl.layout.*;
import borland.jbcl.control.*;
import borland.jbcl.dataset.*;

public class DataModule1 implements DataModule {
  private static DataModule1 myDM;

  public DataModule1() {
    try {
      jbInit();
    }
    catch (Exception e) {
      e.printStackTrace();
    }

  }

  void jbInit() throws Exception{
  }

  static public DataModule1 getDataModule() {
    if (myDM == null)
      myDM = new DataModule1();
    return myDM;
  }
}
```

The two notable features of this code are the presence of a private static variable named *myDM*, and a public static method named *getDataModule()*. The method *getDataModule()* tests whether or not the private variable has been assigned an instance of the data module, and if not, creates and returns an instance. If an instance has previously been created, the method returns that instance. It is this variable and method that permit the *DataModule* class to return the same instance of this class to two or more objects. In other words, this static method calls the data module's constructor only if no instance of the data module already exists.

Your next step is to add data access components to the data module.

Adding Components to the Data Module

To add components to the data module, use the following steps:

1. Select the DataModule1.Java file in the Navigation pane.

2. Click the Design tab of the Content pane to open the UI Designer.

3. Click the Data Access tab of the Component Palette. From the Data Access page, add one *Database* component and one *QueryDataSet* component to the design. These added components appear under the Data Access node in the Component Tree in the Structure pane as described in the last chapter.

4. Select the *Database* component from the Component Tree. Move to the Properties page of the Inspector and click in the *connection* property field until a button with an ellipsis appears (...). Click this ellipsis to display the Connection dialog.

5. From the Connection dialog, click the Choose URL button and choose jdbc:odbc:dataset tutorial.

6. Next, enter **SYSDBA** in the Username field.

7. In the Password field, enter **masterkey**.

8. Click the Test connection button to verify that all information is entered correctly. The word "Success" appears beneath the Test connection button if a connection to the local InterBase server can be successfully opened.

9. Return to the UI Designer by clicking OK.

10. Now select the *QueryDataSet* from the Component Tree.

11. Move to the Properties page of the Inspector and click in the *query* property field until a button with an ellipsis appears (...). Click this ellipsis to display the Query dialog.

12. On the Query dialog, set the Database field to database1 by selecting it from the drop-down list. In the SQL Statement field, enter the following SQL statement:

    ```
    SELECT * FROM CUSTOMER
    ```

13. Click the Test query button to test the query. When it is correct, the message "Success" will appear beneath the Test query button.

14. Click OK to close the Query dialog. Now select Build|Make Project to compile the data module.

The data module is now all set to be used by one or more frames.

8

NOTE: You can check the Asynchronous execution checkbox on the Query dialog to instruct JBuilder to execute the query in a thread. An asynchronous query permits the user to see and work with data as soon as the query returns its first few rows. However, the query may continue to return rows even while the user works with the data, possibly providing the user with an incomplete picture of their data. When a query executes asynchronously, you can use the *dataLoaded* event handler for the query dataset to signal that the query has completed its execution.

Using a Data Module from a Frame

You can easily provide any frame or dialog with access to this data module. You do this by declaring a variable to be of the type of the data module, and then initializing this variable with an instance of the data module's class. This initialization can be done with either a call to the data module's static *getDataModule()* method or with a call to the data module's constructor.

This particular example being developed here is intended to demonstrate how to share a data module between two or more frames. Consequently, the *getDataModule()* method is the initializer of choice, since it will either create the first instance of the data module or return an existing instance of it.

The following steps demonstrate how to add a call to *getDataModule()* to the *Frame1* declaration:

1. Select Frame1.java in the Navigation pane.
2. Click the Source tab to display the Editor in the Content pane.
3. From the Structure pane, select *Frame1*, the top-level node. This will move your cursor in the Editor to the *Frame1* declaration.
4. Insert a new line immediately below the line that reads

    ```
    public class Frame1 extends DecoratedFrame {
    ```

5. In the newly added line, enter the following statement:

    ```
    DataModule1 datamod = DataModule1.getDataModule();
    ```

The source code in the Editor will look like that shown in Figure 8-2.

Linking Data Aware Controls to a Data Module

Once a data module has been added to a frame and initialized, you can set the *dataSet* property of any of the data aware controls on that frame to a *DataSet* object on the data module. To demonstrate this, perform the following steps:

1. Click the Design tab to display the UI Designer.

2. Select the status bar object on the frame in the UI Designer.

3. Using the Properties page of the Inspector, select the status bar's *dataSet* property, and then select datamod.QueryDataSet1 from the *dataSet* drop-down list.

TIP: In the first version of JBuilder, the UI Designer will appear to be out of sync with the code since the UI Designer only uses compiled JavaBeans, not the source code for them. If you open the *dataSet* property's drop-down list, and datamod.QueryDataSet1 is not available, save your changes and close the project. Then, open the project again. This time, the *dataSet* property will display the dataset from the data module. If it does not, close JBuilder and then reopen it. Now the *dataSet* property drop-down list will surely display the data module's query dataset.

4. It is time to add some additional data aware controls to *Frame1*. Begin by first selecting the bevel panel on *Frame1*, and setting its *layout* property to BorderLayout.

5. Add a *NavigatorControl* to the bevel panel so that it is aligned North, and a *GridControl* so that it is aligned Center. (See Chapter 5 for a description of placing components into a border layout.)

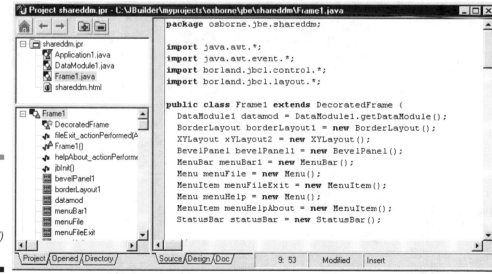

The *datamod* variable is initialized with a call to *getDataModule()*

Figure 8-2.

8

6. Using the Properties page of the Inspector, set the *dataSet* property of both the *GridControl* and the *NavigatorControl* to datamod.QueryDataSet1.

At this point, the application's frame is data aware. The data returned by the query on the data module should appear in the frame as shown in Figure 8-3.

To continue this example, it is necessary to add another frame to this application. This new frame will be used to display a single row from the same dataset that is displayed in the grid control. Furthermore, since this second frame will share the same instance of the dataset, the single-row view and the view displayed in the grid control will stay synchronized to the same row.

Sharing a Data Module with Another Frame

To add another frame to the application, and have it share the same instance of the data module, use the following steps:

1. Use the Frame Wizard to add an additional frame to the application.

2. Select Frame2.java in the Navigation pane. Select the Design tab of the Content pane to active the UI Designer. *Frame2* itself will be selected. Using the Properties page of the Inspector, set its *exitOnClose* property to False.

The configured *Frame1* displays data from the data module

Figure 8-3.

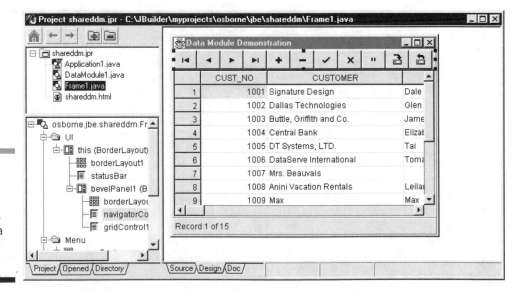

3. Click the Events tab of the Inspector to display the Events page. Add an event handler to the *windowClosing* event. Add the following single line to the generated event method:

```
dispose();
```

4. Click the Design tab to return to the UI Designer. With the *Frame* still selected, sets its *layout* property to BorderLayout.

5. Click the Controls tab of the Component Palette and add a *StatusBar* component to the *Frame*, aligning it South. Add a *NavigatorControl*, aligning it North. Finally, from the Containers page of the Component Palette add a *BevelPanel* and align it Center. Your *Frame2* should now look like that shown in Figure 8-4.

6. Now add the data module instance variable to *Frame2* using steps similar to those you used to add the data module to *Frame1*. Specifically, with Frame2.java selected in the Navigation pane, click the Source tab of the Content pane and then move to the *Frame2* declaration (by selecting the top-level node in the Component Tree, labeled *Frame2*). Insert a new line in the *Frame2* declaration statement, and add the following code to that line:

```
DataModule1 datamod = DataModule1.getDataModule();
```

7. Now that this data module has been added, select the status bar and set its *dataSet* property to datamod.QueryDataSet1. Do the same for the *NavigatorControl*.

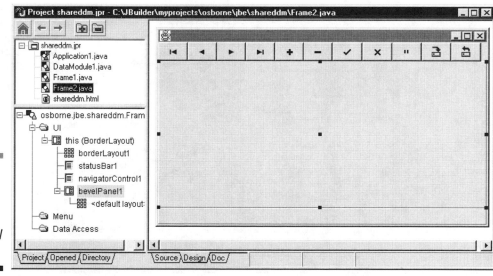

Frame2 with a *StatusBar*, a *BevelPanel*, and a *NavigatorControl*

Figure 8-4.

8

8. It is now time to add the UI components that can be used to display a single-row view. To do this, it is necessary to add controls that display single column values (as opposed to the *GridControl*, which displays multiple rows of data). An ideal component for this purpose is the *FieldControl*. In addition, you will want to place some *java.awt.Label* components onto the bevel panel as well in order to identify the columns being displayed in the *FieldControl* components. Begin by clicking the AWT tab of the Component Palette to display the AWT page. Place onto the bevel panel four *Label* components, one at a time. As you place each one, set its *text* property using the Properties page of the Inspector. This *text* property should be set to **Customer ID** for the first label, **Customer** for the second, **Contact First Name** for the third, and **Contact Last Name** for the fourth label.

9. Next, select the Controls page of the Component Palette and add four *FieldControl* components, placing them to the right of each label. When you are done, *Frame2* should look like that shown in Figure 8-5.

10. Now it is time to configure the *FieldControl* objects to display data. Begin by selecting *fieldControl1* in the Component Tree of the Structure pane. Using the Properties page of the Inspector, set its *dataSet* property to datamod.QueryDataSet1, and enter its *columnName* property as **CUST_NO**. For the remaining *FieldControl* objects, select each one in turn and set its *dataSet* property to datamod.QueryDataSet1, and *columnName* to the corresponding column names, which are **CUSTOMER**, **CONTACT_FIRST**, and **CONTACT_LAST**, respectively. *Frame2* is now complete.

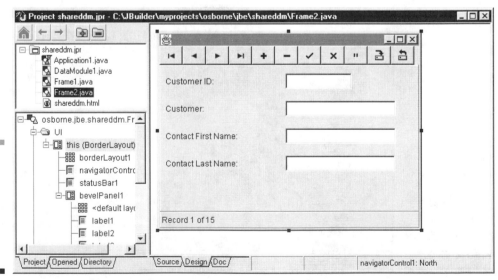

Label and *FieldControl* objects placed to display a single-row (record) view

Figure 8-5.

11. Return to *Frame1,* select its menu bar, and double-click on the menu bar node in the Component Tree to activate the Menu Designer. Insert a new menu into the menu bar. Place this item between File and Help and set its label to **View**. (See Chapter 3 for more information on creating and modifying menus.)

12. Now insert a new menu item into the View menu, and enter **Single Record** for its label.

13. With the Single Record menu item still selected, move to the Events page of the Inspector and add an *actionPerformed* event handler. Modify the generated method to look like the following:

```
void menuItem1_actionPerformed(ActionEvent e) {
  Frame2 singleRec = new Frame2();
  singleRec.pack();
  singleRec.setVisible(true);
}
```

This project is done. Select File|Save All to save your work. Next, click the Run button on the JBuilder toolbar. *Frame1* appears first, with its *GridControl* displaying multiple records. To display the single-record view, select View|Single Record from the application's main menu. Notice that when the single-record view appears, it displays the record that is active in *Frame1,* even if you have used the navigator control to move to a record other than the first record. Figure 8-6 displays these two frames, synchronized to a common record.

If you now navigate the query using the navigator control on either *Frame1* or *Frame2*, you will observe that as you navigate, both frames stay synchronized to the same record.

Two frames are synchronized to the same record by sharing an instance of a data module

Figure 8-6.

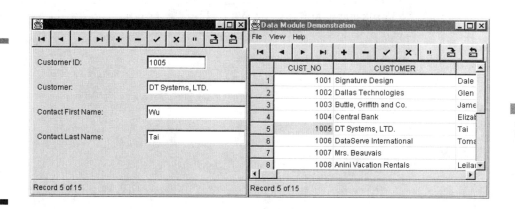

8

Using Multi-Instance Data Modules

Frame2 in the preceding example used the same instance of the data module as *Frame1*, and therefore shared a single cursor with *Frame1* as well. If two or more frames must display completely separate cursors to the database, there are two options. One is to place two or more storage datasets on a data module, one for each of the frames. Another is to create a separate instance of the data module. The following example expands on the preceding example, adding a new frame that will use a separate instance of the data module.

To create this example, add a new frame, *Frame 3,* to the project. Follow the steps described in the preceding section in this chapter entitled "Sharing a Data Module with Another Frame." The only difference you will perform is in step 6, where you add an instance variable for the data module to *Frame3*. Instead of initializing the data module instance variable to an existing instance (if it exists), you want to initialize it with a new instance of the data module, created using the data module's constructor. Therefore, instead of entering the line of code shown in step 6 of "Sharing a Data Module with Another Frame," enter the following line of code:

```
DataModule1 datamod = new DataModule1();
```

Once you have completed step 10 for your new *Frame3,* you will want to add code to *Frame1* that will permit you to display *Frame3*. To do this, return to *Frame1* by selecting Frame1.java in the Navigation pane. Click the Design tab of the Content pane to open the Designer and select *menuBar1* in the Component Tree.

With the Menu Designer displayed, add a new menu item to the View menu, and enter **New Data Module** for its label. (See Chapter 3 for more information on creating and modifying menus.)

With this new menu item still selected, move to the Inspector, select the Events page, and add an event handler to the *actionPerformed* event. Add the following code to the generated event:

```
void menuItem2_actionPerformed(ActionEvent e) {
  Frame3 newMod = new Frame3();
  newMod.pack();
  newMod.setLocation(300,300);
  newMod.setVisible(true);
}
```

Save your changes to this project, and then run it. From the menu bar on *Frame1*, select View|New Data Module. A copy of *Frame3* opens. You can now move freely between *Frame1* and *Frame3*, and navigate the CUSTOMER table from either frame. As you navigate, notice that each frame can display a different current record (row), as shown in Figure 8-7. Unlike when a single instance of the data module is used, each frame in this example has a separate cursor.

The one problem with this example, however, is that each instance of the data module has a separate instance of the database. As a result, each time a new instance of the data module is instantiated, a new connection to the database is established. In many types of applications, database connections are limited in number. In fact, if you are using the Local InterBase Server that ships with JBuilder, you can have only a maximum of two simultaneous connections. In most cases, two connections are adequate for performing limited testing of an application.

This limitation is immediately obvious if you select View|New Data Module a second time from *Frame1*. If you do so, you will see the error dialog shown in Figure 8-8.

Creating Database Modules

The primary advantage of multiple-instance data modules is that they permit you to easily instantiate two or more cursors to the same table without having to explicitly place and configure separate datasets. As shown in the preceding section, however, placing a database on a multiple-instance data module has a drawback.

There are two general solutions that solve the problem with using multiple databases. One is to place multiple datasets on a single data module, and use a different dataset from this single-instance data module from different

Frame1 and *Frame3* use different instances of *DataModule1*, permitting them to display different records (rows)

Figure 8-7.

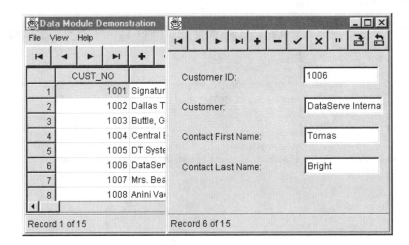

8

frames. The drawback to this solution is that you must anticipate how many frames you will permit to be open simultaneously, as well as manage which frame gets which dataset. In addition, you must still place and configure each dataset on the single-instance data module. For example, if you decide that a maximum of five data-accessing frames can be open simultaneously, you must place at least five datasets onto the single data module. Each dataset on this data module, however, can easily share a common database.

Another solution, one that is far more flexible, is to make use of two data modules. One of these is a single-instance data module that holds a database (or one database for each server you need to access). The second is a multiple-instance data module, one that holds the dataset or datasets that will make use of the database or databases in the single-instance module.

The following section describes how to create a project in which a single-instance data module holds one or more databases, and is shared by one or more multiple-instance data modules that contain datasets.

NOTE: There is a third alternative, which is to use *DataSetView* components for each of the views of a single dataset. Each dataset view maintains its own cursor. Also, some servers require that you have one connection for each query. For these servers, using two or more dataset views is the only way to view multiple instances of a table without creating separate connections. Using dataset views is described in Chapter 9.

Each database instance uses a separate connection. You cannot exceed the number of connections allowed by your server

Figure 8-8.

Creating Data Modules that Share a Database

By creating a data module, and placing in it only a database, you permit two or more additional data modules to employ that database. This approach minimizes the number of connections required to access your data.

To demonstrate the use of a single-instance database data module, begin by creating a new application, as described earlier in the section "Creating the Initial Project." In step 3, where you enter the name of the project, enter **C:\JBuilder\myprojects\osborne\jbe\databasemodule\ databasemodule.jpr**. Continue to step 4, where you should set the Title field to **Database Data Module Demonstration**.

After creating the initial project, your next step is to create the data module for the database.

Creating the Database Data Module
To create a database data module, use the following steps:

1. Add a new data module to your project by selecting File|New and then double-clicking the Data Module icon (Data Module Wizard). JBuilder displays the New Data Module dialog.

2. In the New Data Module dialog, set the Class Name field to **DatabaseModule**. Click OK to continue.

3. DatabaseModule.java is now selected in the Navigation pane. Open the UI Designer by clicking the Design tab of the Content pane.

4. Add one *Database* component from the Data Access page of the Component Palette to the data module by dropping it into the Component Tree.

5. Configure the *Database* component by selecting *database1* in the Component Tree. Move to the Properties page of the Inspector, select *connection,* and click its ellipsis button to activate the Connection dialog.

6. From the Connection dialog, set Connection URL to **jdbc:odbc:dataset tutorial**, set Username to **SYSDBA**, and set Password to **masterkey**. Click the Test connection button to verify that your connection works.

7. Click OK to close the Connection dialog.

The database data module is now configured. The next step is to create one or more dataset data modules. In this demonstration, only one dataset data module is created.

8

Creating the Dataset Data Module

To create a dataset data module, perform the following steps:

1. Add a new data module to your project by selecting File|New and then double-clicking the Data Module Wizard. JBuilder displays the New Data Module dialog.

2. In the New Data Module dialog, set the Class Name field to **DataSetModule**. Click OK to continue.

3. DataSetModule.java is now selected in the Navigation pane. Open the UI Designer by clicking the Design tab of the Content pane.

4. Add one *QueryDataSet* component from the Data Access page of the Component Palette to the data module by dropping it into the Component Tree.

5. The next step in creating the dataset data module is to add an instance variable of the type *Database* to the data module, and initialize it to the instance of the database that appears in the database data module. To do this, make sure that DataSetModule.java is selected in the Navigation pane, then click the Source tab in the Content pane.

6. From the Structure pane, select the top-level node, labeled *DataSetModule*. This will move the cursor in the Editor to the data module declaration.

7. Insert a new line in the Editor immediately below the line that reads:

    ```
    public class DataSetModule implements DataModule{
    ```

8. On the newly entered line, enter the following statement:

    ```
    Database database1 = DatabaseModule.getDataModule().database1;
    ```

This statement declares a new instance variable of the type *Database*. This variable is initialized with a reference to the *Database* instance variable, *database1*, declared in the database data module (an instance of which is returned using *getDataModule*).

Although the database data module's instance variable is declared using the default visibility (it is neither public nor private), it is visible to the dataset data module since both reside in the same package. If these two data modules were declared in separate packages, it would be necessary to declare a public getter method for the data module. This getter method, which should be named *getDatabase1()*, would return the instance of *database1* in the database data module. Furthermore, it would be this getter method that you would call to initialize the *Database* instance variable on the dataset data module. If there were more than one *Database* instance variable on the data module, you would need to declare one public getter method for each *Database* instance variable.

TIP: You should consider creating public getter methods for each database in your database data module anyway. Doing so is in keeping with the spirit of Java, and gives you a means to use your database data modules from other packages in the future without further modification. The database data module defined in the databasemodule project on the code disk includes such a method. This method is declared as follows:

```
public borland.jbcl.dataset.Database getDatabase1() {
  return database1;
}
```

Now that the *Database* is available to the dataset data module, you can define the query dataset's *query* property.

9. Click the Design tab of the Content pane and then select *queryDataSet1* in the Component Tree.

10. Move to the Properties page of the Inspector and select the *query* property, and click its ellipsis button to activate the Query dialog.

11. Unfortunately, in this initial version of JBuilder the Query dialog is not capable of recognizing the *Database* instance that you just created in step 8. Consequently, you will not be able to set the database using the Database field's drop-down list on the Query dialog. Setting the database for the *QueryDescriptor* used to set the query must be done in code. (Doing this is described in step 14.) However, you can set all other properties available on the Query dialog. Enter the following statement in the SQL Statement field:

```
SELECT * FROM CUSTOMER
```

12. Since the Database option was not set, it is not possible to test this query. Continue as if the query is successful by clicking the OK button on the Query dialog.

13. Accepting the Query dialog causes JBuilder to enter the following line of code in the *jbInit()* method:

```
queryDataSet1.setQuery(
  new borland.jbcl.dataset.QueryDescriptor(null,
  "SELECT * FROM CUSTOMER", null, true, false));
```

14. This statement is correctly formed in all respects, except that **null** appears as the first actual parameter of the *QueryDescriptor* constructor. Here is where you need to manually place your reference to the *Database* instance variable. To do this, erase the first occurrence of **null**, and replace it with the variable name **database1**. (If you gave your

8

Database instance variable a different name in step 8, use that name instead.) Your revised *setQuery()* method call should look like the following:

```
queryDataSet1.setQuery(
  new borland.jbcl.dataset.QueryDescriptor(database1,
  "SELECT * FROM CUSTOMER", null, true, false));
```

Your dataset data module is now complete. Each time you instantiate a new instance of this data module, it will create and execute a new instance of the query dataset. However, regardless of how many of these query datasets you create, they all will share the common database, permitting all of them to use a single connection to your database server (if the data you are accessing is on a database server).

The following is the completed source code for the dataset data module:

```
package osborne.jbe.databasemodule1;

import java.awt.*;
import java.awt.event.*;
import borland.jbcl.layout.*;
import borland.jbcl.control.*;
import borland.jbcl.dataset.*;

public class DataSetModule implements DataModule{
  Database database1 = DatabaseModule.getDataModule().database1;
  private static DataSetModule myDM;
  QueryDataSet queryDataSet1 = new QueryDataSet();

  public DataSetModule() {
    try {
      jbInit();
    }
    catch (Exception e) {
      e.printStackTrace();
    }
  }

  void jbInit() throws Exception{
    queryDataSet1.setQuery(
      new borland.jbcl.dataset.QueryDescriptor(database1,
      SELECT * FROM CUSTOMER", null, true, false));
  }

  static public DataSetModule getDataModule() {
    if (myDM == null)
      myDM = new DataSetModule();
```

```
      return myDM;
  }

  public borland.jbcl.dataset.QueryDataSet getQueryDataSet1() {
    return queryDataSet1;
  }
}
```

Using a Dataset Data Module

In the preceding section, a database data module as well as a dataset data module were configured. The following steps demonstrate the use of a dataset module. These steps are similar to the preceding steps listed in the section entitled "Using Multi-Instance Data Modules." However, this description, with the appropriate modifications, will be repeated here since it is brief.

1. Add a new frame to the project. Follow the steps described in the earlier section in this chapter entitled "Sharing a Data Module with Another Frame." The only variation you should employ is in step 6, where you add an instance variable for the data module to *Frame2*. Instead of initializing the data module instance variable to an existing dataset data module (if it exists), you want to initialize it with a new instance of the dataset data module. You do this by calling the dataset data module's constructor in the initializer part of the *DataModule* declaration. Therefore, instead of entering the line of code shown in step 6 of "Sharing a Data Module with Another Frame," enter the following line of code:

   ```
   DataSetModule datamod = new DataSetModule();
   ```

2. Once you have worked through all 10 steps described previously in "Sharing a Data Module with Another Frame," you will want to add code to *Frame1* that will permit you to display *Frame2*. To do this, return to *Frame1* by selecting Frame1.java in the Navigation pane. Click the Design tab to open the UI Designer, and double-click *menuBar1* in the Component Tree.

3. In the Menu Designer, insert a new menu between File and Help. For the label of this new menu, enter **View**. (See Chapter 3 for more information on creating and modifying menus.)

4. Add a new menu item to the View menu. Set the label of this menu item to **Record**.

5. With the menu item labeled Record still selected (select it if it is not selected), move to the Events page of the Inspector and add an *actionPerformed* event handler. Add the following code to the method assigned to this event handler by JBuilder:

8

```
void menuItem1_actionPerformed(ActionEvent e) {
    Frame2 frame = new Frame2();
    frame.pack();
    frame.setVisible(true);
}
```

This example is now complete. Save your project and then run it by clicking the Run button in JBuilder's toolbar. When *Frame1* opens, select View|Record. After a moment, an instance of *Frame2* appears. Return to *Frame1* and select View|Record again. Repeat this step once more to open a third instance of *Frame2*. Unlike the preceding example of a multiple-instance data module, this project permits three or more different frames containing data to be displayed simultaneously, as shown in Figure 8-9. Each of these frames has its own cursor, since each uses a separate instance of the query dataset. Due to the single-instance database data module, however, they share a common database.

Creating Master-Detail Views

The databases that you create using JBuilder are often relational databases. Relational databases store data in two or more related tables. For example, customer information is stored in a customer table, employee information is stored in an employee table, and sales information is stored in a sales table.

Since these multiple tables are related, it is natural to want to display one record from one table alongside one or more related records from another

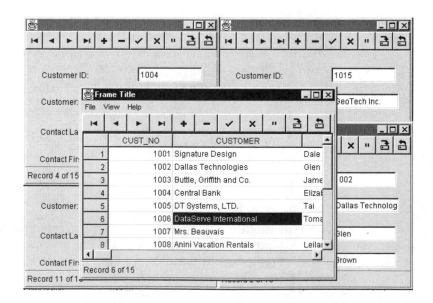

Many frames and many datasets using a single database

Figure 8-9.

table. For example, you might want to view the record for a single customer, and at the same time see that customer's sales records. This type of data view is referred to as a one-to-many view or a master-detail view.

The datasets in JBuilder are designed to permit you to easily create master-detail views of your data. In fact, building a basic master-detail view requires no code at all. All of the necessary configuration can be done using the properties of the storage datasets you use.

Creating a Single-Frame Master-Detail View

The following steps demonstrate how to create a master-detail view on a single frame. They begin by setting up the project. Next, the master-detail data module is created. Finally, the frame on which the master-detail view will be displayed is designed.

 NOTE: While the following steps could make use of a database data module and a dataset data module, as described in the preceding section, this was not done in this case in order to simplify the demonstration. If you want, you can modify the demonstration to make use of a database data module.

Starting the Master-Detail Project

Use the following steps described early in this chapter in the section entitled "Creating the Initial Project," with the following modifications. First, in step 3 set the File field on the Project Wizard to **C:\JBuilder\myprojects\osborne\jbe\masterdetail\masterdetail.jpr**. Second, in step 4 set the Title field to **Master-Detail Demonstration**.

With the basic project created, you are ready to build the master-detail data module.

Creating the Master-Detail Data Module

Use the following steps to create the master-detail data module:

1. Select File|New and then double-click the Data Module icon (Data Module Wizard).
2. Accept all defaults from the Data Module Wizard. Click OK to continue.
3. With DataModule1.java selected in the Navigation pane, click the Design tab of the Content pane.
4. Click the Data Access tab of the Component Palette to display the Data Access page, then drop one *Database* component and two *QueryDataSet* components into the Component Tree.

8

5. The next steps duplicate those described earlier in this chapter in the section "Adding Components to the Data Module." Rather than repeating those steps here, return to that section and complete steps 4 through 14.

   With the database and the first query dataset configured, you are ready to configure the second query dataset. This query dataset will display the detail records.

6. Make sure that the UI Designer is displayed (click the Design tab) and select *queryDataSet2* in the Component Tree.

7. Select the *query* property on the Properties page of the Inspector and click the ellipsis to activate the Query dialog.

8. Set the Database field to database1. In the SQL Statement field, enter the following SQL statement:

   ```
   SELECT * FROM SALES WHERE (CUST_NO = :CUST_NO)
   ```

   This query is what is called a *parameterized* query. A parameterized query includes one or more parameters, which are placeholders for values that will be defined at runtime. Within a parameterized query, a parameter is a label that is preceded by a colon. In the preceding query, the parameter is :CUST_NO. In some types of parameterized queries, a parameter is indicated by a single question mark ("?"). These types of parameterized queries do not use a label. Parameterized queries that use a question mark are discussed in Chapter 9.

   When creating a detail query dataset, each label used for each parameter must match a column name in the master query dataset exactly. This requirement is satisfied in this query, since the column name CUST_NO appears in the master table CUSTOMER. Furthermore, in this query only one parameter is required, since the CUSTOMER and SALES tables are related based on only one column. However, when your master and detail tables are related based on two or more columns, you must supply one parameter for each of the associated columns.

9. Since this query includes a parameter, it is not possible to test it before defining the *masterLink* property on the Inspector. Click OK to close the Query dialog.

10. Select the *masterLink* property in the Inspector and click the ellipsis to activate the MasterLink dialog, shown in Figure 8-10.

11. Your first step is to set the Master Dataset field to the dataset that constitutes the master table of the master-detail relationship. In this case, set Master Dataset to *queryDataSet1*. Doing so will update the Master Link Columns list and the Detail Link Columns list to display the column name CUST_NO. This MasterLink dialog determined this information from the parameterized query. The only change you need

to make is to check the Delay fetch of detail records until needed checkbox. Click OK to accept the MasterLink dialog. In response, JBuilder creates a *MasterDetailDescriptor* object, which it sets to the *masterLink* property of the query dataset. It does this by adding the following line of code to the data module's *jbInit()* method:

```
queryDataSet2.setMasterLink(
  new borland.jbcl.dataset.MasterLinkDescriptor(
  queryDataSet1, new String[] {"CUST_NO"},
  new String[] {"CUST_NO"}, true));
```

The data module is now complete and the master-detail relationship for the data has now been defined. To continue with this example, you need to design the frame or frames on which to display the data. In the following section, you will learn how to create a single frame that will display rows from both the master and the detail tables. In a later section, you will learn how to display detail rows on a separate frame.

Designing the Master-Detail Frame

A frame designed to display a master-detail relationship must include one set of controls to display data from the master table and one set to display data from the detail table. In many cases, it is desirable to display only a single

Use the MasterLink dialog to link a detail *QueryDataSet* to a master *QueryDataSet*

Figure 8-10.

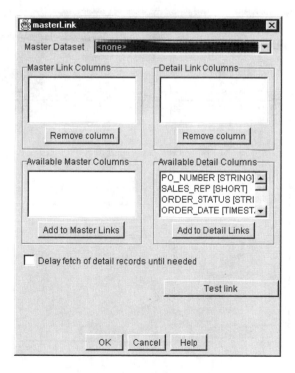

8

row from the master, and many rows from the detail. The following steps demonstrate how to create a master-detail view using a *borland.jbcl.control.SplitPanel* component.

1. *Frame1* already contains a bevel panel. From the Containers page of the Component Palette, select a *SplitPanel* component and drop it into the bevel panel.

2. Next, select a *BevelPanel* component and drop it into the *SplitPanel*. The bevel panel will align itself to take up the entire split panel.

3. Now select a *GridControl* from the Controls page of the Component Palette. Starting from the left side of the split panel, drag your mouse down and to the right, and then release the mouse button to drop a grid control into the lower part of the split panel. Your frame should now look like that shown in Figure 8-11.

4. Add two *Labels* (at a minimum), one at a time, to the bevel panel. Set the *text* property of the first label to **Customer ID:** and the second label to **Customer**. Then add a *FieldControl* to the right of each label, setting the *dataSet* property of both field controls to datmod.QueryDataSet1. Next, set the *columnName* property of the first field control to **CUST_NO**, and the *columnName* property of the second field control to **CUSTOMER**.

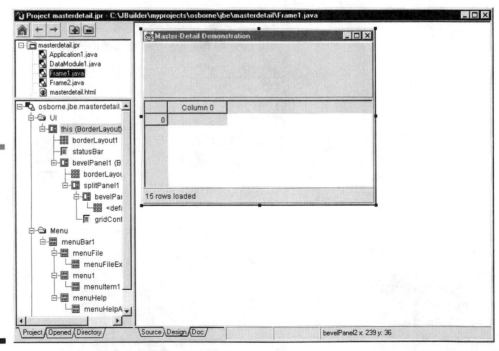

A split panel permits you to define separate, resizable regions on a frame, making it ideal for a master-detail view

Figure 8-11.

5. Now select the grid control and set its *dataSet* property to datmod.QueryDataSet2.

The master-detail view is complete. Save your work and run the project. Once running, your frame should look like that shown in Figure 8-12.

As it stands, the navigator control only works with the master records. Since this control is the only means that we have provided for the user to resolve changes made to the database, we should make this control available to both the master and the detail. With the way that this frame is designed, this can easily be achieved by adding code to the grid control's *focusGained* and *focusLost* event handlers.

6. To do this, select the grid control in the UI Designer. From the Inspector, display the Events page and add a *focusGained* event handler. Add the following code to the generated method:

```
void gridControl1_focusGained(FocusEvent e) {
  navigatorControl1.setDataSet(datmod.getQueryDataSet2());
  statusBar.setDataSet(datmod.getQueryDataSet2());
}
```

7. Now add an event handler to the *focusLost* event for the grid control and enter the following code in the generated method:

```
void gridControl1_focusLost(FocusEvent e) {
  navigatorControl1.setDataSet(datmod.getQueryDataSet1());
  statusBar.setDataSet(datmod.getQueryDataSet2());
}
```

A completed master-detail frame

Figure 8-12.

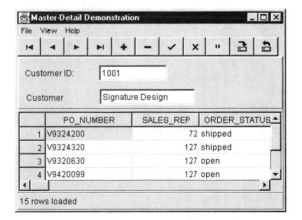

8

These two event handlers permit both the navigator control and the status bar to operate for both tables in the master-detail relationship.

Creating Master-Detail Views with Multiple Frames

It was not necessary to place the master and detail views on the same frame. In fact, sometimes it is desirable to have them displayed on separate frames. This technique is demonstrated by adding another frame to the project masterdetail.jpr, and displaying on it the sales information. While this makes the sales information redundant, since it appears on *Frame1* already, it nonetheless demonstrates an alternative approach that you can take to creating these multitable views.

1. Add another frame to the project using the Frame Wizard.

2. Add a *DataModule1* instance variable to the generated frame, and initialize it with a call to the data module's *getDataModule()* method.

3. Set the *exitOnClose* property for this frame to False, and add a *windowClosing* event handler from which you add a call to *dispose()*.

4. Set the *layout* property of the bevel panel to BorderLayout. Place a *NavigatorControl*, a *StatusBar*, and a *GridControl* on this frame, aligning them North, South, and Center, respectively.

5. Set the *dataSet* property for each of these components to datmod.QueryDataSet2.

   That's it. Since the master-detail link between the two query datasets has already been established, creating a detail view on a separate frame is as easy as creating a frame of an unlinked table. All you need to do now is add a menu item to *Frame1* and create an *actionPerformed* event handler for it that displays *Frame2*.

6. Add a new menu to the *Frame1* menu bar. Insert this menu between File and Help, and set its label to **View**. Add a menu item to this new menu, and set its label to **Sales**.

7. Add an *actionPerformed* event handler to the Sales menu item, and enter the following code in the generated method:

```
void menuItem1_actionPerformed(ActionEvent e) {
  Frame2 salesFrame = new Frame2();
  salesFrame.setSize(400,200);
  salesFrame.setVisible(true);
}
```

Configuring Data Controls

Data controls permit you to display, edit, and post changes to data retrieved from a database. Up to this point, however, the examples presented here have used only a few of the many features that the data access components offer. This section provides you with a sample of the properties and techniques that you can employ at design time to more effectively use data in your JBuilder applications. Furthermore, these techniques require the addition of no code. (For a discussion of features that rely primarily on the use of event handlers, see the following chapter.)

This section is not intended to be a complete reference to the design-time features of the database-related components. Such coverage would have required an entire book. Instead, a small selection of representative topics is considered. These topics include requiring user login, sorting data, using a *DataSetView* component, creating persistent columns, and using the *LocatorContol* component. For information on other data-related, design-time configurations, refer to the online JBCL reference.

Each of the topics covered in this section is demonstrated using a new project. Therefore, before you begin, you should use the following steps to create this new project:

1. Use the steps described earlier in this chapter in the section "Creating the Initial Project," with the following modifications. In step 3, set the File field on the Project Wizard to **C:\JBuilder\myprojects\osborne\jbe\ designtimedata\designtimedata.jpr**, and in step 4 enter **Design Time Database Features** in the Title field.

2. Add a data module. Add to it one *Database* component and two *QueryDataSet* components from the Data Access page of the Component Palette. Configure the database to use the JDBC-ODBC bridge, as described earlier in this chapter. Also, configure both query datasets as described earlier in this chapter. Make one of them use the query **SELECT * FROM CUSTOMER**, and the other use **SELECT * FROM EMPLOYEE**.

3. Add a *DataModule1* instance variable to the *Frame1* class, and initialize it using the data module's *getDataModule()* method.

4. On *Frame1*, set the bevel panel's *layout* property to BorderLayout. Place within this bevel panel one *BevelPanel* component from the Container page of the Component Palette, and one *GridControl* component from the Controls page. Using the Properties page of the Inspector set the new bevel panel's *constraints* to North, and the grid control's *constraints* to Center. Next, set the *dataSet* property of both the grid control and the status bar to datmod.queryDataSet1.

8

5. Next, place within the bevel panel that is constrained to North one
   NavigatorControl from the Controls page and one *BevelPanel* from the
   Containers page. Now, with the bevel panel in which you placed these
   two components, set its *layout* property to BorderLayout. Then set the
   navigator control's *constraints* to North, and the added bevel panel's
   constraints to Center. Finally, set the navigator control's *dataSet* property
   to datmod.queryDataSet1.

When you are done, *Frame1* should look similar to the one shown in
Figure 8-13.

NOTE: Due to the absence of any controls in the bevel panel that
appears beneath the navigator control, the grid control may be drawn too
small to be usable. In a later example in this section, a control will be placed
in the bevel panel, and it will redraw correctly. Until that happens, you
may need to resize the frame at runtime to be able to see the contents of the
grid control.

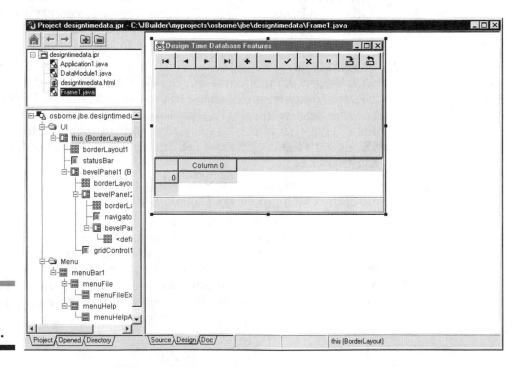

The new
project
Figure 8-13.

Requiring User Login

You establish a connection to a database using a *ConnectionDescriptor*. This object is created using the Connection dialog shown in Figure 8-14. By default, the Prompt user password checkbox is not checked, which causes JBuilder to write the password to the Java file in the call to the *ConnectionDescriptor* constructor. For example, in the preceding master-detail project example, JBuilder wrote the following line to the DataModule1.java file:

```
database1.setConnection(
  new borland.jbcl.dataset.ConnectionDescriptor(
  "jdbc:odbc:dataset tutorial", "SYSDBA", "masterkey",
  false, "sun.jdbc.odbc.JdbcOdbcDriver"));
```

Due to the inclusion of the password in the *ConnectionDescriptor* constructor, the user is not prompted for the password to the server at runtime. While this may seem like a convenience, it is a gross security violation. First, the password resides in the uncompiled Java file without being encrypted. Second, the compiled class includes this password, and unless the class file is obfuscated, the password is potentially discoverable. Third, any user using the application has unchallenged access to the database server, even those who are unauthorized to have this access. And finally, each user probably has their own password, rather than the one that you enter to access the server at design time.

When you place a checkmark in the Prompt user password checkbox, the password is omitted from the *ConnectionDescriptor* constructor, and **null** appears in its place instead. Furthermore, the user is shown the following

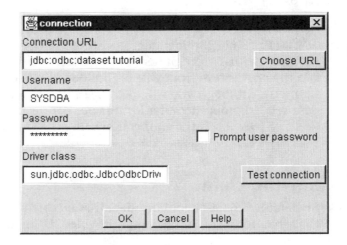

The Connection dialog
Figure 8-14.

8

dialog when the database first attempts to establish a connection to the server.

To demonstrate this in the current project, select DataModule1.java in the Navigation pane and then in design mode, select *database1* in the Component Tree. Select *connection* in the Properties page of the Inspector. Click the ellipsis that appears in the *connection* field to display the Connection dialog shown in Figure 8-14. Uncheck the Prompt user password checkbox.

Now run this project by selecting Run|Run. Before *Frame1* is displayed, the password dialog appears. Enter **masterkey** in the password field and click OK to continue. If you typed the password correctly, the application will continue loading normally. If you fail to enter a correct password, the database is not opened.

As a rule, you should ensure that the Prompt user password checkbox is checked on the Connection dialog. Although this means that you must explicitly open the Connection dialog and enter the password to the server each time you begin working on your project (if you want to access the data at design time), you will not be inadvertently exposing the database's password to discovery.

NOTE: Since JBuilder does not store the password when you check Prompt user password, it losses its connection to the database each time you run the application from within JBuilder. While this is annoying, it is harmless. Although you will likely see error messages when setting data-related properties after losing your connection, you can either ignore them or reestablish the connection using the Connection dialog.

Sorting Data

By default, a dataset contains data that is sorted by the sort order defined in the table from which the data is provided. Using the *sort* property on the

Properties page of the Inspector, you can specify that the data be sorted on one or more fields. (The *sort* property makes use of a reference to a *SortDescriptor*.) This sort can be in either ascending or descending order, as well as be either case sensitive or not.

To demonstrate the use of a sort descriptor, select *queryDataSet1* (from the data module) in the Component Tree and then select the *sort* property in the Properties page of the Inspector. Click the ellipsis that appears to display the Sort dialog shown in Figure 8-15.

The Sort dialog lists the currently defined columns in the Available columns list, and the columns that define a custom sort order in the Sorted columns list. To define a custom sort, select the fields you want to sort on in the Available columns list and then click the Add to Sort button.

NOTE: The Available columns list will be empty, or may contain only persistent fields, if you have not executed the query associated with the selected query dataset. If no fields are displayed, close the Sort dialog, open the Query dialog (by selecting the *query* property in the Inspector and clicking the displayed ellipsis), and then click the Test query button on the Query dialog. If the query fails, you may need to select the database component being used by the query, open its Connection dialog (by selecting the *connection* property in the Inspector and clicking the displayed ellipsis), and enter the password. After doing so, you should be able to test the query successfully, and then view all available fields in the Sort dialog.

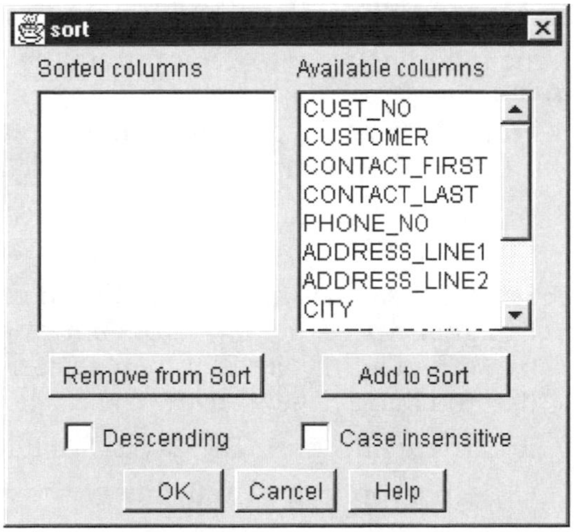

Use the Sort dialog to select a default sort order

Figure 8-15.

8

From the Sort dialog, select CONTACT_LAST and CONTACT_FIRST, one at a time, and click the Add to Sort button. Click OK when you are done.

Now run the project. When *Frame1* opens, notice that the data is sorted by CONTACT_LAST and CONTACT_FIRST.

Using DataSetView Components

JBuilder provides you with the *DataSetView* component to permit you to create customized views of your data. A dataset view gets its data from a storage dataset, but does not necessarily use that dataset's sort, nor does it necessarily display all of that dataset's columns.

There are two principal uses for a dataset view. The first is to provide a common object from which two or more data aware components get their data, permitting you to easily change which data the controls use without having to call the *setDataSet()* method of each control. For example, it is very common to include a navigator control, a grid control, and a status bar control on a frame. Assuming that you have at least two query datasets on your data module, changing these controls from displaying one dataset to another would require at least three method calls (one for each control) if you do not use a dataset view. However, if all three of these controls use a dataset view, and that dataset view points to one of the query datasets, you can switch to viewing the other dataset simply by calling the dataset view's *setStorageDataSet()* method.

The second use for a dataset view is to provide several alternative views of a single dataset. For example, you may want to extract all of a customer's records only once, but be able to display two different sort orders for this data on a single frame. To do this, you would use a single query dataset and two dataset views. Both dataset views would use the same query dataset's data, but employee different sort orders.

Use the following steps to demonstrate the use of a dataset view:

1. From the Data Access page of the Component Palette, begin by placing a *DataSetView* component onto the data module.

2. Using the Properties page of the Inspector, set the dataset view's *storageDataSet* property to queryDataSet1.

3. Select Frame1.java in the Navigation pane, and then view it in the UI Designer. Select the navigator control, the grid control, and the status bar, one at a time, and set their *dataSet* property to datmod.DataSetView1 using the Properties page of the Inspector.

4. Run the application. The CUSTOMER table is displayed in the frame.

5. Close the application and change the dataset view to use queryDataSet2.

6. Run the application again. This time it displays the employee table.

 NOTE: Changing the dataset used by a *DataSetView* at runtime through code is described in the following chapter.

Creating Persistent Columns

A persistent column is a *Column* object whose properties you have set at design time. These properties are then used at runtime to control the display and behavior of the column.

Columns define the display attributes of the columns of a dataset. In addition, they act as a store for metadata (data about the data), including the data type, precision, and so forth, of the columns in your table.

 NOTE: *Column* objects do not give you access to the data stored in the corresponding column of a table. The *ReadRow* and *ReadWriteRow* objects do that.

When you set a column at design time, JBuilder adds an instance variable for that column to your frame's class, and uses that variable to set the properties. Assuming that you set only some of the properties of a column at design time, the *Column* object defines the remaining properties at runtime based on data it retrieves from the dataset. If you do not set any properties of a column at design time, the *Column* object is not created until runtime, and all of its properties are set based on the underlying table.

There are several reasons for creating persistent columns. First, defining column properties at design time permits you to easily define and maintain the characteristics of a column, such as its display format, read-only status, color, font, and validation event handlers. Second, you can manually define the metadata at design time, and instruct the column not to download metadata at runtime. This is particularly valuable if your connection is slow, and retrieving the metadata is a time-consuming process.

The drawback to creating persistent columns is that they can affect the display order of the columns in a dataset when viewed using a tabular control, such as a *GridControl*. This occurs because each time a dataset is provided data, it deletes any column objects that are not persistent, creating new columns to hold the newly provided data. Each time this happens, the persistent columns become the first columns in the dataset, even if this order differs from the order in the table from which the data is being

8

provided. For example, the CUST_NO column is the first column in the CUSTOMER table. However, if you set a property for only one of the columns for a dataset that queries the CUSTOMER table, and that column is not the CUST_NO column, the CUST_NO column will not be the first visible column in the table if the dataset's data is displayed in a grid control.

Another side effect of using persistent columns is that their order in the table is determined by the order in which their properties are set. That is, the first column you set a property for in the UI Designer will end up being the first column in the table, the second column you set a property for will be the second, and so forth. This order is determined by the call to the dataset's *setColumns()* method, which is passed an array of columns. Fortunately, you can easily edit this method call in your code if you want your columns to appear in an order that differs from the order in which you modified your column properties.

Due to the effects produced by using persistent columns, you will want to either avoid setting properties at design time, or create persistent columns for those columns whose order you want to control. Furthermore, you can simplify this process by changing the column properties in the same order as you want them displayed in a grid control.

NOTE: If you do need to display your data in a grid control, the order of the columns only affects column-related method calls that use the column's ordinal position. Hopefully, the column-ordering effect of setting properties at design time will be modified in future versions of JBuilder.

Use the following steps to demonstrate the effects of setting column properties at design time:

1. Select DataModule1.java in the Navigation pane.

2. If you followed the preceding example and set the dataset view's *storageDataSet* property to queryDataSet2, now set its *storageDataSet* property back to queryDataSet1 using the Properties page of the Inspector.

3. Select *queryDataSet1* in the Component Tree of the Structure pane, and then expand that node by clicking this node's plus sign (+). (If no columns appear, you may have to set your database connection, and reexecute the query using the Connections dialog and the Query dialog, respectively, as described earlier in this chapter.)

4. Select CONTACT_LAST. Using the Properties page of the Inspector, set its *required* property to True and its *background* property to LightGray.

5. Select CONTACT_FIRST, and set its *required* property to True and its *background* property to LightGray using the Properties page of the Inspector.

6. JBuilder adds the following statements to the data module's declaration:

```
Column column1 = new Column();
Column column2 = new Column();
```

And the following code to its *jbInit()* method:

```
column1.setBackground(Color.lightGray);
column1.setColumnName("CONTACT_LAST");
column1.setDataType(borland.jbcl.util.Variant.STRING);
column1.setReadOnly(true);
column2.setBackground(Color.lightGray);
column2.setColumnName("CONTACT_FIRST");
column2.setDataType(borland.jbcl.util.Variant.STRING);
column2.setReadOnly(true);
queryDataSet1.setColumns(new Column[] {column2, column1});
```

The instance variables for the persistent *Column* objects also appear in the Structure pane.

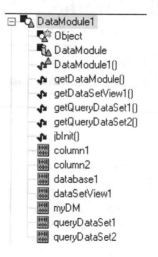

 TIP: For information about column properties, including display masks, refer to the online JBCL documentation in JBuilder.

8

Now, save your work and run the project. Notice that the CONTACT_FIRST and CONTACT_LAST columns are the first columns displayed in the *GridControl,* as shown in Figure 8-16.

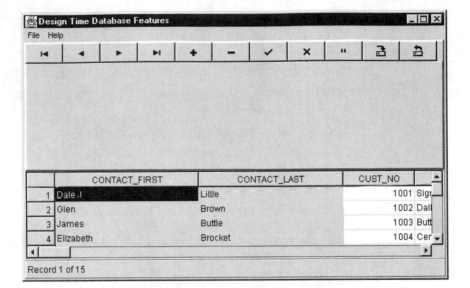

Persistent columns affect the display order of columns in a *GridControl*

Figure 8-16.

Using the LocatorControl

You use the *LocatorControl* to provide users with the ability to easily search columns in a database for a particular row of data. For example, assuming that the user knows the last name for a customer contact, you can provide a locator control that permits the user to enter the contact's last name, moving the table's cursor to the row containing that customer.

The locator control has two primary properties that affect its usage. The first is the *dataSet* property, which defines the dataset that will be searched. The second is the *columnName* property, which can be optionally set to the name of one of the columns in the dataset.

If you set the *columnName* property of a locator control, that control will only search the specified column in the dataset. If you leave this property blank, the locator control will search the current column in the database. For example, if the user moves their cursor to the Customer column in a grid control immediately before entering a value in a locator control, the locator control will search the Customer column for the entered value. By comparison, if the user moves their cursor to the CUST_NO column, the locator control will then search that column.

When searching on a text column, the locator control performs an incremental search of the table. Specifically, it will perform a best-match locate after each character is entered. If the user first presses the letter **G**, the locator control will locate the first row whose value starts with G (or the closest thing to it). If the next character the user enters is an **R**, the locator control finds the row that begins with GR. This search is case-insensitive if the user enters all characters in lowercase letters, and is case-sensitive otherwise.

If the column being located on is not a text field, the search is not performed until the user presses ENTER. For example, the user must press ENTER before the locator control will search in a column containing numbers or dates.

NOTE: When the value the user is entering is not an exact match to a unique value in a column, it is almost always necessary for the user to sort the column being searched. If the table being searched is displayed in a *GridControl,* the user can sort the column by clicking on the column heading.

The following steps demonstrate the use of the locator control.

1. Add a *Label* component to the bevel panel that appears immediately above the grid control. Using the Properties page of the Inspector, enter **Search for:** for this label's *text* property.

2. From the Controls page of the Component Palette, add a *LocatorControl* to the immediate right of the label. Use the Properties page of the Inspector to set this locator control's *dataSet* property to datmod.DataSetView1.

Save your work and run the application by selecting Run|Run. Move to the CUSTOMER column and click its heading to sort that column alphabetically. Once the column has been sorted, click in the CUSTOMER column in order to make it active. Now move to the locator control and enter the letter **d**. The locator control moves to the customer whose name is DT Systems, LTD. Now enter the letter **a**. The customer Dallas Technologies is selected. Finally, enter the letter **t**. The customer DataServe International is located, as shown in Figure 8-17.

NOTE: When the *LocatorControl* finds a match, the user can click the up and down arrows to find the previous and next matches.

Now move to the CUST_NO column. Click its heading to sort by CUST_NO. Type **1010** in the locator control and press ENTER. After you press ENTER, the locator control locates the record (row) whose CUST_NO value is 1010.

This section has explored only a fraction of the properties and techniques that permit you to add features to your JBuilder database applications

8

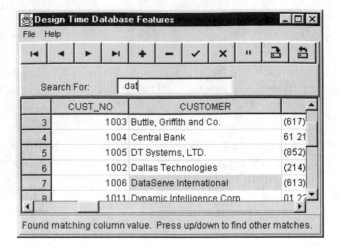

The locator
control
performs
searches on
your datasets
Figure 8-17.

without programming. The next chapter looks at a selection of features that
require you to add code to your project.

CHAPTER 9

Programming Database Functionality

The database features described in the preceding chapters were easily used with little or no need to write code, being controlled instead by the properties of the data-related objects. The advantage of controlling objects through the use of properties is that these features are easier to implement and more convenient to maintain. Fortunately, there are quite a few features that can be defined through the use of properties alone.

Nonetheless, there are some capabilities that you will want to add to your application that require the addition of code. This chapter provides you with an introduction to some of the features that must be programmed. However, please note that the techniques demonstrated here represent but a small selection of those that you can add. They were selected to provide a representative selection of programmable database features.

CD-ROM: The project files and package names for the projects for this chapter are listed at the beginning of each new example. Note, however, that jbedc is the subdirectory used on the CD-ROM. See Appendix C for information on installing and using the files on this book's CD-ROM.

Preparing for this Chapter's Examples

Each of the projects demonstrated in this chapter requires some setup. For instance, several of the applications described here need to include a frame and a data module. The frame for each of these applications needs to include a menu bar, a status bar, a grid control, and a navigator, at a minimum. An example of such a project was created in Chapter 8, in the section "Using a Data Module."

Several other projects in this chapter make use of a similar frame, but must also include a bevel panel in which the navigator control and an embedded bevel panel will appear. A frame similar to this was created in Chapter 8, in the section "Configuring Data Controls."

Because the steps to all of the projects used in this chapter, with the exception of the very last project, are described in Chapter 8, they will not be repeated here. Instead, each of the following sections in this chapter will indicate which of these two basic projects you will need to create in order to demonstrate the described technique.

You can save yourself some time when working through these examples by first creating one example of each of the two basic projects, and then making a copy of the required project for a new example project at the beginning of each demonstration. (The alternative is to simply re-create each example from scratch, using the steps described in Chapter 8. While this is more time consuming, and increases the chance of accidentally omitting steps, you might want to re-create each example from scratch simply for the practice.) The following steps describe how to create the two basic projects, and how to copy them:

1. Create the basic project described in the section "Using a Data Module" in Chapter 8. However, enter the project filename (described in step 3 of

"Creating the Initial Project") in the File field as **C:\JBuilder\myprojects\osborne\jbe\basic1\Basic1.jpr**. Complete all steps described in the sections "Creating the Initial Project," "Adding the Data Module," "Adding Components to the Data Module," "Using a Data Module from a Frame," and "Linking DataAware Controls to a Data Module." Select File|Save All to save this new project.

2. Create the second basic project, as described in the section "Configuring Data Controls" in Chapter 8. The project filename entered in the File field should be **C:\JBuilder\myprojects\osborne\jbe\basic2\Basic2.jpr**. When done, select File|Save All to save this project.

3. When a copy of one of these two projects is called for, use the Windows Explorer to create a new subdirectory under myprojects. Ideally, you would place it under myprojects\osborne\jbe*projectname*, where *projectname* is the name of the project. You do this by selecting the folder named jbe under the c:\JBuilder\myprojects\osborne folder, then selecting File|New Folder from the Explorer's main menu. Next, copy all of the files associated with the basic project (Basic1 or Basic2) to this directory, and then change the package name that appears in each of the Java files to the appropriate package name. For example, in the first demonstration described in this chapter, you will be instructed to create a project named c:\JBuilder\myprojects\osborne\jbe\savedata\savedata.jpr based on the project Basic1. To do this, you would first use the Windows Explorer to create a subdirectory named savedata under the c:\JBuilder\myprojects\osborne\jbe directory. Then, still using the Windows Explorer, you should select all of the files from the directory c:\JBuilder\myprojects\osborne\jbe\basic1, then select Edit|Copy from the Explorer's main menu. Next, select the directory named c:\JBuilder\myprojects\osborne\jbe\savedata, then select Edit|Paste from the Explorer's main menu to paste a copy of the files.

TIP: For assistance using the Windows Explorer, select Help|Help Topics from the Explorer's main menu.

Next, you need to load the Basic1 project from the c:\JBuilder\myprojects\osborne\jbe\savedata directory. Then, selecting each Java file in the project one at a time, set its package name to osborne.jbe.savedata (or whatever package is appropriate for the described project). The modified package statement will look like the following:

```
package osborne.jbe.savedata;
```

In addition, you will want to change the name of the project from Basic1 to savedata (or whatever project name the given demonstration calls for). You do this by selecting the project name Basic1.jpr in the Navigation pane and selecting File|Rename from JBuilder's menu. Enter the new project name in the File name field of the Save As dialog. Also rename the .html file associated with the project from Basic1.html to savedata.html (or the appropriate project name).

Saving Data

When a dataset is opened, its rows are automatically fetched in a process called *providing*. Any changes a user (or your code) makes to this data are stored locally, and will be lost if not explicitly resolved back to the database from which it was provided. In the database examples demonstrated so far in this book, the user is responsible for remembering to click the Save button from the navigator control in order to save their data. However, if the user forgets to perform this essential step, all of their changes to the data are lost.

There are two general steps to ensuring that a user does not lose their changes. The first is to automatically save your user's unresolved data when they close the frame on which their data aware controls are displayed. While this is the easiest approach, it is not always safe to assume that a user wants to save their data.

The second technique is to check for unresolved changes when the frame is closing. If at least one change has not been either resolved or discarded, you prevent the frame from closing and display a message to the user asking them to either resolve or cancel their changes before attempting to close the frame again. It is this technique that is demonstrated in the following example.

Detecting Unresolved Rows

In order to determine whether changes have been made to rows, it is necessary to look for deleted rows, inserted rows, and updated rows, each in a separate step. Each step requires that you pass a *DataSetView* instance to the *getDeletedRows()*, *getInsertedRows()*, or *getUpdatedRows()* methods, and then test the value returned by that dataset view's *getRowCount()* method. This technique is demonstrated in the following example, which also demonstrates how to prompt the user to save or discard changes before closing an application.

CD-ROM: The completed project savedata.jpr can be found in the osborne\jbecd\savedata subdirectory.

To create this example, use the following steps:

1. Create a new project, named **savedata.jpr**, based upon the project named Basic1.jpr, as described earlier in this chapter (or follow the steps outlined in the section "Using a Data Module" in Chapter 8 to create this new project). Set the *title* property of the frame to **Saving Data.**

2. Import the borland.jbcl.dataset package by adding the following statement to the existing **import** statements at the top of the Frame1.java file:

```
import borland.jbcl.dataset.*;
```

3. Select Frame1.java in the Navigation pane and click the Design tab on the Content pane to open the UI Designer.

4. Add a *Message* component from the Dialogs page of the Component Palette to *Frame1*. Select *message1* in the Component Tree and then move to the Properties page of the Inspector. Set its *frame* property to **this**, its *message* property to **Save or cancel changes before closing**, and its *title* property to **Problem**.

5. Next, select *this* in the Component Tree. Use the Properties page of the Inspector to set the *closeOnExit* property to False.

6. With *this* still selected, move to the Events page of the Inspector and click twice in the *windowClosing* event field and enter the following code in the generated method for this event handler:

```
void this_windowClosing(WindowEvent e) {
  DataSetView ds = new DataSetView();
  QueryDataSet qds = datmod.getQueryDataSet1();

  if (qds.isEditing()) {
    qds.post();
  }

  try {
    qds.getDeletedRows(ds);
    if (ds.getRowCount() > 0) {
      message1.show();
      return;
    }
    qds.getInsertedRows(ds);
```

9

```
    if (ds.getRowCount() > 0) {
      message1.show();
      return;
    }
    qds.getUpdatedRows(ds);
    if (ds.getRowCount() > 0) {
      message1.show();
      return;
    }
  }
  catch (DataSetException ex) {
    DataSetException.handleException(ex);
  }
  System.exit(0);
}
```

This code first ensures that any modifications to the current row are saved to the dataset before proceeding. It then checks for each type of modification using the appropriate get rows method such as *getDeletedRows()*. The get rows methods populate a dataset view with those rows from the specified dataset that have been edited in the specified way. For example, *getDeletedRows()* creates a dataset view containing the deleted rows. If this code detects that there are any rows in one of the three generated dataset views, it displays a message and exits the method. Only when no edits are detected does the *System.exit(0)* statement get executed.

7. Finally, select *menuFileExit* in the Component Tree. On the Events page of the Component Inspector, select its *actionPerformed* event handler and press ENTER to move to its associated method in the source code. Delete the existing line that reads:

```
System.exit(0);
```

and replace it with a call to the *windowClosing* event handler you created in step 6. This is done using the following code:

```
public void fileExit_actionPerformed(ActionEvent e) {
  this_windowClosing(
    new WindowEvent(this,
      java.awt.event.WindowEvent.WINDOW_CLOSING));
}
```

This code has the effect of calling the event handler you created for the frame's *windowClosing* event. As a result, the code attached to the *windowClosing* event handler will be executed whether the user attempts to close the window by clicking on the Close icon or by selecting File|Exit from the application's menu bar.

Save your project by selecting File|Save All and run it by selecting Run|Run. Next, delete a row, and then select File|Exit. The dialog shown in Figure 9-1 will warn you that you have changes that have not been resolved. Click OK to return to the application. Now select the right-most button on the Navigator to fetch new rows, which discards any unsaved changes. Select File|Exit again. This time the application closes.

Saving and Canceling Changes

The preceding example demonstrated how to detect that changes were not saved. It did not, however, demonstrate how to save or cancel those changes programmatically.

You save changes to a storage dataset either by using its *saveChanges()* method or the *saveChanges()* method of the database to which the storage dataset is connected. In the following example, the use of the database's *saveChanges()* is demonstrated, since this overloaded method permits you to automatically perform the save operation within a transaction. By beginning a transaction before saving changes, and committing the transaction when the save is complete, the changes are saved in an all-or-none fashion.

Changes are canceled by requesting a new set of rows from the database. This is done through the use of the dataset method *refresh()*. This method is also used to retrieve a new batch of rows after a call to the *saveChanges()* method. Calling *refresh()* after a call to *saveChanges()* is not a requirement, but it does serve to clear out the row changes from the cache where they are stored. In this particular demonstration, if you fail to call *refresh()* after saving changes, the *getDeletedRows()*, *getInsertedRows()*, and *getUpdatedRows()*

The application displays this Problem dialog if you attempt to close it without saving your data
Figure 9-1.

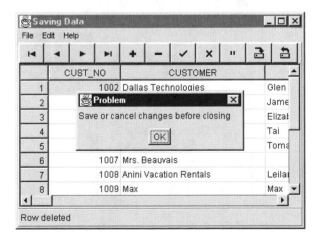

methods will still return nonempty datasets, since these methods return the rows still in the cache.

The following example builds on the project savedata.jpr by adding menu items that permit the user to save or discard their changes.

Begin with the project savedata.jpr created in the preceding section. Use the following steps to add two menu items to this project's menu bar: one that saves changes, and another that cancels changes.

1. Select Frame1.java in the Navigation pane.

2. From the Component Tree, select *menuBar1*. Right-click it and select Activate designer from the popup menu.

3. From the Menu Designer, select the File menu and then insert a new menu item immediately above the menu item labeled Exit. Enter **Save Changes** for the label of this new menu item.

4. Add another menu item below the new item labeled Save Changes. Enter **Cancel Changes** for the label of this new menu item.

5. Add a separator bar between the menu items labeled Exit and Cancel Changes. Your menu bar in the Menu Designer will now look like the one shown in Figure 9-2.

6. Select the menu item labeled Save Changes and use the Events page of the Inspector to add an *actionPerformed* event handler to it. Enter the following code to the method generated by JBuilder:

Two menu items and a separator bar added using the Menu Designer
Figure 9-2.

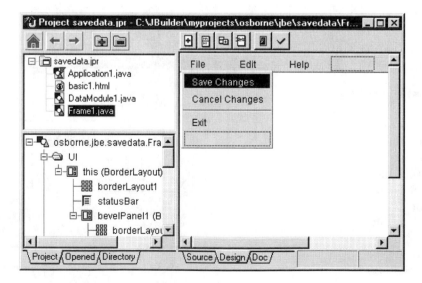

```
void menuItem1_actionPerformed(ActionEvent e) {
  Database db = datmod.getQueryDataSet1().getDatabase();
  QueryDataSet qds = datmod.getQueryDataSet1();
  try {
    db.saveChanges(new DataSet[] {qds},true);
    qds.refresh();
  }
  catch (DataSetException ex) {
    DataSetException.handleException(ex);
  }
}
```

This method operates by calling the *saveChanges()* method of the database that the query dataset is using. The version of *saveChanges()* used in this example accepts two parameters. The first parameter is an array of *DataSet*s. The second parameter is a boolean value. When this boolean parameter is passed the value **true**, a transaction is initiated prior to saving the changes and automatically committed once the changes have been posted. If the value **false** is passed, no transaction is used. After the call to *saveChanges()*, the dataset is refreshed using the *refresh()* method.

7. Now create an *actionPerformed* event handler for the menu item labeled Cancel Changes. Add the following code to the method generated by JBuilder:

```
void menuItem2_actionPerformed(ActionEvent e) {
  try {
    datmod.getQueryDataSet1().refresh();
  }
  catch (DataSetException ex) {
    DataSetException.handleException(ex);
  }
}
```

Unlike the event handler attached to the menu item labeled Save Changes, this event hander does not call *saveChanges()*. Instead, it merely calls *refresh()*, which causes all current rows to be discarded (including changes), and receives a new set of rows that are provided by the database. As a result, the changes are discarded and the cache is emptied.

Navigating a Dataset

The data that is stored in a dataset can be navigated—that is, traversed—row by row. For example, it is possible to specifically make the first row in a dataset the current row. Furthermore, you can instruct a dataset to change the current row by moving to the next row, the previous row, the last row, or a specific row, based on the row's position within the dataset. It is even possible to move to a particular row based on the contents of the row. This technique involves the use of the dataset *locate()* method.

What is particularly interesting about row navigation is that it is supported by datasets even though the database from which data is retrieved may not support it. This is because the navigation being provided by the dataset is being performed on the stored rows of the dataset, and does not involve the row position within the table itself.

Basic Table Navigation

The following example demonstrates simple table navigation by creating an event handler that will scan through all rows in the dataset. In order to scan you begin by moving to the first row in the dataset. You then move to the next row repeatedly until you have arrived on the final row in the database. This is an operation you might perform in order to perform some systematic conversion on every row in a database, such as converting the values in one of the columns to all uppercase characters. Performing this conversion is described in the following section.

Use the following steps to add an event handler to the project savedata.jpr that will scan all rows in the CUSTOMER table.

1. Starting with the project savedata.jpr created in the preceding example, select Frame1.java in the Navigation pane and then click the Design tab to display the UI Designer.

2. Select *menuBar1* in the Component Tree. Right-click it and select Activate designer from the popup menu to activate the Menu Designer.

3. Insert a new menu into the menu bar, between File and Help. Enter **Edit** for the label of this new menu.

4. Add a menu item to the Edit menu. Enter **Scan Table** for the label of this menu item.

5. With this new menu item still selected, use the Events page of the Inspector to add an *actionPerformed* event handler. Enter the following code into the method generated by JBuilder:

```
void menuItem3_actionPerformed(ActionEvent e) {
  DataSet ds = datmod.getQueryDataSet1();
  try {
    if (ds.isEmpty()) return;
    ds.first();
    while (true) {
      //do some process
      if (ds.atLast()) break;
      ds.next();
```

```
      } // while (true)
  }
  catch (DataSetException ex) {
    DataSetException.handleException(ex);
  }
}
```

As you inspect this code, keep in mind that the method *atLast()* returns **true** when you arrive at the last row, not when you attempt to move beyond it. Consequently, if you are scanning in order to perform an operation on each row, you need to perform your operation before testing *atLast()*, otherwise you might not perform your operation on the last row. Also, it is not necessary to scan an empty table.

The code presented here performs all of the necessary steps. First, it calls the dataset method *isEmpty()*, which returns **true** if the dataset has no rows. If *isEmpty()* returns **true**, the method is exited. If the table is not empty the **while** loop is entered. This loop performs the desired action, then tests to see if the cursor is on the last row. If not, *next()* is called and the loop is repeated. When the last row is detected, the loop is exited.

Save your changes by selecting File|Save All and run this project by selecting Run|Run. From the application's main menu, select Edit|Scan Table. Regardless of which row was current when you made this menu selection, the cursor will move to the first row of the dataset. Then, you will observe the grid control rapidly navigating forward one row at a time, until it eventually stops at the last row.

NOTE: While observing a table being scanned is somewhat entertaining, you typically want to avoid displaying in UI components the data from a dataset that is being scanned. You will want to avoid this because regardless of which platform that application is running on, repainting the screen after moving to a different row is a very time-consuming process and dramatically reduces the speed of the scan.

Editing a Dataset

As mentioned in the preceding section, one of the reasons for scanning a dataset is to perform some operation on the data in each row. For example, you might want to ensure that the value in a particular column is in uppercase. The following demonstration shows you how to edit the rows you are scanning.

As you learned in Chapter 7, the *StorageDataSet* class descends from *ReadWriteRow* (actually, its immediate superclass is *DataSet*, which descends directly from *ReadWriteRow*). Using the methods of a *ReadWriteRow*, it is possible to change the data in the current row.

NOTE: Rather than scanning a dataset to make changes to rows, sometimes it is far more efficient to execute a query that changes the data in your dataset. Queries almost always outperform table navigation when it comes to data transformation since a query can leverage the power of a database server to perform any required changes to the data.

While there are a number of methods that you can use, some of which permit you to assign values to an entire row in a single statement, the methods that assign values to individual columns are the easiest to use. For example, the *ReadWriteRow* class declares a group of methods whose names are *setString()*, *setDate()*, *setDouble()*, and so forth. These methods permit you to assign a value to a column, based on the data type of the column. For example, if the column is of type string, you use *setString()*. Alternatively, if the column is of type date, you use *setDate()*.

Each of these set methods is overloaded. They all include two versions, both taking two parameters each. One of the methods takes an integer and a string, while the second takes two strings. For the version that accepts an integer and a string, the integer identifies the column position of the column being edited, and the string contains the value being assigned to the column. When you use the version that accepts two strings, the first string contains the name of the column, and the second contains the value you are setting to the column.

For example, assuming that *queryDataSet1* is an instance variable that points to a query result that returns values from the CUSTOMER table, the following statement assigns the value BORLAND INTERNATIONAL to the column named CUSTOMER:

```
queryDataSet1.setString("CUSTOMER", "BORLAND INTERNATIONAL");
```

Furthermore, assuming that the CUSTOMER column is the second column in the CUSTOMER table's structure, the following version of *setString()* is equivalent to the preceding:

```
queryDataSet1.setString(1, "BORLAND INTERNATIONAL");
```

NOTE: Remember that the first column in the table is associated with the integer 0, the second is associated with the integer 1, and so forth.

Reading values from individual columns is equally simple. The *ReadRow* class declares a collection of get methods that correspond to the set methods. These methods are named *getString()*, *getDate()*, *getDouble()*, and so forth. Like their set method counterparts, these methods are also overloaded. You can pass either an integer value or a string to identify the column you want to get the value of. If you pass an integer, the integer you pass specifies the column position of the column whose value is returned. When you use the version that accepts a string parameter, the value of the column whose name matches the string you pass is returned.

NOTE: Changes made to a column are not resolved to the underlying table until you call the *saveChanges()* method.

The following steps demonstrate how to add row editing to the project savedata.jpr that you have been building up to this point in this chapter.

1. Using the Menu Designer, add two new menu items to the Edit menu on *Frame1*. Enter **Uppercase State/Province Field** for the label of the first new menu item. Enter **Lowercase State/Province Field** for the label of the second new menu item.

2. Add an *actionPerformed* event handler to the menu item labeled Uppercase State/Province Field, the first menu item added. Enter the following code in the generated method:

```
void menuItem4_actionPerformed(ActionEvent e) {
  DataSet ds = datmod.getQueryDataSet1();
  try {
    if (ds.isEmpty()) return;
    ds.first();
    while (true) {
      ds.setString("STATE_PROVINCE",
        ds.getString("STATE_PROVINCE").toUpperCase());
      ds.post();
      if (ds.atLast()) break;
      ds.next();
    } // while (true)
  }
```

```
    catch (DataSetException ex) {
      DataSetException.handleException(ex);
    }
  }
```

3. Next, add an *actionPerformed* event handler to the menu item labeled Lowercase State/Province Field. Enter the following code into the generated method:

```
void menuItem5_actionPerformed(ActionEvent e) {
  DataSet ds = datmod.getQueryDataSet1();
  try {
    if (ds.isEmpty()) return;
    ds.first();
    while (true) {
      ds.setString("STATE_PROVINCE",
        ds.getString("STATE_PROVINCE").toLowerCase());
      ds.post();
      if (ds.atLast()) break;
      ds.next();
    } // while (true)
  }
  catch (DataSetException ex) {
    DataSetException.handleException(ex);
  }
}
```

4. Save your changes by selecting File|Save All and then run the application by selecting Run|Run. Select Edit|Lowercase State/Province Field. After the scanning ends, scroll to the right until the STATE_PROVINCE field is visible. Notice that it is now in all lowercase characters. Convert the data back to its uppercase values by selecting Edit|Uppercase State/Province Field. This time, the table is scanned and the rows are converted back again.

Customizing Data Views

JBuilder provides you with a number of different ways that you can modify the view of the data that the user sees. This section provides you with an introduction to several of the techniques that you can use to customize the view of the data. These include controlling which storage dataset is used by a dataset view, creating calculated fields, and filtering datasets.

Switching Between Dataset Views at Runtime

In the preceding chapter you learned that you can use a *DataSetView* component to easily control which storage dataset's data is displayed in two or more data aware UI components. To restate the issue, if you have two or more data aware controls on a frame and you want to change them to use an alternative storage dataset, and these controls are set to use a query dataset, you need to change the dataset property of each of the controls. However, if all of the data aware controls on a frame use a dataset view as their dataset, you can simply change the dataset view to use an alternative storage dataset, thereby changing which dataset is used by all controls that use the dataset view.

In Chapter 8, you learned how to create and use a dataset view at design time. This section describes how to change the *storageDataSet* property of a dataset view at runtime, providing you with a means to easily reuse a grid control for many different tables.

CD-ROM: The completed project datasetview.jpr can be found in the osborne\jbecd\datasetview subdirectory.

To create this example, use the following steps:

1. Create a new project, named **datasetview.jpr**, based upon the project named Basic1.jpr, as described at the outset of this chapter (or follow the steps outlined in the section "Using a Data Module" in Chapter 8 to create this new project). Set the *Frame1* title to **Using DataSetViews**.

2. Select Frame1.java in the Navigation pane and then click the Source tab of the Content pane. In the Editor, add the following statement to the **import** statements in the source code:

```
import borland.jbcl.dataset.*;
```

3. Select the file DataModule1.java in the Navigation pane and click the Design tab of the Content pane to load the UI Designer. From the AWT page of the Component Palette, add one *QueryDataSet* component and one *DataSetView* to the Component Tree. Set this dataset view's *storageDataSet* property to queryDataSet1.

4. Next, select *queryDataSet2* in the Component Tree. From the Properties page of the Inspector, select *query* and click the ellipsis button to display the Query dialog. On this dialog, set the Database field to database1 and enter the following SQL statement in the SQL Statement field:

```
SELECT * FROM EMPLOYEE
```

5. Select Frame1.java in the Navigation pane, then select the Design tab of the Content pane to load the UI Designer.

6. Select the navigator control, the grid control, and the status bar, and set the *dataSet* property for each of these objects to datmod.dataSetView1.

7. Select *menuBar1* in the Component Tree, then right-click it and select Activate designer from the popup menu.

8. In the Menu Designer, add a new menu to the menu bar between the menus labeled File and Help. Enter **View** for the label of this new menu.

9. Add a new menu item to the View menu. Enter **Employee** for the label of this new menu.

10. Select the Employee menu item, then use the Events page of the Inspector to create an *actionPerformed* event handler for it. In the method generated by JBuilder, enter the following code:

```
void menuItem1_actionPerformed(ActionEvent e) {
  DataSetView1 dsv1 = datmod.getDataSetView1();
  try {
    if (menuItem1.getLabel() == "Employee") {
      menuItem1.setLabel("Customer");
      dsv1.close();
      dsv1.setStorageDataSet(datmod.getQueryDataSet2());
      dsv1.open();
    }
    else {
      menuItem1.setLabel("Employee");
      dsv1.close();
      dsv1.setStorageDataSet(datmod.getQueryDataSet1());
      dsv1.open();
    }
  }
  catch (borland.jbcl.dataset.DataSetException ex) {
    DataSetException.handleException(ex);
  }
}
```

This code uses the *label* property for the menu item under the View menu to determine which storage dataset to assign to the dataset view. If the menu item is labeled Employee, the menu item label is switched to Customer, the dataset view is closed using the *close()* method, and then *queryDataSet2* is assigned to the dataset view using the *setStorageDataSet()* method. If the label already is set to Customer, the label is changed to Employee, the dataset view is closed, and *queryDataSet1* is assigned to the dataset view. After assigning a new storage dataset to the dataset view, the dataset view is reopened using the *open()* method.

Save your work by selecting File|Save All and run this project by selecting Run|Run. Initially, the CUSTOMER table is displayed in the grid control, as shown in Figure 9-3. Both the status bar and the navigator control are defined for this table as well. Select View|Employee to switch the grid control, the navigator control, and the status bar to use the EMPLOYEE table.

Calculated Fields

Calculated fields permit you to display data in a column, even though that data is not stored in the dataset to which the column belongs. This data is calculated, often based on data in other columns in the same dataset. Consequently, calculated fields are ideal when information that is useful to the user can be calculated based on the stored data.

There are three steps to creating a calculated field. These are as follows:

1. Create a new, persistent column for a dataset.
2. Set the *calcType* property of the new column to calculated.
3. Write a *calcFields* event handler for the dataset in which this calculated column appears. The code that you add to the event handler assigns the value to the calculated field. In most cases, this value is based on one or more columns (fields) in the current row.

The following example demonstrates how you can easily create a calculated field that displays the full name of the contact person listed in the CUSTOMER table. This full name is calculated based on the data in the CONTACT_FIRST and CONTACT_LAST columns.

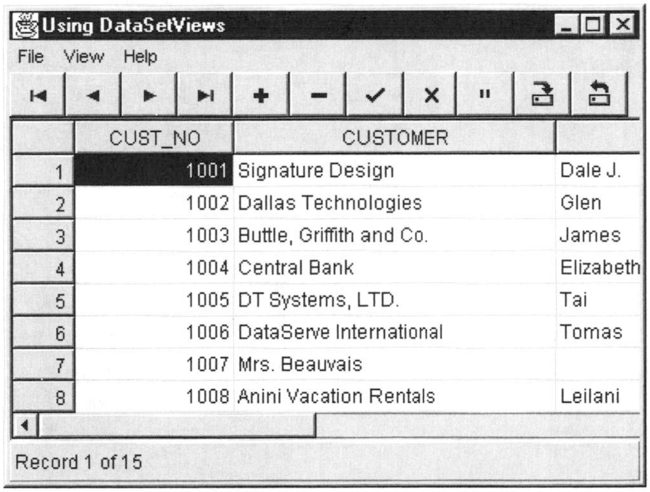

The application displaying the first of two query datasets

Figure 9-3.

1. Create a new project, named **calcfields.jpr**, based upon the project named Basic1.jpr, as described at the outset of this chapter (or follow the steps outlined in the section "Using a Data Module" in Chapter 8 to create this new project). Set the Frame1 title to **Creating a Calculated Field**.

2. Select DataModule1.java in the Navigation pane, then expand the *queryDataSet1* node in the Component Tree, as shown in Figure 9-4.

3. From this expanded node, select the node that reads <new column>.

4. In the Properties page of the Inspector, set the *columnName* property of this new column to CONTACT_NAME.

5. Still using the Properties page of the Inspector, set the *calcType* property of this new column to calculated.

6. Select *queryDataSet1* in the Component Tree, move to the Events page of the Inspector, and add a *calcFields* event handler. Enter the following code to the generated method in the source code:

```
void queryDataSet1_calcFields(ReadRow readRow,
    DataRow dataRow, boolean boolean1)
    throws DataSetException{
    dataRow.setString("CONTACT_NAME",
```

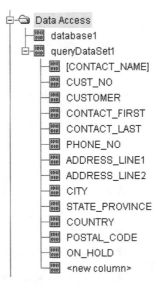

The expanded *queryDataSet1* node

Figure 9-4.

```
                    readRow.getString("CONTACT_FIRST") + " " +
                    readRow.getString("CONTACT_LAST"));
    }
```

The *calcFields* event handler is passed three parameters. The first parameter is a *ReadRow* that contains the values in the current fields. A read row is read-only, which prevents you from attempting to set values to any of the noncalculated fields in the dataset. The second parameter, a *DataRow*, contains those calculated columns to which you can set values. The final parameter is a boolean value that indicates whether the current row has been posted yet or not. When *boolean1* is true, the row has been posted. You can use this value when you only want to perform calculations only on either posted or un-posted rows.

The preceding code sets the CONTACT_NAME column in the data row parameter to a value that is a concatenation of the read row's CONTACT_FIRST and CONTACT_LAST columns.

Save this project by selecting File|Save All and then run it by selecting Run|Run. The calculated column appears as the first field of the grid control, due to its being the only persistent column in the dataset. As shown in Figure 9-5, this calculated column contains the full name of the contact, based on the data in the CONTACT_FIRST and CONTACT_LAST columns.

NOTE: Calculated columns are read-only, meaning that you cannot enter data into them.

Calculated columns are calculated based on other columns in the current row

Figure 9-5.

	CONTACT_NAME	CUST_NO	CUSTOMER
1	Dale J. Little	1001	Signature Design
2	Glen Brown	1002	Dallas Technologies
3	James Buttle	1003	Buttle, Griffith and Co.
4	Elizabeth Brocket	1004	Central Bank
5	Tai Wu	1005	DT Systems, LTD.
6	Tomas Bright	1006	DataServe International
7	Mrs. Beauvais	1007	Mrs. Beauvais
8	Leilani Briggs	1008	Anini Vacation Rentals

Creating a Calculated Field

Record 1 of 15

Data

.g a query dataset, normally all rows returned by the query, up to
.num number of rows (specified by the *maxRows* property), are
.e. However, there are times when it is desirable to retrieve all rows,
.play only a subset. For example, while all sales rows are retrieved by a
y, creating a consistent view of the table contents, it is possible to limit
display of rows to a subset of those retrieved. JBuilder's filtering feature
.sily provides this capability.

A filter only affects the display of rows. That is, it neither adds nor removes
rows from the underlying table. Furthermore, the filter is automatically
reexecuted for each row as it is added to a query dataset. If you add a new
row to a filtered query dataset, but the filter does not include the data
contained in the added row, that new row will apparently disappear when it
is posted, even though it will be resolved to the underlying table if and when
the inserts are resolved.

You define a filter using the *filterRow* event handler associated with a dataset.
This event handler is executed for each row that JBuilder is attempting to
display, and it permits you to either permit or deny the display of that row.

The *filterRow* event handler generated by JBuilder is passed two parameters.
The first is a *ReadRow* parameter, and it provides you with access to the
contents of the row. You use this information to inspect the data to
determine if it contains values that you want to display in the filtered view.
The second parameter is a *RowFilterResponse* instance. If you want to permit
the row for which the *rowFilter* event handler is executing to display, you call
the row filter response method *add()*. The *RowFilterResponse* class also has an
ignore() method, but ignoring a row is the default response, which makes the
ignore() method one that you rarely need to call.

The following example demonstrates how to create a *rowFilter* event handler
to display a subset of the provided rows. In this case, the SALES table will be
used. Although the query dataset will retrieve all rows from this table, the
project that you create will permit a user to choose to display only the
shipped rows, open rows, or waiting rows, or any combination of these rows.

CD-ROM: The completed project filterdata.jpr can be found in the
osborne\jbecd\filterdata subdirectory.

To create this example, use the following steps:

1. Create a new project, named **filterdata.jpr**, based upon the project
   named Basic2.jpr, as described at the outset of this chapter (or follow

the steps outlined in the section "Configuring Data Controls" in Chapter 8 to create this new project). Set the *Frame1* title to **Filtering Data Demonstration**.

2. The frame of this application must have a means of communicating which rows to display. The user will control this through the use of *CheckboxControl* components that you will place on that frame. In order to permit these changes to be transmitted to the data module, you need to declare a boolean array for the data module, as well as a set method that can be called to set elements of this array. To do this, select DataModule1.java in the Navigation pane, then select the Source tab of the Content pane. Add the following array declaration to the data module's class declaration:

```
boolean[] checkFlags = {true, true, true};
```

When done, your data module declaration should look like this:

```
public class DataModule1 implements DataModule{
  private static DataModule1 myDM;
  Database database1 = new Database();
  QueryDataSet queryDataSet1 = new QueryDataSet();
  QueryDataSet queryDataSet2 = new QueryDataSet();
  boolean[] checkFlags = {true, true, true};
}
```

3. Next, add a public method that permits the elements of the *checkFlags* array to be changed. To do this, add the following public method to the *DataModule1()* class:

```
public void setCheckFlags(int flag, boolean newValue) {
  checkFlags[flag] = newValue;
}
```

4. Now click the Design tab of the Content pane to activate the UI Designer. Select *queryDataSet1* in the Structure pane, then move to the Properties page of the Inspector. Select *query* in the Inspector and then click the ellipsis button to display the Query dialog. Change the statement in the SQL Statement field to the following:

```
SELECT * FROM SALES
```

5. With *queryDataSet1* still selected, move to the Events page of the Inspector and select the *filterRow* event field to generate its event handler. Enter the following code in the generated method:

```
void queryDataSet1_filterRow(ReadRow readRow,
  RowFilterResponse rowFilterResponse)
  throws DataSetException{
```

9

```
if (readRow.getString("ORDER_STATUS").
  equals("open") && checkFlags[0]) {
  rowFilterResponse.add();
} else if (readRow.getString("ORDER_STATUS").
  equals("shipped") && checkFlags[1]) {
  rowFilterResponse.add();
} else if (readRow.getString("ORDER_STATUS").
  equals("waiting") && checkFlags[2]) {
  rowFilterResponse.add();
}
}
```

This event handler evaluates the contents of the current row's ORDER_STATUS field. If the field contains a value that corresponds to a flag in the *checkFlags* array, the row filter response *add()* method is called. Any row for which this method is not called does not appear in the query dataset.

6. Now select *Frame1* in the Structure pane. Add the following statement to the list of **import** statements in Frame1.java:

```
import borland.jbcl.dataset.*;
```

7. Next, click the Design tab to activate the UI Designer for *Frame1*. Add three *CheckBoxControl* components to the bevel panel that appears beneath the navigator control. Set the *label* property of *checkboxControl1*, *checkboxControl2*, and *checkboxControl3* to **open**, **shipped**, and **waiting**, respectively. Set the *checked* property of each to True.

Frame1 should now look like the one shown in Figure 9-6.

8. Add an *itemStateChanged* event handler to *checkboxControl1,* and enter the following code into the generated method:

```
void checkboxControl1_itemStateChanged(ItemEvent e) {
  try {
    datmod.setCheckFlags(0,
      checkboxControl1.isChecked());
    datmod.getQueryDataSet1().refilter();
  }
  catch (DataSetException ex) {
    DataSetException.handleException(ex);
  }
}
```

9. Add a similar event handler to *checkboxControl2* and *checkboxControl3*. The one difference is the parameters you pass to the *setCheckFlags()* method. The method you enter for *checkboxControl2* should call

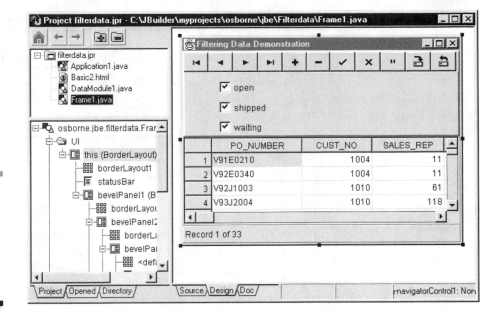

```
setCheckFlags(1,checkboxControl2.isChecked());
```

and the method you enter for *checkboxControl3* should call

```
setCheckFlags(2,checkboxControl3.isChecked());
```

The effect of these three event handlers is to set the corresponding element of the *checkFlags* array, and then call the *refilter()* method for the query dataset. Calling *refilter()* causes the *rowFilter* event handler to reexecute. When this event handler reexecutes, it uses the new values in the *checkFlags* array to control which rows are visible.

This project is complete. Save your work by selecting File|Save All and then run the project by selecting Run|Run. When *Frame1* is displayed, resize it so that you can see the ORDER_STATUS field. Initially, all rows will be displayed, as shown in Figure 9-7. Uncheck the checkbox labeled shipped. The corresponding flag is set to false, and the filter is reexecuted. As a result, the shipped orders are not added, and are absent from the filter. The filtered data is displayed in Figure 9-8.

Customizing Queries

The datasets used in the examples described in this book have all been *QueryDataSet* components. This class provides you with the greatest flexibility in accessing and manipulating data. For example, you can use a single *QueryDataSet* component to generate any number of different queries,

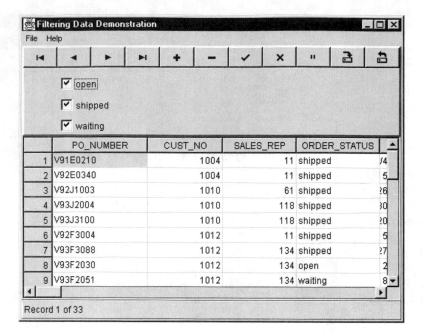

When you first
run the
application,
all rows are
displayed
Figure 9-7.

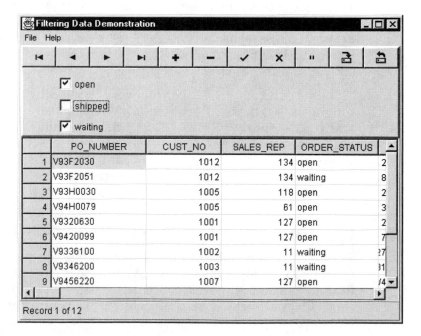

Uncheck the
shipped
checkbox to
suppress the
display of
shipped rows
Figure 9-8.

including queries that select specific rows from a table, queries that create new tables, queries that join data from multiple tables, and so forth. This is because a SQL (Structured Query Language) statement defines a query's operation. SQL is a powerful, standardized language for defining and manipulating data.

NOTE: The SQL statements used in this book have been very similar, typically only selecting all columns and rows from a specified table. While this use has been intentional, it fails to convey the richness of SQL. If you are unfamiliar with using SQL, you should consult one of the many good books that discuss SQL in detail. Since JDBC uses ANSI92-compliant SQL, make sure that the book you choose covers this version of SQL.

The following sections describe how to get more out of the query datasets you use in your JBuilder applications. In the first section, you will learn how to dynamically change your SQL statements at runtime. This approach provides you with the greatest level of flexibility. In the second section, you will learn how to create parameterized queries. While parameterized queries are less flexible than dynamically changed queries, they provide exceptional performance, in addition to giving you enough flexibility to satisfy most of your querying needs.

Defining Query Strings

The SQL statement that you enter into the Query dialog is a string. JBuilder uses this string to define your query as it appears in the call to the *QueryDescriptor* constructor that it uses in the *setQuery()* method of your query dataset. For example, the *setQuery()* statement that JBuilder generates for the query dataset created in the project Basic1.jpr looks like the following:

```
queryDataSet1.setQuery(
  new borland.jbcl.dataset.QueryDescriptor(database1,
  "SELECT * FROM CUSTOMER", null, true, false));
```

The *QueryDescriptor* constructor takes five arguments. The first is the database that contains the tables being queried, and the second is a string that specifies the query statements to execute. The third parameter is a *ParameterRow* object, which is **null** in the preceding example (since this query is not a parameterized query. Parameterized queries are discussed in the following section). The fourth parameter is a boolean value that indicates whether or not the query should be executed automatically when the query dataset is opened. The fifth parameter controls whether the query will be executed asynchronously (in a separate thread). The preceding statement specifies that the query will execute automatically when opened, and will not execute asynchronously.

In order to create a completely flexible query, you can call the *setQuery()* method from an event handler, and pass it a new *QueryDescriptor* constructor. Within this constructor, the string that appears in the second parameter can consist of any valid string, including a string literal or even one that you construct by concatenating several strings together. The only requirement is that your string must constitute a syntactically correct SQL statement. If so, the next time the query is executed, the results produced will be those specified by the string.

There are four steps to changing the SQL statements for a query at runtime. These are as follows:

1. Close the query dataset using the *close()* method.

2. Call the query dataset's *setQuery()* method, passing to it a new *QueryDescriptor* object. Include in the second parameter of the *QueryDescriptor* the string that defines the new query. The SQL statement defined by this string can be any valid SQL statement, even one completely unrelated to the previous SQL statements used in the last execution of the query dataset.

3. Use the query dataset's *executeQuery()* method to reexecute the query.

4. Use the query dataset's *open()* method to reopen the query dataset.

Use the following steps to create a project that dynamically changes the contents of a query dataset at runtime, reexecuting the new query and then displaying the results to the user.

CD-ROM: The completed project dynamicquery.jpr can be found in the osborne\jbecd\dynamicquery subdirectory.

1. Create a new project, named **dynamicquery.jpr**, based upon the project named Basic1.jpr, as described at the outset of this chapter (or follow the steps outlined in the section "Using a Data Module" in Chapter 8 to create this new project). Set the *Frame1* title to **Dynamic Query Demonstration**.

2. Select Frame1.java in the Navigation pane and then add the following statement to the list of **import** statements in Frame1.java:

```
import borland.jbcl.dataset.*;
```

3. Click the Design tab on the Content pane to load the UI Designer.

4. Select *menuBar1* in the Component Tree. Right-click it and select Activate designer from the popup menu to load the Menu Designer. In the Menu Designer, add a new menu to the menu bar between the menus labeled File and Help. Enter **View** for the label of this new menu.

5. Add a new menu item to the View menu. Enter **Employee** for the label of this menu item.

6. Select the Employee menu item, then use the Events page of the Inspector to create an *actionPerformed* event handler for it. In the method generated by JBuilder, enter the following code:

```
void menuItem1_actionPerformed(ActionEvent e) {
  QueryDataSet qds = datmod.getQueryDataSet1();
  Database db = qds.getDatabase();
  try {
    qds.close();
    if (menuItem1.getLabel().equals("Customer")) {
      menuItem1.setLabel("Employee");
      qds.setQuery(new QueryDescriptor(db,
        "SELECT * FROM CUSTOMER",null,false,false));
    } else {
      menuItem1.setLabel("Customer");
      qds.setQuery(new QueryDescriptor(db,
        "SELECT * FROM EMPLOYEE",null,false,false));
    }
    qds.executeQuery();
    qds.open();
  }
  catch (DataSetException ex) {
    DataSetException.handleException(ex);
  }
  gridControl1.setDataSet(qds);
}
```

The code segment begins by closing the query dataset using a call to its *close()* method. Then, the code uses the *label* property of the newly created menu item to determine which table is currently being displayed in the grid control. If the label reads Customer, it is necessary to change the query so that it displays the CUSTOMER table. This is done by calling *setQuery()*, passing to it the *QueryDescriptor*. The *QueryDescriptor,* in this case, defines a query that returns all rows and columns from the CUSTOMER table.

This *QueryDescriptor* also specifies no *ParameterRow* object (passing **null** instead), and indicates that the query should not be opened automatically, nor should it be executed asynchronously.

9

If the menu item's label is not Customer, a different *QueryDescriptor* is passed in the call to the *setQuery()* method. This *QueryDescriptor* defines a query that selects all rows and all columns from the EMPLOYEE table.

Once the new *QueryDescriptor* is set using *setQuery()*, the *executeQuery()* method executes the new query, and then the query dataset is opened again. Finally, the grid control's *setDataSet()* method is called to reset the grid control to the query dataset. Technically, you should not have to perform this last step. However, if you fail to call the grid control's *setDataSet()* method, the grid never displays the results of the new query.

Select File|Save All to save this project and then select Run|Run. Once the application is running, select View|Employee. The query is changed dynamically, switching from the CUSTOMER table to the EMPLOYEE table. Now, select View|Customer. The query is again redefined, and the view changes from the EMPLOYEE table back to the CUSTOMER table.

It should be noted that this approach produces a result similar to the one shown earlier in this chapter in the section "Switching Between Dataset Views at Runtime." However, while these two techniques produce similar results, the underlying mechanism is dramatically different. When switching between dataset views, the dataset view is simply switching between open queries, each of which displays data retrieved when the query was opened. Using this dynamic query technique, a single query is reexecuted repeatedly, forcing new data to be fetched with each execution. Consequently, using dataset views permits the switching between two or more static datasets, while generating queries dynamically permits complete flexibility in the selection of data rows.

Parameterized Queries

A parameterized query is one that permits flexible row selection using a parameter in the WHERE clause of a SQL statement. A parameter is a placeholder for a value in the WHERE clause and need not be defined until just before the query is executed.

There are two types of parameters that can appear in a parameterized query, parameters based on name and parameters based on position. Parameters based on name are identified by placeholders that appear as a text label preceded by a colon. For instance, in the following SQL statement the parameter is named **cust**:

```
SELECT * FROM CUSTOMER
WHERE (CUST_NO = :cust)
```

Position parameters do not have labels. Instead, they are represented by question marks (?). The following SQL statement is similar to the preceding one, except that it uses a position parameter rather than a named parameter:

```
SELECT * FROM CUSTOMER
WHERE (CUST_NO = ?)
```

Parameterized queries can use either named parameters or position parameters, but not both in the same SQL statement.

In order to execute a parameterized query, it is necessary to supply a value for each parameter prior to the execution of the query. This is done using a *ParameterRow* object. This object, which is a *ReadWriteRow* descendant, must include exactly one column for each parameter required by the query.

You define a *ParameterRow* object for a query by passing it to the *QueryDescriptor* constructor. As you might recall from the preceding section, the third argument in the *QueryDescriptor* constructor is a *ParameterRow* object (**null** was passed in the examples presented in that section). Depending on the types of parameters used in the query, the values assigned to the columns of the *ParameterRow* object are assigned to the query's parameters either by name or by ordinal position.

Parameterized queries are less flexible than dynamic queries, since they can be designed to affect row selection only. (Every aspect of a dynamic query can be changed, including which tables are queries and even the type of operation. For example, a dynamic query can at one moment be a SELECT query, and a DELETE query in the next.) However, parameterized queries that are executed repeatedly are executed much faster than dynamic queries. This occurs because it is not necessary for a parameterized query to be *prepared* between one execution and the next, even when the values of the parameters change. (Preparation is a necessary, two-step process that prepares the server for executing a query.) By comparison, a dynamic query must be prepared each time it is executed. In addition, unlike with dynamic queries, a parameterized query does not have to be closed before it is executed.

The following steps demonstrate how to create and execute a parameterized query. However, in order to simplify this example, it is necessary to create a project that places the database and query dataset on the frame itself, and not on a data module. (Using a data module for this example would require many more steps, and this example has enough steps as it is. However, in practice, you will want to use a data module for your parameterized queries.)

CD-ROM: The completed project paramquery.jpr can be found in the osborne\jbecd\paramquery subdirectory.

1. Begin by closing all projects.

2. Select File|New to display the New page of the Object Gallery. Double-click the Application icon.

3. From the Project Wizard dialog, set the File field to **C:\JBuilder\myprojects\osborne\jbe\paramquery\paramquery .jpr** and then click Finish to display the Application Wizard.

4. Click the Next button to move to the Step 2 page of the Application Wizard. Set the Title field to **Parameterized Query Demonstration**. Next, enable the Generate menu bar, Generate status bar, and Center frame on screen checkboxes. Click Finish to complete the Application Wizard.

5. Select Frame1.java in the Navigation pane. In the Editor, add the following statement to the **import** statements in the source file:

    ```
    import borland.jbcl.dataset.*;
    ```

6. Click the Design tab to open the UI Designer. From the Data Access page of the Component Palette, drop a *Database* and a *QueryDataSet* component into the Component Tree.

7. Select the *Database* component in the Component Tree. From the Properties page of the Inspector, select *connection* and click the ellipsis button to display the Connection dialog.

8. From the Connection dialog, click Choose URL and select jdbc:odbc:dataset tutorial. Next, enter **SYSDBA** in the UserName field and in the Password field enter **masterkey**. Return to the UI Designer by clicking OK.

9. Now select the *QueryDataSet* in the Component Tree.

10. Select *query* in the Properties page of the Inspector and then click the ellipsis button to display the Query dialog.

11. Set the Database field to database1. In the SQL Statement field, enter the following SQL statement:

    ```
    SELECT * FROM CUSTOMER
      WHERE (COUNTRY = :CTRY)
    ```

12. Click OK to return to the UI Designer.

13. Select the status bar in the UI Designer, and set its *dataSet* property to queryDataSet1 using the Properties page of the Inspector.

14. Select the bevel panel in the UI Designer and set its *layout* property to BorderLayout using the Properties page of the Inspector.

15. Place into this bevel panel one new bevel panel, constrained to North, and a grid control, constrained to Center. (Set the *constraints* using the Properties page of the Inspector.) Your frame should now look like the one shown in Figure 9-9.

16. Place a *Label* from the AWT page of the Component Palette within the bevel panel and align it to North. Set this label's *text* property to Country.

17. Next, from the Controls page of the Component Palette, place a *FieldControl* component to the right of the label. Set the field control's *text* property to **USA**.

18. Now, from the AWT page place a *Button* to the right of the field control. Enter **Get Customers From Country** for the button's *label* property. Your frame should now look like the one shown in Figure 9-10.

19. Select Frame1.java in the Navigation pane again. Click the Source tab to display it in the Editor. Add a *ParameterRow* instance variable named *pm* to the frame's class declaration. This line should look like the following:

```
ParameterRow pm = new ParameterRow();
```

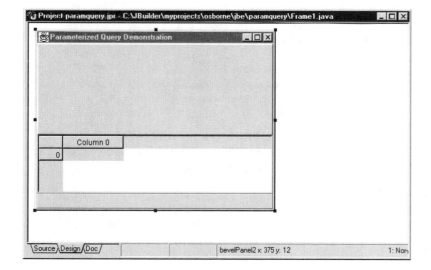

A bevel panel and a grid control are placed in a bevel panel

Figure 9-9.

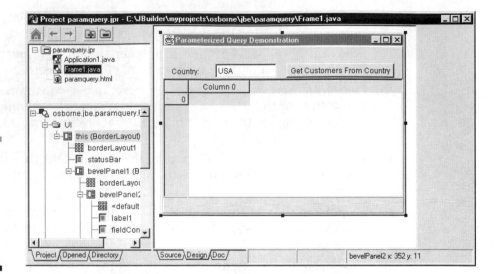

The controls
are in place
for the
parameterized
query
demonstration
Figure 9-10.

This is how your frame's class declaration should now look:

```
public class Frame1 extends DecoratedFrame {
  BorderLayout borderLayout1 = new BorderLayout();
  BevelPanel bevelPanel1 = new BevelPanel();
  MenuBar menuBar1 = new MenuBar();
  Menu menuFile = new Menu();
  MenuItem menuFileExit = new MenuItem();
  Menu menuHelp = new Menu();
  MenuItem menuHelpAbout = new MenuItem();
  StatusBar statusBar = new StatusBar();
  Database database1 = new Database();
  QueryDataSet queryDataSet1 = new QueryDataSet();
  BorderLayout borderLayout2 = new BorderLayout();
  BevelPanel bevelPanel2 = new BevelPanel();
  GridControl gridControl1 = new GridControl();
  Label label1 = new Label();
  FieldControl fieldControl1 = new FieldControl();
  Button button1 = new Button();
  ParameterRow pm = new ParameterRow();
```

20. Now move to the *jbInit()* method. Here, you need to initialize the
parameter row. This needs to be done before the *setQuery()* statement is
executed. Locate the statement that reads

```
queryDataSet1.setQuery(
  new borland.jbcl.dataset.QueryDescriptor(
  database1, "SELECT * FROM CUSTOMER
  WHERE (COUNTRY = :CTRY)", null, true, false));
```

21. Begin inserting in the line preceding this *setQuery()* statement. These inserted lines should contain the following code:

```
pm.addColumn(new Column("CTRY", "",
  borland.jbcl.util.Variant.STRING));
pm.setString("CTRY","USA");
```

The first line adds a column named CTRY to the parameter row. This column name matches the named parameter that appears in the query. The last line sets the value of this parameter to the initial value USA.

22. Next, modify the *setQuery()* statement to use the parameter row that you defined in the preceding code. Replace the reference to **null** with the name of the parameter row. Also, change the fourth parameter, which controls when the query is executed, to **false**. The modified call to *setQuery()* should look like the following:

```
queryDataSet1.setQuery(
  new borland.jbcl.dataset.QueryDescriptor(
  database1, "SELECT * FROM CUSTOMER
  WHERE (COUNTRY = :CTRY)", pm, false, false));
```

23. Finally, you need to add an event handler to the button placed on the frame earlier in this example. Click the Design tab of the Content pane to open the UI Designer. Select the button, move to the Events page of the Inspector, and add an *actionPerformed* event handler. Enter the following code into the generated method:

```
void button1_actionPerformed(ActionEvent e) {
  try {
    pm.setString("CTRY",fieldControl1.getText());
    queryDataSet1.executeQuery();
  }
  catch (DataSetException ex){
    DataSetException.handleException(ex);
  }
  gridControl1.setDataSet(queryDataSet1);
}
```

This code assigns the value the user enters into the field control to the CTRY column of the parameter row. The query is then reexecuted by calling the query dataset's *executeQuery()* method. Finally, the grid control's *setDataSet()* method is called to force the grid control to update its display.

The project is now complete. Select File|Save All to save your work and run the project by selecting Run|Run. When it is first displayed, the grid control is blank, as shown in Figure 9-11, since the query has not yet been executed.

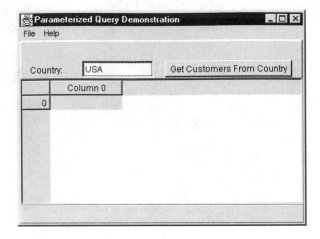

The grid control is blank since this query is not automatically executed
Figure 9-11.

Click the button labeled Get Customers From Country. This assigns the value from the field control to the parameter row and executes the query. Only the rows that match the country USA are displayed, as shown in Figure 9-12.

Now enter **Italy** into the field control (make sure to enter it using this exact combination of upper and lowercase letters). You must press ENTER after entering the country name. Then, click the Get Customers From Country button again. This time, the one customer from Italy is displayed in the grid control.

This concludes the discussion of database-specific topics. In the following chapters the discussion returns to general JBuilder topics, beginning with using threads.

Click the Get Customers From Country button to execute the query
Figure 9-12.

CHAPTER 10

Creating and Using Threads

Have you ever wanted to write programs that do spell
checking while the user types? Perform database queries
without freezing the user interface? Perform complex
calculations using idle time? Threads provide an ideal
mechanism for accomplishing these goals and more
because a multithreaded program can execute more than
one piece of code at the same time.

Developing for a multithreaded environment takes some getting used to since most developers have experience writing code that executes in a strictly sequential fashion. For example, complete step A, then proceed to step B, and finally to step C. Even code developed to deal with an event-driven environment like Windows typically takes care of one task at a time, processing an individual event to completion before proceeding to the next one. For example, redraw a window, process a single keystroke, then a mouse click, and so on.

Multitasking and multithreading are related but subtly different concepts. Both are typically implemented by scheduling rapid switches between several sequential tasks to give the illusion of simultaneous execution. In a multitasking environment, this allows an operating system to manage a number of entirely independent programs at once. The programs themselves do not need to be aware of the process since each is given its own private space in memory and the operating system hides the details of managing the screen, files, and other shared resources.

Multithreading is typically implemented inside of a multitasking environment, and builds on this foundation by allowing a single program to perform more than one action at a time. A thread is used to represent each of these actions, and is executed independently of all other threads. Creating and destroying threads is a simple and efficient operation, allowing an application to start a thread to deal with a background task and then dispose of it when the task is complete. While multithreading is a very powerful tool, it does introduce some new issues for a developer to be concerned about. Notably, since all of the threads within a program share the same memory space, you need to be aware of the possible interactions when two or more threads try to manipulate the same data.

The Multithreaded Code Trade-Off

Not every application or applet needs to be heavily multithreaded. Designing, developing, and debugging threaded code can take significantly longer than single-threaded code. You will want to determine if the benefits clearly outweigh the risks for your particular situation before undertaking developing multithreaded code.

Multithreading Benefits

The advantages of threaded code all derive from the ability to eliminate delays:

10

♦ A multithreaded server processing a lengthy request can continue to service additional requests without waiting for the original transaction to complete.

♦ A user saving or printing a document can continue to browse through or make changes to the document.

♦ A data entry application saving a record to a database can continue to accept user input for the next record.

Multithreading does not allow individual tasks to be completed any faster. In fact, individual tasks will be performed at the same speed or slower: printing will take at least as long, and saving a record to a database over a wide area network will still be painfully slow. The benefits come from allowing more than one task to be overlapped. In other words, multithreading allows you as the developer to use the computer's CPU more efficiently by partitioning the application among threads. For example, in an application you can assign one thread to perform lengthy background processing while another thread is used to get user input. Because time would normally be wasted waiting for input, multithreading results in an overall performance benefit. It is easiest to achieve clear benefits in areas like those listed previously, where delays are the result of waiting for peripherals, such as network or disk interaction.

NOTE: Operating systems that support multiple processors can actually allocate threads to different processors, achieving performance benefits even for CPU-intensive tasks.

Multithreading Pitfalls

If it's that easy, why don't developers do everything in background threads so the user never has to wait for a task to be completed? First, there are practical limits on the number of threads that an operating system can manage efficiently. Second, there is significant additional complexity inherent in creating a thread-safe application.

The first of these is pretty straightforward. While there is no hard limit on the number of threads you can create and manage, the performance of most operating systems begins to degrade when faced with a large number of threads to schedule. In practice, lightweight applications should use only a handful of threads, and even large applications should typically use less than 20 concurrent threads.

The second issue, thread-safe development, deals with the inherent problems in running more than one piece of code simultaneously in a shared memory space. Locking mechanisms must be provided to prevent data from becoming corrupted when two or more threads attempt to manipulate the same information at the same time. The introduction of the locking raises issues about performance and the potential for deadlock, a situation that can cause one or more threads to wait forever for an event that will never occur.

JBuilder and Multithreaded Development

JBuilder supports all of Java's threading capabilities, but offers only a few threading-specific tools of its own. The Debugger, discussed in Chapter 11, provides a detailed view of what is happening inside a multithreaded application or applet, and there are classes in the JBCL (JavaBeans Component Library) that create and manage threads on your behalf.

Even though there aren't many features of JBuilder aimed specifically at creating multithreaded code, it is still an important technique for anyone looking to take full advantage of JBuilder. Not only can it be used to great advantage as discussed earlier, it is a requirement that all JavaBeans be developed in a thread-safe manner.

The remainder of this chapter focuses on standard Java features for multithreading and the helpful *borland.jbcl.util.Timer* class that can be used to trigger a periodic event in a background thread.

Multithreaded Development in Java

One of Java's unique characteristics is the high level of support for multithreaded development. There are features built into the language for creating and managing threads and for managing data in a thread-safe fashion. The Java runtime and standard packages make extensive use of these features to provide some degree of parallelism automatically, but you will likely want to learn how to take control of the capability within your own code.

The Thread Class

The class *java.lang.Thread* provides a mechanism for creating, managing, and destroying threads in Java code. This *Thread* class hides all of the details of creating operating system threads, or emulating them on systems that do not have native support for threads. Because *Thread* is a part of the core Java classes, it is guaranteed to be present on any system that has a Java runtime environment.

The following code is all that is required to create and start a thread:

```
Thread thread = new Thread();

thread.start();
```

Instances of the *Thread* class are created like any other objects, in this case using the constructor that takes no parameters. Creating a thread object does not immediately create an operating system thread and begin execution. It merely creates an object that can be used to start and manage the thread. Additional methods could be used to configure the thread prior to actually starting it. The *start()* method must be invoked to actually create an operating system thread and begin execution.

After executing the *start()* method of a thread, execution actually proceeds simultaneously from two entirely different points in a Java program. The code immediately following the *start()* method executes as if the method returned immediately, but the task associated with the new thread starts at the same time, proceeding in parallel. The newly created thread executes until its task is complete, at which time the operating system thread associated with the thread object is stopped. The thread object provides a set of methods to test the state of the executing thread and control its execution.

The default behavior associated with the *Thread* class is to do nothing. Clearly, there needs to be a way to specify the code to be executed when the thread starts. As it happens, there are two techniques available. A thread instance can delegate its task to another object, or a subclass of *Thread* can be created that performs a specific task.

Extending the Thread Class

When a thread is actually started, it invokes the thread object's *run()* method to carry out the desired task. Overriding the *run()* method in a subclass is all it takes to create a useful background process:

```java
class CountingThread extends Thread {
  private TextField countField;

  public CountingThread(TextField field) {
    countField = field;
  }

  public void run() {
    for(int counter = 1; counter < 100; counter++) {
      countField.setText(String.valueOf(counter));

      try {
        sleep(200);
      }
```

```
      catch(InterruptedException ex) { }
    }
  }
}
```

The new class adds a private *countField* variable that is used to keep track of a text field that will be manipulated by the thread. The sole constructor requires an instance of the *TextField* class as its parameter and stores the reference for use when the thread actually executes. The *run()* method counts from 1 to 100, displaying each number within the text field and then pausing for 200 milliseconds before displaying the next value. The *sleep()* method used to pause briefly is inherited from the *Thread* class. The exception handler surrounding the method is required, but need not do anything meaningful with the exception.

This counting thread can easily be incorporated into an applet or application. An event handler for an action, such as a button being pressed, could start the counter by including the following code:

```
new CountingThread(textField1).start();
```

Since the *start()* method returns immediately without waiting for the thread to complete, the counter would run while still allowing user interaction with the interface.

Delegating a Thread's Task

Often, it is convenient to be able to place the code describing a thread's task in another object rather than creating a *Thread* subclass. The delegate object must belong to a class that implements the *java.lang.Runnable* interface, which describes only a *run()* method.

The following class performs the same task as the *Thread* subclass in the previous example, but uses a *TextField* subclass with corresponding changes to the *run()* method. The code that invokes the *setText()* method is now simpler as the object is simply invoking its own method. On the other hand, the code that invokes the *sleep()* method is more complex because it needs to use the static method *currentThread()* to get a reference to the object representing the currently executing thread.

```
public class CountingField extends TextField
implements Runnable {
  public void run() {
    for(int counter = 1; counter < 100; counter++) {
      setText(String.valueOf(counter));

      try {
```

```
        Thread.currentThread().sleep(200);
      }
      catch(InterruptedException ex) { }
    }
  }
}
```

A standard thread instance can be created to delegate its task to any object that implements *Runnable*, such as an instance of *CountingField*, by using a constructor that takes a single parameter:

```
new Thread(countingField1).start();
```

As before, execution continues from two places after the *start()* method is invoked. The counting process begins in a background thread, and execution also proceeds from the line after the call to the *start()* method.

Sample Threaded Project

The following example creates an application to demonstrate the threading concepts introduced so far in this chapter:

1. Select File|New Project to display the Project Wizard. In the File field, enter the name **c:\JBuilder\myprojects\osborne\jbe\thread\Thread.jpr** and click the Finish button.
2. Select File|New, and double-click the Application icon on the New page in the Object Gallery.
3. On the Step 1 page of the Application Wizard, enter **ThreadApplication** in the Class field and click the Next button. On the Step 2 page, enter **ThreadFrame** in the Class field for the Frame Class and click Finish.
4. Select the ThreadFrame.java file in the Navigation pane and click the Design tab.
5. Select the AWT tab on the Component Palette and place two *java.awt.TextField* components on the frame in the UI Designer, one above the other.
6. In the Component Tree in the Structure pane, select *textField1* and hold down the SHIFT key while selecting *textField2* to extend the selection to cover both components. Use the Properties page of the Inspector to change the *columns* property to **20** for both of these components at once.

7. Place a *java.awt.Button* from the AWT page of the Component Palette below the two text fields. Use the Properties page of the Inspector and change its *label* property to **Start Counters**.

8. Double-click on the button object to create an action event handler for it, and edit the event handler to match the following source code:

```
void button1_actionPerformed(ActionEvent e) {
  new CountingThread(textField1).start();
  new CountingThread(textField2).start();
}
```

9. Add the *CountingThread* class to the source file by pressing CTRL-END to move to the last line in the Editor, press ENTER to add a blank line, and add the following code:

```
class CountingThread extends Thread {
  private TextField countField;

  public CountingThread(TextField field) {
    countField = field;
  }

  public void run() {
    for(int counter = 1; counter < 100; counter++) {
      countField.setText(String.valueOf(counter));

      try {
        sleep(200);
      }
      catch(InterruptedException ex) { }
    }
  }
}
```

10. Select Run|Run, press SHIFT-F9, or click the Run button on JBuilder's toolbar to start the application. Pressing the Start Counters button in this application will start two simultaneous counting threads, as shown in Figure 10-1.

Thread-Safe Development

The term "thread-safe development" refers to the use of techniques that prevent data corruption when more than one thread attempts to manipulate the same information at the same time. The problem may not be obvious at first, but consider a trivial code example consisting of a class with a single method:

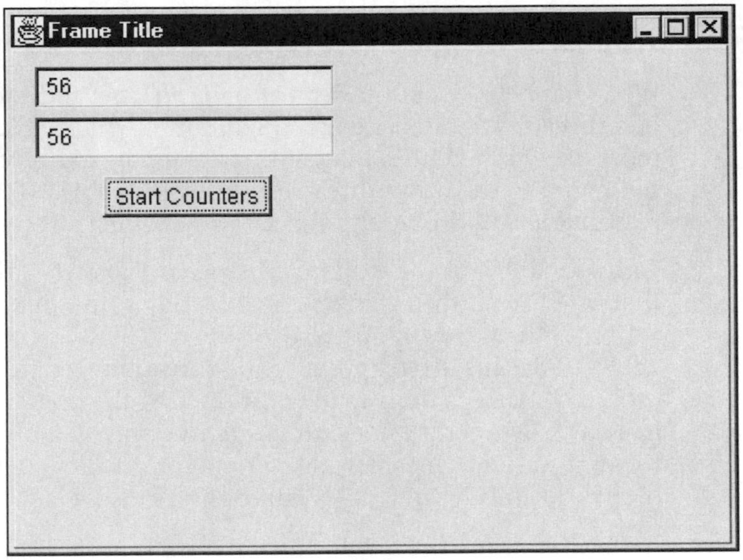

Two threaded
counters
running
simultaneously
Figure 10-1.

```
public class Counter {
  private int counter = 0;

  public int increment() {
    return ++counter;
  }
}
```

When executed, this *increment()* method actually performs the steps shown in Table 10-1. The type of action performed when calling *increment()* from a single thread is shown in the first column: Load *counter,* Add one (to increment *counter*), and Save *counter.* The Temp Value column shows the value at the top of the Java Virtual Machine (VM) stack, where it keeps the value it has loaded from *counter* before adding to it and putting it back. The

Calling
increment()
from a Single
Thread
Table 10-1.

Action	Temp Value	*counter* Value
Load *counter*	0	0
Add one	1	1
Save *counter*	1	1

counter Value column shows the values of the *counter* variable for the actions. These steps look reasonable enough, and certainly achieve the desired result.

What happens when the same *increment()* method is called from more than one thread? That depends on the order in which the steps are executed. The most likely outcome is that all three steps are executed in one thread before switching to the other thread, as shown in Table 10-2. Again, the steps look reasonable and the results are certainly correct.

Unfortunately, in the example shown in Table 10-2 there is no guarantee that one thread won't interrupt the other in the middle of performing its actions. When this happens, the results are less encouraging, as shown in Table 10-3. This interruption of the thread processing is obviously a problem. There is no way to control when the operating system will choose to switch between threads, resulting in unpredictable code that sometimes works and sometimes fails. As you might imagine, debugging this kind of problem can be extremely frustrating because it is so unpredictable.

Calling *increment()* from Two Threads, Best-Case Scenario
Table 10-2.

Thread One Action	Temp Value	Thread Two Action	Temp Value	*counter* Value
Load *counter*	0			0
Add one	1			1
Save *counter*	1			1
		Load *counter*	1	1
		Add one	2	1

Calling *increment()* from Two Threads, Worst-Case Scenario
Table 10-3.

Thread One Action	Temp Value	Thread Two Action	Temp Value	*counter* Value
Load *counter*	0			0
	0	Load *counter*	0	0
	0	Add one	1	0
	0	Save *counter*	1	1
Add one	1			1
Save *counter*	1			1

Consider what could happen when two methods attempt to modify a more complex data structure simultaneously. The implications are frightening, but there is a solution to the dilemma. All would be well if a thread could acquire some sort of exclusive lock on the data, perform a complete operation, and then release the lock.

All of the standard Java packages are designed to be entirely thread safe. Java also makes this easy to accomplish in your own classes by providing several simple techniques for implementing thread synchronization. These methods are described next.

Synchronized Methods

Method declarations can include the modifier **synchronized** to indicate that the method requires an exclusive lock on the object it is invoked on. The class introduced earlier can be made thread safe by applying this modifier to its *increment()* method:

```
public class Counter {
  private int counter = 0;

  public synchronized int increment() {
    return ++counter;
  }
}
```

When a synchronized method is invoked, it waits until it can acquire the necessary lock before performing its task. The lock is automatically released when it exits, whether the method returns gracefully or throws an exception.

Consider the scenario introduced earlier in Table 10-3. If you use the new locking scheme with this scenario, you may see the threading behavior shown in Table 10-4. As a result of this locking scheme, no two synchronized methods may be invoked on the same object at the same time. One will always wait for the other to complete before proceeding. A nonsynchronized method does not require a lock, so it may execute at the same time as a synchronized method.

The trivial approach to making a class thread safe is to make every method synchronized, but this can lead to deadlock situations and performance degradation, as discussed later. Methods that read but do not alter information typically do not need to be synchronized, nor do methods that alter information exclusively through synchronized methods.

Thread One Action	Temp Value	Thread Two Action	Temp Value	*counter* Value
Wait for lock				0
Load *counter*	0			0
	0	Wait for lock		0
Add one	1			1
Save *counter*	1			1
Release lock				1
		Load *counter*	1	1
		Add one	2	1
		Save *counter*	2	2

Calling a Synchronized *increment()* from Two Threads, Worst-Case Scenario
Table 10-4.

Implications for Class Methods

A synchronized static method acquires a lock on the class, not on an individual instance of the class. As a result, no two synchronized static methods may execute at the same time, though a synchronized instance method may be invoked concurrently with a synchronized class method.

Synchronized Code Blocks

Synchronized code blocks provide a way for a developer to explicitly lock an object while executing a series of statements. Before getting into the details of how this is accomplished, it is important to understand why it might be necessary.

Synchronized methods are useful when the developer of a class wants to enforce the integrity of data manipulated by methods of a class. Each synchronized method acts as an atomic operation—an indivisible set of changes—to the underlying data.

There is another technique that can be used when a developer who is simply using an existing class wants to enforce data integrity on a larger scale by treating several method invocations as a single atomic operation. For example, there is no single synchronized method to find and replace a string in a *TextArea* component. To replace all occurrences of the string "jb" with "JBuilder", you might use the following code:

```
while(true) {
  String text = textArea1.getText();
  int    pos = text.indexOf("jb");

  if (pos == -1) break;
  textArea1.replaceRange("JBuilder", pos, pos+2);
}
```

This example retrieves the current text and searches for an occurrence of the string in question. If the string is not found, the process ends; otherwise, the string is replaced and the process begins again.

There is a subtle problem with this code. While *getText()* and *replaceRange()* are both synchronized methods, the lock on the text area is released briefly between checking the text and replacing the string. If a user's keystroke is processed between these two calls, the text will have been changed and the position of the string to be replaced may no longer be accurate. Again, the problem is that there is no single synchronized method that performs both actions.

The keyword **synchronized** can also be used as a statement to lock an object while executing statements within a code block. The keyword must be followed by parentheses around a reference to the object to be locked, and the code block in curly braces that should be executed before the lock is released. The last example can be corrected as follows:

```
synchronized (textArea1) {
  while(true) {
    String text = textArea1.getText();
    int    pos = text.indexOf("jb");

    if (pos == -1) break;
    textArea1.replaceRange("JBuilder", pos, pos+2);
  }
}
```

Performance Considerations

Not surprisingly, the addition of locking and unlocking behavior means that it takes much longer to invoke a synchronized method than a typical method. The actual performance hit varies from one Java VM to another, but is significant enough to be a concern when designing Java code. Avoiding the performance hit requires either single-threaded access to classes or careful design to minimize the number of synchronized methods used.

A design can certainly incorporate single-threaded access to objects that are not thread safe, but note that in Java this is the exception rather than the rule. Classes that deliberately neglect thread safety should document this fact very clearly. Instances of such a class can still be used from any thread, but no two threads should attempt to access these objects at the same time.

It is much more efficient to invoke a single synchronized method that performs a number of tasks than to invoke several synchronized methods in sequence. If you find a common sequence of method invocations, consider redesigning the class in question to include private unsynchronized implementations of these methods, and add a single public synchronized method that calls them in sequence.

Deadlocks

A multithreaded program that suddenly stops responding may have run into a deadlock situation. Deadlock occurs when two or more threads encounter a situation where they are waiting for resources to be unlocked that are held by other threads caught in the deadlock situation. All threads involved will wait forever for an event that will never occur.

The most common example of this occurs with two threads, as shown in Table 10-5. In this example, thread one successfully locks object A, and thread two successfully locks object B. Thread one then attempts to lock object B, finds that it is locked and begins to wait for it to become unlocked. Thread two attempts to lock object A, finds that it is also locked, and begins to wait for it to become unlocked. These two threads have become deadlocked.

There is no simple rule for avoiding deadlock situations. You should definitely consider the possibility when designing your code and try to avoid situations where it might occur.

Thread One	Thread Two
Lock A	
	Lock B
Lock B	
	Lock A

The Classic Deadlock Situation
Table 10-5.

NOTE: The locking mechanism in Java is smart enough to prevent a thread from waiting for itself to release a lock. This is extremely important, because otherwise you could never call a synchronized method from another synchronized method in the same object! A thread that tries to lock an object it has already locked merely increments a lock count and proceeds. The lock will only be released when it has been unlocked as many times as it was originally locked.

10

Managing Threads

The *Thread* class includes methods for controlling the behavior of a thread. There are two basic techniques for getting a reference to a thread object in order to manage its operating system thread:

♦ To influence another thread after creating it, keep a reference to the thread object created when starting the thread.

♦ To influence the current thread, use the *Thread* class's static method *currentThread()* to obtain a reference to the thread object.

The methods described are documented in greater depth in JBuilder's online help.

Starting and Stopping Threads

There are four basic methods for starting and stopping threads. The *start()* method is used to create a new operating system thread in conjunction with a thread object. The *stop()* method causes the specified thread to experience a *java.lang.ThreadDeath* exception to forcibly terminate it. The *pause()* method puts a thread on hold until the *resume()* method causes it to continue executing.

There are several additional methods that also deal with the execution of a thread. The *sleep()* method puts a thread on hold for a specified period of time. A thread's *sleep()* can be interrupted with the *interrupt()* method. Lastly, the state of an existing thread can be tested with the *isAlive()* method. This method will return **true** only if the thread has been started and has not yet completed its task or been forcibly stopped.

Controlling Thread Priorities

The method *setPriority()* can be used to change the priority of a thread, while *getPriority()* retrieves the current setting. The priority of a thread is an integer value that determines the amount of CPU time it gets, with higher-priority threads getting preference over lower-priority threads. When a new thread is created, it inherits the priority of the thread that created it. There are three constants that define standard priority values: *Thread.MIN_PRIORITY*, *Thread.MAX_PRIORITY*, and *Thread.NORM_PRIORITY*.

Daemon Threads

The Java interpreter exits when there are no longer any non-daemon threads running. A daemon thread is therefore useful for performing a noncritical background task that can be interrupted at any time if the application is shutting down. A newly created thread is not by default a daemon thread unless the thread that created it was a daemon thread. The *setDaemon()* method can be used to change the state of a thread, but it must be set before starting the thread. The *isDaemon()* method can be used to test if an existing thread is a daemon thread.

 NOTE: The initial thread created when a Java application starts is a non-daemon thread.

The Timer Class

The *borland.jbcl.util.Timer* class is a convenient way to perform periodic background tasks without manually creating and managing the necessary threads. There is a single shared thread used to dispatch all registered tasks, which helps minimize the number of threads used in an application even when dozens of background tasks are scheduled. You never actually create an instance of the *Timer* class because the methods needed to schedule tasks are both static methods, associated with the class itself rather than an instance of the class.

 NOTE: Since a single thread is used to dispatch all events controlled by the timer, the tasks performed should be very short. If an individual task requires more time, it should create a thread of its own when invoked so that the timer thread can be released to deal with other timed events.

To schedule a new period task, use the static *startTimer(TimerClient, eventId, period, repeat)* method. The first parameter must be a reference to an object that implements the *borland.jbl.util.TimerClient* interface. This interface defines a single method, *timerEvent()*, that will be triggered to perform the actual task. The *eventId* parameter is an integer value that is passed to the *timerEvent()* method so that a single timer client can implement more than one task. The *period* parameter is an integer value measuring the length of time in milliseconds before the task is executed. The final parameter, *repeat*, is a boolean value that specifies whether the task is to be executed indefinitely or just once.

This method implies a two-step process for dealing with periodic tasks. First, a class implementing the *TimerClient* interface needs to be created to perform the task. For example, the following class defines a client that prints a message to the console every time an event is fired:

```
class MessageClient implements borland.jbcl.util.TimerClient {
  public void timerEvent(int timerId) {
    System.out.println("Timer ID "+timerId+"was invoked");
  }
}
```

Second, one or more calls to *startTimer()* must be used to schedule the tasks. This example will use a single instance of the *MessageClient* class as the timer client for two timers, the first firing every second, the second firing twice per second:

```
MessageClient client = new MessageClient();

Timer.startTimer(client, 0, 1000, true);
Timer.startTimer(client, 1, 500, true);
```

To stop a repeating task, invoke the static method *stopTimer(TimerClient, eventId)*. This method stops the timer created for the specified timer client and identifier.

NOTE: The timer maintains a reference to each timer client, which prevents the client from being garbage collected unless the timer is stopped.

Sample Timer Project

The following example demonstrates the use of a timer to perform background tasks similar to those introduced in the previous sample project. Using the timer mechanism requires slightly less code and uses fewer threads, resulting in a cleaner implementation:

1. Select File|New Project to display the Project Wizard. In the File field, enter the name **c:\JBuilder\myprojects\osborne\jbe\thread\Timer.jpr** and click the Finish button.

2. Select File|New and double-click the Application icon on the New page in the Object Gallery.

3. On the Step 1 page of the Application Wizard, enter **TimerApplication** in the Class field and click the Next button. On the Step 2 page, enter **TimerFrame** in the Class field for the Frame Class and click Finish.

4. Select the TimerFrame.java file in the Navigation pane and click the Design tab.

5. Select the AWT tab on the Component Palette and place two *java.awt.TextField* components on the frame in the UI Designer, one above the other.

6. In the Component Tree in the Structure pane, select *textField1* and hold down the SHIFT key while selecting *textField2* to extend the selection to cover both components. Use the Properties page of the Inspector to change the *columns* property to **20** for both of these components at once.

7. From the AWT page of the Component Palette, place a *java.awt.Button* below the two text fields. Use the Properties page of the Inspector to change its *label* property to **Start Timers**.

8. Double-click on the button in the UI Designer to create an action event handler for it. Edit the event handler to match the following source code:

```
void button1_actionPerformed(ActionEvent e) {
  Timer.startTimer(new CountingClient(textField1),
    0, 200, true);
  Timer.startTimer(new CountingClient(textField2),
    0, 200, true);
}
```

9. Add the *CountingClient* class to the source file by pressing CTRL-END to move to the last line of the Editor, press ENTER to add a blank line, and add the following source code:

```
class CountingClient implements TimerClient {
  private TextField countField;
  private int counter = 1;

  public CountingClient(TextField field) {
    countField = field;
```

10

```
    }

    public void timerEvent(int timerId) {
      countField.setText(String.valueOf(counter++));
      if (counter++ == 100) {
        Timer.stopTimer(this, timerId);
      }
    }
  }
```

10. Press CTRL-HOME to move to the top of the file in the Editor and add the following line below the existing **import** statements:

    ```
    import borland.jbcl.util.*;
    ```

11. Select Run|Run, press SHIFT-F9, or click the Run button on JBuilder's toolbar to start the application. Pressing the Start Timers button in this application will start two timers that run in the generic timer background thread, as shown in Figure 10-2.

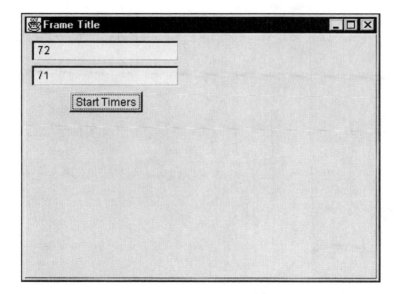

The timer
thread running
two timed
events
Figure 10-2.

CHAPTER 11

Debugging JBuilder Applications and Applets

The JBuilder Debugger is an invaluable tool that helps you locate problems and remove errors in your project source code. This chapter describes the features of the Debugger and how to use them. It starts with basic debugging topics, including types of errors, preparing your projects for debugging, and starting and stopping the Debugger. Next, the debugging interface is presented and the features that allow you to follow and control code execution and examine data values are covered in detail. Finally, tips are suggested for dealing with errors and other common problems that can crop up during development.

CD-ROM: The example project for this chapter, Debbuging.jpr, can be found in the osborne\jbecd\debugging subdirectory. See Appendix C for information on installing and using the files on the CD-ROM that accompanies this book.

Debugging Basics

Java compilers are designed to catch a wide variety of problems long before code execution. As a result, syntax errors, uninitialized variables, and unreachable code should never cause problems at runtime. The design of Java itself eliminates another category of errors by using sophisticated garbage collection techniques to reduce memory leaks and eliminate situations where deallocated memory is inadvertently accessed.

While these compiler benefits certainly help improve the likelihood that your code will run correctly if it compiles, there are still a variety of errors that you may make during development. There are two categories of errors you can make in your code that the compiler cannot catch: runtime errors and logic errors.

Runtime and Logic Errors

A runtime error appears when you run your application or applet and it encounters an unexpected situation. The statements in your code may be syntactically correct and valid according to the compiler, but when executed, cause an abnormal termination of program flow due to the error. This results in an exception being thrown. You can eliminate many runtime errors with preventative or proactive coding to test for conditions and handle exceptions that could potentially arise. The Debugger is especially useful for locating runtime errors since you can follow and control the execution of your code to diagnose where in the code the runtime error is occurring.

An application or applet that runs without throwing exceptions can still fail to produce the results you expect. If, for example, your application needs to display a subset of records produced by a query, the query could execute without throwing an exception and still produce an incorrect record set due to the use of the wrong query parameters. These kinds of problems, errors in programming logic, can be the most difficult to track down, and the Debugger is indispensable in assisting you with locating these errors. To help you find these errors, you will want to use the debug features that allow you to follow and control code execution as well as the features that allow you to examine data values along the way.

 TIP: Since runtime and logic errors arise from different sources, they require different approaches to correct or prevent them. For suggestions on dealing with runtime and logic errors, see the later sections in this chapter "Tips for Common Java Problems" and "Defensive Programming: Testing Invariant Conditions."

11

Preparing for a Debugging Session

For the Debugger to work, you need to instruct the compiler to place additional debugging information in class files. This is the default behavior, one that there is rarely any need to change. To check that the debug information is compiled with your project, open the project and select File|Project Properties. On the Project page, ensure that the Include Debug Information option is checked.

You may also want to define other options for debugging your project, as described in the following sections.

Using the Execution Log

When JBuilder runs Java code, it records textual output in the execution log or a console window. The default for every new project is to display a console window while the code is running, which means that this information is lost once the application has finished running. When debugging Java code, however, JBuilder still allows the console window to be displayed, but it also records output and other information in the execution log. You can display the execution log window, shown in Figure 11-1, by selecting View|Execution Log.

The execution log records output on a tabbed page named after the class used to start an application or the HTML file used to start an applet. Running the same application or applet more than once results in new output being appended to the end of an existing page so that information from multiple test runs can be captured. The text on the pages is also editable so that you can include additional notes or selectively remove information that is no longer of interest. When you exit JBuilder, the execution log is emptied, but you can save the log information in a text file by right-clicking in the output area of the execution log shown in Figure 11-1, and selecting Save to File from the popup menu.

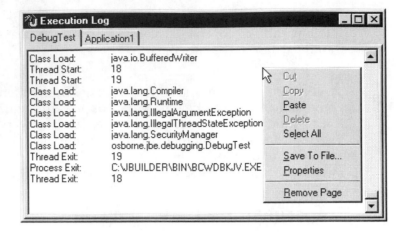

Execution log
window with
captured
output and
popup menu
Figure 11-1.

The Log Properties dialog shown in Figure 11-2 allows you to choose the kind of information that is recorded in the execution log during debugging. To display this dialog, right-click in the output area of the execution log shown in Figure 11-1, and select Properties from the popup menu.

The execution log can also be used to capture output while running an application outside of the Debugger. To do this, select Run|Parameters to display the Run|Debug page of the project's Properties dialog, shown in Figure 11-3, and select the option labeled Send run output to Execution Log.

NOTE: The execution log options shown in Figure 11-2 only affect debugging output. Only normal program output will be recorded in the log when not in debug mode.

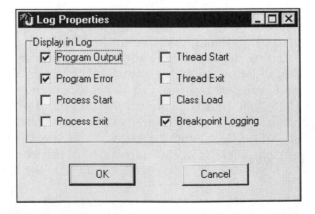

Log properties
dialog
Figure 11-2.

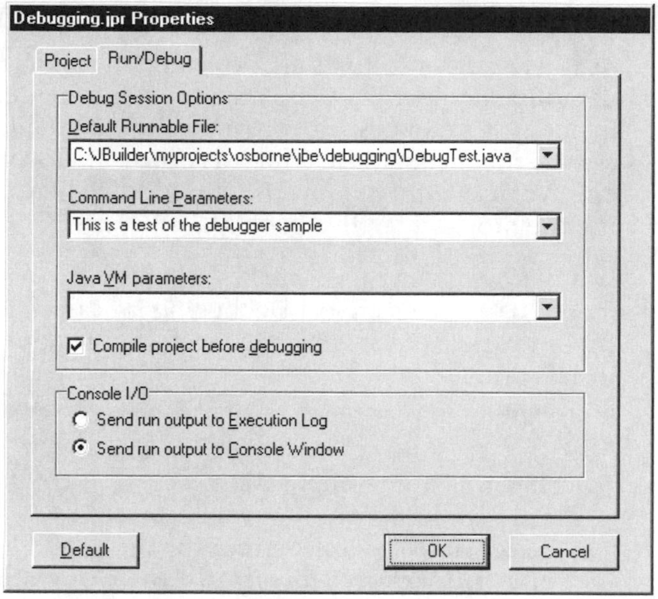

11

The
Run/Debug
page of the
project's
Properties
dialog
Figure 11-3.

[Screenshot: Debugging.jpr Properties dialog]

Debugging.jpr Properties

Project | Run/Debug

Debug Session Options

Default Runnable File:
C:\JBuilder\myprojects\osborne\jbe\debugging\DebugTest.java

Command Line Parameters:
This is a test of the debugger sample

Java VM parameters:

☑ Compile project before debugging

Console I/O
○ Send run output to Execution Log
● Send run output to Console Window

Default   OK   Cancel

Changing the Default File to Debug

A debugging session typically begins with the project's *default runnable file*. If
this file is not explicitly set, the file is selected for you by JBuilder, which
searches for a Java source file containing a class that has a *main()* method,
and failing that, an HTML file. If you need to change the default selected for
you by JBuilder, select Run|Parameters to display the Run/Debug page of the
project's Properties dialog (see Figure 11-3). Select the desired file in the
Default Runnable File field.

Setting Command-Line Arguments

If the application you want to debug accepts command-line arguments, you
may configure these in JBuilder prior to starting the application. To
configure command-line arguments, select Run|Parameters to display the
Run/Debug page of the project's Properties dialog (see Figure 11-3). Fill in
any string of parameters in the Command Line Parameters field.

CAUTION: Setting command-line arguments for a project may prevent
applets from running correctly. If a single project contains both application
and applet code, remove any command-line arguments before attempting to
run or debug the applet.

Creating a Sample Buggy Application

As the Debugger features are presented in this chapter, the examples that demonstrate a particular task use the following sample application, which includes several bugs. The program should list all of the words passed on the command line, but instead it lists every other word, starting with the second one. You can either follow the steps shown here to create this application, or use the project from this book's CD-ROM.

CD-ROM: This project Debbuging.jpr can be found in the osborne\jbecd\debugging subdirectory. See Appendix C for installation instructions.

To create the sample application:

1. Select File|New Project from the menu and in the File field enter **c:\JBuilder\myprojects\osborne\jbe\debugging\Debugging.jpr**. Click Finish.

2. Select File|New, select Class, and click the OK button.

3. On the displayed New Object dialog, leave the Package set to osborne.jbe.debugging. At Class Name, enter **DebugTest** and uncheck the Generate default constructor checkbox. Click OK to create the new file.

4. Edit the file to match the code shown here:

```
package osborne.jbe.debugging;

public class DebugTest {
  public static void main(String[] args) {
    new DebugTest().printArray(args);
  }

  public void printArray(Object array[]) {
    System.out.print("{");
    for (int index = 1; index < array.length; index++) {
      if (index > 1) System.out.print(", ");
      System.out.print(array[index]);
      index += 1;
    }
    System.out.println("}");
  }
}
```

Since this sample application expects parameters, it needs to be configured as described in the last section. To set the command-line parameters:

1. Select Run|Parameters to display the project's Properties dialog with the Run|Debug page displayed (see Figure 11-3).
2. Enter the string **This is a test of the debugger sample** in the Command Line Parameters field, and click OK to accept these settings.

Starting the Debugger

11

The JBuilder Debugger can be started in a number of different ways, as follows:

♦ Select Run|Debug
♦ Click the Debug button on JBuilder's toolbar
♦ Press F9
♦ Right-click on a file in the Navigation pane and select Debug from the popup menu

If an HTML file is selected, it is assumed that it contains an <APPLET> tag and this file is used to start the Debugger as described in the next section. If a Java source file is selected, and that file contains a class with a *main()* method, JBuilder attempts to debug the class with the same name as the source file. If none of the above are true, as when the project file or a Java source file not containing a *main()* method is selected, the default runnable file is used as a starting point for the Debugger.

JBuilder will normally ensure that the most recent version of the code to be executed has been compiled before starting a debugging session. If changes have been made, the compiler will automatically be invoked and a failed compilation will abort the debugging attempt. This automatic compilation can be disabled for a project by selecting Run|Parameters and disabling the Compile project before debugging checkbox.

Debugging Applets

To allow JBuilder to debug applets, the default runnable file may be an HTML file that contains an <APPLET> tag rather than a Java source file. You can then use any of the methods described in the last section to start debugging an applet.

When a debugging session is started for an HTML file, the simple *appletviewer* application included in the Java Developer's Kit is started and JBuilder is automatically used to debug whatever applet the appletviewer loads. The initial release of JBuilder cannot be used to debug applets running in a Java-enabled Web browser.

CAUTION: JBuilder cannot debug applets that do not override the *init()* method inherited from *java.applet.Applet*. If a dialog is displayed with the message "Unable to debug" after exiting the appletviewer, this is often the cause of the problem. Overriding *init()*, even with an empty method body, allows the JBuilder Debugger to attach itself to the applet correctly.

Stopping the Debugger

To stop debugging your project, select Run|Program Reset, or click the Reset button, which appears as a stop sign on the debugging toolbar. Resetting terminates the Java session containing the applet or application controlled by the Debugger and allows the operating system to close opened files, release resources, and reclaim allocated memory. This process does not remove any breakpoints or watches you may have placed.

The Debugging Interface: Debug and Watch Tabs

When you start debugging a project, the Debugger appears in the form of two additional AppBrowser tabs (the Debug tab and the Watch tab) at the bottom-left corner of the window, as shown in Figure 11-4. These are the only obvious indications that JBuilder is debugging code in a particular project. The Debug tab displays the main debugging view and contains the Thread and Stack pane, the Data pane, and the Source pane. You view running threads and method calls in the Thread and Stack pane, and inspect data in the Data pane. The Source pane displays the execution point in the appropriate source code.

Selecting the Watch tab displays the Watch view of the Debugger, as shown in Figure 11-5. It contains the Source pane and the Watch pane, which is used for watching program values. The two tabs share the same debugging toolbar and have similar functionality. Both tabs' features are discussed in detail in the sections that follow.

To see how the two tabs appear at the start of debug mode, and disappear when the project is no longer being debugged, try the following steps with the sample debug application:

1. Select Run|Debug "DebugTest".

Thread and Stack pane

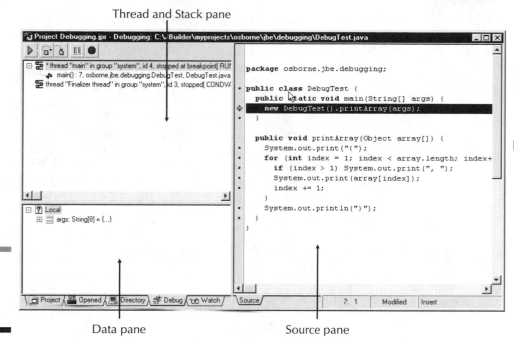

The
Debugger's
Debug tab
Figure 11-4.

Data pane

Source pane

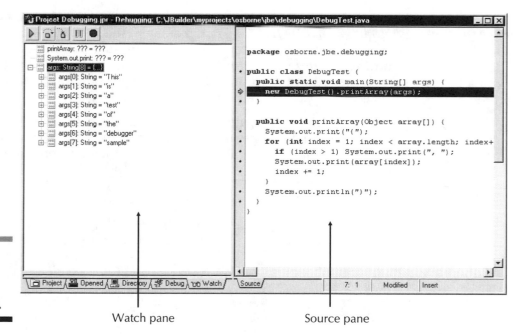

The
Debugger's
Watch tab
Figure 11-5.

Watch pane

Source pane

2. Click the available tabs at the lower left of the AppBrowser, Project, Opened, Directory, Debug, and Watch tabs, to see how the appearance of the AppBrowser changes.

3. Select Run|Program Reset to exit debug mode. Note that the Debug and Watch tabs disappear when you exit the Debugger.

The Debugger provides developers assistance in two main areas: following the execution of code in an application, and examining the state of data at any point during the debugging session. Given these two capabilities, you can validate the behavior of even the most complex code. The next section describes debugging features that allow you to follow and control code execution. The later section "Examining Data" describes the features for examining data values.

Following Code Execution

Watching an application execute provides only crude hints about what is actually happening behind the scenes. Thousands of lines of code may execute between visible changes in an application's interface, making it nearly impossible to determine the exact path that the code follows. A time-honored approach to resolving this problem is to litter the code with statements that produce a textual log as execution passes through key points, but this process is usually a tedious waste of time.

JBuilder's Debugger gives you the opportunity to observe exactly what code is executing, line by line. The Run menu and the debugger toolbar provide control over your application's execution, running one or more lines before returning to a frozen state for further examination. None of these options change the order of execution, they merely control how much detail about the execution path will be visible.

The buttons on the debugging toolbar are merely alternatives to some of the debugging menu items, providing shortcuts, from left to right, for Run|Debug, Run|Step Over, Run|Trace Into, Run|Pause, and Run|Program Reset menu items.

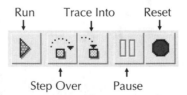

The Execution Point

When the Debugger is initially activated, it automatically halts program execution before the first line of an application's *main()* method or an applet's *init()* method is executed. At this point, the Java code execution is paused, leaving the developer in control of the Debugger's features. The line of code that will be executed next is highlighted with a green arrow in the left margin of the source code, as shown in Figure 11-4.

It is possible to browse through source code while in debug mode, possibly losing track of the execution point. At any time, the display can be returned to a state where the green arrow is visible by selecting Run|Show Execution Point from the menu.

11

Controlling Execution

Each of the options described here resumes code execution until specified conditions are met, at which point the Debugger will pause again and put the developer back in control. This process can be interrupted at any time by selecting Run|Program Pause, by clicking the Pause button in the debugging toolbar, or by triggering a breakpoint as described later in this chapter. The following debugging options can be found on the Run menu.

Debug

Debug resumes execution without a specified stopping point. The same effect can be achieved by pressing F9, clicking on the Debug button on the JBuilder toolbar, or clicking on the Run button on the debugging toolbar.

Trace Into

Trace Into executes the current line and pauses before the next line of code to be executed. The next line will be one of the following:

◆ If the current line invokes other methods, the next line will be the first line of the method called.

◆ If an exception is thrown when executing the current line, the next line will be the first line of the appropriate exception handler.

◆ If the current line is the last line of a method, the next line will be the line of code immediately following the call to the current method.

◆ If none of the above apply, the next line will be the line immediately following the current line.

Alternative ways to choose Trace Into are to press F7 or to click the Trace Into button on the debugging toolbar.

Step Over

Step Over starts executing the current line and pauses before the line below it in the source code. Despite its name, Step Over does not actually bypass any code, it simply allows you to execute all code invoked by the current line before pausing. Alternative ways to choose Step Over are to press F8 or clicking the Step Over button on the debugging toolbar.

Run to Cursor

Run to Cursor resumes execution and pauses again before executing the line the cursor is currently placed on.

Run to End of Method

Run to End of Method resumes execution and pauses again before returning from the method currently executing.

Controlled Execution Example

The following steps demonstrate several mechanisms for controlling code execution using the sample application created earlier in this chapter. Make sure that the Debugging.jpr project is open and that command-line parameters have been configured as described earlier in the section "Creating a Sample Buggy Application."

1. Exit debug mode, if necessary, by selecting Run|Program Reset or by clicking the Reset button.

2. Select View|Execution Log and move the execution log window to a place on the screen where you can watch output as the program executes without other windows obscuring your view. It may be necessary to move or resize the AppBrowser as well.

3. Select Run|Debug "DebugTest" from the menu to start the Debugger. The green arrow indicating the execution point should be pointing to the following line (see Figure 11-4):

   ```
   new DebugTest().printArray(args);
   ```

4. Select Run|Step Over, or click the Step Over button on the debugging toolbar. Note that the execution log shows the complete output from the *printArray()* method. This is because the Step Over option allows all code invoked by the current line to execute to completion before pausing again.

5. To stop the application, select Run|Program Reset or click the Reset button on the debugging toolbar. Select Run|Debug "DebugTest" to start the debugging process again.

6. This time, select Run|Trace Into. The execution point moves to the line:

```
public class DebugTest {
```

This line indicates that the default constructor is being executed. In classes that do not explicitly declare any constructors, the compiler declares one on your behalf. The debugger cannot display the appropriate line in source code because it isn't actually included in the source. The class declaration is compiled as if the line class declaration line was as follows:

```
public class DebugTest { public DebugTest() { }
```

7. Select Run|Trace Into again. The execution point jumps to the first line of *printArray()*. Keep an eye on the execution log, and this time use the Trace Into button on the debugging toolbar to achieve the same effect, clicking the button a total of eight times to see the effect of the **for** loop.

8. Keep watching the execution log as you select Run|Run to End of Method from the menu. The execution point moves to the closing brace of the method after executing the remaining code in the method.

9. Select Run|Program Reset or click the Reset toolbar button to terminate the debugging session.

11

Selectively Disabling Method Tracing

Developers often need a middle ground between the behavior of Trace Into and Step Over. Even a single line of code may implicitly invoke a number of methods, some of which are of interest for debugging purposes, others of which are assumed to be bug-free. You can specify classes that should be skipped for tracing purposes using the List of Packages and Classes With Tracing Disabled dialog. Since Step Over always skips all methods invoked by the current line, this option only affects the Trace Into feature.

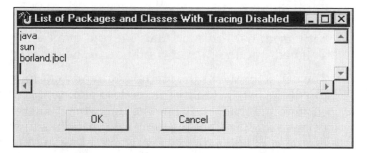

While not currently in a debugging session, View|Loaded Classes displays this dialog, which contains a list of packages and classes for which tracing will be disabled during the next debugging session. Adding a fully qualified class name such as **java.lang.String** disables tracing for all methods belonging to that specified class. Specifying a package name such as

java.lang disables tracing for all methods belonging to classes in the named package *and all other packages starting with the same prefix,* in this case, *java.lang* and *java.lang.reflect.* By default, JBuilder disables tracing for all classes in the java, sun, and borland.jbcl packages.

NOTE: If you remove the java, sun, and borland.jbcl packages from the list and try using Trace Into to walk all the way through the sample application, it will take you a very long time. Typically, you will want to keep these packages in the tracing disabled list.

This list cannot be changed while you are debugging an application or applet. In debug mode, selecting View|Loaded Classes displays the Loaded Classes dialog, indicating which currently loaded classes have tracing disabled:

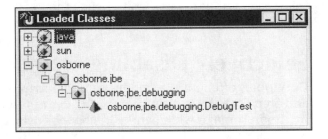

Threads and Execution Stacks

The Thread and Stack pane shown in Figure 11-6 provides a wealth of information about the state of an application or applet. Each active thread is displayed, and beneath each thread is its *call stack.* Each thread is presented with its unique thread id, plus a thread name and group name if one is assigned, and the current condition of the thread.

The call stack shows the method currently executing in each thread at the top of the list, including the method name, class name, source file, and current line number. Below the current method is the method it was called from, including all of the same information, and so forth. In Figure 11-6, for example, *printArray()* is currently executing in the thread named main, and *printArray()* was called from the method *main().* Double-clicking on any method in the call stack moves to the correct line in the Source pane and allows data within that context to be examined, as described later in this chapter.

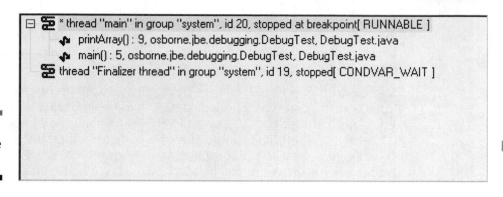

The Thread
and Stack pane
Figure 11-6.

11

Aside from the main thread, there is also a finalizer thread shown in the Figure 11-6 example. This is a thread created by the Java Virtual Machine to assist with the garbage collection process, and is one of many threads that Java and the standard packages create on your behalf. Don't be surprised if a graphical application has a half-dozen threads executing that you weren't aware of before you invoked the Debugger. It's just the normal state of affairs.

Using Breakpoints

Typically, a *breakpoint* is placed on a line of code and causes the Debugger to automatically stop prior to executing the line and await further instructions. JBuilder supports this simple type of breakpoint and expands on the notion in three significant ways:

♦ JBuilder breakpoints can be placed on lines of code, but can also be defined for exceptions. Exception breakpoints are invoked anywhere in the application that an exception meeting the description is thrown.

♦ Conditions and pass counts can be used to further control when the breakpoint is triggered.

♦ Breakpoints may perform a wider variety of actions than merely halting execution.

Placing and Removing Breakpoints

To place a breakpoint, click to the left of a line of code in the visible margin. The line is highlighted in red and the breakpoint symbol, a large red bullet, is displayed in the margin, indicating the presence of a breakpoint on that line of code. Click on the breakpoint symbol to remove the breakpoint for that line.

When running in debug mode, the Debugger will automatically pause before executing that particular line of code. Any number of breakpoints can be placed, and JBuilder will remember where breakpoints were placed when you exit, restoring those breakpoint definitions when JBuilder is launched again. Breakpoint settings are saved globally in JBuilder, not on a project-by-project basis.

Some caution needs to be exercised in placing breakpoints, since not every line of source code corresponds to generated code. During a debugging session, the source code displayed in the Source pane will include a small blue dot at the left of each line of source code for which instructions were actually generated by the compiler. The Debugger will ignore breakpoints placed on any other line, such as a comment or a blank line.

Viewing and Manipulating Breakpoints

Select View|Breakpoints to display the Breakpoints window, shown in Figure 11-7, which displays the currently defined breakpoints. You can also modify characteristics of breakpoints, either for all breakpoints or for an individual breakpoint.

To modify a specific breakpoint, right-click on the breakpoint to display the popup menu of available options shown in Figure 11-7. Breakpoints can be removed entirely, or merely disabled, leaving a placeholder without actually affecting anything during a debugging session. Disabled breakpoints are useful since you can later re-enable them when needed.

To modify all breakpoints, right-click in the white area of the Breakpoints window to display a popup menu with the following option for all breakpoints: Disable All, Enable All, Remove All, Expand All, and Collapse All. Once breakpoints have been assigned to named groups, the group names appear at the top level, with the associated breakpoints grouped beneath them. The Expand All and Collapse All items provide a quick way to show or hide all grouped breakpoints.

Breakpoints
window with
popup menu
Figure 11-7.

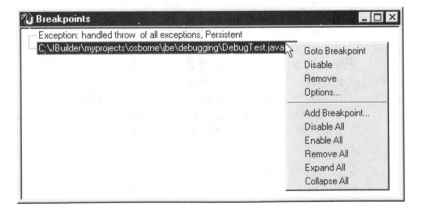

Modifying Breakpoint Options

When the Options menu item shown in Figure 11-7 is selected, a Breakpoint Options dialog is displayed with two tabbed pages: Breakpoint Definition and Action. The Breakpoint Definition page, shown in Figure 11-8, describes the situation that triggers the breakpoint, and can be used to define two distinct kinds of breakpoints: *source* breakpoints and *exception* breakpoints. A source breakpoint is placed on a specific line of a source file. An exception breakpoint is triggered for exceptions meeting specified criteria. At Breakpoint Type, set the type of breakpoint you are modifying by clicking either the Source Breakpoint or the Exception Breakpoint radio button.

The options at the top of the Breakpoint Definition page differ depending on whether you are modifying a source or an exception breakpoint. The Source File and Line Number fields allow you to change the location of a source breakpoint. For an exception breakpoint, you can specify one of three options: Unhandled Exception Throw, All Handled Exception Throws, or Handled Throw of Class. For the final option, a class name for the exception type must be provided. The controls in the bottom half of the dialog are the same for both source and exception breakpoints.

11

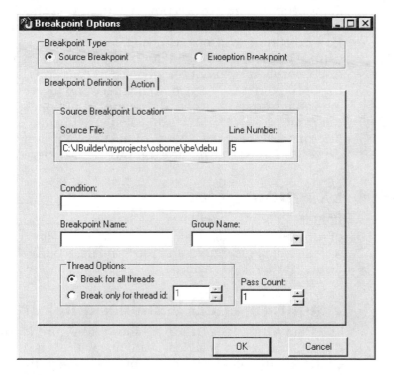

The
Breakpoint
Definition
page of the
Breakpoint
Options dialog
Figure 11-8.

The Breakpoint Name field allows you to name the breakpoint if desired. You can also organize breakpoints into groups using the Group Name field. Any breakpoint may also be restricted to a specific thread using Thread Options. The Condition field allows the definition of a boolean expression that will be evaluated every time the breakpoint is reached, with the breakpoint being ignored if it evaluates to false.

TIP: Evaluating an expression may take a second or two, and so it is best to avoid using the conditional breakpoint feature in frequently executed code.

Lastly, a Pass Count may be specified. Every time the breakpoint is reached, an internal counter is incremented, and the breakpoint is only acted upon when the counter matches the value specified. A value of 1 indicates that the breakpoint's action should always be invoked, a value of 2 indicates that it should be invoked every other time it is reached, starting with the second occasion, and so forth. This feature can be extremely useful for debugging problems that occur only after a number of iterations through a code loop.

The Action page of the Breakpoint Options dialog, shown in Figure 11-9, allows you to specify the action or actions that should be taken when a breakpoint is encountered. The most common action is selected with the Halt execution checkbox, which merely suspends execution and puts you in control of the Debugger. Additional options can display dialogs, enable or disable other breakpoints or groups of breakpoints, and record the fact that the breakpoint was reached in the execution log. If you check the Log breakpoint occurrence checkbox, you can optionally enter an expression in the Expression field. If the expression is left blank, JBuilder still logs information about the context of the breakpoint. If the field includes a valid expression, the value of the expression is also logged.

Examining Data

JBuilder provides a flexible array of tools for examining and altering the state of running Java code. There are automatic displays of local variables, watches, data inspectors, and the Evaluate/Modify dialog. Each type of display is discussed in turn.

Examining Local Variables and Parameters

The Data pane of the Debug tab shown in Figure 11-10 automatically displays the values of all local variables within the current execution context. This includes local variables declared within the current method,

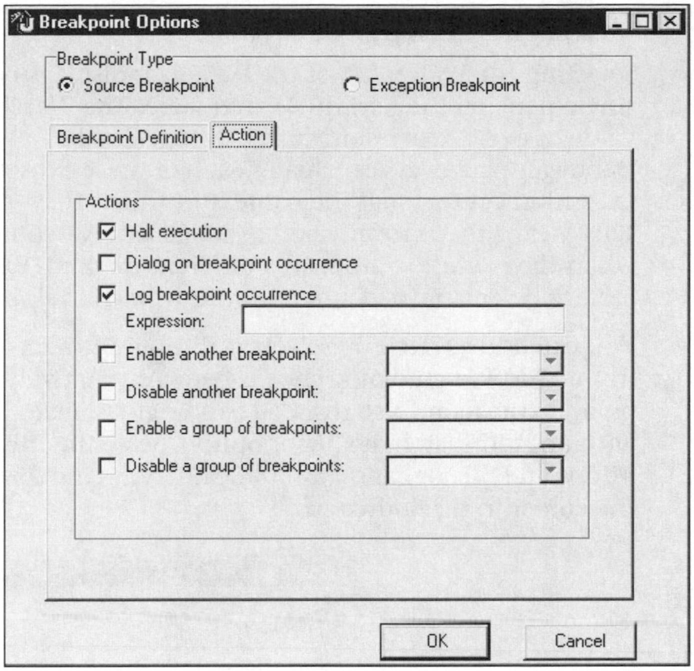

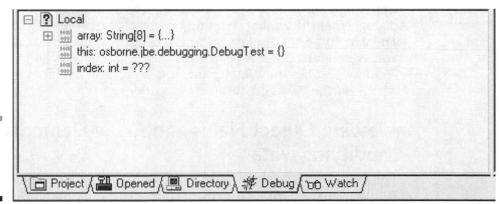

The Action
page of the
Breakpoint
Options dialog
Figure 11-9.

11

parameters passed to the method, and implicit parameters such as the value
of the special keyword **this**.

In the situation shown in Figure 11-10, the three variables that are displayed
include the loop counter *index*, the parameter *array*, and **this**. The definition
of the *index* variable has not yet been reached, so it is displayed as having an
unknown value.

The
Debugger's
Data pane
Figure 11-10.

Watching Expressions

Selecting the Watch tab of the Debugger displays the Source pane and a single pane on the left, the Watch pane. The Watch pane is a display of the value of every expression currently registered as a *watch*. Each time the Debugger pauses, it reevaluates each of these expressions within the current execution context, *not* the context in which they were originally defined. This means that a local variable added as a watch may not be meaningful when the execution stops in a different method. Expressions whose values cannot be determined are displayed with the value "???".

You can add a watch by selecting Run|Add Watch and typing an expression in the Add Watch dialog shown here. Alternatively, you can place the cursor on an expression in source code and right-click to bring up a popup menu with an Add Watch at Cursor option. Selecting this option displays the same Add Watch dialog, and automatically types in whatever expression contains the cursor in the Source pane.

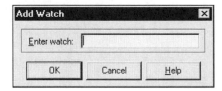

If you right-click on an expression listed in the Watch pane, a popup menu with a variety of options is displayed. These options include Edit Watch for altering the watch expression and Remove Watch for deleting the watch entirely.

Data Inspectors

The amount of screen space available within the Watch pane can be quite restrictive. You can create a free-floating window, a data inspector, for watching a single expression. To do so, select Run|Inspect, and in the Inspect dialog, enter the symbol. Pressing OK creates a free-floating data inspector. The data inspector displays information in the same format as in the Debug and Watch tabs, but can be freely resized and moved as an independent window. Just like the Watch pane, this expression's value is updated whenever the Debugger suspends execution.

Viewing Object Fields and Array Elements, and Modifying Data

The Debug tab, Watch tab, and data inspector all share a number of other abilities. Any complex datatype, such as an array or an object, can be expanded to display individual elements as shown here. If any of these elements or fields represent arrays or objects, they in turn may be expanded, ad infinitum.

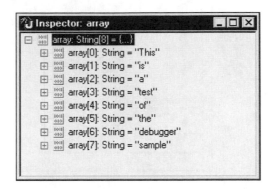

Right-clicking on a data element presents a popup menu of options appropriate to the selected data element and the context it appears in. Some of these options are as follows:

♦ To add a field or array element to the Watch pane, select the Watch option.

♦ A new data inspector can be created with the Inspect option.

♦ Boolean values include a Toggle Value option to change their values.

♦ Non-boolean primitive types can be modified with a Modify Value option and the subsequent dialog.

♦ The expanded view of a large array will normally constrain itself to a subset of the elements available. The popup menu for the array itself includes an Adjust Range menu option to allow a different or larger range to be presented.

Evaluating and Modifying Expressions

The Evaluate/Modify dialog shown in Figure 11-11 presents an alternate interface for evaluating expressions and modifying the value of expressions that represent primitive data elements. To display this dialog, select Run|Evaluate/Modify. This interface can be convenient when you are examining a number of successive expressions that do not need to persist as watches or data inspectors. If you are interested in a particular expression, you can then use the buttons along the bottom of this dialog to record it to the execution log, add it as a watch, or create a data inspector for it.

Fixing the Buggy Sample Application

The sample application created at the beginning of this chapter has one simple bug—it fails to print the first element passed on the command line. The following steps use a breakpoint and basic data examination techniques to identify the source of the problem and correct it.

1. Exit debug mode, if necessary, using Run|Program Reset, and remove any existing breakpoints from the source code.

2. Ensure that the command-line parameters are set up correctly as the string **This is a test of the debugger sample**.

3. The line that prints the array elements is not printing the correct element the first time, so in the Source pane, click to the left of the line in question to place a breakpoint:

```
System.out.print(array[index]);
```

4. Select Run|Debug "DebugTest" from the menu to start the Debugger.

5. Click the Run button on the debugging toolbar to execute until the breakpoint is reached. The green arrow should now be pointing at the line listed in step 3.

6. Look at the Data pane in the lower right and note that *index* is indeed equal to 1. There isn't much space to examine the array, so right-click on *array* in the lower-right pane and select Inspect from the menu.

7. Expand the array in the new data inspector window by clicking on the plus icon to the left of the name *array*. The elements of the array will be displayed beneath it.

8. Why isn't element 1 in the array the first item on the command line? Because Java arrays always begin with element number 0, as clearly displayed in the data inspector. That's one mystery solved, and fixing it requires a simple change to the **for** loop in the *printArray()* method to start with a 0 index:

```
for (int index = 0; index < array.length; index++) {
```

9. Click the Run button on the debugging toolbar once more to execute until the breakpoint is reached. If you made the correction listed in step 8, JBuilder will ask if you want to recompile the application, forcing the debugging session to start again from the beginning. Click the No button. The green arrow should now be pointing at the line listed in step 3.

10. Why doesn't the next word in the command line get printed? It is because the index has been incremented twice since the value of *index* is now three. A quick look at the code confirms that the **for** loop increments the index and so does the final line of code inside the loop. Commenting out this superfluous line solves the problem:

```
// index += 1;
```

NOTE: The final source code for Debugging.jpr is shown in the next section.

Defensive Programming: Testing Invariant Conditions

Not all bugs get discovered since their visible effects can be very subtle. Worse, the cause of some overt bugs can be so obscure as to be nearly impossible to trace, even with the best tools, because they only occur under complex circumstances that are difficult to duplicate. What can a conscientious developer do to improve the odds of finding and eradicating these kinds of problems?

One approach is to use defensive programming techniques, embedding code whose sole purpose is to identify potential problems at the earliest possible point in your code. This code typically tests for invariant conditions, or what the rest of us call assumptions. If a method is designed to work only with positive values for parameters, include tests to make certain that this is the case. If code assumes that values in two variables should be related, provide a test to ensure that the relationship is valid. Assumptions that prove to be incorrect can lead to very strange behavior in otherwise well-mannered code.

11

Unfortunately, debugging code tends to inflate an application while simultaneously slowing it down. With Java, both code size and performance are critical. In C and C++, a special macro, ASSERT, is commonly used to get around these problems. The macro expands as debugging code when compiled one way, and does not result in any code at all when compiled for final delivery. Since Java lacks the C preprocessor, the same solution isn't available. There simply is no easy solution with a standard Java compiler.

Luckily, the compiler included in JBuilder has a unique feature, the Exclude Class compiler option, designed for just this purpose. Your code will still be standard Java code and the compiled code will still be standard Java byte code, but the JBuilder compiler can automatically omit your debugging instructions when generating production code.

The Exclude Class Compiler Option

Select File|Project Properties to display the Project page of the project's Properties dialog. The Exclude Class field allows you to specify a class to eliminate all references to static methods of that particular class. Any class named in the Exclude Class field will be treated in this fashion at compile time. So long as all debugging code exists in the form of references to static methods of a single class, changing this Exclude Class field can disable it all before you ship your final code.

As a part of the JBCL (JavaBeans Component Library), JBuilder provides the *borland.jbcl.util.Diagnostic* class that includes a variety of static methods designed for exactly this purpose. Only the methods related to invariant testing are described next, so review the JBuilder documentation for additional features of the class.

The Diagnostic Class

The online documentation for the *Diagnostic* class covers a wide range of methods that can be used for debugging purposes. The method *check()* provides the basic behavior necessary for invariant testing. Two overloaded versions of the method exist:

♦ *Diagnostic.check(boolean parm)* prints the message "check failed" to the execution log and throws a *borland.jbcl.util.DiagnosticCheckException* if *parm* is not true.

♦ *Diagnostic.check(boolean parm, String message)* behaves similarly, but also includes the supplied message in the execution log and as the message in the exception instance.

Enhancing the Sample Application with an Invariant Test

The sample application used in this chapter makes one significant assumption. The *printArray()* method assumes that the array in question is not a **null** reference. The following additions add an explicit test for this case:

1. Import the *Diagnostic* class by adding the following line below the package statement:

```
import borland.jbcl.util.Diagnostic;
```

2. Add the invariant test before the first line of the *printArray()* method:

```
Diagnostic.check(array != null,
    "printArray called with a null parameter");
```

11

The revised source code is shown in Figure 11-12. As with all invariant tests, the change should have no affect on the application, because *printArray()* isn't supposed to be called with a **null** parameter. If at some point this assumption was violated, the test would catch the situation immediately and draw attention to the problem.

The resulting compiled class file occupies 1,128 bytes when compiled without excluding the *Diagnostic* class. When the value **borland.jbcl.util.Diagnostic** is specified for the Exclude Class field and

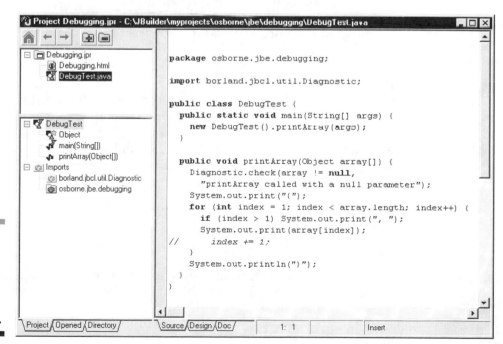

Sample
application
with invariant
testing
additions
Figure 11-12.

the class is recompiled, the resulting file occupies only 987 bytes. Eliminating the constant variable *String*, the boolean expression, and the invocation of the *check()* method has made a noticeable impact in the size of the class file and improved the performance as a bonus. The code is still present in the source and could be reinstated at any time to provide a "checked" version that detects problems when they occur for debugging purposes.

Tips for Common Java Problems

Although JBuilder provides a comprehensive set of debugging facilities, the process of debugging can still be a very labor-intensive one. No tool will actually find the bugs for you—the best you can hope for is that they merely make the true situation as obvious as possible. This section provides tips for finding remaining problems in your code, which typically fall into one of three categories: unhandled exceptions, flaws in program logic, and problems in foundation technology. Along with the proactive coding techniques discussed in the last section, the tips in this section attempt to aid your debugging efforts so that you can correct and perfect your code.

Unhandled Exceptions

The Java compiler forces the developer to write code to deal with any exception that doesn't descend from *java.lang.RuntimeException*, so only this exception's descendants can remain unhandled. The most frequently encountered *RuntimeException* subtypes, their causes, and possible solutions are as follows.

java.lang.NullPointerException

Any attempt to reference a field or method of an object reference, or the length field or an indexed element through an array reference, can result in a *NullPointerException* if the reference value is currently **null**. Unless the reference is obviously initialized to a non-null value before being used, it's good practice to include a test to ensure that a reference is valid before using it. The most obvious technique is to use an explicit test as shown here:

```
if (object != null) {
  object.doSomething();
}
```

Another equally valid technique is to use the **instanceof** operator. This operator will always evaluate to false if the left-hand side has a value of **null**.

```
if (object instanceof InterestingClass) {
  object.doSomething();
}
```

java.lang.ArrayIndexOutOfBoundsException

Java arrays have a fixed length, so any attempt to read or write to an element beyond the end of an array results in an *ArrayIndexOutOfBoundsException*. A common mistake leading to this exception is to use the array's *length* as an upper bound for a loop. The first element in a Java array has an index of zero, so the last element has an index equal to the length *minus one*. This method will always throw one of two exceptions:

```
public int lastValue(int[] values) {
  return values[values.length];
}
```

The usual result will be an *ArrayIndexOutOfBoundsException* because the index for the last element should be `values.length-1`, but that isn't the only potential problem with this code. Specifically, the value **null** can be passed for `values` and will result in a *NullPointerException*.

java.lang.ClassCastException

An explicit typecast is always checked for validity at runtime, and will result in a *ClassCastException* if the reference does not refer to a compatible type. The following code will compile, but will throw an exception at runtime:

```
public void castingProblem() {
  Object object = new Object();

  System.out.println((String) object);
}
```

This problem commonly arises when invoking a method whose return type is *Object* and the developer assumes that the object is of another type and attempts to treat it as such. The **instanceof** operator can be used to test object types wherever there is any doubt about the compatibility of two types.

```
public void castingSolution() {
  Object object = new Object();

  if (object instanceof String)
    System.out.println((String) object);
}
```

java.lang.ClassNotFoundException

If a class is present on the class path at compile time, the Java compiler will allow references to the class, assuming that it can be found at runtime. If the class is missing at runtime, a *ClassNotFoundException* will be thrown the first time it is actually used. Deploying code that depends on JBCL or JGL (Generic Collection Library for Java) classes without installing the class libraries themselves is one common source of this error, as is an incorrectly configured class path.

java.lang.SecurityException

Code that runs in an application may not run correctly as an applet. A *SecurityException* is thrown any time code attempts to violate the security constraints imposed by the applet runtime environment. One common cause of this is JBCL's attempt to load a resource such as an image that has not been correctly deployed with an applet. If the image cannot be found on the Web server, the subsequent attempt to load it directly from a file will result in a *SecurityException*.

Finding Logic Errors

An application that runs without throwing exceptions can still fail to produce the desired result. This kind of problem in program logic usually needs to be carefully traced using the Debugger to examine the nature of the problem. While the problems described here may only form a small percentage of the logic errors you will encounter, they are a few of the particularly insidious mistakes that even the most experienced Java developer can make.

References to Obsolete Class Files

Java compilers will compile code that references to a class so long as there is a valid corresponding class file on the class path. This becomes a problem when a class is renamed, moved to a new package, or deleted from a source code after being successfully compiled. The now obsolete class remains on the class path along with the new class file, and code that refers to the old class is still considered legal by the compiler even though it no longer exists in source form.

It seems that the only solution to this is to periodically delete all class files in JBuilder's output path to make sure that they can be regenerated from source code. Doing so periodically, and certainly after every major overhaul of class and package names, can help eliminate this surprising type of error. While deleting class files generated by JBuilder is safe, it always pays to be cautious when deleting files to avoid losing any of your work. As always, regular backups help reduce the risk of loss.

Comparing Object Values with the = = Operator

The reference equality operator == (two equal signs) does not test whether two objects contain the same value, merely whether the two references refer to the same object. This mistake is an especially common one with instances of *java.lang.String*. Code that compares *String* instances and other objects using the reference equality operator (==) can lead to surprising results as shown next.

```
String first = "HELLO", second = first.toUpperCase();

System.out.println("== says " + (first == second));
System.out.println("equals() says " + first.equals(second));
```

The first test using the reference equality operator, (first == second) returns **false** because these are two different strings whose values just happen to be identical. The *equals()* method for *String* does the right thing, comparing the actual contents of the two strings, and returns **true** in this example. Note that it isn't safe to assume that the *equals()* method will work for every class! The default implementation inherited from *java.lang.Object* actually uses the reference equality operator to do the comparison, and must be overridden by an individual class to offer any improvement.

Comparing Boolean Values with the = Operator

Accidentally using the assignment operator = when attempting to compare boolean values results in some surprising behavior. At a glance, this code looks reasonable, but the use of the wrong operator changes its meaning dramatically.

```
boolean flag = true;

if (flag = false) {  // Should be 'if (flag == false) {'
  doSomething();
}
```

This code actually changes the value of flag to **false**, and then tests the value, finds it to be false, and fails to execute *doSomething()*. The compiler can't help because this is completely legal code. All you can do is read your code carefully when it seems to be doing something counterintuitive.

Problems in Foundation Technology

When every other possibility of error has been eliminated in your source code and you still have problems, sometimes it may mean you have found a bug or problem in one of the foundation technologies your code relies upon.

11

Unfortunately, as Java is a very new technology, this isn't entirely unlikely. Newsgroups are a good place to compare your experiences with other Java developers who may be able to provide additional insight or workarounds. JavaSoft keeps a list of known bugs in the core Java technologies on their Web site and solicits bug reports from the development community.

Abnormally Terminating a Java Application

Some types of bugs result in applications that will not exit gracefully and must be terminated abruptly. This is easy when you are running a program under JBuilder's Debugger. Select Run|Program Reset or click the Reset button on the debugging toolbar to bring the current debugging session to a premature halt.

When running a program outside of the Debugger, more drastic measures may be necessary. If a console window for the application is present, you can click on the window and press CTRL-C to bring the Java interpreter to a halt. Unfortunately, the console window is not present if you have elected to send program output directly to the execution log as described earlier in this chapter. In this situation, you will need to find and shut down the *javaw* task using a technique appropriate to your operating system.

Under Windows NT, the task manager can be displayed by pressing CTRL-SHIFT-ESC. The *javaw* task will be listed on the Processes tab. Select the task and press the End Process button to stop it. Under Windows 95, a similar task list can be displayed by pressing CTRL-ALT-DELETE once, keeping in mind that pressing this key sequence a second time will reboot Windows 95. Always exercise caution when stopping tasks, and treat these techniques as a last resort, remaining aware that stopping the wrong task can easily result in data loss.

CHAPTER 12

Deploying Java Applications and Applets

The process of creating a Java application or applet results in the creation of many small files arranged in a deep directory hierarchy. Every class is stored a separate file, as are all of the images and sounds associated with those classes. A dozen files is typical for a trivial example, hundreds for a medium-sized project, and thousands or even tens of thousands for large projects.

This organization has significant advantages. The lengthy link cycle required by traditional compiled languages after every single change is not necessary with Java. Every class is loaded when it is needed from its own class file. A Java program can locate and use classes that were added after the original installation. Classes can even be installed while a program is running and still be used by that program.

There are also drawbacks to this approach. A single missing file can result in runtime errors that are difficult or impossible to recover from. Installing all of the necessary files becomes critical when deploying Java code, but determining which files are necessary can be a difficult task. There are also inherent inefficiencies in managing a large number of small files rather than one large file.

You can use JBuilder's Deployment Wizard to assist in addressing some of these issues when deploying applets or applications. However, this tool cannot be relied upon to solve the problem entirely. The best approach is to use the Deployment Wizard to perform much of the predictable work, and then manually solve the remaining problems.

Deployment Concepts

JBuilder is an environment for creating pure Java code, and as such it shares all of the advantages and limitations of Java code deployment. The remainder of this chapter is designed to address the following fundamental concerns common to all Java applications and applets:

♦ How are the necessary classes loaded?

♦ How are additional resource files such as image files and sound files loaded?

♦ How efficient is the distribution mechanism?

♦ What can I legally deploy and under what restrictions?

There is no single answer for any of these questions, but rather a variety of choices and guidelines for selecting the best answer in a given situation. The rest of this chapter addresses the underlying issues and introduces useful techniques instead of attempting to provide a single deployment recipe.

Loading Classes: The Class Path

As discussed at the beginning of this chapter, Java loads classes when they are first needed. The Java VM (Virtual Machine) brings the code into memory the first time that it encounters any reference to the class—such as when an instance is constructed, or code refers to a static method or variable belonging to the associated class.

How does the Java VM find the class? It searches all of the locations listed on the *class path* for the class in question. The class path contains a list of directories and uncompressed archive files in either zip or JAR (Java Archive) format, typically separated by semicolons. A typical class path might look something like this:

```
c:\jbuilder\java\lib\classes.zip;c:\jbuilder\redist\jbcl-rt.zip;
c:\jbuilder\redist\jgl.zip;c:\jbuilder\redist\jclass.zip;
c:\jbuilder\myclasses;.
```

This class path includes the standard Java packages from classes.zip, Borland's JBCL (JavaBeans Component Library) runtime classes from jbcl-rt.zip, ObjectSpace's JGL (Generic Collection Library for Java) from jgl.zip, and the KL Group's JClass library from jclass.zip. These archives are followed by the default directory JBuilder uses to store compiled class files. Last on the path is a single period that is interpreted as a reference to the current directory.

In order to load the class *java.lang.String*, for example, the search begins with the archive classes.zip. The Java VM looks inside the zip file to see if it contains an archived copy of the file java\lang\String.class. Note that the package the class belongs to is translated into a set of nested directories, and the class file itself must have the traditional .class extension. In this instance, the Java VM finds the class, loads it, and proceeds without searching the remainder of the path.

Consider a second example, the search for the class *osborne.jbecd.layout.FlowLayoutSample* used in Chapter 5. This class will not be found in the first three locations on the class path, which are the archive files classes.zip, jbcl-rt.zip, and jgl.zip. The search then proceeds with the next entry on the class path, the directory c:\jbuilder\myclasses. The package hierarchy and class name are added to the root directory and the Java VM looks for the class file itself in c:\jbuilder\myclasses\osborne\jbecd\layout\FlowLayoutSample.class. If the examples from the CD-ROM have been installed in the default directory as described in Appendix C, the class file will be found in this location. Failing this, the process will be repeated for the fifth entry on the class path, which is a reference to the current directory. Once again, the Java VM will look for the appropriate file in a subdirectory of the current directory derived from the package to which the class belongs.

12

Class Loading for Applets

Within a Web browser, the process of loading classes is very similar, but adds a slight twist. As a first step, the browser searches the class path in the usual way, loading classes that can be found on the path from the local hard drive. This allows code such as the standard Java packages to be installed locally to avoid downloading them every time they are needed. If a class cannot be found on the traditional class path, the browser looks to the Web for the class definition.

Every applet is loaded in response to discovering an <APPLET> tag in an HTML (HyperText Markup Language) document. This tag may include additional information about the location that the browser should search for classes that cannot be located locally. Each applet has a URL (Uniform Resource Locator), an address on a Web server that it uses as its code base, a root location to use when searching for class files. If the code base is not explicitly defined in the <APPLET> tag, it defaults to the directory the HTML file itself was loaded from.

The <APPLET> tag may optionally list one or more URLs for archive files available over the Web. The browser will download any archive files specified, and searches them in the order they were specified for the desired class file. If none of the archives contains the necessary class, the browser will attempt to download the class file from a URL derived from the code base. The browser's cache may be used to eliminate the download time when the same class is needed again.

NOTE: See Chapter 6 for further details on the <APPLET> tag and related applet concepts.

Setting the Class Path

The technique used to set the class path depends on the individual Java VM or browser. The Java VM supplied with the JDK (Java Developer's Kit) uses an environment variable named CLASSPATH, while Microsoft's VM reads the value from the Windows registry. Both allow the class path to be overridden by passing a command-line parameter to the program used to start a Java application, but the syntax for doing so is different. Consult the documentation for the VM or browser you intend to deploy to for further details.

Within JBuilder, the class path for the current project can be viewed and modified by selecting File|Project Properties. The Class Path text field can be edited directly, or the Edit button to the right can be pressed to display a more sophisticated interface for altering the path. The default class path for new projects can be set in exactly the same way by selecting Tools|IDE Options. These changes only affect execution within the JBuilder environment.

Loading Resources

A resource in Java can take one of two forms:

♦ A collection of data stored in an independent file that is loaded by an application or applet. Typical examples of resources include image files in GIF (Graphic Interchange Format) or JPEG (Joint Photographic Experts Group) formats.

♦ A collection of data provided by a related collection of class files, each of which provides data internationalized, or translated, for a different locale.

Java code that is unable to access the required resource files at runtime may run incorrectly or fail to run at all depending on the amount of exception-handling code designed to detect the condition. Including the necessary resource files during deployment is just as important as distributing the necessary class files. All of the same techniques apply, except that there are no tools to automatically detect and include the necessary resource files.

12

The getResource() Method

Just like classes, resources can be loaded from individual files or located in a JAR file. Resources are typically loaded using the *java.lang.Class* method *getResource()* or another method that calls this method. Resources are loaded from locations relative to a particular class. For example, when configuring a *borland.jbcl.control.ButtonBar*, the image location is listed as the string "image" by default. Assuming that this is a relative path, the *getResource()* method automatically attempts to locate the necessary images by the same means as the *ButtonBar* itself: from an archive file, a local file on disk, or a Web server, searching in the subdirectory borland\jbcl\control\image.

Distribution Efficiency

The ability to create an archive file to combine class and resource files into a single file is the single most effective tool for increasing the convenience of distributing applications and reducing the time required for downloading applets. The benefits of bundling everything into a single convenient archive file are significant:

♦ Keeping track of a large number of small files wastes disk space under any operating system. Some operating systems are less efficient at allocation than others, using a multiple of 32K or more for every file, large or small. Multiply that waste by thousands of tiny class files and the loss becomes significant.

♦ There is a significant amount of fixed overhead in requesting a file from a Web server. As a result, Web servers can deliver information more efficiently as a single large file than as a large number of small files.

It is recommended that you simply package everything needed into a single archive file and consider the drawbacks of this approach only if one of the following becomes an issue:

♦ For small- to medium-sized projects, the majority of code in the archive file will come from the class libraries that ship with JBuilder. When delivering numerous applications or applets based on the same core classes, making multiple copies of the information wastes disk space and can actually increase download time. It may be advantageous to create an archive file that contains code shared between multiple projects since both applications and applets can load classes from more than one archive file.

♦ An entire archive file must be downloaded before the applet contained within it can be executed. You can reduce the initial download time by placing rarely used classes on the Web server as individual files to be loaded as needed. This technique should be used carefully since it will take significantly more time to download these classes as individual files if they are needed.

Redistribution Licensing

It is extremely important to make certain that you have the legal right to distribute someone else's code before doing so. The REDIST.TXT file installed with JBuilder describes the detailed terms for deploying Borland's own JBCL, ObjectSpace's JGL, and the KL Group's JClass Beans.

The Deployment Wizard

JBuilder's Deployment Wizard includes several related features in one convenient tool. It automatically creates zip and JAR files that combine the classes and resources in your project into a single deployable file. The wizard can also detect most interclass dependencies and incorporate the required classes into the same archive file.

To use the Deployment Wizard, select Wizard|Deployment Wizard from JBuilder's menu, make the appropriate selections in the dialog shown in Figure 6-1, and click the Finish button.

The Select Files to Deploy list contains all of the files and packages included in the project. The entire list is selected by default, but individual items can be removed from the selection by holding down the CTRL key and clicking on the item or items that you want to remove. The HTML files included in a project are typically not deployed, and can be deselected to reduce the size of the archive file. When Java source files are listed, the wizard automatically scans the source file to determine which class files to deploy. The source files themselves are never included in the archive file.

The Deploy Dependencies checkbox controls whether the wizard searches for interclass dependencies and attempts to include these required classes in the resulting zip or JAR file. The two checkboxes below Deploy Dependencies control the classes that are excluded from the deployment process. By default, all JBCL and JGL classes are excluded from the archive file, based on the assumption that these classes will be deployed in their own zip files as provided by Borland. Disabling one or both checkboxes forces the required classes to be included in the archive file. The core Java classes included with the JDK are always excluded from the archive file.

The radio buttons for the Deploy as option control the type of file that is created. The only significant difference between the zip and JAR file formats created by the wizard is that JAR files include a special manifest file listing their contents. The manifest can be manually edited to take advantage of additional JAR capabilities not directly supported by JBuilder, including the designation of a trusted applet. Refer to the online JDK documentation in JBuilder (select Help|Java Reference) for a further discussion of the JAR format and manifest files.

12

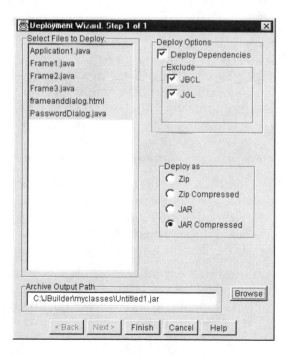

The
Deployment
Wizard
Figure 12-1.

NOTE: Several popular unzip tools, including WinZip 6.2, cannot extract files from archives produces by the JBuilder or the JDK jar.exe utility. You may need to get a newer version of a zip tool if you experience difficulty using your existing unzipping utility.

When the desired options have been selected, specify the desired filename in the Archive Output Path field and click the Finish button to create the archive file.

The Deployment Wizard's Limits

Limitations of the Deployment Wizard in the initial release of JBuilder prevent it from correctly determining dependencies for classes that have been loaded into JBuilder's Java VM for a variety of reasons. To be safe, you should always quit and restart JBuilder before using this wizard. Also, the wizard can take several minutes to complete the deployment process if the Deploy Dependencies checkbox is checked. Be patient and wait for the Deployment Wizard dialog to disappear before proceeding with other tasks in JBuilder.

You should always do a Build|Make Project before invoking the Deployment Wizard. This is important because the wizard uses the most recently compiled files and does not check to see if there have been changes made to the source code.

CAUTION: In the initial release of JBuilder, the Deployment Wizard does not fully support the use of a new language feature in JDK 1.1 referred to as inner classes. Since JBuilder will never automatically generate an inner class declaration, this may not be a problem if you do all of your development in JBuilder. However, if you use inner classes, you will need to add these class files manually.

The wizard can only detect dependencies between classes that are recognized at compile time, neglecting two other kinds of dependency. The first kind is a required resource file, such as an image or sound file. These files will only be included if the project file directly references them. The second type is a class whose identity is determined at runtime.

In addition to the standard techniques for referring to a class in code, a class file may be loaded with the *java.lang.Class* method *forName()*. This method accepts a single string argument that contains a fully qualified class name, loads the class file in question, and returns a reference to a special object that represents it. The method is rarely used in JDK 1.1 code, with two notable exceptions:

♦ JDBC (JavaSoft Database Connectivity) drivers are typically loaded by name and will not be included by the wizard.

♦ Subclasses of *java.util.ResourceBundle*, which are used for internationalization purposes, are also loaded by name.

Ideally, all of the necessary classes and resources should be bundled into one or more zip or JAR files for deployment purposes. You can eliminate one source of difficulty by always including your own Java source files and resources in every project that requires them. The classes and resources used by JBCL, JGL, and JClass should be dealt with differently, depending on whether an application or an applet is being deployed.

12

Deploying Applications

A Java application can easily be deployed using a minimal set of classes in the application's JAR file accompanied by archive files that include the necessary runtime support class and resource files. Including the full runtime libraries ensures that none of the JBCL or JGL files are missing from the distribution. The following steps illustrate a process that can be used to deploy any Java application:

1. Create an application JAR file containing all of the required classes and resources, but excluding JDK, JBCL, and JGL classes.

   Save all files, build the project to make sure the class files are up to date, and quit JBuilder to ensure a clean deployment. Restart JBuilder, load the desired project, and select Wizard|Deployment Wizard to start the deployment process. Select the Deploy as JAR option, since compressed JAR files are only supported for applets. You may also want to specify a different Archive Output Path before proceeding. Click the Finish button and wait for the Deployment Wizard to complete its task.

2. Install the application JAR file on the target system.

   Copy the entire application JAR file to a standard location on the target system. For installation on a network, choose a location on the network that is visible to all systems to avoid installing files on each computer individually.

3. Install the JBCL and JGL archive files on the target system.

   Copy the versions of the libraries designed for redistribution to a standard location on the target system. These files are installed with JBuilder as C:\JBuilder\redist\jbcl-rt.zip and C:\JBuilder\redist\jgl.zip.

NOTE: The JClass runtime classes are not included in this process because the Deployment Wizard will include them in the application JAR. There is no checkbox to exclude the JClass classes from the dependency tracking process. A future version of JBuilder may include this ability, in which case the file jclass.zip would also need to be placed in the target directory.

4. Make sure the target platforms have a standard Java VM installed.

   A minimal Java VM called the JRE (Java Runtime Environment) is available from JavaSoft. You can use this VM or any other Java 1.1-compliant VM to distribute applications. The JRE must be installed on every computer the Java application will be deployed to. Other Java runtime VMs may have different requirements.

5. Create a standard way to launch the application that does not depend on the configuration of the target computer.

Configuring the CLASSPATH and executable search path on every machine is a thankless and time-consuming task. Fortunately, it is easy to create an application launching script that does not require any prior configuration of the target machine. This process works whether the application and support files are installed on a local drive or a network drive.

A single command line can be triggered from a shortcut under Windows 95 or NT 4.0, a shell script in UNIX, or any comparable mechanism in another environment. To create the shortcut in Windows, right-click on the desktop and select New|Shortcut. Specify the command line shown here in the wizard that appears, click the Next button, and give the shortcut a name. Click the Finish button to complete the process.

```
"C:\Program Files\JavaSoft\jre\1.1\bin\jrew.exe" -classpath
 "C:\Program Files\JavaSoft\jre\1.1\lib\rt.jar;
C:\java\lib\jbcl-rt.zip;C:\java\lib\jgl.zip;
C:\Java\Example.jar" example.ExampleApp
```

NOTE: This command is actually a single line that has been formatted to fit the printed page. For the example to work, this complete command must be entered without carriage returns, there must be a space before the text shown on the second line, and there must not be a space between the text shown on the other consecutive lines. You may consider executing this line from a batch file.

The example uses the executable jrew.exe to start the Java VM without creating a console window. Applications that require a console window for text-based interaction should use jre.exe instead.

This shortcut makes the following assumptions that can easily be adjusted for the actual target environment:

♦ That the JRE is in use and has been installed in C:\Program Files\JavaSoft\jre\1.1. This installation includes the jrew.exe and jre.exe as well as the core Java classes in the rt.jar file.

♦ That the JBCL and JGL archive files are installed in C:\java\lib.

♦ That the application JAR file is Example.jar and is stored in C:\java\Example.jar.

♦ That the class used to start the application is *ExampleApp* in the package called example, so that the fully qualified class name specified is *example.ExampleApp*.

12

Deploying Applets

A Java applet can be deployed in one of several ways, each of which has its advantages and disadvantages. The trade-offs involved in deploying a single archive file, multiple archive files, and individual class and resource files are discussed prior to introducing the deployment steps for each technique. Finally, there is a brief discussion of combining these techniques for addressing the various browser limitations.

Single Archive Applets

Creating one archive allows for the simplest conceptual form of delivery, since a single download from a Web server brings with it everything that is needed by the applet. The approach requires a complete map of your code's class and resource dependencies, a task that the Deployment Wizard can help with but not resolve completely. Finding a solution to the problem of deploying the JBCL's resource files is a necessary part of the deployment process.

Combining all of the necessary files into a single archive file is effective when:

♦ You can take the time to test your applet and know for certain that the archive file isn't missing the necessary class or resource files.

♦ The resulting archive file is significantly smaller than the combination of all necessary archive files, (described under "Multiple Archive Applets"), and visitors who may have slow links to your Web server will use the applet.

The following steps illustrate a process that can be used to deploy a Java applet in a single archive file.

1. Extract the JBCL's image resource files into your source path.

   Unfortunately the Deployment Wizard cannot extract the necessary image resource files from the JBCL archive for you. It is necessary to manually extract these images for inclusion in your project. You will need to perform this step only the first time you use this technique since the files can be used from any project.

   From a DOS command line, execute the steps in the following command listing. The first step configures your environment so that the command-line tools included with JBuilder can be used. The second and third lines ensure that the files will be extracted into your source path. The final line uses the JDK jar.exe tool to perform the extraction.

   ```
   c:\JBuilder\bin\setvars c:\JBuilder
   c:
   cd \JBuilder\myprojects
   jar -xf c:\jbuilder\redist\jbcl-rt.zip
    borland\jbcl\control\image borland\jbcl\view\image
   ```

NOTE: The above listing includes four commands, each of which must be entered separately. The last two lines are actually a single line that has been formatted to fit the printed page. For the example to work, this complete command must be entered without carriage returns, and there must be a space before the text shown on the fifth line.

2. Add the JBCL's image resource files to your project.

   Open your project and click on the Add to project button on the AppBrowser toolbar to display the File Open / Create dialog. Click on the Package type and enter **borland.jbcl.control.image** in the Name field. Click OK to add the package to your project. Repeat the process for the package name **borland.jbcl.view.image**.

   The Deployment Wizard will now deploy these image files with the applet. These are the only resource files required by the libraries that ship with JBuilder. There are a total of 21 image files that add roughly 5K to a compressed archive file.

TIP: If you take a moment and examine the AppBrowser, you will find that the packages added to the project appear as nested subtrees within the project. The same technique can be used to organize large projects by including nothing but package names immediately under the project file in the Navigation pane.

3. Create an application JAR file containing all of the required class and resource files, including JBCL and JGL classes, but excluding JDK classes.

   Save all files, build the project to make sure the class files are up to date, and quit JBuilder to ensure a clean deployment. Restart JBuilder, load the desired project, and select Wizard|Deployment Wizard to start the deployment process. Disable the Exclude JGL and Exclude JBCL checkboxes to ensure that these class files are deployed. You may also want to specify a different Archive Output Path before proceeding. Click the Finish button and wait for the Deployment Wizard to complete its task.

4. Copy the applet archive to your Web server.

   Choose a URL path on your Web server to store applet archives and use it as a repository for all of your JAR files. It is highly recommended that you actually set up and use a Web server for your tests, resulting in a URL path like http://servername/Java/, where servername is the network name for your server.

   If you cannot use a Web server, you can use a URL path like file://c:\Java\ to refer to files on your local hard drive. For the remainder of this chapter, we will refer to files in the path using URLs in the former notation http://servername/Java/, and leave it to you to convert to the latter format as needed.

   The method used to get files to the server differs from one to the next, so consult your server's documentation for details on how to manage this process. If you are using a Web server managed by an ISP (Internet Service Provider) on your behalf, the ISP will provide details about how to transfer files.

   The remainder of this example uses the archive URL http://servername/Java/SingleArchive.jar.

5. Create an HTML container file for the applet and put it on the server.

   The following HTML code incorporates the applet into a 500 × 400 pixel rectangular region within a simple Web page:

```
<APPLET
  WIDTH=500
  HEIGHT=400
  ARCHIVE=/Java/SingleArchive.jar
  CODE=package.name.ClassName.class>
</APPLET>
```

The path /Java/Example.jar is a relative path, meaning that this applet will be loaded from the archive file in the specified location using whatever server the HTML file itself was loaded from. The fully qualified class name

12

package.name.ClassName must be replaced with the actual package and class name for the *Applet* subclass in the archive file.

Make this file accessible from http://servername/TestSingle.html. Any Java 1.1-compliant browser should now be able to load and view the applet by loading the HTML document. See Chapter 6 for a discussion of issues regarding limitations of browsers available as of this writing.

Multiple Archive Applets

Delivering the complete JBCL and JGL libraries along with the applet code has its appeal. With a complete delivery, it becomes impossible to leave out class or resource files from these libraries' archive files. Though the archive files aren't small, once downloaded they will be placed in the browser's cache to eliminate the need to download them again immediately for another applet.

Deploying applet-specific code and resource files in one JAR file and standard class libraries as additional archive files is effective when:

♦ You want to be certain that all necessary class and resource files are available without investing a lot of time and effort.

♦ Internal users or visitors who have a high-speed connections to your Web server will use the applet.

♦ Several applets all require the same class libraries.

The following steps illustrate a process that can be used to deploy a Java applet as multiple archive files:

1. Create an application JAR file containing all of the required class and resource files, excluding JDK, JBCL, and JGL class files.

   Save all files, build the project to make sure the class files are up to date, and quit JBuilder to ensure a clean deployment. Restart JBuilder, load the desired project, and select Wizard|Deployment Wizard to start the deployment process. The default settings are appropriate for this style of applet deployment, although you may want to specify a different Archive Output Path before proceeding. Click the Finish button and wait for the Deployment Wizard to complete its task.

2. Copy the applet archive to your Web server.

   The remainder of this example uses the archive URL http://servername/Java/MultiArchive.jar.

3. Copy the redistribution archives to your Web server.

Place the file installed in C:\JBuilder\redist\jbcl-rt.zip at http://servername/Java/jbcl-rt.zip. Repeat the process with C:\JBuilder\redist\jgl.zip and http://servername/Java/jgl.zip.

4. Create an HTML file to contain the applet and put it on the server.

The following HTML code incorporates the applet into a 500 × 400 pixel rectangular region within a simple Web page:

```
<APPLET
  WIDTH=500
  HEIGHT=400

ARCHIVE=/Java/MultiArchive.jar,/Java/jbcl-rt.zip,/Java/jgl.zip
  CODE=package.name.ClassName.class>
</APPLET>
```

The difference between this HTML file and the previous example is that the fourth line contains a comma-delimited archive list that includes not only the applet archive file, but also the standard class libraries required to support the applet. Make this file accessible from http://servername/TestMulti.html. Again, any Java 1.1-compliant browser should now be able to load and view the applet by loading the HTML document.

12

Individual File Applets

Prior to Java 1.1, the only standard way to download classes and resources was to download a single file at a time. This approach has the advantage of just-in-time delivery, reducing the amount of information that needs to be distributed to start an applet, but delivering data in small chunks turns out to be extremely inefficient over a wide area network such as the Internet.

Deploying applet code as a collection of individual class and archive files is effective when:

♦ The user's browser does not correctly support the use of archive files or does not support the use of multiple archive files.

♦ The class or resource files delivered in this fashion are needed infrequently.

The easiest way to create a file structure containing all of the necessary directories and files is to expand all of the archives that would normally be used in a multiple archive applet deployment. This can be accomplished using the jar.exe tool included with JBuilder. The necessary steps are as follows:

1. Create an application JAR file containing all of the required class and resource files, excluding JDK, JBCL, and JGL class files.

   Save all files, build the project to make sure the class files are up to date, and quit JBuilder to ensure a clean deployment. Restart JBuilder, load the desired project, and select Wizard|Deployment Wizard to start the deployment process. The default settings are appropriate for this style of applet deployment, although you may want to specify a different Archive Output Path before proceeding. Click the Finish button and wait for the Deployment Wizard to complete its task.

2. Expand the JBCL, JGL, and applet archive files.

   From a DOS command line, execute the steps listed following this paragraph. The first line configures your environment so that the command-line tools included with JBuilder can be used. The next three lines create a C:\Java directory and set it as the current directory. The next three lines use the JDK (Java Development Kit) jar.exe tool to extract the contents of the necessary archives. Replace the reference to C:\JBuilder\myclasses\Example.jar in the last line with the Archive Output Path specified in step 1.

   ```
   c:\JBuilder\bin\setvars c:\JBuilder
   c:
   mkdir \Deploy
   cd \Deploy
   jar -xf c:\jbuilder\redist\jbcl-rt.zip
   jar -xf c:\jbuilder\redist\jgl.zip
   jar -xf c:\jbuilder\myclasses\Example.jar
   ```

3. Copy the entire file and directory hierarchy to your Web server.

   Copy the whole file and directory hierarchy under C:\Java to http://servername/Java/.

4. Create an HTML file to contain the applet and put it on the server.

   The following HTML code incorporates the applet into a 500×400 pixel rectangular region within a simple Web page:

   ```
   <APPLET
     WIDTH=500
     HEIGHT=400
     CODEBASE=/Java
     CODE=package.name.ClassName.class>
   </APPLET>
   ```

The difference between this HTML file and those in the previous examples is that it specifies a code base for loading individual files rather than providing a list of archive files. Make this file accessible from http://servername/TestFiles.html. Once more, any Java 1.1-compliant browser should now be able to load and view the applet by loading the HTML document.

Combining Techniques

The archive-based and individual file approaches to distributing an applet are not mutually exclusive. Even though the applet is deployed using one or more archive files, the individual files may still be provided as a fallback. Combining archive-based and individual file techniques is really a best-of-both-worlds approach. This has the following advantages:

◆ It allows browsers that do support archive files to use the efficient archive download approach since archive files are used in preference to individual files.

◆ It still works with browsers that do not properly support archive files or that do not support more than one archive file.

◆ Class or resource files that were missed when creating a single archive file deployment can still be found as individual files since the technique discussed in the previous section provides all files in the support libraries.

◆ Infrequently used class files can be trimmed from the applet archive file to reduce the download size. These class files will still be downloaded as individual files when they are actually needed.

The necessary steps are as follows:

1. Follow steps 1–3 outlined previously in the section "Individual File Applets" to create the safety net of class and resource files.

2. Follow steps 1–4 outlined previously in the section "Single Archive Applets" to create a single deployment archive file for your applet.

3. Create an HTML container file for the applet and put it on the server.

   The following HTML code incorporates the applet into a 500 × 400 pixel rectangular region within a simple Web page:

```
<APPLET
  WIDTH=500
  HEIGHT=400
  ARCHIVE=/Java/SingleApplet.jar
  CODEBASE=/Java
  CODE=package.name.ClassName.class>
</APPLET>
```

The HTML file combines references to the archive and code base . The archive file will be downloaded and searched first, but failure to find a class or resource file will cause the code base to be searched next. Make this file

12

accessible from http://servername/TestCombo.html. You should now be able to load and view the applet using a Java 1.1-compliant browser.

Advanced Deployment Topics

This chapter is intended to serve as a good starting point in understanding the issues inherent to Java code deployment. There are certainly numerous additional topics that could be covered, quite possibly enough to fill a book of their own. Each of these possible topics builds on the basic principles outlined earlier in the chapter, so you should be well equipped to begin investigating the subject on your own.

Two topics of particular interest are worth discussing: deploying database applications and applets, and deploying for an environment that supports only the older Java 1.02 standard.

Database Applications and Applets

JBuilder's DataExpress architecture uses JDBC for database access. The JDBC API (Application Programming Interface) in turn requires a driver to communicate with the database used to store data. Deploying the appropriate driver is critical for a database application or applet. The driver must be included in an archive or directory on the class path in order to function correctly.

Some of the readily available drivers and specific deployment issues are discussed in the following sections.

The JDBC-ODBC Bridge Driver

Java 1.1 ships with a trivial driver that provides access to ODBC (Open Database Connectivity) data sources through JDBC. As this is the only driver shipped with the JDK, it is commonly the first driver used in attempting to write Java database applications and applets. Unfortunately, it is a poor choice for two reasons and should not be considered practical for real-world deployment:

♦ The bridge driver requires ODBC to be previously configured on the target machine.

♦ To enforce security, the bridge driver cannot be used from an applet unless it is a signed applet that the browser has been configured to trust.

InterClient

The InterBase database included with JBuilder Professional and Client/Server has a 100 percent Java JDBC driver called InterClient. This driver can be downloaded free of charge from http://www.interbase.com and used to deploy Java applications and applets.

DataGateway for Java

Borland has developed a middleware product that includes a 100 percent Java JDBC driver and server software to allow Java applications and applets to connect to a wide variety of databases. More information on DataGateway for Java can be found on Borland's JBuilder Web site at http://www.borland.com/jbuilder. You can go to Borland's Web site from within JBuilder by selecting Help|Borland Online.

Deploying for Java 1.02

The limited availability of Java 1.1-compliant Web browsers makes widescale deployment of JDK 1.1 applets unattractive for the very near future. This problem is self-correcting, since major browser vendors have committed to Java 1.1 support, but it does create the need to support and perhaps even write Java 1.02 code.

12

NOTE: See Chapter 6 for a discussion of Web browser capabilities and limitations.

JBuilder is geared towards Java 1.1 development, but the compiler does generate byte code that is compatible with Java 1.02. JBuilder will import and compile existing Java code without problems. Newly added code must follow a single rule: it cannot reference classes and methods introduced in Java 1.1. A good Java reference such as *Java 1.1: The Complete Reference* (Osborne/McGraw-Hill) is critical for finding a complete description of the changes introduced in the newer Java release. You can also select Help|Java Reference from within JBuilder to view the JDK Documentation and supplement references for JDK 1.1.

This simple rule of not referencing classes and methods in Java 1.1 has numerous implications:

♦   Many methods and some classes supported by Java 1.02 will be flagged by the compiler with deprecation warnings. These can be ignored.

♦   The event-handling model in Java 1.02 is completely different from Java 1.1. You cannot use JBuilder's UI Designer to create Java 1.02-compliant event-handling code.

♦   JBCL components rely heavily on Java 1.1 features and cannot be used in code designed to run with only Java 1.02 support.

Finally, applets deployed in this manner cannot be deployed as archives. Standardized zip and JAR archive file support is a Java 1.1 addition.

CHAPTER 13

JavaBeans Basics

You've been reading about working with and manipulating components throughout this book. However, this chapter focuses specifically on the JavaBeans components and standards; in other words, the JavaBeans component model, which was implemented in the JDK (Java Developer's Kit) version 1.1. This chapter focuses on how to take advantage of existing JavaBeans by describing the interface to each of these attribute types. Since this chapter ties together many concepts of working with and manipulating components, you may find that some of the descriptions here are similar to those in other chapters, and you are referred back to the other chapters for more detail on particular topics. Chapter 14 discusses creating or writing new JavaBeans by implementing the patterns that describe the attributes of the JavaBeans.

The JavaBeans Standard

Development tools of the past have often included their own proprietary component model. Each vendor had their own ideas about how the technology should work and incorporated these ideas into their own languages or grafted them onto existing languages. With the second major release of JDK version 1.1, Sun introduced the JavaBeans component model. Adoption of the JavaBeans standard by all Java development tools would help unify the Java component market and prevent this kind of fragmentation.

The JavaBeans standard describes how a component should be written in Java, and how a graphical design tool should work with components to take advantage of their functionality. With a single standard in place, creators of components can address a broad market since their components should work in any tool that supports the standard. Similarly, new development tools can take advantage of a wide range of existing components.

Component Technology Overview

The introduction of component-based development has arguably been the most successful recent step towards achieving true code reuse on a large scale. Learning how to use a function or class library takes a lot of time, requires a lot of documentation, and is something that beginners find difficult to learn to do effectively. Components, by contrast, vastly simplify the process of accomplishing difficult tasks and are effective tools for beginners and experts alike.

Component Philosophy

Components are more than just classes. They are classes that follow a set of standards and adhere to a philosophy about code reuse. They can be manipulated directly in a graphical environment, should be expected to work reliably under a wide variety of conditions, and require relatively little training to use effectively.

When creating JavaBeans components, it is important to keep in mind that each component should provide flexible, useful functionality through a simple interface. Ideally, each Bean should be "beginner proof" so as to encourage exploration and experimentation.

JavaBeans Concepts: Design Patterns

The Java language doesn't contain any specific syntax for the creation of Beans. A Bean is really a class, or cooperating set of classes, written following a specific coding style. The style dictates specific patterns that must be followed in order for a JavaBeans-aware tool to be able to discover the Bean's attributes. JBuilder looks for elements that follow these design patterns, infers these attributes, and presents the user with the necessary tools to manipulate the Bean.

The design patterns JBuilder and other JavaBeans-aware development tools look for describe attributes that are collectively referred to as the PME (Property Method Event) model. All of the following terms should be familiar, as these concepts were introduced in earlier chapters, but they are presented here as a quick reminder:

♦ A *property* is a named value associated with a Bean that can be manipulated by a developer in the design environment and by code at runtime. Unlike a variable, reading or writing a property can have additional side effects. This is obvious when changing a property that affects the Bean's visible appearance, such as its color, because the Bean will automatically redraw itself to reflect the change. Other kinds of side effects can be implemented as well, though the impact may be more subtle. The Bean's creator determines the nature and extent of these side effects.

♦ A Bean *method* is just like a method in any other class. Methods can be used to control the behavior of a Bean at runtime, but JBuilder does not provide any way to invoke a method at design time.

♦ An *event* is a notification sent from a Bean to interested observers when a predefined situation occurs, such as text being edited or a button being pressed. This design allows standard components such as buttons and text fields to delegate responsibility for what happens under these circumstances to another object. The JBuilder design environment allows Bean events to be connected to an event handler method in a container object such as a frame or dialog.

 NOTE: Properties, methods, and events are also covered in Chapter 3. Refer to that chapter for additional information. Note that properties, methods, and events are also used in examples throughout this book.

13

JavaBeans Terminology

The JavaBeans specification divides Beans into two categories. There are *invisible Beans*, which are not seen by the user at runtime, and there are *visible Beans*, which define part of the user interface of a Java program. Both share the same PME model and are defined using the same design patterns. The difference is that visible Beans inherit from the *java.awt.Component* class or one of its subclasses. This ancestor class provides many basic characteristics, including the ability to be drawn inside a container and to be controlled by the container's layout manager.

JBuilder sometimes uses the term *component* to refer to either type of Bean, despite the fact that only visible Beans actually descend from the *Component* class. The Component Palette contains Beans of both types, so JBuilder uses the qualified terms *UI component* and *non-UI component* as substitutes for the terms visible Bean and invisible Bean.

TIP: The Borland terminology is easier for people who are not immersed in Java development to understand. You are much more likely to obtain funding to purchase "non-UI components" than "invisible Beans."

In JBuilder, both types of components appear in the Component Tree while in design mode, as shown in Figure 13-1. The frame itself is a UI component,

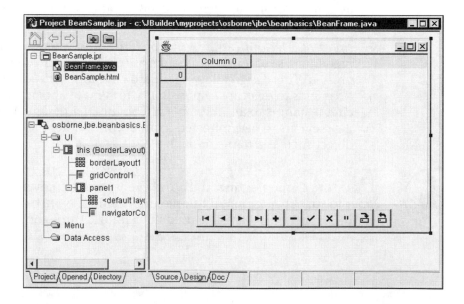

The
Component
Tree

Figure 13-1.

as are the grid control, navigator control, and panel. The border layout manager, database, and query dataset are all non-UI components.

Any type of component can be selected using the Component Tree, but only UI components can be selected and directly manipulated through the UI Designer. Any selected component can be manipulated using the Inspector to modify properties and events for components.

The Bean Info Alternative

Not all JavaBeans follow the design patterns described in this chapter, though it is highly recommended that they do so. A special class, known as the component's Bean info class, can be used to describe a component that does not follow the normal conventions. Bean info can also be used to describe other characteristics of a component and is discussed in more depth in Chapter 14.

Using Beans in JBuilder

JBuilder allows components to be created and manipulated either visually or in code. Changes made to the visual design in the UI Designer will automatically generate the corresponding code, and changes to code are visually reflected in the UI Designer. This flexible approach to RAD (Rapid Application Development) is what Borland refers to as their *two-way tools* architecture.

The following three sections include a discussion of the source code style that JBuilder generates and expects to find when parsing Java source code for creating Bean instances, using Bean properties, and understanding Bean events. Again, you may find that many of these concepts seem familiar since they are also described in earlier chapters in this book.

13

Creating Bean Instances

A component must be created before its properties and event handlers can be set. Dropping a component from the Component Palette on the UI Designer or into the Component Tree while in design mode (the Design tab is selected in the Content pane) automatically generates code to declare an instance variable and create the component instance. Placing UI components also generates code to position them within the appropriate container.

When a *Button* component, such as a *java.awt.Button* instance, is added to a frame, as shown in Figure 13-2, JBuilder will add the following line to the frame's instance variable declarations:

```
Button button1 = new Button();
```

When attempting to parse Java code in order to translate it into a visual design, JBuilder looks for the same pattern. The following are requirements for any component that can be seen and manipulated through the Component Tree and the Inspector:

♦ There must be object references via instance variables that belong to the public class that the UI Designer is working with. For the *Button* component in Figure 13-2, for example, *button1* is the name of its instance variable. This is the object reference.

♦ It must include an initializer.

If both of these conditions are met, a component whose name is derived from the name of the instance variable will be displayed in the Designer.

NOTE: JBuilder assumes that the initializer uses a constructor with no parameters to create an object. It also assumes that the object created is of the same type as the variable declaration. An initializer that creates objects of a different type or passes parameters to the constructor may result in a presentation at design time that does not match the runtime presentation, but will otherwise cause no ill effects.

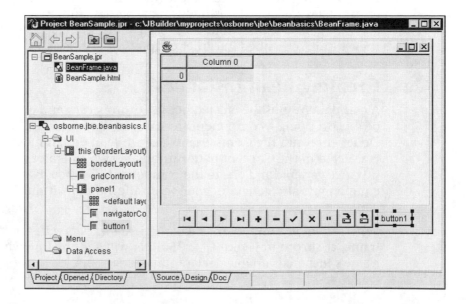

Creating a
java.awt.Button
instance
Figure 13-2.

If necessary, JBuilder will also generate an **import** statement to allow the component to be referred to by its class name alone:

```
import java.awt.*;
```

NOTE: JBuilder can parse component declarations that use either fully qualified class names or rely upon imports like the one just shown.

In addition to the component declaration and imported package, JBuilder will also add a line for a UI component that places it within a parent container. For example, the *Button* component in Figure 13-2 was added to a panel, resulting in the following line in the frame's *jbInit()* method:

```
panel1.add(button1, null);
```

The *add()* method is invoked on the button's immediate parent, passing the component to be added to the container and any constraints appropriate to the layout manager in use.

13

NOTE: Details on the formats used for various layout managers are presented in Chapter 5.

JBuilder always generates calls to *add()* that take two parameters, as shown in this example. It can parse both this format and calls to the *add()* method that take only a single parameter, implying a **null** constraints value.

Using Bean Properties

The Java language does not have any formal syntax for declaring properties. What a Bean describes as a property is actually defined by implementing *accessor methods* that follow a standard design pattern. This section will start by introducing the accessor methods for simple properties, and subsequent sections will refine this concept by introducing indexed, bound, and constrained properties.

NOTE: For more information on setting properties and accessor methods, refer to Chapter 3.

A simple property can have a *getter* method, a *setter* method, or both. The getter method for a property has a name that begins with the prefix "get" followed by the name of the property, with the lowercase letter that starts the property name capitalized. For example, the method *getColor()* is the getter method for the *color* property. The type of the property is derived from the return type for the getter method, which must not be **void**. The getter method for a simple property takes no parameters.

NOTE: Boolean properties may use the prefix "is" rather than "get" for their getter method. The boolean property *visible* is tested with the method *isVisible()*.

The setter method for a property follows a similar convention, starting with the prefix "set" followed by the property name. For example, the *color* property's setter method is *setColor()*. The return type for the setter method must be **void**, and the method must accept a single parameter of the same type as the property itself.

The interface definition for the pair of methods describing a read/write *color* property is as follows:

```
public Color getColor()
public void setColor(Color color)
```

A property with a getter method but no setter method is a read-only property. The converse, a write-only property, is extremely rare and has only a setter method. Most properties are read-write properties with both a setter method and a getter method. When a component is selected in design mode, JBuilder displays only the read-write properties on the Properties page in the Inspector. The properties for an instance of *java.awt.Button* are shown in Figure 13-3.

When the Inspector is used to modify a property value, JBuilder generates a line of code in the *jbInit()* method to implement the change. If a line of code in *jbInit()* exists that sets the property, the line is replaced; otherwise, a new line is generated. Figure 13-3 shows a change to the *label* property for *button1*, which generates the following code:

```
button1.setLabel("Quit");
```

JBuilder can only parse lines that follow the same basic format—a constant expression passed to the property's setter method.

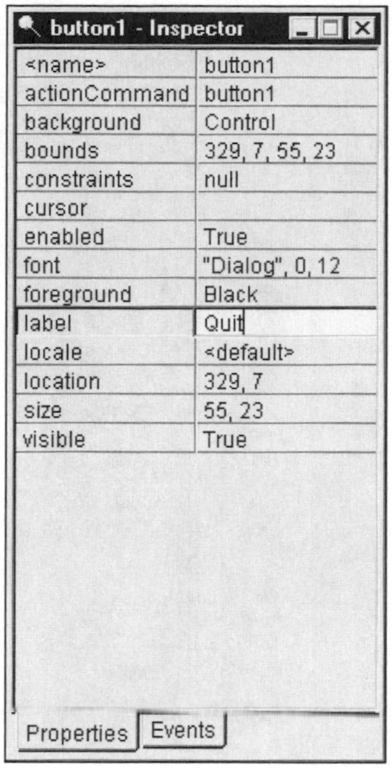

button1 - Inspector	
<name>	button1
actionCommand	button1
background	Control
bounds	329, 7, 55, 23
constraints	null
cursor	
enabled	True
font	"Dialog", 0, 12
foreground	Black
label	Quit
locale	<default>
location	329, 7
size	55, 23
visible	True

Properties | Events

Properties of a
java.awt.Button
instance
Figure 13-3.

13

Understanding Bean Events

From a component's point of view, an event is a situation that other objects
might want to be notified about. Dispatching events to other objects allows
very simple, elegant components to be developed; a button component need
only look and act like a button, notifying another object when it is clicked.
A developer can define new behavior that occurs as a result of clicking the
button every time the reusable component is put to use.

JBuilder allows the set of events associated with a component to be viewed
using the Inspector when the Design tab is selected in the Content pane
(design mode). Clicking on the Events tab of the Inspector displays the
Events page with a list of events for the currently selected component. The
events available for an instance of *java.awt.Button* are shown in Figure 13-4.

The design pattern for an event incorporates several elements: an event
listener interface, an event object, and a pair of registration methods. These
features are described in the following sections.

NOTE: For additional information on events and event handlers, refer to
Chapter 3.

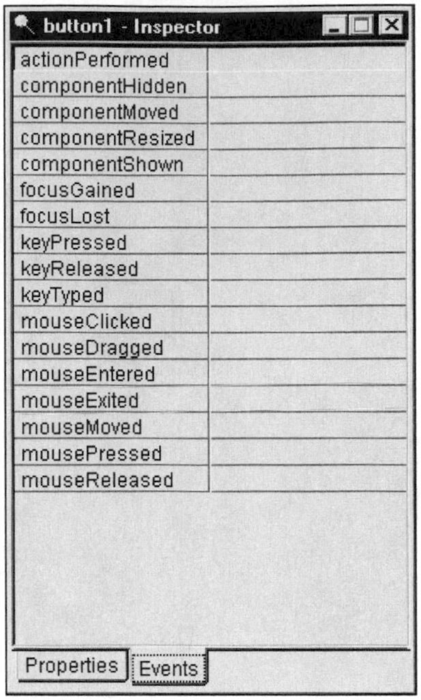

button1 - Inspector	
actionPerformed	
componentHidden	
componentMoved	
componentResized	
componentShown	
focusGained	
focusLost	
keyPressed	
keyReleased	
keyTyped	
mouseClicked	
mouseDragged	
mouseEntered	
mouseExited	
mouseMoved	
mousePressed	
mouseReleased	

Properties | Events

Events of a
java.awt.Button
instance
Figure 13-4.

The Listener Interface

Each event is associated with a single method that is triggered in all listeners when the event occurs. In order to provide a consistent data type for all listeners that include the event method, the JavaBeans standard introduces listener interfaces. These interfaces must extend the *java.util.EventListener* interface.

NOTE: By convention, listener interface names include the suffix "Listener."

No methods are inherited from the *EventListener* interface. Each method declared as a part of the interface is associated with a single event and is named after the event. For example, the listener interface used by buttons for the *actionPerformed* event is *java.awt.event.ActionListener*:

```
public interface ActionListener extends EventListener {
  public void actionPerformed(ActionEvent e);
}
```

This may sound like a lot of work, but unless you are creating your own components that introduce new event types, all of the work has been done for you. There are a number of practical benefits to this scheme:

♦ A single object can listen to any number of events because each event type invokes a different method.

♦ A single listener interface can define a number of related events, guaranteeing that any listener object implements methods to deal with all of the events.

Event methods typically accept a single parameter—an event object that provides additional information about the event.

The Event Object

Each type of event may have unique information about the event that it needs to pass to event handlers. This information is recorded in an event object that belongs to a subclass of *java.util.EventObject*. All event objects inherit a *getSource()* method that is used to identify the component that triggered the event, and component authors are free to define fields and methods as a part of their event object's class in order to pass additional information to event handlers.

13

As an example, the *actionPerformed* event handler for a button passes an instance of *java.awt.event.ActionEvent* that also includes the following: an event id, the *actionCommand* property of the button, and the state of the modifier keys at the time the action took place.

NOTE: By convention, *EventObject* subclass names include the suffix "Event."

Event Registration Methods

A listener must be registered with a component before it will receive event notification. The event pattern defines a pair of methods for each listener interface supported by a component. To derive the method names, the prefixes "add" and "remove" are added to the capitalized listener interface name. Both methods take a single parameter—a reference to an object that implements the listener interface. Neither method returns a value. For example, the *Button* class registers listeners that implement *ActionListener* through the following two methods:

```
public void addActionListener(ActionListener listener)
public void removeActionListener(ActionListener listener)
```

Many component architectures restrict the delegation process to notifying a single object when an event occurs. The JavaBeans standard encourages the use of multicast notification, allowing any number of objects to receive notification when the event occurs. Calling the appropriate registration method more than once registers more than one listener.

Support for multicast events is recommended, but not required. The overhead involved in keeping track of a list of listeners may be unacceptable for performance and memory-conscious components. A component that wants to support a single listener for an event, referred to as a unicast event, may declare a registration method that throws a *java.util.TooManyListeners* exception if a second listener is added before the first is removed.

Event Adapters

As flexible as the basic event-handling architecture is, there are still limitations. A single listener can implement multiple interfaces in order to respond to any number of different events, but if it is registered with two components for the same type of event, a single method will receive both notifications.

It would be ideal if every event went to a different event-handling method. JBuilder implements the solution recommended by the JavaBeans specification. Rather than directly dispatching events to the desired object, special classes, sometimes referred to as event adapters, are created to receive the event and forward it to the desired method. In this manner, two buttons on a frame can trigger different frame methods because they use different adapter classes.

Figure 13-5 shows the Events page in the Inspector during the creation of an *actionPerformed* event handler for a button. In response to this, JBuilder automatically adds the *quitApplication()* method to the frame class displayed in the UI Designer:

```
void quitApplication(ActionEvent e) {

}
```

According to the concepts introduced earlier in this section, there must be a few other steps involved in transferring control to this method when the button is pressed. Sure enough, two other changes took place automatically by JBuilder. First, one line of code was added to the *jbInit()* method to register a listener:

```
button1.addActionListener(new
    BeanFrame_button1_actionAdapter(this));
```

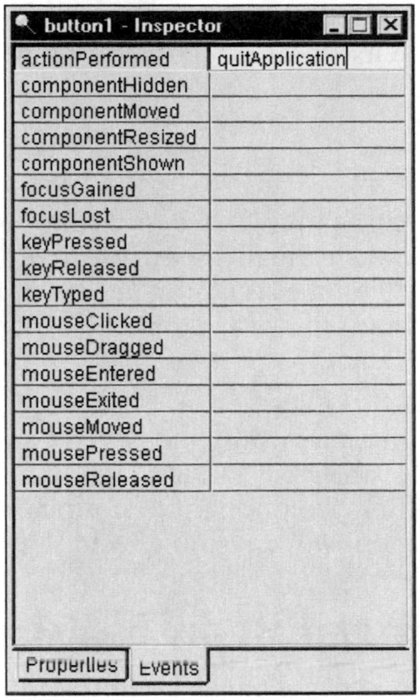

button1 - Inspector ▢ ▢ ✕

actionPerformed	quitApplication|
componentHidden	
componentMoved	
componentResized	
componentShown	
focusGained	
focusLost	
keyPressed	
keyReleased	
keyTyped	
mouseClicked	
mouseDragged	
mouseEntered	
mouseExited	
mouseMoved	
mousePressed	
mouseReleased	

Properties | Events

Creating an
actionPerformed
event handler
Figure 13-5.

13

The listener is an instance of *BeanFrame_button1_actionAdapter*. This class was automatically generated by JBuilder to dispatch *ActionListener* methods from *button1* to instances of the frame class being defined—the class *BeanFrame* in this case. This naming convention guarantees that all adapters will be given unique names. The second change is the adapter class code segment JBuilder generated for you. The generated adapter class looks like this:

```
class BeanFrame_button1_actionAdapter implements
  java.awt.event.ActionListener {
  BeanFrame adaptee;

  BeanFrame_button1_actionAdapter(BeanFrame adaptee) {
    this.adaptee = adaptee;
  }

  public void actionPerformed(ActionEvent e) {
    adaptee.quitApplication(e);
  }
}
```

Whenever an instance of this adapter class has its *actionPerformed* method invoked, it calls the *quitApplication()* method of whatever object was passed to it during construction. A glance back at the line in *jbInit()* confirms that the frame itself was passed as the construction parameter:

```
button1.addActionListener(new
  BeanFrame_button1_actionAdapter(this));
```

Does event handling have to be this complicated? Not necessarily. When writing code manually, there are many shortcuts that you can take depending on the situation, but when JBuilder generates code on your behalf, it opts to use a very flexible, consistent approach instead.

The Default Event

A component may designate one of its events as the default event. JBuilder will create an event-handling method for the default event when you double-click a component that is placed in the UI Designer. Double-clicking a component will have no effect if it does not define a default event.

Advanced Bean Features

The features described so far in this chapter are incredibly flexible. The entire JBCL (JavaBeans Component Library) was created using these techniques. In fact, neither the AWT (Abstract Windowing Toolkit) nor the JBCL runtime components make use of the indexed, bound, or constrained properties introduced in this advanced section. Nor does JBuilder itself provide any special visual design support for these features. The material presented in this section is provided for the sake of completeness because it is a part of the JavaBeans standard.

Indexed Properties

Indexed properties are a special extension for simple properties whose types are arrays. A simple property may deal with any data type, primitive, object, or array, but the basic getter and setter methods provide only the ability to replace the entire property at once.

This is sufficient for primitive types since they represent a single value. Special behavior isn't necessary for object types, either, as they may have their own properties. This means that only array properties have no mechanism for associating behavior with the reading and writing of individual elements.

A simple read-write string array property, *friends*, could be implemented with the usual two access methods, as shown here:

```
public String[] getFriends()
public void setFriends(String[] friends)
```

This simple property *friends* can be turned into an indexed property by overloading the existing accessor methods, providing a total of four accessors for a read-write indexed property. The new accessors have an integer index as their first parameter, specifying an element of the array property to operate on as shown here:

```
public String getFriends(int index)
public void setFriends(int index, String friend)
```

NOTE: The indexed accessor methods can only be used to read and change existing elements of the array. To change the size of the array, the simple setter method must be called with a whole new array of the desired size.

Bound Properties: Detecting Changes

All property modifications are performed through accessor methods, which can easily implement any desired side effect (behavior) within the scope of a single component. JavaBeans extends this concept to allow any number of objects to receive notification when a bound property is changed. A Bean that provides bound properties incorporates one or more of the design patterns described in this section.

13

All of these patterns use the basic event pattern established earlier in the chapter. A pair of registration methods allows any object that implements the *java.beans.PropertyChangeListener* interface to receive notification after a bound property changes.

After a bound property is modified, all of the registered *PropertyChangeListener* objects have their *propertyChange()* methods invoked. This method accepts a single parameter, a *java.beans.PropertyChangeEvent*, that can be queried to determine what object is being modified, which of its properties has changed, what the original value was, and what the new value is.

All Bound Properties

The first design pattern allows a listener to register interest in all bound properties of a Bean. The only way to know which properties are bound is to check the Bean documentation.

```
public void addPropertyChangeListener(
  PropertyChangeListener listener)
```

```
public void removePropertyChangeListener(
  PropertyChangeListener listener)
```

Any Bound Property

The second design pattern allows a listener to register interest in a specific bound property by passing a property name as one of its parameters. As with the first pattern, the only way to know for certain which properties can be bound is to check the Bean documentation.

```
public void addPropertyChangeListener(
  String propertyName,
  PropertyChangeListener listener)
```

```
public void removePropertyChangeListener(
  String propertyName,
  PropertyChangeListener listener)
```

Specific Bound Property

The final design pattern provides a pair of methods for each bound property rather than using a single pair of methods for all bound properties. The following examples illustrate the specific interface used for a bound *color* property:

```
public void addColorListener(
  PropertyChangeListener listener)
```

```
public void removeColorListener(
  PropertyChangeListener listener)
```

Constrained Properties: Validating Changes

Components can easily enforce their own rules about legal values for properties. A property setter method will typically throw an exception if an illegal value is passed for the new property value. This is sufficient for most occasions, but there are times when it would be convenient if other objects could provide additional validation rules. The JavaBeans specification allows for the definition of constrained properties to support this behavior.

A Bean that provides constrained properties declares that the setter method can throw a *java.beans.PropertyVetoException*, as shown here:

```
public void setColor(Color color) throws
  PropertyVetoException
```

A Bean that provides constrained properties also incorporates one or more of the design patterns described in the next sections. All of these patterns use the basic event pattern established earlier in the chapter. A pair of registration methods allows any object that implements the *java.beans.VetoableChangeListener* interface to receive notification after a constrained property changes.

Before a constrained property is modified, all of the registered *VetoableChangeListener* objects have their *vetoableChange()* methods invoked. This method accepts a single parameter, a *java.beans.PropertyChangeEvent*, that can be queried to determine what object is being modified, which of its properties is changing, what the current value is, and what the new value will be. When notified, any listener that wants to reject the change need only throw a *java.beans.PropertyVetoException*.

All Constrained Properties
The first design pattern allows a listener to register interest in all constrained properties of a Bean.

```
public void addVetoableChangeListener(
  VetoableChangeListener listener)

public void removeVetoableChangeListener(
  VetoableChangeListener listener)
```

Any Constrained Property
The second design pattern allows a listener to register interest in a specific constrained property by passing a property name as one of its parameters.

```
public void addVetoableChangeListener(
  String propertyName,
  VetoableChangeListener listener)

public void removeVetoableChangeListener(
  String propertyName,
  VetoableChangeListener listener)
```

Specific Constrained Property
The final design pattern provides a pair of methods for each constrained property rather than using a single pair of methods for all constrained properties. Each pair of methods will have a unique name derived from the constrained property they are associated with. The examples below illustrate the specific interface used for a constrained *color* property:

13

```
public void addColorListener(
  VetoableChangeListener listener)

public void removeColorListener(
  VetoableChangeListener listener)
```

Customizers

A JavaBeans customizer defines a special user interface for manipulating an entire Bean rather than dealing with one property at a time.

NOTE: The initial release of JBuilder does not provide any support for invoking customizers associated with Beans.

Installing JavaBeans Components

JBuilder comes with numerous JavaBeans components installed, but it can be further extended with the addition of third-party and custom components. The Component Palette can be configured by selecting Tools|Configure Palette or by right-clicking on the Component Palette tabs and selecting the Properties option from the popup menu.

TIP: Components do not actually need to be added to the Component Palette to get visual design support. Any valid JavaBeans component on the project's class path can be added manually as an instance variable using JBuilder's usual conventions. The Component Tree, UI Designer, and Inspector will automatically detect and work with the new component in design mode.

Modifying Pages of the Component Palette

You can modify the components that appear on the pages in the Component Palette by either adding components to a page or removing components from a page. In addition, you can add an entirely new page to the Component Palette. To do all of these modifications to the Component Palette, you use the Palette Properties dialog, which contains three pages.

Figure 13-6 shows the Pages page of the Component Properties dialog. The left side of the dialog, labeled Pages, presents a list of the tabs that appear on the Component Palette. The right-side list labeled Components shows the components that appear under the tab selected in the Pages list. The Add, Remove, Properties, Move Up, and Move Down buttons affect the most recently selected item in either the Pages list or the Components list and are described next.

TIP: Double-clicking on any item in either the Pages list or the Components list has the same effect as selecting that item and clicking the Properties button.

When the most recent selection is on the left-hand side:

◆ The Add button prompts for a name for a new palette tab and adds it to the bottom of the list.

◆ The Remove button removes the selected palette tab.

◆ The Properties button prompts for a new name and renames the selected tab.

◆ The Move Up and Move Down buttons move the selected tab up or down in the list. Use these buttons to arrange the order of the tabbed pages in the Component Palette. Tabs are displayed on the Component Palette in the same order they appear in the Pages list shown in Figure 13-6.

13

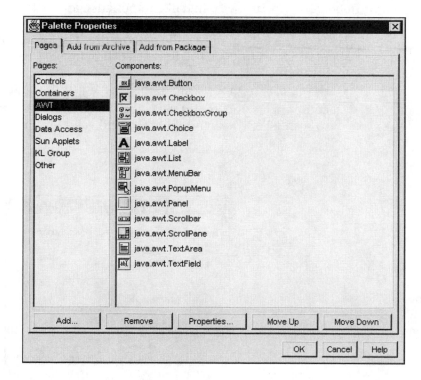

The Pages page of the Palette Properties dialog
Figure 13-6.

When the most recent selection is on the right-hand side:

♦ The Add button is disabled. The Add from Archive and Add from Package pages on the Palette Properties dialog are used to add components to the Component Palette.

♦ The Delete button removes the selected component from the palette. The component remains on disk; its button icon representation is simply removed from the Component Palette.

The Properties button displays a dialog that allows you to choose the icon for the selected component. This dialog allows an image file to be selected, or JBuilder can query the component's Bean info to retrieve an appropriate image, as shown in Figure 13-7.

♦ The Move Up and Move Down buttons move the selected component up or down in the list. Components are displayed under the appropriate tab in the Component Palette in the same order they appear in the list.

Installing Beans from Archives

Figure 13-8 shows the Add from Archive page of the Palette Properties dialog. This page allows you to install components packaged in zip or JAR (Java Archive) files from any location, including removable media or over a network connection. To install components, follow these steps:

1. Type the full zip or JAR file path in the Select a JAR or ZIP file field and press ENTER, or click the Browse button and use the resulting dialog to locate the file.

2. In the Packages found in archive list, select the package that contains components you are interested in installing. It may take a few seconds to scan all of the components to find valid JavaBeans.

Item
Properties
dialog for a
component
Figure 13-7.

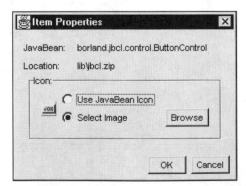

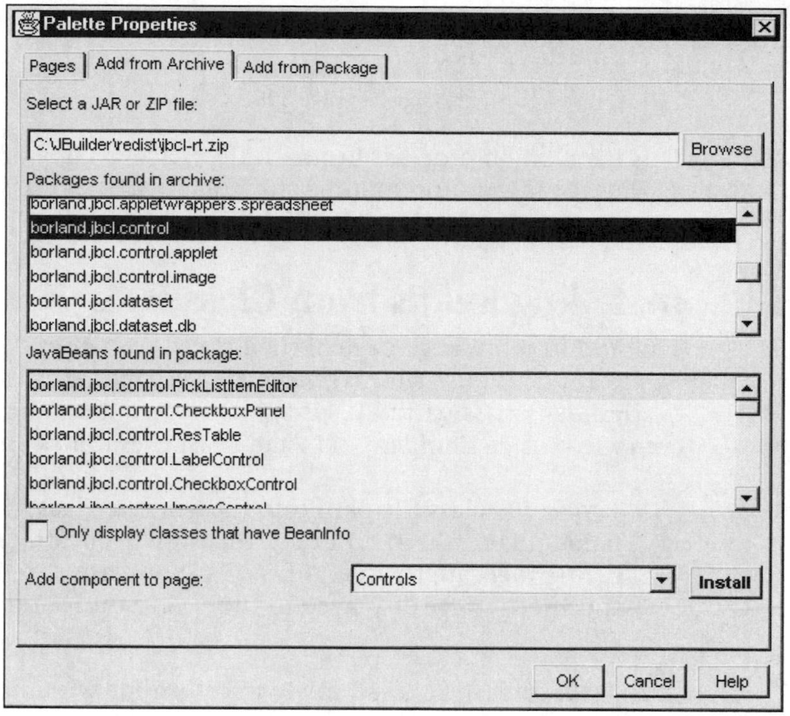

Palette Properties

Pages | Add from Archive | Add from Package |

Select a JAR or ZIP file:

C:\JBuilder\redist\jbcl-rt.zip   Browse

Packages found in archive:

borland.jbcl.appletwrappers.spreadsheet
borland.jbcl.control
borland.jbcl.control.applet
borland.jbcl.control.image
borland.jbcl.dataset
borland.jbcl.dataset.db

JavaBeans found in package:

borland.jbcl.control.PickListItemEditor
borland.jbcl.control.CheckboxPanel
borland.jbcl.control.ResTable
borland.jbcl.control.LabelControl
borland.jbcl.control.CheckboxControl
borland.jbcl.control.ImageControl

☐ Only display classes that have BeanInfo

Add component to page: Controls ▼   Install

OK   Cancel   Help

The Add from
Archive page
of the Palette
Properties
dialog
Figure 13-8.

13

3. If the list includes numerous classes, you can try narrowing the list by checking the option labeled Only display classes that have Bean info. Note, however, that not every valid JavaBean has a BeanInfo class, so this process may hide components of interest. You can always turn this option back off by unchecking it.

4. Select the component or components of interest from the JavaBeans found in package list. You can select more than one component by holding down the CTRL key while selecting components, or select ranges of components by holding the SHIFT key while clicking on items.

5. The next step is to place the components on a page in the Component Palette. Select the page you wish to add the components to from the Add component to page drop-down list.

6. Click the Install button. Once installation is complete, you will see the message "Installation complete" displayed in the dialog.

NOTE: If you just click the OK button instead of the Install button, your selection will not be installed.

7. Repeat the appropriate steps given here until all desired components have been installed.

8. Click OK to return to JBuilder.

This installation process automatically places a copy of the archive in c:\JBuilder\beans and modifies JBuilder's internal class path to include the newly added archive.

Installing Beans from Class Files

The Add from Package page of the Palette Properties dialog is shown in Figure 13-9. You use this page to install components that exist as .class files on JBuilder's class path. This is typically used for components that have been compiled inside JBuilder. To install .class files follow these steps:

1. Type a full class file path into the Select a .class file from the package field and press ENTER, or click the Browse button and use the resulting dialog to locate the file. A list of all the classes in the package you specified is now displayed in the JavaBeans found in package list.

NOTE: This file is used solely to determine which package classes are being installed from. The exact class selected in this step does not matter since all classes along the class path in the selected package will be displayed for the next step.

2. If the list includes numerous classes, you can try narrowing the list by checking the Only display classes that have BeanInfo option. Not every valid JavaBeans has a Bean info class, so this process may hide components of interest. You can always turn this option back off by unchecking it.

3. Select the component or components of interest from the JavaBeans found in package list. You can select more than one component by holding down the CTRL key while clicking items, or select ranges of components by holding the SHIFT key while clicking items.

4. Use the Add component to page drop-down list to select the page of the Component Palette you wish to add the components to.

5. Click the Install button. Once installation is complete, you will see the message "Installation complete" displayed in the dialog.

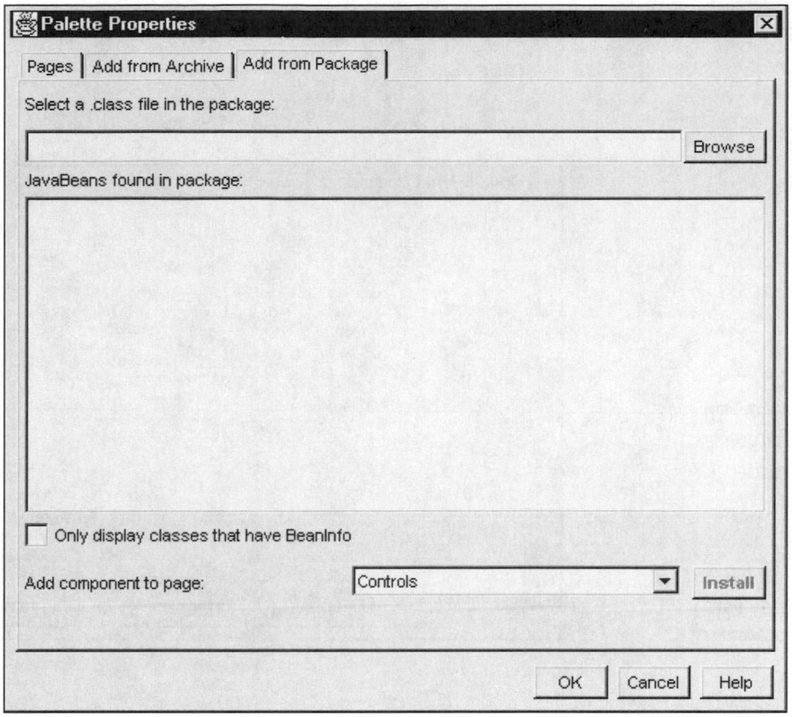

The Add from
Package page
of the Palette
Properties
dialog
Figure 13-9.

NOTE: If you just click the OK button instead of the Install button, your
selection will not be installed.

6. Repeat the appropriate steps given here until all desired components
   have been installed.
7. Click OK to return to JBuilder.

This installation process does not make a duplicate of the class files required.
It is assumed that the necessary class files will be available on the class path
when they are needed.

Converting Applets into JavaBeans

JBuilder includes an interesting facility for automatically converting an
applet to a Bean. This is the Create Applet Wrapper Wizard. To display this
wizard, you select Wizards|Wrap Applet. The first page of the wizard is
shown in Figure 13-10. In the Package field, enter a package name for the

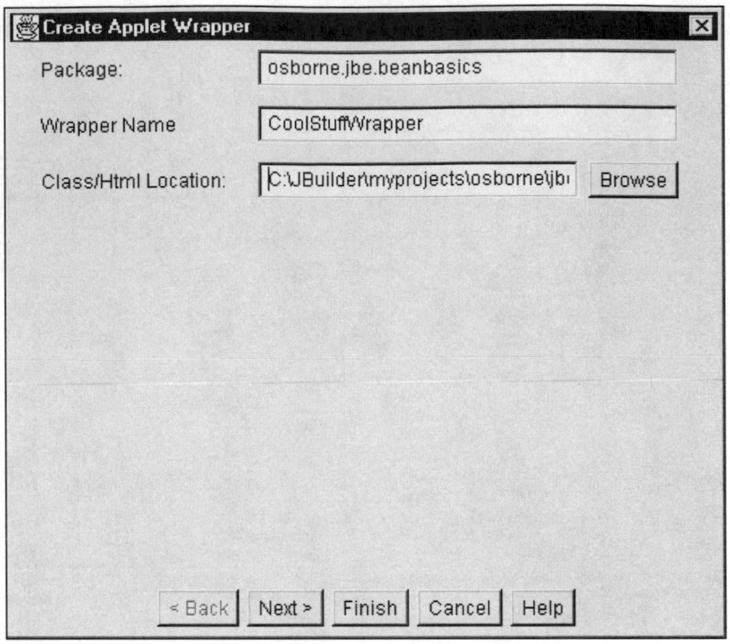

The first page
of the Create
Applet
Wrapper
Wizard
Figure 13-10.

newly created component. In the Wrapper Name field, enter a class name for the newly created component. In the Class/Html Location field, enter the full path of the applet class file or an HTML file that references the class. If you don't know the full path, you can click the Browse button to use a dialog to find the file. Click the Next button to proceed the second page of the wizard.

Figure 13-11 shows the second page of the Create Applet Wrapper Wizard. On this page, you will see that the wizard attempts to discover all of the applet's parameters as reported by the applet's *getParameterInfo()* method and displays them in an editable grid. Make any desired changes to the default values that will be used for the encapsulated applet by editing the Parameter and Value columns. When you are done, click the Finish button.

The newly created Bean provides a complete support environment for the applet, including emulation of parameters normally acquired from an HTML page. For each parameter specified on the second page of the Create Applet Wrapper Wizard shown in Figure 13-11, a property is generated in the new component. Changes to these properties will automatically stop and restart the applet to show the effect of the new property value.

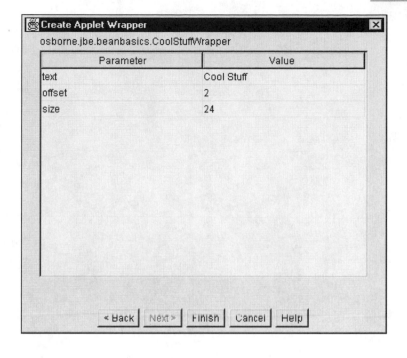

The second
page of the
Create Applet
Wrapper
Wizard
Figure 13-11.

The newly created component is a fully compliant JavaBean that can be installed as described earlier in this chapter in the section "Installing JavaBeans Components."

CHAPTER 14

Writing JavaBeans

The collection of components installed in the Component Palette by default is a fantastic starting point for Java developers. However, JBuilder can easily be enhanced with the addition of more components, adding either the components that come with JBuilder or commercially available components to the Component Palette. As introduced in Chapter 13, new components can be added to the Component Palette as long as they are designed following the JavaBeans standard.

This chapter focuses on creating your own JavaBeans components to extend the JBuilder environment. These components may be for your own use or for use by other developers. The last chapter introduced the basic patterns that give a component additional structure beyond a normal class. This chapter builds on these concepts by expanding on the component philosophy introduced in the last chapter, and focuses on the implementation details specific to the component writing endeavor. It also discusses the process of creating and testing JavaBeans components within the JBuilder environment.

Component Writing Philosophy

In Chapter 13, the section "Component Philosophy" introduced a few basic ideas about what a component should be in order to provide the full benefits of reusable component technology. As a component user, a JBuilder developer can enjoy these benefits without worrying about how they came about. As a component developer, however, you take on the responsibility of making a component robust, easy to use, and consistent.

Living up to these responsibilities takes quite a bit of work, but the potential benefits are enormous. One developer can solve a complex problem thoroughly and provide a simple interface for others to use, in effect packaging his or her expertise for component reuse by other developers. Achieving this goal requires an expenditure of effort to make sure that the right interface is presented to developers who intend to make use of the component. There are no fixed rules about component design, but the guidelines described in the following sections should serve as a good starting point for all component developers.

Ease of Use

The components you write need to be easy for other developers to use. Component developers should hide complexity, choose clear concise names, provide reasonable defaults, and eliminate opportunities for incorrect usage of the component. Each of these recommendations is discussed individually in the following sections.

Hiding Complexity

Internal complexity within a component can often be hidden behind a simpler conceptual interface. For example, the implementation for a component that has optional horizontal and vertical scrollbars introduces two boolean properties: *horizontalScroll* and *verticalScroll*. This interface could be simplified by replacing these two properties with a single integer property, *scrollBars*, and four constant values: NONE, HORIZONTAL, VERTICAL, and BOTH. In general, it takes more work for an individual developer to create a simple interface, but it will benefit all of the developers who will use the component.

Choosing Clear Names

The names chosen for properties, methods, and events should be immediately meaningful. While not every name can be entirely self-explanatory, a developer using your component should not have to refer to the documentation more than once to remember what a given property is good for. For example, a component could have two color properties named *color1* and *color2*, but developers would always be forgetting which was which. Naming the same properties *fillColor* and *outlineColor* would eliminate the problem.

Providing Reasonable Defaults

The most commonly used options should be the default values for properties so that a developer can drop the component in place and make use of it immediately with minimal customization. For example, the *visible* property for all UI components in JBuilder defaults to **true** based on the assumption that they will most often be visible.

The one exception to this guideline is that property settings that invoke lengthy or slow operations should not be used as defaults.

Eliminating Incorrect Usage

The possibility of developers using a component incorrectly can easily happen, and as such eliminating incorrect usage deserves special attention. A component should be designed so that there is no wrong way to use it. First, no special initialization or cleanup process should ever be necessary for a component. The constructor should perform any necessary initialization, without requiring an additional method to be called, and the component should not do anything that would prevent it from being garbage collected when it is no longer needed by the object that created it.

14

Interdependencies between properties should be automatically managed. If a change to one property makes a value in another property invalid, it should automatically change that property to a valid value. For a counterexample, create several *Checkbox* components and a *CheckboxGroup* component. Set the *checked* property for all of the checkboxes, and then set their *checkboxGroup* properties to refer to the same checkbox group. The result is a single set of radio buttons, all of which are on, which is an illegal state. The *checked* property should have been set to **false** when the checkboxes were added to a group that already contained a checked item. This is an example of bad design in the AWT (Abstract Windowing Toolkit).

Last, whenever possible, it should be possible to set properties in any order. Developers should not have to learn the "right" order to set properties in your component to use it effectively.

Robust Components

Creating robust components means that they should be thread-safe, perform exhaustive exception handling, and provide meaningful messages to report error conditions. Components should also be tuned for efficient behavior in a variety of situations. Each of these goals is discussed next.

Thread-Safety

The JavaBeans specification requires that a component be completely thread-safe. Methods that modify the internal state of a component should be declared **synchronized** to prevent data corruption, and other methods should act in a way that will yield consistent results in the presence of multiple threads. Refer to Chapter 10 for a discussion of thread-safe development techniques in Java.

Handling Exceptions

When an exception occurs, a component writer may be tempted to simply declare that the exception may be thrown, but this is often not enough. If an exception occurs while modifying the internal variables of the component, it is important that the variables be restored to a consistent state so that a developer using the component can recover. A component should never enter a "broken" state where it can no longer be used due to an error condition.

Reporting Errors

When an exception is thrown from within a component, the exception message must provide enough information to allow the developer using the component to correct the problem. Meaningful error messages should describe conditions that can be changed outside of the component to correct the problem.

Performance Tuning

A component developer should take extra care in ensuring that components are as efficient as possible. The developers using third-party components will quickly become dissatisfied with slow components, or components that use excessive amounts of memory or other resources. Keep in mind that since your code will be used in a wide variety of situations and by developers with different levels of expertise, worst-case scenarios are worth considering.

Consistency Among Components

Consistency among components means that components should look and act similarly to reduce the amount of effort developers need to invest to use them effectively. To accomplish this, inherit as much behavior as possible and carefully design all new behavior to fit into the standards established by the standard Java components.

Inheriting Behavior

A component designer should borrow heavily from existing classes by inheriting from the class that provides the largest subset of desired functionality without introducing undesirable characteristics. After examining existing classes, you may want to redesign your component to take advantage of an ancestor class that is a close fit. In practice it is often better to accomplish 95 percent of the goal while maintaining consistency with other familiar components than to achieve 100 percent but force users and developers to learn a new way of doing things.

Choosing Names

It is important to be familiar with all of Java's naming conventions, and stick to the standard Java usage as much as possible. Keep in mind the following:

♦ Class names begin with a capital letter. Examples: *Button* and *GridControl*.

♦ Method, variable, and property names begin with a lowercase letter. Examples: *getLabel()*, *width*, and *label*.

♦ Event names begin with a lowercase letter and are typically presented in the past tense to represent an event that has just occurred. Examples: *windowClosed* and *actionPerformed*. Events that represent actions that have not yet been performed are the exception, and use names like *windowClosing*.

Component Writing Overview

14

The remainder of this chapter focuses on the specific tasks required to write and test a new component in the JBuilder environment. There are three steps that are necessary for each and every component:

1. Define the component class in terms of an appropriate ancestor class.

2. Add new properties for the component.

3. Create appropriate events for the component.

There are also two optional steps that can help further refine the component's behavior at design time in JBuilder:

4. Design a Bean info class.

5. Polish the component configuration process with custom property editors.

Each of these steps is discussed in depth in one or more of the sections that follow.

Defining the Class

Every JavaBeans component begins with a class declaration, but the declaration for a component must follow a few simple restrictions:

◆ First, the class must be declared public.

◆ Second, a public constructor that takes no parameters is required.

The class must be public so that code inside other packages can instantiate and manipulate components belonging to the newly defined class. The component may in turn use additional classes internally that are not declared public.

A public zero-parameters constructor is required so that a visual design environment that has no special knowledge about a particular component can create instances of the component. Any number of additional constructors may be provided at any visibility level for manual coding convenience.

These simple rules mean that even the following class can be considered a legal component:

```
public class NothingComponent {
}
```

The class *NothingComponent* is public, meeting the first requirement, and the compiler will automatically generate a zero-parameters constructor for any class that does not explicitly declare a constructor of its own, meaning that the second requirement is met as well. The parent class in this case, *java.lang.Object*, doesn't provide any inherited properties or events, leading to a rather uninteresting component. Typically, you will pick a more feature-rich class as the starting point for a new component.

Picking a Parent Class

JavaBeans components can descend from any class, even *Object*, as shown in the previous example. The only requirement in picking a parent class is that all visual Beans—what JBuilder calls UI components—must descend from *java.awt.Component* or one of its subclasses. Any other parent class will result in an invisible Bean, a non-UI component.

A trivial UI component inherits properties that determine its position and size, and will be automatically positioned by its parent layout manager. The simplest possible UI component looks like this:

```
public class NothingUIComponent
  extends java.awt.Component {
}
```

JBuilder's Treatment for the Container Class

JBuilder provides additional behavior for descendants of *java.awt.Container*. When a container subclass is used in a visual design, additional components can be placed within the container and JBuilder will generate appropriate calls to the container's *add()* method to establish the relationship. A trivial container appears as follows:

```
public class NothingContainer
  extends java.awt.Container {
}
```

It is sometimes desirable to use a container subclass for a component but avoid this additional behavior. JBuilder will disable this additional functionality if the container subclass implements the interface *borland.jbcl.util.BlackBox*. The *BlackBox* interface does not define any methods—just adding the name to the component class's **implements** clause is sufficient to tell JBuilder to suppress the normal container behavior. The simplest component that descends from *Container* without actually acting like a container at design time is as follows:

```
public class NothingNonContainer
  extends java.awt.Container
  implements borland.jbcl.util.BlackBox {
}
```

14

NOTE: Interfaces that do not contain any methods are often used in the manner just described to designate that instances of a class should receive special treatment. Code can use the **instanceof** operator to determine if an object belongs to a class that includes the specific interface. These interfaces are sometimes called *marker interfaces*.

Defining a Class with BeansExpress

JBuilder includes sample snippets of code for defining new components, referred to collectively as BeansExpress. A new component can be created by selecting File|New to display the Object Gallery, selecting the BeansExpress page, and then double-clicking on the New Bean icon.

JBuilder responds by creating a new Java source file in the current project, called NewBean.java, in the current project that contains the following class definition:

```java
public class NewBean extends BeanPanel
  implements BlackBox{
  BevelPanel bevelPanel1 = new BevelPanel();
  BorderLayout borderLayout1 = new BorderLayout();
  XYLayout xYLayout1 = new XYLayout();

  public NewBean() {
    try {
      jbInit();
    }
    catch (Exception e) {
      e.printStackTrace();
    }
  }

  public void jbInit() throws Exception{
    bevelPanel1.setLayout(xYLayout1);
    this.setLayout(borderLayout1);
    this.add(bevelPanel1, BorderLayout.CENTER);
  }

  // Example properties
  private String example = "Example1";

  public void setExample(String s) {
    example=s;
  }
  public String getExample(){
    return example;
  }

  // Example event
  public static final String EXAMPLE_EVENT
    = "ExampleEvent";
  protected void fireExampleActionEvent() {
    //Args:  event source,event ID, event command
    processActionEvent(new ActionEvent(this,
```

```
                ActionEvent.ACTION_PERFORMED, EXAMPLE_EVENT));
    }
}
```

This component uses *borland.jbcl.control.BeanPanel* as its ancestor. The *BeanPanel* class is a container, allowing other components to be added to it in order to create a complex aggregate component. This is the easiest way to get started with component design in JBuilder. A simple constructor and *jbInit()* method provide complete support for visual placement and configuration of components within the new custom component. Clicking the Design tab brings up the UI Designer that displays the component's contents. By default, the new component contains only a *BevelPanel* placed in the center of the custom component by using a *BorderLayout* layout manager. The *BevelPanel* itself uses an *XYLayout* for rapid prototyping.

The new component implements the *BlackBox* interface so that once the component's contents have been designed, developers actually using the component cannot place additional components within it. The remainder of the class definition includes sample methods and events that will be discussed in later sections.

The *BeanPanel* class used as the parent class adds a number of additional features to the basic container: event-handling support for *actionPerformed* events and numerous methods designed to be overridden. The event-handling support will be discussed later, but the additional methods are discussed immediately.

BeanPanel Keyboard Events

To deal with individual keyboard events, you need only override one or more of the following methods: *processKeyTyped()*, *processKeyPressed()*, and *processKeyReleased()*. The *processKeyTyped()* method is the most frequently used, as it is automatically invoked repeatedly when auto-repeat is invoked as a key is held down.

BeanPanel Mouse Events

To deal with individual mouse events, you need only override one or more of the following methods: *processMouseClicked()*, *processMousePressed()*, *processMouseReleased()*, *processMouseEntered()*, *processMouseExited()*. As the *processMouseClicked()* method is invoked automatically when the mouse is pressed and released without being moved, the *processMousePressed()* and *processMouseReleased()* methods usually are used only to manage dragging operations.

14

BeanPanel Mouse Motion Events

Two additional mouse-related events provide additional detail about mouse movements within the component: *processMouseMoved()* and *processMouseDragged()*. Both methods indicate mouse motion, but the *processMouseDragged()* method is invoked when the mouse button is currently held down.

Sample Component Development Using BeansExpress

This example creates a new component using BeansExpress, and uses the UI Designer to create unique presentation and behavior: a list control, a text field, and a button that adds strings to the list control.

1. Select File|New Project to display the Project Wizard. At the File field, enter **c:\JBuilder\myprojects\osborne\jbe\writingbeans\ BeanProject.jpr**. Click the Finish button to create the new project.

2. Select File|New to display the Object Gallery, select the BeansExpress page, and double-click the New Bean icon. JBuilder will create and select the file NewBean.java.

3. The first thing you should do with the new component is to rename it. Modify the source code in the Editor by selecting the class name *NewBean* and replacing it with **SimpleBean**. The constructor must also be edited to match the class name. Find the declaration of *NewBean()* and replace it with *SimpleBean()*. Lastly, the public class name and filename must match, so use File|Rename to change the file to **c:\JBuilder\myprojects\osborne\jbe\writingbeans\ SimpleBean.java**.

4. Click the Design tab, select *bevelPanel1* from the Component Tree, and press DELETE to remove the component.

5. Click the Controls tab of the Component Palette, select a *ListControl*, and click in the center in the UI Designer to place it.

6. Use the Properties page of the Inspector to change the list control's *editInPlace* property to False.

7. Click the AWT tab of the Component Palette, select a *Panel*, and place it at the bottom in the UI Designer, using the status bar to verify that the constraint South will be used.

8. Use the Properties page of the Inspector to change *panel1's layout* property to GridBagLayout.

9. Select a *TextField* from the Component Palette and click on *panel1* in the Component Tree to place it on the panel.

10. Select a *Button* from the Component Palette and click to the right of the text field in the UI Designer. Set the button's *label* property to **Add** using the Inspector.

11. Select *textField1* using the Component Tree or the UI Designer. Right-click the text field object and select Constraints from the menu. Using the constraints editing dialog, specify a fill value of Horizontal, an X weight of 1.0, and a value of 8 for all four insets. Click OK to save these settings.

12. Select *button1* using the Component Tree or the UI Designer. Right-click the text field and select Constraints from the menu. Using the constraints editing dialog, specify a right inset value of 8. Click OK to save this setting.

The UI Designer should appear similar to the one shown in Figure 14-1.

13. Double-click the button in the UI Designer to create an *actionPerformed* event handler, and edit the source code to match the following:

```
void button1_actionPerformed(ActionEvent e) {
  listControl1.addItem(textField1.getText());
}
```

14

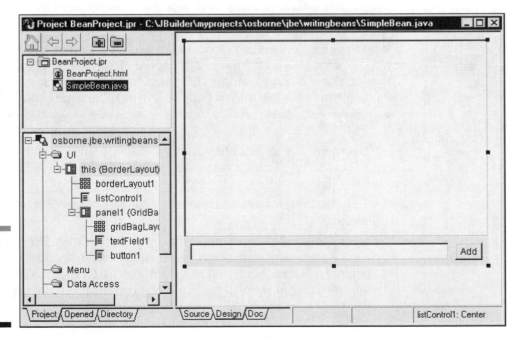

Visual design for the *SimpleBean* component

Figure 14-1.

14. Select Build|Make to compile the component. Components must be compiled before JBuilder can display them inside another container at design time.

15. Select File|Save All to save your progress. You will need to extend this project in the next section.

Testing the Sample Component

The sample component SimpleBean created in the last section can easily be installed and tested in the same project. The following steps install the component, create a frame to test the component in, and add the component to the frame:

1. Make sure the project c:\JBuilder\osborne\jbe\writingbeans\ BeanProject.jpr is open in the current AppBrowser.

2. Select Tools|Configure Palette to display the Palette Properties dialog.

3. Click the Add from Package tab and click the Browse button. Find the file c:\JBuilder\myclasses\osborne\jbe\writingbeans\SimpleBean.class and click the OK button to list all potential components in the same package.

4. Select osborne.jbe.writingbeans.SimpleBean from the list, and select the Other page from the drop-down list. Click the Install button to finish installing the component and then click OK to close the Palette Properties dialog.

NOTE: JBuilder can only load a class file once during a given session. If you make changes to a component that has already been displayed by the Designer, those changes will not be reflected when the component is displayed inside a container at design time until you quit and restart JBuilder.

5. Select File|New and double-click the Frame icon on the New page of the Object Gallery. Enter **TestFrame** in the Class Name field and then click OK.

6. Click the Design tab and then select the Other tab of the Component Palette.

7. Select the *SimpleBean* component on the Other page. Next, place two *SimpleBean* components onto the form by clicking and dragging to specify their size. Note that the Component Tree shows only *simpleBean1* and *simpleBean2*, and not the components they used

internally. The implementation details are hidden, as they are for any other component.

8. Select File|Save All to save your progress.

The frame created in this process should appear as shown in Figure 14-2.

Defining Properties

Properties can be added to a component by simply adding the appropriate getter and setter methods to the class as described in Chapter 13. These methods must be public, and both a getter and a setter method must be present before JBuilder will display the property in the Inspector.

The code provided by BeansExpress for a new component introduces a single *example* property, a string with a default value of Example1. To verify that JBuilder displays this correctly, make sure the project BeanProject.jpr created earlier in this chapter is loaded and the file TestFrame.java is selected, then click the Design tab. Select *simpleBean1* and look in the Inspector at the *example* property. This property is displayed with its default value and can be edited like any other string property, and JBuilder automatically adds code to *jbInit()* when changes are made.

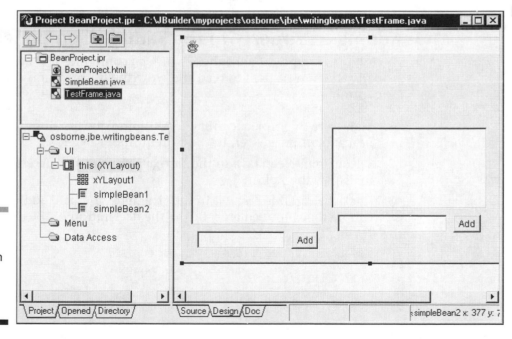

14

Multiple instances of *SimpleBean* in the UI Designer
Figure 14-2.

A look at the provided getter and setter methods indicates that the property is internally stored in a private variable named *example*:

```
private String example = "Example1";

public void setExample(String s) {
  example=s;
}
public String getExample(){
  return example;
}
```

Any number of additional properties can be defined by declaring additional getter and setter methods that follow the standard design patterns. The use of an instance variable to store the property value isn't required; any mechanism can be used to store and retrieve the value. It could be written to and read from disk, communicated to a server, or passed to another object.

NOTE: Don't forget to remove the example property included by BeansExpress before delivering your component. You can comment out or remove this example property from all future components by directly editing the New Bean snippet in c:\JBuilder\snippets\NewBean.java.

Adding a Property to the Sample Component

The following steps enhance the *SimpleBean* component by adding an *items* property that can be used to read and write the list of strings displayed in the list control:

1. Make sure the project c:\JBuilder\osborne\jbe\writingbeans\ BeanProject.jpr is open in the current AppBrowser.

2. Select SimpleBean.java in the Navigation pane and click the Source tab to display the Editor.

3. Click the variable *example* in the Structure pane and add the following two methods immediately before the declaration of the *example* variable:

   ```
   public String[] getItems() {
     return listControl1.getItems();
   }

   public void setItems(String[] items) {
   ```

```
        listControl1.setItems(items);
    }
```

4. Select Build|Make to recompile the *SimpleBean* component.

5. Select File|Save All to save your progress. Quit and restart JBuilder to allow the updated component to be displayed and manipulated in the UI Designer.

6. JBuilder should automatically display your project when it restarts. If not, open the project c:\JBuilder\myprojects\osborne\jbe\ writingbeans\BeanProject.jpr.

7. Select the file TestFrame.java in the Navigation pane and click the Design tab. Select *simpleBean1* in the Component Tree and use the Properties page of the Inspector to change the *items* property to a list of three items: **One**, **Two**, and **Three**. The list control within the component will automatically reflect the change.

As shown in the final step, the newly added property can be used to indirectly read and write the list of strings contained in a subcomponent that is completely encapsulated within *SimpleBean*.

Defining Events

The JavaBeans event pattern is one of the more complicated patterns, requiring two methods in your component and an additional public listener interface and public event object class. Optional extensions to the pattern can further extend the implementation. With at least three public components, the full definition actually spans three or more Java source files.

Luckily, it isn't all that common that you will want to declare a new event type. The *BeanPanel* class used by BeansExpress inherits component, container, key, mouse, and focus events, and also implements action event registration and dispatch. The purpose of an action event is component specific, so you can use the event in any way you desire.

Within a single event type, additional parameters in the event object can be used to distinguish among different meanings for the event. The component created by BeansExpress includes a definition for a single type of action event by using a pubic constant for the *actionCommand* property of the event object:

```
// Example event
public static final String EXAMPLE_EVENT
  = "ExampleEvent";
```

14

To actually trigger the event, the component also includes a method that creates the event object and processes it.

```
protected void fireExampleActionEvent() {
  //Args:  event source,event ID, event command
  processActionEvent(new ActionEvent(this,
    ActionEvent.ACTION_PERFORMED, EXAMPLE_EVENT));
}
```

A component needs only to trigger the *fireExampleActionEvent()* method in whatever circumstances are appropriate to the event you define.

Dispatching Action Events from the Sample Component

The following steps will dispatch the example action event every time the Add button is clicked immediately after adding the contents of the text field to the list control:

1. Make sure the project c:\JBuilder\osborne\jbe\writingbeans\ BeanProject.jpr is open in the current AppBrowser.

2. Select the file SimpleBean.java in the Navigation pane and click the Source tab to display the Editor.

3. Select *button1_actionPerformed()* in the Structure pane and edit the method to match the following:

```
void button1_actionPerformed(ActionEvent e) {
  listControl1.addItem(textField1.getText());
  fireExampleActionEvent();
}
```

4. Select Build|Make to compile the updated component.

The updated component is now ready to be integrated into your applications and applets.

Tips on Defining New Events

Unfortunately, the New Event Bean snippet on the BeansExpress page of the Object Gallery is not a good example of how to introduce event handling into your components. It fails to deal with events properly in a multithreaded environment and could result in erratic behavior of your component.

Developing a complete event listener and multicast registration and dispatch mechanism is beyond the scope of this book. For a good example, look at

BeanPanel's implementation of *ActionListener* events, including the *borland.jbcl.util.ActionMulticaster* class.

Bean Info Classes

The JavaBeans specification allows a visual design environment to infer a lot about components from design patterns, but not everything can be inferred. More sophisticated components need to be able to communicate additional information to the environment, and this is accomplished through a special class that implements the *java.beans.BeanInfo* interface.

When JBuilder examines a component, it also searches for another class that belongs to the same package, starts with the same name, and includes the suffix "BeanInfo." The class *borland.jbcl.control.GridControl*, for example, has a companion class called *GridControlBeanInfo* that belongs to the same package.

Bean info can be used to describe the following:

♦ More detailed information about properties and events, including property editors and floating hints that appear when the cursor is positioned over a property or event in the Inspector.

♦ A default event, which JBuilder creates a handler for when a developer double-clicks the component in the Designer. For example, a button's default event is *actionPerformed*.

♦ A default property, which is currently not used by JBuilder.

♦ A customizer for the component, which is currently not used by JBuilder.

♦ An icon for the component.

14

Using BeansExpress to Define Bean Info Classes

A Bean info class can be created by selecting File|New to display the Object Gallery, selecting the BeansExpress page, and double-clicking on the Bean Info icon. JBuilder responds by displaying a Paste Snippet dialog so you can customize this snippet before adding it to your project. A Parameters button on the dialog allows the name of the Bean info class and the name of the class it describes to be defined separately.

NOTE: The Bean info class must be named using the convention described at the beginning of this section. Entering incorrect information into the snippet parameters will yield code that will compile but be ignored by JBuilder because it cannot find the Bean info class under the expected name.

The Bean info snippet is quite long, so it is presented with commentary interrupting the code as needed:

```
// This snippet creates a bean info shell for the
// specified class. Example descriptors can be
// commented out to enable specific bean info
// functionality.

// Snippet Note: Use the parameter button to change the
// name of the bean class.

package  osborne.jbe.writingbeans;

import java.beans.BeanInfo;
import borland.jbcl.util.BasicBeanInfo;

public class SimpleBeanBeanInfo extends BasicBeanInfo {
```

This snippet was given the class name *SimpleBeanBeanInfo* so that it could describe the *SimpleBean* component developed throughout this chapter. It inherits from *BasicBeanInfo*, which provides a trivial implementation of the *BeanInfo* interface that responds to the appropriate methods by returning values stored in instance variables.

The default values for these variables force the normal process of searching for design patterns to determine the existence of properties, methods, and so forth. An overridden constructor for the Bean info class is used to selectively change the defaults where different information is desirable:

```
public SimpleBeanBeanInfo() {
    beanClass = SimpleBean.class;
```

JBuilder doesn't make use of Bean customizers, so this line will likely remain commented out in all of your Bean info classes:

```
    /*
    customizerClass=null; //Optional customizer class
    */
```

The *eventSetDescriptors* variable shown next describes the event sets appropriate for this component. It contains an array of arrays of strings. Each subarray should contain four strings, providing the following values for each set of events associated with the class:

♦ The display name of the set of events.

♦ The interface that listeners implement in order to receive events belonging to this set. Note that this is incorrectly referred to as an event listener class in the comments that are automatically generated.

♦ The name of the method used to register listeners. This can be used to implement components that do not follow the standard design patterns, but this practice is not recommended.

♦ The name of the method used to remove listeners from the registered list. Again, the standard patterns are strongly recommended.

```
/**
     * The event information for your JavaBean.
     * Format:   {{"EventSetName", "EventListenerClass",
     *               "AddMethod", "RemoveMethod"}, ...}
     * Example: {{"ActionListener",
     *               "java.awt.event.ActionListener",
     *               "addActionListener",
     *               "removeActionListener"}, ...}
     */
    /*
    eventSetDescriptors = new String[][] {
      {"ActionListener",
       "java.awt.event.ActionListener",
       "addActionListener", "removeActionListener"},
    };
    */
```

The *eventListenerMethods* variable shown next describes the names of the events associated with each event set, since an event set can include any number of individual events. It contains another array made up of arrays of strings. Each array relates to the corresponding event set described by *eventSetDescriptors*, so there must be the same number of entries and they must occur in the same order.

14

The subarrays, however, can each contain any number of strings, each one naming a different event-handling method associated with the relevant event set:

```
/**
     * The names of each event set's listener methods.
     * Format:   {{"listener1Method1",
     *               "listener1Method2",
     *               "listener1Method3", ...}, ...}
     * Example: {{"actionPerformed"}, ...}
     */
    /*
    eventListenerMethods = new String[][] {
      {"actionPerformed"},
```

```
};
*/
```

Counting through the methods listed in the *eventListenerMethods* array and storing the appropriate index in the *defaultEventIndex* variable can specify the default event. Remember that the first method's index is zero, and a negative value is used to indicate that there is no default event:

```
/**
    * The index of the default event for your JavaBean.
    */
defaultEventIndex = -1;
```

The *propertyDescriptors* variable shown next describes the properties for this component. It contains an array made up of arrays of strings. Each subarray should contain four strings, providing the following values for each property associated with the class:

◆ The display name of the property.

◆ A short description of the property, displayed as a floating hint by JBuilder when the cursor pauses over an entry in the Inspector.

◆ The name of the method used to read from the property, or **null** if the property is write-only. This can be used to implement components that do not follow the standard design patterns, but this practice is not recommended.

◆ The name of the method used to write to the property, or **null** if the property is read-only. Again, the standard patterns are strongly recommended.

```
// Property Info

 /**
  * The property information for your JavaBean.
  * Format:  {{"PropertyName",
  *             ""PropertyDescription", "ReadMethod",
  *             "WriteMethod"}, ...}
  * Example: {{"fontSize",
  *             "Get the font size (points)",
  *             "getFontSize", "setFontSize"}, ...}
  */
 /*
 String[][] propertyDescriptors = new String[][] {
   {"fontSize", "Get the font size (points)",
     "getFontSize", "setFontSize"},
```

```
  };
  */
```

The default property value is assigned similarly to the default event, but JBuilder ignores this value:

```
/**
  * The index of the default property for your
  * JavaBean.
  */
defaultPropertyIndex = -1;
```

Additional descriptive information for methods can be provided through the *methodNames* and *methodParameters* variables, but JBuilder does not use the information:

```
// Method Info

/**
  * The method names (non-properties) for your
  * JavaBean.
  * Format:  {"method1", "method2", "method3", ...}
  * Example: {"fillRect", "eraseRect", "close",
  *           "open"}
  */
methodNames = new String[] {"fillRect", "eraseRect",
  "close", "open"};

/**
  * The method parameters for each of your
  * JavaBean's methods.
  * Format:  {{"method1Parameter1",
  *            "method1Parameter2", ...}, ...}
  * Example: {{"java.awt.Graphics",
  *            "java.awt.Rectangle", ...}, ...}
  */
/*
methodParameters = new String[][] {
  {"java.awt.Graphics", "java.awt.Rectangle"},
};
*/
```

14

JBuilder can use the icons provided here, or it can use external images assigned when the Component Palette is configured. These icons must be instances of the *java.awt.Image* class:

```
// Icon Info

/**
 * A 16x16 color icon for your JavaBean.
 */
iconColor16x16 = null;

/**
 * A 32x32 color icon for your JavaBean.
 */
iconColor32x32 = null;

/**
 * A 16x16 monochromatic icon for your JavaBean.
 */
iconMono16x16 = null;

/**
 * A 32x32 monochromatic icon for your JavaBean.
 */
iconMono32x32 = null;
```

More than one Bean info instance can be used to describe a single
component. This is typically used so that inherited information does not
need to be described again in a subclass's Bean info implementation:

```
// Additional Info

/**
 * Any additional BeanInfo for this JavaBean.
 */
/*
additionalBeanInfo = new BeanInfo[0];
*/
  }
}
```

Defining Bean Info for the Sample Component

The component developed so far can be customized to provide more
information about its two new properties through a Bean info class. The
steps shown add a floating hint to the two properties:

1. Make sure the project c:\JBuilder\osborne\jbe\writingbeans\
   BeanProject.jpr is open in the current AppBrowser.

2. Select File|New to display the New page of the Object Gallery. Click the BeansExpress tab, and double-click the Bean Info icon to display the Paste Snippet dialog.

3. Click the Parameters button to change the snippet's settings. Change the Name for the Bean info class field to **SimpleBeanBeanInfo**, and the Bean class field to **SimpleBean**. Click the OK button to accept these settings.

4. The Paste Snippet dialog is automatically updated to reflect the changes. Click OK to add the new SimpleBeanBeanInfo.java file to your project.

5. Select the SimpleBeanBeanInfo.java file in the Navigation pane and click the Source tab to display the Editor. Search for the *propertyDescriptors* declaration and edit it to match the following source code:

```
/*
String[][] propertyDescriptors = new String[][] {
  {"example", "A meaningless property", "getExample",
    "setExample"},
  {"items", "The current list of items", "getItems",
    "setItems"},
};
*/
```

6. Remove the comment markers /* and */ from above and below the declaration so that this source code will be compiled.

7. The snippet contains an erroneous initial "String[ ][ ]" that causes this code to declare a local variable rather than change the value of the appropriate instance variable. You need to remove this type declaration.

The final, edited version should appear as follows:

```
propertyDescriptors = new String[][] {
  {"example", "A meaningless property", "getExample",
    "setExample"},
  {"items", "The current list of items", "getItems",
    "setItems"},
};
```

8. Select Build|Make to compile the Bean info class.

9. Select File|Save All to save your progress. Quit and restart JBuilder to allow the updated information to be read by the UI Designer.

10. JBuilder should automatically display your project when it restarts. If not, open the project c:\JBuilder\myprojects\osborne\jbe\ writingbeans\BeanProject.jpr.

14

11. Select the file TestFrame.java in the Navigation pane and click the Design tab. Select *simpleBean1* in the Component Tree and examine the Inspector. The only properties displayed are those provided by Bean info, and pausing the mouse pointer over either *example* or *items* causes the appropriate hint to be displayed.

Property Editors

JBuilder displays and modifies properties through the Inspector while in design mode. Different properties have different presentations, may include lists of possible values, and may present dialogs to capture additional information. The different means of editing properties are expressed through property editors.

JBuilder defines standard property editors for the following types:

◆ The boolean primitive type presents a drop-down list with selections of True and False.

◆ The remaining primitive types, byte, short, int, long, char, float, and double, are edited as character strings with appropriate validation.

◆ The *java.lang.String* class accepts any sequence of characters.

◆ The type *String[]* displays a multiline text entry field, allowing any number of strings to be displayed and edited.

◆ The type *String[][]* displays a two-dimensional grid and provides controls for determining the size of the two dimensions as well as the contents of each of the subarrays.

◆ The classes *java.awt.Insets*, *java.awt.Point*, *java.awt.Dimension*, and *java.awt.Rectangle* all use an editor that displays a comma-delimited list of numbers. Editing is performed as for a normal string, with the individual values retrieved after validating the results.

◆ The classes *java.net.URL*, *java.awt.Color*, and *java.awt.Font* all display a dialog that provides for creation of an appropriate object.

◆ The classes *java.awt.LayoutManager* and *java.awt.MenuShortcut* display a drop-down list of the appropriate values.

JBuilder also defines many custom property editors for use internally. You may want to examine these editors for ideas on defining your own property types.

CHAPTER 15

The Model-View Architecture

The concepts introduced in this chapter assume that you have spent some time familiarizing yourself with the JBuilder development environment and have created several Java applications and applets. Once you are comfortable with the basic components in JBuilder, then it is time to peek under the covers and see what tools are available for the advanced JBuilder developer.

This chapter discusses the basic concepts behind the component architecture of the JBCL (JavaBeans Component Library)—specifically, the model-view architecture. Topics covered include understanding the model-view architecture and why it is important for your development work, using models and views, understanding and implementing interfaces, and managing selection and subfocus. Once you understand the fundamental concepts and examples presented in this chapter, you will have the background necessary to delve more deeply into specific topics of interest.

JBCL Component Philosophy

The user-interface components included in the JBCL are typical of the Borland approach to software development: The components are easy to use for the beginner, yet flexible enough to be useful to an expert. The first-time developer will find that it takes very little effort to drop a component in place and start using it. That's part of the appeal of all RAD (Rapid Application Development) tools, the ability to do productive work immediately after picking up the product. A typical user interface can be constructed very quickly, and standard approaches to the likes of database access come just as easily. This kind of accessibility allows you to focus on the unique aspects of the problem at hand.

That's usually when it becomes apparent that the accessibility of the product is also its Achilles heel. Trivial development is easy enough, but complex problems are made even more complex because you need to fight the limited nature of the underlying architecture. Luckily, JBuilder's designers focused on providing flexible solutions, not just easy ones. Each and every JBCL control acts as a gateway to a sophisticated architecture for managing and representing data.

Rather than using a single object to represent a control, the architecture used divides the responsibility among many smaller objects. One object knows how to store information, another knows how to display it, still another knows how to manage selections in complex user-interface elements, and so forth. Each of these concepts will be examined in turn in this chapter.

Separating Models and Views

The basic philosophy behind the model-view architecture, as depicted in Figure 15-1, is to separate data storage from the visual representation of the data—that is, the user interface or *view* of the data. In order to display the user interface, the view retrieves the data it represents from the model used to store the data. When changes are made through the user interface, the altered information is once again stored in the model. The goal of a model is

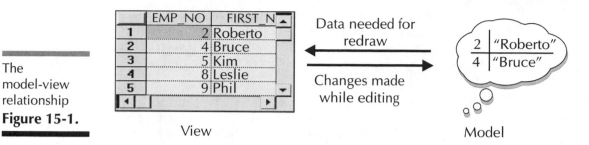

to provide a mechanism for the storage of information whose visual representation is managed by one or more views.

Why divide these two mechanisms, model and view? The first reason is that applications frequently need to be able to display more than one visual representation of the same data. For example, an order entry system might have several ways of showing customer information. When viewing a list of customers, only the customer names may be displayed. When reviewing a particular customer's file, a more detailed summary of the customer information is displayed beside a scrolling list of order summaries. Detailed customer information is edited through a third kind of interface, and so on. What happens when several views of a single customer record are open and the customer data is changed in one or more of the views, either by the same user or by different users? Ideally, the updates are displayed immediately in all open views that show the same data. Writing code to keep separate copies of the information synchronized would be a tedious and potentially error-prone task. However, if the information is stored in one location with three separate ways of viewing it, the goal of easily maintaining consistent data becomes much easier to achieve.

The second reason is that being able to use more than one representation of data for a single visual interface also turns out to be useful. Many development environments offer several kinds of scrolling lists, one for lists of textual information in memory, perhaps another for graphical information, and yet another for information maintained in a database. Ideally, a single scrolling list could be used to access data in many different forms. This ideal can be realized once there is a standard for exchanging information between the visual representation and the data storage mechanism.

In JBuilder, a model contains data, while a view makes the information accessible and may allow the data to be modified. This is the model-view relationship initially shown in Figure 15-1. Once a view is associated with a model, the view is automatically notified of changes to the data. This ensures that no matter how many views there are of the same data, the data

15

displayed in these views is always consistent. Your code interacts with the model to control changes to the data and determine when and how the views are notified of changes. An example of views sharing a model is shown in Figure 15-2. The next section describes how you use models and views in JBuilder.

JBuilder is not the first or only product to use this model-view architecture to create flexible user-interface classes. This architecture is used in SmallTalk, among other languages, and works well within any sophisticated object-oriented language.

A Shared Model

The model-view architecture is extremely flexible but can be intimidating in its implementation, especially for the developer not familiar with object-oriented designs that solve problems by dividing tasks among many small objects. Fortunately, the JBCL components provided on the Controls page of the Component Palette simplify the process by automatically creating both the view and model when a component is dropped in the UI Designer. The *TextFieldControl* component, for instance, is actually a subclass

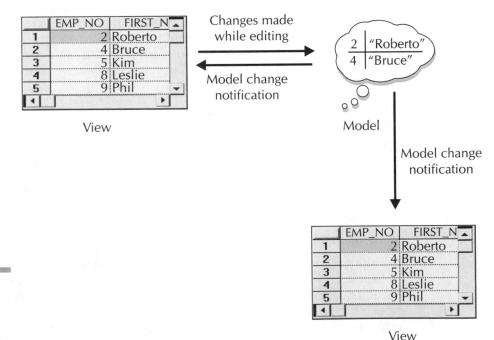

Two views
sharing a
model

Figure 15-2.

of the view *TextFieldView* that automatically creates a model of type *SingletonModel* to contain the text entered into the field.

Although by default each component has its own private model, you can change the model currently being used. You can do this by setting the *model* property of the component to refer to any appropriate model object. This overrides the default behavior so that from that point onward, the component uses the new model. The following example demonstrates this effect:

CD-ROM: You can find the finished project ModelView.jpr in the osborne\jbecd\modelview subdirectory. Ideally, you would want to follow along with the examples so that you can see the intermediate steps. See Appendix C for information on installing and using the files on the CD-ROM that accompanies this book.

1. Select File|New Project to display the Project Wizard. Enter **C:\JBuilder\myprojects\osborne\jbe\modelview\ModelView. jpr** in the File field for the name of your project. Click the Finish button.

2. Select File|New and then select the Application icon from the New page of the Object Gallery. On the Step 1 page of the Application Wizard, enter **osborne.jbe.modelview** in the Package field and **ModelViewApp** in the Class field. Click the Next button to move to the Step 2 page. On this page, enter **ModelViewFrame** in the Class field and **ModelView Chapter** in the Title field. Leave all other settings with their default values and click the Finish button.

3. Select ModelViewFrame.java in the Navigation pane and click the Design tab to display the UI Designer. Click the Controls tab on the Component Palette and place two *TextFieldControl* components in the frame, one above the other.

4. Use the Properties page of the Inspector to set the component properties as shown here:

Component Name	Property	Set to
textFieldControl1	columns	20
textFieldControl2	columns	20

5. Click the Source tab to switch to the source view and add the following line to the end of the *jbInit()* method. This line uses the *setModel()* method to tell the second field, *textFieldControl2,* to use the model created by the first field, *textFieldControl1:*

15

```
textFieldControl2.setModel(
  textFieldControl1.getModel());
```

6. Run the application by selecting Run|Run, by pressing SHIFT-F9, or by clicking the Run button on the toolbar. Observe what happens when you make a change in either of the fields and press TAB or ENTER. If you type an entry in one of the text fields and press TAB or ENTER, the other text field immediately shows the same entry.

The fields remain synchronized because they are sharing the same underlying data, the same model. A *TextFieldControl* displays information from the model and permits editing, and then updates the model when the change is complete. Once a change to the model is made, all views connected to the model automatically detect the change and display the new information. The nature of the underlying model is still not obvious since you are relying on the component to create and manage it, but it is clear that the two components are tied to the same underlying data (the same model) as originally shown in Figure 15-2.

Components Are Models, Too

While an instance of *TextFieldControl* can be asked for a reference to its model via the *getModel()* method, the JBCL components on the Controls page of the Component Palette also include another convenient technique for accessing the model. The control itself implements all of the methods required for the underlying model and simply passes requests on to whatever model it happens to be using. This means that the control itself can be treated as if it were a model.

To demonstrate this for yourself, find and comment out the following lines of code in the *jbInit()* method and then add the new line of code shown here:

```
//textFieldControl2.setModel(
//  textFieldControl1.getModel());
textFieldControl2.setModel(textFieldControl1);
```

Rather than asking for the field's model and passing it as a parameter, this code just passes a reference to the field itself as the model.

If you select Run|Run to compile and test the new code, you will find that it behaves identically to the example shown in the last section. This technique has one distinct advantage. In the first example, changing the model used by *textFieldControl1* would have no effect on *textFieldControl2*. To change both fields to a new model would require two calls to *setModel()*. In the second example, when the model used by *textFieldControl1* is changed, both controls start using the new model because *textFieldControl2* indirectly uses whatever model is connected to the first field.

Using the Lightweight View Components

The parent class of *TextFieldControl* is *TextFieldView,* a lightweight view component that is generally lacking in the little touches that make a component easy to use in a visual environment. *TextFieldView* does not automatically create a private model, cannot be treated as a model itself, and does not include any of JBuilder's data aware capabilities.

Many of the JBCL components have similar lightweight view ancestor classes. These can be very useful when you are trying to produce an applet that minimizes the amount of code that needs to be downloaded, or are attempting to squeeze a little extra performance out of a Java-based application or applet. If you don't need the extra baggage included in the *TextFieldControl,* why use it? JBuilder does not expose these pure view components on the default Component Palette, but they can be added to the palette or used directly in code.

Adding TextFieldView to the Component Palette

Like every component in the JBCL, the *TextFieldView* is a true JavaBeans component and can be added to the Component Palette. The following steps add the *TextFieldView* component to a new Component Palette page called Views.

 TIP: As you become more familiar with JBuilder, you will find more and more components that you would like to be able to use directly by adding them to the Component Palette. In fact, less than 10% of the JavaBeans included in the JBCL are provided on the default Component Palette when you install JBuilder! See Chapter 13 for information on installing and using JavaBeans components.

15

1. Select Tools|Configure Palette to display the Pages page of the Palette Properties dialog. Click the Add button to display the Add Page dialog. Enter **Views** in the Page name field and click OK.

2. Click the Add from Archive tab and then click the Browse button. Next, you want to select the file JBCL.zip. If you used JBuilder's default install location, the file/directory path should be C:\JBuilder\lib\jbcl.zip. Either enter **C:\JBuilder\lib\jbcl.zip** in the File name field and press ENTER or select the file JBCL.zip, which is in the lib directory under your JBuilder directory. Note that when you return to the Add from Archive page, the directory/file path is displayed in the field called Select a JAR or ZIP file.

TIP: Most developers find that using the mouse to select files is easy and quick. However, you can also type in this information as described in step 2, or even enter it at the Add from Archive page. At the Select a JAR or ZIP file field, enter the path **C:\JBuilder\lib\jbcl.zip** and then press ENTER to display the packages in this file.

3. In the Packages found in archive list, select borland.jbcl.view. All of the lightweight JBCL view components are contained in this package and are displayed in the second list, as shown in Figure 15-3.

4. In the JavaBeans found in package list, select borland.jbcl.view.TextFieldView.

5. At the Add component to page field, select the Views page if it is not already displayed in this field. Click the Install button. Once the message "Installation complete" is displayed in the dialog, click the OK button to return to the AppBrowser.

Your Component Palette now has a Views tab and the *TextFieldView* component appears on the Views page.

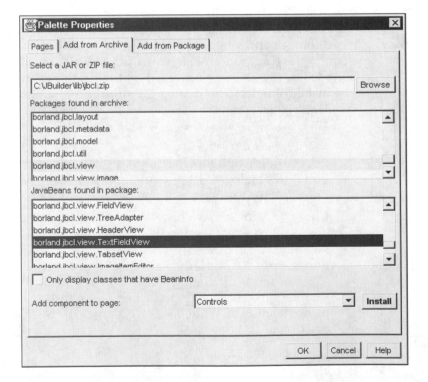

Adding the
TextFieldView
component
Figure 15-3.

Putting the

Once the *Texu·* ... ,le in the Component Palette, it can be dropped in pla·· ... and assigned a model. This final step is necessary because the ι·· ... ·mponent does not have a private model of its own.

1. Select the file ModelViewFrame.java in the Navigation pane and select the Design tab to display the UI Designer.

2. Click the Views tab of the Component Palette. Drop a *TextFieldView* component in the UI Designer, placing it below the two existing fields.

3. Select *textFieldView1*, either in the Component Tree or by selecting the *TextFieldView* object in the UI Designer. On the Properties page of the Inspector, set the columns property to 20.

4. Click the Source tab to display the Editor. At the bottom of the *jbInit()* method, add the following statement to connect the new field to an existing model:

```
textFieldView1.setModel(textFieldControl1);
```

5. Select Run|Run to compile and execute the newly updated application. When you type an entry in any of the fields and press ENTER or TAB, the other fields display the same entry. This is because the third field shares the model used by the other two fields and acts in a manner indistinguishable from them.

JBCL's Four Basic Models

JBuilder's components are built using one of four standard models, shown in Figure 15-4. All four models follow some of the same conventions, but each is capable of representing a different kind of underlying structure:

The four types of models are designed to represent different information structures:

♦ A *singleton* model contains a single object.

♦ A *vector* model contains a list of objects.

♦ A *matrix* model contains a two-dimensional array of objects.

♦ A *graph* model contains a hierarchy, or tree, of objects.

Each of these models can contain objects of any type. The *TextFieldControl* component in the last example uses a singleton model containing an instance of the *String* class as its data object. Other components use different types of models containing data types appropriate to their behavior. Many of the simpler interface objects store data using a singleton model, while *ListControl*

15

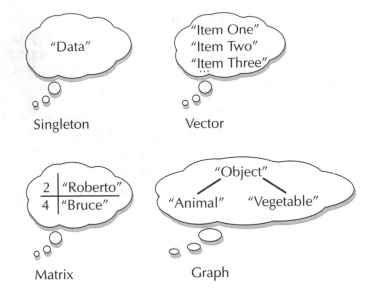

Four basic
model types
for JBuilder
components
Figure 15-4.

uses a vector model, *GridControl* uses a matrix model, and *TreeControl* uses a graph model.

Model Interfaces and Classes

Remember, the basic goal of a model is to provide a mechanism for the storage of information whose visual representation is managed by one or more views. Java code needs to interact with the model to change its contents, find out about its current contents, or control when views will be notified about changes. As long as these basic tasks can be accomplished, it doesn't matter how the data is stored or where, so JBuilder defines a set of interfaces that describe how other objects interact with each of the model types.

To make the architecture as flexible as possible, JBCL describes each of these models as a collection of *interfaces* rather than *classes*. Any class can be used as a model as long as it implements the correct interface.

There are actually two interfaces for each type of model—one interface that supports read-only access and an extended interface that allows read/write access for applying modifications. In addition to the two interfaces, JBCL makes life easy for the developer by including a basic implementation class for each of the read/write interfaces. All of the interfaces and classes for the standard model types are shown in Table 15-1, and are a part of the borland.jbcl.model package.

Model Type	Read-Only Interface	Read/Write Interface	Basic Implementation Class
Singleton	*SingletonModel*	*WritableSingletonModel*	*BasicSingletonContainer*
Vector	*VectorModel*	*WritableVectorModel*	*BasicVectorContainer*
Matrix	*MatrixModel*	*WritableMatrixModel*	*BasicMatrixContainer*
Graph	*GraphModel*	*WritableGraphModel*	*BasicGraphContainer*

The following example demonstrates how to create an instance of the basic implementation class for the singleton model, a simple model for storing a single item. The model is then associated with the first text field control.

1. Create a new model for the fields by adding the following code after all other lines in *jbInit()*:

```
WritableSingletonModel newModel =
  new BasicSingletonContainer();
newModel.set("I am stored in a model!");
textFieldControl1.setModel(newModel);
textFieldControl1.touched();
```

2. Make sure that the borland.jbcl.model package is imported by adding the following line beneath the existing **import** statements at the top of the file:

```
import borland.jbcl.model.*;
```

3. Compile and execute the application by selecting Run|Run from the menu. The application should run in the same way as before, but the initial value for all three fields will be the string "I am stored in a model!"

15

The code added creates a new model, sets its initial value, replaces the model used by the first field (which is in turn used indirectly by the other two fields), and notifies all views connected to the field that the model has changed by invoking the model's *touched()* method. The *touched()* method is included in all of the JBCL models, and invoking *touched()* is the usual technique for telling a model that its views need to be notified of changes.

Most changes to a model will invoke the *touched()* method automatically, but in this example the model was modified before being associated with any views.

Creating a Custom Model

The previous example demonstrates the use of the class *BasicSingletonContainer,* but any class that implements the *SingletonModel* interface can be used for a read-only field. Likewise, any class that implements the *WritableSingletonModel* interface can provide read/write storage for the field. You can choose between implementing each of the necessary methods in their own classes or inheriting from classes that already provide implementations for most of the methods.

To demonstrate how easy it is to create and use a new model, the following example defines a model that automatically converts all strings to uppercase. By overriding the only method that can change the value stored in the model, it is guaranteed that strings containing lowercase letters will never be stored in the model.

Remember that a model can contain objects of *any* type. Consequently, the explicit test and typecast shown in the following example are required for a well-behaved model.

1. Select the file ModelViewFrame.java in the Navigation pane and place the cursor in the Editor. Press CTRL-END to move to the bottom of the file and press ENTER to add a new line.

2. Type the following class definition into the Editor:

```
class StringCapsModel
  extends BasicSingletonContainer {
  public void set(Object value) {
    if (value instanceof String)
      value = ((String) value).toUpperCase();
    super.set(value);
  }
}
```

3. Find and comment out the following lines of code that create a *BasicSingletonContainer* model and add the extra lines that create an instance of the new model as shown here:

```
//WritableSingletonModel newModel =
//  new BasicSingletonContainer();
WritableSingletonModel newModel =
  new StringCapsModel();
```

4. Select Run|Run to compile and test the example to see how the fields behave. All three fields now display "I AM STORED IN A MODEL!" You can type lowercase letters in any of the fields, but as soon as the information is actually stored in the model behind the scenes, the text you typed in is converted to uppercase.

Learning More About Models

All of the JBCL models are documented in the JBuilder online help. The JBCL Reference contains complete descriptions of the methods for each of the read-only and read/write models. This documentation is invaluable for developers, whether you are creating a new implementation of a model or just interacting with an existing model.

Remember that the JBCL components on the Controls tab implement the model's methods to allow direct manipulation of the underlying data, so everything you learn about models can be applied directly to these controls as well.

Suppressing Model Change Events

Every time the model is updated, all views connected to it are automatically updated. This behavior is convenient when you are writing code that makes one change at a time, but can become problematic when making a large number of changes at once. When making large numbers of changes, it would be convenient to be able to suppress the automatic model change events that update views until after all of the desired changes have been made.

T IP: When dealing with vector, matrix, or graph models, it is advisable to use *enableModelEvents()* to avoid visible side effects when making multiple changes to the data.

The application created in the following steps builds a list of items to be displayed without using event suppression to demonstrate the problem.

Make the following additions to ModelViewFrame.java:

1. Select ModelViewFrame.java in the Navigation pane and click the Design tab.

2. Click the Controls tab on the Component Palette, and add a *ListControl* below the three text fields. Next, place two *ButtonControl* instances to the right of the list. Your design should look similar to the one shown in Figure 15-5.

3. Use the Properties page of the Inspector to set the component properties as shown here:

15

Component Name	Property	Set to
buttonControl1	label	Add
buttonControl2	label	Clear

4. Double-click the Add button object in the UI Designer to create an *actionPerformed* event handler for it. Enter the following code into the event handler in the Editor:

```
for (int counter = 1; counter <= 100; counter++) {
  listControl1.addItem(String.valueOf(counter));
}
```

5. Click the Design tab to switch back to the design mode and then double-click the Clear button object to create an *actionPerformed* event handler for it. Type the following code into the *actionPerformed* event handler:

```
listControl1.removeAll();
```

6. Run the application and click the Add and Clear buttons. The Clear button only performs a single action, so the results are displayed instantly. However, the event handler for the Add button makes 100 changes to the model. When you click the Add button, the display is updated after each and every change, resulting in a slow process that

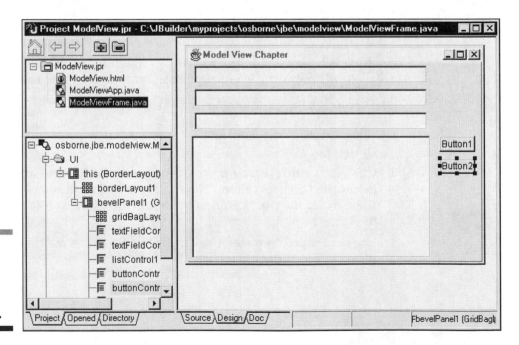

Model-view test application interface

Figure 15-5.

flickers noticeably. Clearly, it is important to be able to temporarily suspend these automatic updates.

You can use the *enableModelEvents()* method to enable and disable automatic updates. All of the existing JBCL models include an *enableModelEvents()* method that requires a single boolean parameter. Events are disabled when **false** is passed as the parameter, so that the model no longer notifies views of changes. Events can be reenabled by calling the model with **true** as its parameter. When events are reenabled, all views are automatically notified that changes may have occurred and their contents are redisplayed.

The use of the *enableModelEvents()* method is shown in the following example:

1. Change the Add button's event handler to match the following:

   ```
   listControl1.enableModelEvents(false);
   for (int counter = 1; counter <= 100; counter++) {
     listControl1.addItem(String.valueOf(counter));
   }
   listControl1.enableModelEvents(true);
   ```

2. Select Run|Run to compile and test the resulting application.

Note that this code calls *enableModelEvents()* with **false** as its parameter to disable updates before making all 100 changes, and calls *enableModelEvents()* again with **true** as its parameter to reenable events afterwards. Pressing the Add button now results in a quick update after all changes have been made. The same technique can be used with any of the JBCL controls, not just with *ListControl* components.

View Managers: Dealing with Disparate Data Types

15

The basic model-view mechanism works very well when a view can be designed to work with a particular type of data. It is true that some components can make assumptions about the type of data they will be dealing with, but others cannot. For example, a *TextFieldControl* always displays and edits strings, so there's no need to change the design of this control—it is sufficient for its normal task. In other words, the *TextFieldControl* component knows that it only deals with data of type *String*. Other components such as *FieldControl, GridControl,* and *ListControl* provide more flexibility by being able to deal with a wide variety of data types, and potentially more than one kind of data within the same control.

Rather than providing viewing and editing capabilities for a fixed number of data types, *view managers* in the JBCL provide an open-ended mechanism for dealing with disparate data types. The standard view manager components are a part of the borland.jbcl.model package in the JBCL.

In order to understand how you use view managers, consider again the model-view architecture. The simple form of model view uses two objects, one that handles all user-interface tasks and another that handles storage of all data. What happens when the data stored in the model is of a type that the user-interface component does not understand? Then, a more sophisticated architecture is necessary, and is used by the JBCL controls.

In the JBCL, the view keeps track of an area on the screen where information is presented, either as a simple rectangle in the case of a text field control, or perhaps dividing it into cells in the case of a grid or a list. The model maintains the actual data to be edited as an object or collection of objects. However, neither the view nor the model knows how to draw the data. Instead, the view defers to a third object—called a view manager—to find out about a fourth object—an *item painter*—that knows how to paint a particular cell. Figure 15-6 illustrates this process.

The view manager actually returns an object that implements the *ItemPainter* interface. This item painter actually draws the contents of an individual cell within the control. When the user wants to change the information presented, the view manager returns a fifth object—an *item editor*—that implements the *ItemEditor* interface, which allows changes to be made and reports the results back to the view. This division of labor complicates the picture somewhat, but provides extraordinary flexibility.

There are different view manager interfaces for each of the basic models. This allows a special view manager to take into account not only the *type* or *value* of the data, but also its position within a model, such as the row and column coordinates of a cell in a grid. Writing a custom view manager is fairly straightforward, but typically you can simply pick one of the view

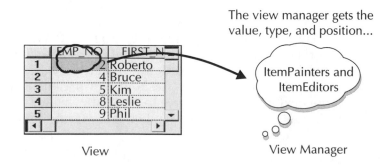

The role of the view manager
Figure 15-6.

managers already implemented within the JBCL as a part of the borland.jbcl.model package.

The *BasicViewManager* class provides a manager sufficient for controls that contain a single uniform type of data. Much more interesting is the *TypedViewManager*, which selects a painter and editor based on the class of the data within an individual cell in the model.

While the *TextFieldControl* component assumes that the data is always of type *String*, the *FieldControl* component uses a view manager and can therefore be configured to deal with a variety of data types. The *ListControl*, *GridControl*, and *TreeControl* components always use view managers, and with a little work can display several types of information concurrently. In the examples that follow, the *ListControl* added to the project earlier in the chapter will be enhanced to provide the ability to display color swatches as well as strings.

Life Without View Managers

Currently, there is no way to add color swatches to the list. There are only buttons to add textual items and clear the list. The first changes we make here are necessary to provide a mechanism for adding instances of *java.awt.Color* to the underlying *VectorModel*.

1. Return to the file ModelViewFrame.java. Modify the Add button's *actionPerformed* event handler to reduce the number of strings added when the button is clicked. Find and comment out the following line in the *actionPerformed* event handler and add the second line:

   ```
   //for (int counter = 1; counter <= 100; counter++)
   for (int counter = 1; counter <= 5; counter++)
   ```

2. Click the Design tab and add two new *ButtonControl* instances below the existing buttons. Change their properties as follows:

Component Name	Property	Set to
button3	*label*	Red
button4	*label*	Green

3. Double-click the Red button and enter the following statement to create an event handler:

   ```
   listControl1.addItem(Color.red);
   ```

4. Create the following event handler for the Green button:

   ```
   listControl1.addItem(Color.green);
   ```

15

5. Compile and test the application by selecting the menu item Run|Run, and observe what happens when the Red and Green buttons are clicked. The correct objects are added to the list, but the default *ItemPainter* and *ItemEditor* translate them to strings like "java.awt.Color[r=255,g=0,b=0]" because the list doesn't yet have a view manager that knows how to deal with any data type except *java.lang.String*.

The TypedViewManager Class

A *TypedViewManager* instance matches an item's class with an *ItemPainter* and *ItemEditor* suited to that class. It also uses a default pair for items that do not have their class registered with the manager. Only three steps are necessary to use a *TypedViewManager*. Firstly, create an instance of *TypedViewManager* using its default constructor. Secondly, add the appropriate data types with the *add()* method. The *add()* method takes three parameters: the class being registered, an *ItemPainter*, and an *ItemEditor*. Lastly, register the view manager with the control through its *SetViewManager()* method.

1. Add the following to the bottom of the *jbInit()* method for the *ModelViewFrame* class in ModelViewFrame.java:

```
TypedViewManager tvm = new TypedViewManager();
tvm.add(String.class, new SelectableTextItemPainter(),
  new TextItemEditor());
tvm.add(Color.class, new ColorItemPainter(), null);
listControl1.setViewManager(tvm);
```

2. Click the Design tab to display the UI Designer. Select *listControl1* and use the Properties page of the Inspector to change its *uniformHeight* property to False.

3. Select Run|Run to compile and test the new application. Observe what happens when colors are added to the list. Notice that the list can deal with both *String* and *Color* objects at the same time. Also note that *String* elements can be edited, while *Color* objects cannot because no item editor was registered. Lastly, note that the item painter is responsible for highlighting the item when selected, and while *SelectableTextItemPainter* knows how to do this, *ColorItemPainter* does not. Luckily, classes that implement the *ItemPainter* interface are extremely easy to write, requiring only two methods; one method describes the preferred size of the item, the other actually paints an object retrieved from the model. Writing an *ItemEditor* is a much more involved process.

Managing Selection and Subfocus

The concept of selection is important for user-interface components that display multiple data elements such as grid, list, and tree objects. In the simplest case, you might be able to sidestep the issue by using a view-only interface in which you only allow users to see data items in the view. However, most often you will also want to allow users to select an individual data item or select multiple data items in the grid, list, and tree objects. The user will typically make a selection and then use menus or other user-interface elements to act on that selection.

The issue is further complicated by the need to deal with keyboard interactions. The user needs to be able to move the cursor within a grid or list without affecting the selection. This cursor location affects where typed data will appear, and can also be used to pick new cells to add to the selection. Windows and Java both use the concept that a single control has keyboard focus. The individual cell within a control that will be affected by keyboard actions is said to have the keyboard subfocus.

The JBCL Approach

In any development environment, the most sophisticated user-interface components are ones that display multiple data elements. For example, grids, lists, and trees all present related data elements through which the user can navigate. Most component sets go a step beyond and provide at least the ability to select an individual data element within the component. Some provide the ability to select more than one element at a time.

JBuilder's JBCL provides a degree of control over the selection behavior of components that is unprecedented, and takes some getting used to. However, once you become comfortable with the flexibility, you will wonder how you ever got along without it.

15

The idea of selection in JBCL is divided into two distinct concepts: the *selection pool* and the *subfocus*. The selection pool contains a list of all of the items—that is, cells—that are currently selected by the user. For example, a list control might contain a list of customer names that the user could highlight individually or in groups. The subfocus describes a single cell, regardless of the type of selection allowed, and indicates the item that will be edited if the user begins to type. The subfocus can be changed by clicking the mouse on a cell or by using arrow keys on the keyboard.

Whenever subfocus is changed using the mouse, the selection pool is automatically changed. Subfocus can be changed without affecting the selection pool by holding down the CTRL key while pressing arrow keys or the TAB key.

The sections below describe how to interact with these two core JBCL concepts.

Subfocus Listeners

Changes in subfocus for a JBCL control can be controlled by a *listener* registered with the control. There are three different listener interfaces in the borland.jbcl.model package for the three model types for which the concept of subfocus is meaningful: *VectorSubfocusListener*, *MatrixSubfocusListener*, and *GraphSubfocusListener*. Each interface includes the same two methods: *subfocusChanging()* and *subfocusChanged()*. The parameters passed to these methods differ depending on the model since each model has a different mechanism for specifying a location for the new subfocus.

The purpose of the *subfocusChanging()* method is to give the listener a chance to reject the subfocus change made as a result of a user action or programmatic change. For example, this could be used to prevent the user from tabbing to a particular column in a grid.

The listener can prevent subfocus from being placed in a cell by throwing a *borland.jbcl.util.VetoException* as a part of the event-handling method. Not only does this prevent the user from changing the contents of a cell, it also prevents the selection pool from being changed when the user clicks on a cell. Enough information is available to veto the new subfocus based on any imaginable criteria. The *subfocusChanged()* method is invoked once all listeners have agreed to allow the change.

In the following example, subfocus is allowed only on the *String* objects in a *ListControl*; other objects stored in the model, such as colors in the example, cannot be selected by the user. Since the list control uses a vector model, the listener must implement the interface *borland.jbcl.model.VectorSubfocusListener*. For the rule to be enforced, the listener must be registered with the control it is interested in through the control's *addSubfocusListener()* method.

In this example, we'll let JBuilder automate this whole process by simply setting an event handler for the *subfocusChanging* event on the Events tab of the Inspector. JBuilder will automatically declare an adapter object that implements the interface and allow you to focus on writing the code that enforces the desired rule:

1. Select the file ModelViewFrame.java in the Navigation pane and click the Design tab.
2. Select the *ListView* object and click the Events tab in the Inspector.
3. On the Events page, click twice in the *subfocusChanging* event field to create an event handler.

4. Add the following code to the newly created event-handling method:

```
int     location = parm1.getLocation();
Object  value = listControl1.getModel().get(location);

if (value instanceof Color)
  throw new borland.jbcl.util.VetoException(
    "Colors cannot be selected");
```

5. Compile and run the application by selecting Run|Run. Click the Add button, then the Green and Red buttons, and then the Add button again. Try selecting a color, either with the mouse or the keyboard. The listener should reject all attempts to select colors, effectively blocking subfocus movement by any means.

Managing the Selection Pool

The current selection is maintained in a special selection pool object. Each model type for which selection is meaningful has two interfaces that a selection pool must conform to, all belonging to the borland.jbcl.model package. The read-only *VectorSelection*, *MatrixSelection*, and *GraphSelection* interfaces are paired with *WritableVectorSelection*, *WritableMatrixSelection*, and *WritableGraphSelection* interfaces, which extend their read-only counterparts with the ability to alter the selection. For instance, a control using a vector model may provide a *VectorSelection* or a *WritableVectorSelection* under different circumstances. The read-only interface will be used in situations where the selection should not be changed.

A complete family of classes is provided that implements the full read/write interface. Vector models can be used with the following selection pool classes:

15

- The *NullVectorSelection* class prohibits any kind of selection.

- The *SingleVectorSelection* class allows only one item in the list to be selected.

- The *BasicVectorSelection* class allows standard multiple selection, including discontinuous selection and range selection. Normally when clicking in a list, the selection is changed to a single item, but clicking and dragging can be used to select ranges of items. The existing selection can also be modified by holding down the CTRL key while clicking to select or deselect individual elements, and holding down the SHIFT key while clicking extends the last range selection made.

Graph models have the corresponding null, single, and basic selection pools, implemented in the *NullVectorSelection*, *SingleVectorSelection*, and *BasicVectorSelection* classes, respectively.

Matrix models include the corresponding *NullVectorSelection*, *SingleVectorSelection*, and *BasicVectorSelection* classes, plus three additional selection pools:

♦ The *RowMatrixSelection* class selects entire rows instead of individual cells when the user clicks in a cell.

♦ The *ColumnMatrixSelection* class selects the entire column containing the cell the user clicks in.

♦ The *CrossMatrixSelection* class selects both the row and the column containing the cell the user clicks in.

The average JBuilder application will have no need for any selection pools beyond the null, single, basic, row, column, and cross variation provided. You do not even need to reference these selection pool classes by name in your code since the JBCL controls include properties like *multiSelect* that automatically pick the correct selection pool. In other words, each control picks and maintains its own selection pool.

It may be useful to share an existing selection pool between two controls, in which case it becomes important to understand the role of the selection pool object. Normally, each control maintains an independent selection pool, even if it is sharing a model with another control. However, you can also have two or more controls not only share the same model, but also the same selection pool. As an example, when in design mode in JBuilder, the Component Tree and UI Designer share a single selection pool. The same set of components is always displayed as selected in both presentations. In similarly complex user interfaces, the techniques demonstrated in the next two sections could be exactly what you need.

Shared Model, Distinct Selection Pool

The first step is to set up two controls to share the same model. The process is the same as the one used for fields shown previously in this chapter in the section "A Shared Model." This example creates another list control, *listControl2*, then uses the *setModel()* method to use the underlying model of the existing list control, *listControl1*:

1. Select ModelViewFrame.java in the Navigation pane and click the Design tab.

2. In the UI Designer, resize the existing *ListControl* object so that it is half its previous width. Next, click the Controls tab of the Component Palette and drop another *ListControl* component in the design, placing

it beside the first list control, *listControl1*. Resize the new component—*listControl2*—to occupy the other half of the space originally occupied by the first list. Your design should look similar to the one shown in Figure 15-7.

3. Click the Source tab and add the following line to the end of the *jbInit()* method to share the first list's model in the source code:

```
listControl2.setModel(listControl1);
```

4. Compile and test the application from the menu by selecting Run|Run. Now the two lists have different view managers and selection pools, but share the same model. The ability to present one underlying set of information in many forms is part of the flexibility of the model-view architecture, but in this case, you will take one more step to share the selection pools.

Shared Selection Pool

The second step is to make the controls share a selection pool using the *setSelection()* and *getSelection()* methods. The JBCL controls that manage vector, matrix, and graph models all have *setSelection()* and *getSelection()* methods. These methods do not actually manipulate the contents of the selection pool as their names suggest, but rather allow the developer to get

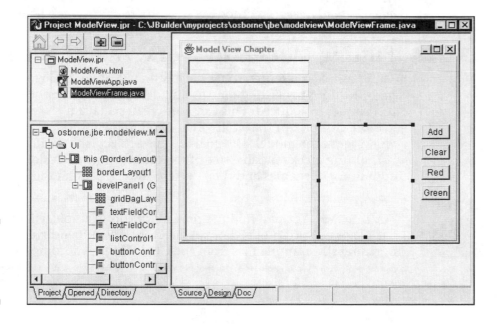

Two list controls side by side

Figure 15-7.

15

and set references to the entire selection pool object. Using this knowledge, all it takes is a single line of code to get the desired result.

1. At the bottom of the *jbInit()* method, add the following line:

```
listControl2.setSelection(listControl1.getSelection());
```

2. Compile and test the results.

This single line of code gets a reference to the selection pool object used by *listControl1*, and directs *listControl2* to use the same object for managing and displaying its selection. The selection can be changed in either list, but both will always highlight the same items to indicate that they are selected. JBuilder itself uses a shared selection for the visual design mode. The hierarchy of components displayed in the Selection pane and the visual design displayed in the Content pane are actually sharing a single graph model and selection pool. This simplifies the process of keeping the information presented and the selection synchronized between the two list controls.

Selection Listeners

Unlike subfocus listeners, selection listeners cannot interfere with the selection process in any way; they can only be informed of changes when they occur. To register a selection listener with a control, you use the *addSelectionListener()* method.

Putting Models to Work: A Java File Browser

The examples presented so far have been trivial, involving simple modifications to existing models and demonstrations of how to apply the techniques introduced. This example creates a Java file browser, and as such is more complex in that it involves developing a working graph model and a working matrix model. The goal for this project is to create a split display, containing an expandable tree of directories on the left side and a grid containing filenames and their corresponding sizes on the right side.

CD-ROM: You can find the project for this example, FileBrowser.jpr, in the osborne.jbecd.modelview subdirectory. See Appendix C for information on using the example files from the CD-ROM that accompanies this book.

This example contains a lot of code, so get ready to spend some time at the keyboard, and take breaks as necessary. To get started, begin a new project as follows:

1. Select File|New Project to display the Project Wizard. Enter **c:\JBuilder\myprojects\osborne\jbe\modelview\FileBrowser.jpr** in the File field and click the Finish button create a new project.

2. Select File|New and select the Application icon from the New page of the Object Gallery to display the Application Wizard. On the Step 1 page in the Application Wizard, leave the Package field set to osborne.jbe.modelview and enter **BrowseApp** in the Class field. Click the Next button to move to the Step 2 page. On this page, enter **BrowseFrame** in the Class field for the name of the Frame Class and enter **Java File Browser** in the Title field. Leave all other settings with their default values and click the Finish button.

The project is created and you are ready to write a graph model.

Writing a Graph Model

The *TreeControl* provides the user interface necessary to browse through a directory structure. While it would be possible to create and populate a *BasicGraphContainer* with the full directory tree, it could take an incredibly long time for a large hard drive. The average user who needs to browse into only a few of the possible branches will hardly appreciate the wasted effort.

It is much more efficient to create a custom class implementing the read-only *GraphModel* and only building branches of the tree as the user browses into them. This technique is sometimes referred to as "lazy" population of a model. In order to fully implement the *GraphModel* interface, it turns out to be necessary to create a second class as well. A quick look at the interface reveals that many of its methods return or accept objects representing individual nodes within the tree. These objects must belong to a class that implements the *GraphLocation* interface. The following source code in the file FileGraphModel.java includes classes that implement both interfaces.

15

1. Select File|New and select the Class icon from the New page of the Object Gallery to display the New Object dialog.

2. On the New Object dialog, leave the Package field set to osborne.jbe.modelview. In the Class Name field, enter **FileGraphModel**. Disable the Generate default constructor checkbox, but leave the Public checkbox enabled. Click OK to create the new file.

3. Edit the file to match the following code. The comments make the code
    clearer, but you may wish to leave them out to save yourself some
    typing.

```java
package osborne.jbe.modelview;

import borland.jbcl.model.*;
import borland.jbcl.util.TriState;
import java.util.Vector;
import java.io.File;
import java.io.FilenameFilter;

/**
 * This is a custom GraphModel that represents a
 * directory tree.
 */

public class FileGraphModel implements GraphModel
{
  FileGraphLocation root = null ;
  GraphModelMulticaster modelListeners =
    new GraphModelMulticaster();

  /**
   * Allow a new root for the hierarchy to be set.
   * When a new root is placed, notify all listeners
   * that the structure of the graph has changed.
   */

  public void setRoot(String path) {
    root = new FileGraphLocation(null, path);
    modelListeners.dispatch(new GraphModelEvent(this,
      GraphModelEvent.STRUCTURE_CHANGED));
  }

  // *** borland.jbcl.model.GraphModel ***

  public GraphLocation getRoot() {
    return root;
  }

  /**
   * Display the name of the directory for each node
   */

  public Object get(GraphLocation location) {
    if (location instanceof FileGraphLocation)
      return ((FileGraphLocation)location).path;
```

```
      return "";
    }

  public GraphLocation find(Object path) {
    return null ;
  }

  public void addModelListener(GraphModelListener
    listener) {
    modelListeners.add(listener);
  }

  public void removeModelListener(GraphModelListener
    listener) {
    modelListeners.remove(listener);
  }
}

/**
 * This is a custom GraphLocation that represents a
 * directory
 */

class FileGraphLocation implements GraphLocation,
  FilenameFilter {
  static final FileGraphLocation[] noChildren =
    ncw FilcCraphLocation[0];

  FileGraphLocation      parent;
  FileGraphLocation[]    children;
  String                 path;

  public FileGraphLocation(FileGraphLocation parent,
    String path) {
    this.parent = parent;
    this.path = path;
  }

  public String getFullPath() {
    if (parent == null) {
      return path;
    }
    else {
      return parent.getFullPath() +
        File.separator + path;
    }
  }
```

15

```
// *** borland.jbcl.model.GraphModel ***

public GraphLocation getParent() {
  return parent ;
}

/**
 * Facilitate lazy evaluation by indicating that there
 * _might_ be children until we know for sure.
 */

public int hasChildren() {
  if (children == null) return TriState.UNKNOWN;
  if (children.length > 0 ) return TriState.YES;
  return TriState.NO;
}

/**
 * Report children as all of our subdirectories by
 * using java.io.File's list() method with a custom
 *  FilenameFilter.
 */

public GraphLocation[] getChildren() {
  if (children == null) {
    String[] subdirectories = new File(
      getFullPath()).list(this);

// Build and preserve an array of children to
// avoid having to repeat this process more than
// once for any given node

children = new FileGraphLocation[
  subdirectories.length];
for ( int index = 0 ; index <
  subdirectories.length ; index++ ) {
  children[index] = new FileGraphLocation(this,
    subdirectories[index]);
  }
}
return children;
}

// *** java.io.FilenameFilter ***

/**
 * Reject all files except directories
 */
```

```
public boolean accept(File dir, String name) {
  return new File(dir + File.separator + name).
    isDirectory() ;
  }
}
```

Examining the Code

Compile the code to make sure there are no problems with it, but don't run the application just yet. Until some user-interface elements have been added to the design, there isn't anything to see, but do look over the code that has been created so far.

The actual *FileGraphModel* class is extremely simple. The only method that isn't a part of the *GraphModel* interface is *setRoot()*, which can be used to change the directory of the root node of the tree. The remaining methods are also quite simple, demonstrating that the *GraphModel* implementation is only responsible for keeping track of the root of the hierarchy, an instance of a class that implements *GraphLocation*. This class also showcases the use of a class provided by Borland for your convenience: *GraphModelMulticaster*. This class maintains a list of objects notified when broadcasting subsequent model events. Specifically, when the root node is changed, this model sends out a notification to every listener for the model indicating that the structure of the tree has changed.

The *FileGraphLocation* class is used to represent each individual node within the hierarchy, including the root. Each node is responsible for describing whether or not it has children and returning an array containing each child node as additional *FileGraphLocation* instances. The *hasChildren()* query can reply with three possible values, defined as constants by *borland.jbcl.util.TriState*. The values YES and NO are obvious enough, but UNKNOWN can be used to describe a situation in which it isn't clear whether or not there are children, such as a branch of the hierarchy that has not yet been explored.

In order to build a list of subdirectories, the *list()* method of the class *java.io.File* is put to use. This method can optionally take a reference to a filter that accepts or rejects particular files. In this case, the *FileGraphLocation* itself acts as a filter, rejecting anything except subdirectories. The actual files within a directory will be taken care of later in this example.

Building a User Interface

The custom *GraphModel* works behind the scenes to provide data for a view that understands the model, so it's time to create a user interface that includes such a view. Thinking ahead, let's place a *TreeControl* on a *SplitPanel*. This leaves the opportunity to add a list of files to the panel later

15

on. Lastly, the *FileGraphModel* needs to be given a root directory to browse from. Using "C:" as shown in this example isn't portable; the directory name doesn't have any meaning on any machine not running DOS or Windows, but it is easier than writing a truly portable example.

1. Select BrowseFrame.java in the Navigation pane and click the Design tab.
2. In the UI Designer, click on the *BevelPanel* object occupying the center of the frame to select it, and press the DELETE key to remove it.
3. Select the Containers tab of the Component Palette and place a *SplitPanel* component in the center of the frame in the UI Designer.
4. Select the Controls tab of the Component Palette and place a *TreeControl* component inside of the *SplitPanel* object in the UI Designer.
5. Click the Source tab to switch to the source view and locate the instance variable declarations at the top of the *BrowseFrame* class. Add the following line after the existing instance variable declarations near the top of the class:

    ```
    FileGraphModel graphModel = new FileGraphModel();
    ```

6. Add the following two lines to the end of *BrowseFrame*'s *jbInit()* method:

    ```
    graphModel.setRoot("C:");
    treeControl1.setModel(graphModel);
    ```

Compile and run the browser to verify that the browser does indeed explore the local hard drive. Remember that only directory names are displayed in the tree at the moment, and that the tree will always indicate that there might be subdirectories under a directory until you actually try to expand a node to find out for certain.

Writing a Matrix Model

The file viewer under construction also needs to be able to display files within a directory. A *GridControl* can provide a neat columnar display for filenames and sizes, and it turns out that read-only *MatrixModel* implementations are easy to write. The model needs to be able to describe the number of rows and columns, and the contents of each cell. The following source code for FileMatrixModel.java describes all of the files in a specified directory.

1. Select File|New and select the Class icon from the New page of the Object Gallery.
2. On the New Object dialog, leave the Package field set to osborne.jbe.modelview. In the Class Name field, enter

FileMatrixModel, and disable the Generate default constructor checkbox. Click OK to create the new file.

3. Once again, edit the file to match the source code shown here:

```java
package osborne.jbe.modelview;

import borland.jbcl.model.*;
import java.util.Vector;
import java.io.*;

public class FileMatrixModel implements MatrixModel
{
  File[] files;
  MatrixModelMulticaster modelListeners =
    new MatrixModelMulticaster();

  public void setDirectory(String path) {
    try {
      String[] filenames = new File(path).list();

      files = new File[filenames.length];

      for (int index = 0; index < filenames.length;
        index++) {
        files[index] = new File(path +
          File.separator + filenames[index]);
      }
    }
    catch(IOException ex) {
      files = null ;
    }

    modelListeners.dispatch(new MatrixModelEvent(
      this, MatrixModelEvent.CONTENT_CHANGED));
  }

  // *** borland.jbcl.model.MatrixModel ***

  public Object get(int row, int column) {
    if (column == 0) return files[row].getName();
    if (column == 1) return
      new Long(files[row].length());
    return null ;
  }

  public MatrixLocation find(Object data) {
    return null;
  }
```

15

```
public int getRowCount() {
    if ( files == null ) return 0 ;
    return ( files.length ) ;
}

public int getColumnCount() {
    return 2;
}

public void addModelListener(MatrixModelListener
    listener) {
    modelListeners.add(listener);
}

public void removeModelListener(MatrixModelListener
    listener) {
    modelListeners.remove(listener);
}
}
```

Examining the Code

Compile this code to verify that it has been entered correctly. The user interface for the file list will be discussed shortly, but look at the model implementation first.

FileMatrixModel instances have a single method for controlling the directory they examine, just like *FileGraphModel*. The *setDirectory()* method scans the specified directory using the unfiltered version of the *list()* method of *java.io.File* and builds a collection of *File* objects. The remaining methods define the matrix itself, fixing the structure at two columns—the filename on the left and size on the right—and a number of rows that is equivalent to the number of files. This class uses an instance of *MatrixModelMulticaster* to track a list of listeners who are notified when the directory for which files are displayed changes.

Extending the User Interface

Next, a grid needs to be added to the display, and a few other details must be taken care of. The list of files displayed in the grid should reflect the current selection in the *TreeControl*. The *subFocusChanged* event can be used to determine when the selection changes, providing a convenient time to invoke the matrix model's *setDirectory()* method.

1. Select BrowseFrame.java in the Navigation pane and click the Design tab.

2. Click the Controls tab of the Component Palette and in the UI Designer, place a *GridControl* component on the right side of the *SplitPanel* object.

3. Select *treeControl1* in the Component Tree. Display the Events page in the Inspector and click twice in the field for the *subfocusChanged* event to create the event handler. In the source code, add the following line to the event handler:

```
matrixModel.setDirectory(((FileGraphLocation)
  e.getLocation()).getFullPath());
```

4. Add the following line to the end of the *jbInit()* method:

```
treeControl1.setModel(graphModel);
```

Done. Or is it? If you run this application, you'll note that only one column is displayed. The *GridControl* is designed to allow only a subset of the columns represented by the actual model to be displayed, and for additional formatting to be added to each column through a *borland.jbcl.view.ColumnView* component. A few more lines are necessary in order to create a pair of these columns and ask the grid to use them through *GridControl*'s *setColumnView()* method.

1. Under the existing **import** statements in BrowseFrame.java (the current file), add a single import for the *ColumnView* component:

```
import borland.jbcl.view.ColumnView;
```

2. Below the declaration of the instance variable *matrixModel*, add the following two lines to declare two *ColumnView* instances:

```
ColumnView fileColumnView = new ColumnView();
ColumnView sizeColumnView = new ColumnView();
```

3. At the end of the *jbInit()* method, you tell the grid about the columns using the following statement:

```
gridControl1.setColumnViews(new ColumnView[]
  {fileColumnView, sizeColumnView});
```

15

4. Compile and test the complete file browser. You may want to add additional features, or just clean up the interface by setting additional properties for the grid and columns. Take your time in reviewing the code to make sure you understand the impact of each line.

Model View in Review

The architecture of JBCL is exciting, powerful, and deep. It should not be necessary to revert to developing custom models, selection pools, and item viewers and editors for every project, but there are times when developing and managing them becomes extraordinarily useful. The topics in this chapter should give you some idea of *what* is possible, and serve as a good starting point for discovering exactly *how* to accomplish your future goals.

APPENDIX A

Java Types, Operators, Literals, and Assignment

If you are new to Java, and especially if you are not already familiar with C/C++, you are probably unfamiliar with the specifics of the Java language. This appendix, in conjunction with Appendix B, is designed to serve as an introduction to the basic elements of the Java language, as well as a refresher for those who have only some familiarity with it.

If you are currently comfortable with Java types and operators, you can skip this appendix. However, if you either do not know Java, or are interested in brushing up on it, you will want to read this appendix and the next one before you read the initial chapters in this book. In addition to types and operators, literals and assignment are also covered in this appendix.

A complete and detailed description of the Java language is beyond the scope of this book. If you are interested in learning more about Java, take a look at *Java 1.1, The Complete Reference* (1997, Osborne/McGraw-Hill). You may also want to consult the Java Language Specification available in JBuilder's online help.

Java Types

Java is actually a simple language with relatively few datatypes and constructs. This is not meant to imply that Java is not powerful. Indeed, Java is a modern, full-featured, object-oriented language capable of creating almost any type of application you might need.

Java types fall into two categories: *primitive* types and *reference* types. Primitive types are the base or elemental types, and are not objects themselves. These include byte, short, int, long, char, float, double, and boolean. These primitive types can be further categorized as integral types (byte, short, int, long, and char), floating point types (float and double), and boolean.

Reference types, on the other hand, are used to refer to objects. There are three variations of reference types. These are object references, interface references, and arrays.

As you work with Java, you might be inclined to conclude that **null** is a type. In fact, it is not. There is, however, a null constant, **null**, which can be used with reference comparison operators to test whether or not a reference has been assigned yet. The constant **null** is discussed later in this chapter.

Integral Primitive Types

The integral types are used to store integers. What distinguishes the various integral types is their range. Byte, for instance, is an 8-bit, signed, two's-complement integer, and is therefore capable of referencing values between -128 and 127. Short, by comparison, is a 16-bit, signed, two's-complement integer whose range is -32,768 to 32,767. In fact, all integral types are signed, two's-complement integers, with the exception of char, which is an unsigned, 16-bit integer used for representing unicode characters (an international set of characters, the first 127 of which represent the ASCII character set). Table A-1 displays the size and range of each of the integral types.

For more information on these types, see the classes *java.lang.Byte, java.lang.Short, java.lang.Integer, java.lang.Long,* and *java.lang.Character.*

Floating Point Primitive Types

There are two floating point primitive types in Java, float and double. Like the integral types, the difference between these two is their range. The type float is a 32-bit, single-precision type, and double is a 64-bit, double-precision type. Both of these types can be represented by negative and positive infinity, as well as by negative and positive zero. In addition, variables of the floating point types can represent values that are not a number, which is represented by the symbol NaN. NaN values are produced by operations such as dividing zero by zero, or negative infinity by positive infinity. The constants POSITIVE_INFINITY and NEGATIVE_INFINITY, as well as NaN, are declared in the *java.lang.Float* and *java.lang.Double* classes. Likewise, the maximum and minimum values for floating point types are represented by the constants MAX_VALUE and MIN_VALUE. The minimum and maximum values for these types are shown in Table A-2.

Although a given floating point type may represent negative and positive zero, these values are considered equivalent in comparisons. Specifically, -0.0 is equal to +0.0.

The float types in Java conform to the IEEE 754 standard, and all operations on values of these types behave as described in that document.

All primitive types have a corresponding *toString()* method that is designed to return a string object that represents the value. (This method is declared in a class that has the same name as the primitive type, but is distinct from it. For example, the class *java.lang.Integer* defines methods that can be used on expressions of type int. It is here that *toString()* is defined for values of the

Type	Size (bits)	Range
byte	8	-128 to 127
short	16	-32,768 to 32,767
int	32	-2,147,483,648 to 2,147,483,647
long	64	-9,223,372,036,854,775,808 to 9,223,372,036,854,775,807
char	16	0 to 65,535

Sizes and Ranges of Integral Types
Table A-1.

Type	Size (bits)	Maximum Value	Minimum Value
Float	32	±3.4028236E+38	±1.4E-45
Double	64	±1.7984828356536 153E+308	±4.9E-324

primitive type int.) This method is automatically called any time a primitive type is concatenated with a *String* object. For example, assuming that there is a *StatusBar* object named *statusBar*, the following statements will display the message "The value of doubleVar is 1.0" in the status bar:

```
double doubleVar = 1.0;
statusBar.setText("The value of doubleVar is "+doubleVar);
```

The Boolean Primitive Type

The boolean primitive type has only two values, *true* and *false*. Unlike some other languages, such as C, values of the integral type cannot be used in expressions that require a boolean value. In other words, in order to use a non-boolean in a boolean expression, you must use an appropriate boolean operator, such as a comparison operator. See *java.lang.Boolean* for more information.

Reference Types

Unlike primitive types, which are used to represent data and are not true objects, reference types are used to reference an object, an implemented interface, or an array. The referent—that is, the item being referenced—may be an object, an object that implements an interface, or an array that you have in your code, or it may be one that is defined in the Java class libraries.

While Java does not support pointer types, a reference is essentially that—a pointer to an object. However, unlike pointers in traditional programming languages, you do not dereference the pointer. Java does this for you.

A variable can be defined as being a reference type, meaning that it is capable of pointing to an instance of a class—that is, an object. If the reference instance variable is not initialized in its declaration, then it is equal to the special constant **null**. For example, assuming that there is a *StatusBar* object named *statusBar,* the following code will display the text "Not yet assigned" in the status bar if the variable *buttonvar* has not yet been assigned to an object, and the value "Already assigned" if it has been assigned:

```
if (buttonvar == null)
   statusBar.setText("Not yet assigned");
else
   statusBar.setText("Already assigned");
```

In the preceding statement, the == character combination (two consecutive equal signs) is a logical comparison operator. The statement buttonvar == null is equal to a boolean true if the referent, *buttonvar* in this example, does not point to an object. Operators are discussed later in this appendix. Control structures, including the **if** statement used in this example, are discussed in Appendix B.

Each object definition includes a *toString()* method that returns a string when the referent is used to concatenate a *String* with another object. If the reference is equal to null, *toString()* returns a string containing the value "null."

This can be demonstrated with a simple example. Imagine that you have a frame on which you have placed two buttons and a status bar. Assume further that you have declared a variable, named *b*, to be of the type *Button*. You declare the variable by placing the statement

```
Button b;
```

in the frame declaration. When you are done adding the variable declaration, your frame might begin like the following code example:

```
public class Frame1 extends DecoratedFrame {
   Button b;
   BorderLayout borderLayout1 = new BorderLayout();
   XYLayout xYLayout2 = new XYLayout();
   BevelPanel bevelPanel1 = new BevelPanel();
   StatusBar statusBar = new StatusBar();
   Button button1 = new Button();
   Button button2 = new Button();
```

Now, add an *actionPerformed* event handler to button1 as follows:

```
void button1_actionPerformed(ActionEvent e) {
    statusBar.setText("The value is "+b);
}
```

Add an event handler to the actionPerformed event of button2 like this:

```
void button2_actionPerformed(ActionEvent e) {
    b = new Button();
```

A

Once you run this application, if you click button1 prior to clicking button2, the Button variable *b* has not yet been assigned, and the message "The value is null" will appear in the status bar. If you click button2, which causes an instance of the *Button* class to be created and assigned to the variable *b*, and then click button1 again, you will see a message similar to the following:

```
The value is java.awt.Button[button2,0,0,0x0,invalid,label=]
```

Operators

Operators are symbols that are used in expressions to modify the value of a simple expression, or to produce a new expression from one or more expressions. For example, the concatenation operator used in the preceding example and represented by a single plus sign (+) acts to create a new *String* object from one *String* and one other object or primitive.

Which operators you can use with a particular expression depends on the type or types of expressions being operated on. For example, there is one set of operators that can be used with integer expressions. Some of these same operators can be used on expressions of the type float, String, and reference. Each of these will be considered separately in the following sections.

Integer Operators

The integer operators can be divided into five categories. These integer operator categories are numeric operators, comparison operators, the conditional operator, cast operators, and the string concatenation operator.

Integer Numeric Operators

The numeric operators are used to change the sign of an integer, perform integer arithmetic, increment or decrement an integer, signed and unsigned shift, bitwise complement, and bitwise comparison. The numeric operators are listed in Table A-3.

Each of these categories of operators is covered in the following sections.

Sign-Changing Operators

The sign-changing operators, + and -, serve to define the sign of a single operand. (Operators that act on a single expression are referred to as *unary* operators.) The - operator changes the sign of the operand, while the + operator has no effect. Consequently, given an integer variable name *i*, the expression:

```
i = -1;
```

Operator Category	Operators
sign changing	-, +
integer arithmetic	+, -, /, *, %
increment	+
decrement	--
shift	<<, >>, >>>
bitwise complement	~
bitwise comparison	&, |, ^

Numeric
Operators
Table A-3.

assigns the value -1 to *i*, and the expression:

```
i = +1;
```

assigns the value 1 to *i*. Since the + operator has no effect on the sign of the operand, the statements:

```
i = -1;
i = +i;
```

result in the assignment of -1 to *i*.

Arithmetic Operators
The integer arithmetic operators operate on two integer operands. Use + to add two integers together, and - to subtract the right operand from the left. The * operator multiplies two operands together, while the / operator divides the left operand by the right.

The % operator returns the integer representing the remainder resulting from the division of the left operand from the right. Consequently, given an integer variable *i*, the following statement assigns the value 2 to *i*:

```
i = 8 % 3;
```

These arithmetic operations can be performed on two integers of different types. When this occurs, the type with the smallest range is promoted to the other type, or int, whichever is smallest (you never get a result of type byte or short from any operation—the smallest result of any of these operators is int). Furthermore, the result is of the same type as that to which the smallest type was promoted. For example, if you multiply a byte by an integer, the

A

resulting value will be of type integer, even if the resulting value can be represented by a value of type byte.

Increment and Decrement Operators

Java defines both increment and decrement operators, which may be used as either a prefix or a postfix. The character combination ++ increments a single operand, while -- decrements it. When these operators are used simply to increase or decrease the value stored in a variable, the prefix and postfix versions are similar, though the postfix is more common.

By comparison, when these operators are used in expressions that are part of a condition used to control a control structure, such as a **while** statement, you will select which version to use based on when you want the operation to occur, either before the evaluation of the condition or following. Specifically, if you want the operator to perform its action prior to the evaluation, use the prefix. On the other hand, if you want the operator to increment or decrement the expression following evaluation, use the postfix.

Consider the following two code segments:

```
int i = 1;
while (++i < 10)
  {//perform some action here}
```

and

```
int i = 1;
while (i++ < 10)
  {//perform some action here}
```

The first **while** loop will execute nine times, while the second will execute ten times. Because the first loop is controlled by an expression that includes the prefix increment operator, *i* is incremented prior to its comparison with the literal 10. In the second example, the incrementation occurs after the boolean comparison is performed.

Bit-Shifting Operators

The shift operators perform bitwise shifting of integer values. The operator appears to the right of the operand, and an integer, indicating the number of bits to shift, appears on the right. For example, the following code segment assigns the value of 4 to the variable *j*:

```
byte i = 1;
byte j = i<<2;
```

This is because *i* is represented by the binary value 00000001, and when it is shifted two bits to the left, the binary value is equal to 00000100, or 4 decimal.

There are three bit-shifting operators in Java. Both the operators >> (shift right) and << (shift left) perform signed bit shifts, with the high-order bits of the >> shift right operations being filled with the sign bit of the operand. The >>> operator (shift right, zero fill), by comparison, performs an unsigned bit shift, with the high-order bits being assigned 0. (Left shift always performs a zero fill.) The following demonstrates the difference between >> and >>> operators:

```
int i = 0xFFFFFFFE;
//i is all ones except the least significant bit, which is zero
//i is initialized to -2 decimal
int j;
j = i>> 1; //signed extension, j is now all ones
//j is equal to -1 decimal
j = i>>>1 ; //unsigned extension, most significant bit is zero
//j is equal to 2,147,483,647 decimal
```

In this code, the variable *i* is assigned an initial value of all 1's, with the exception of a 0 in the least significant bit. When this number is shifted right with sign extension, the least significant bit is dropped and all bits shift right. The most significant bit is replaced by one of the same sign as the previous most significant bit. The resulting value is all 1's, or -1 (remember that int is a 32-bit, two's-complement number).

In the second assignment, the unsigned right shift is used. Since the unsigned right-shift operator always assigns a value of 0 to the most significant bit, the resulting value is all 1's, except for a 0 as the most significant bit. This number is equal to 7FFFFFFF hexadecimal, or 2,147,483,647 decimal.

Using the signed bit-shifting operators, a left shift by 1 is equal to multiplying a value by 2, and a right shift by 1 is equal to dividing a number by 2.

Bitwise Complement Operator

The bitwise complement is performed by the ~ operator. This operator has the effect of performing a one's complement bit transformation. That is, each bit in the operand is toggled from 1 to 0, or 0 to 1. This is demonstrated in the following example. Consider the number 0, which is represented by 32 zeros binary, or 00000000 in hexadecimal. If you take the bitwise complement of 0, the value is -1, which is represented by 32 ones binary, or FFFFFFFF in hexadecimal.

A

The use of the bitwise complement operator is demonstrated in the following code segment. Note the use of hexadecimal notation in the initializer of the variable *b*.

```
int b = 0x7FFFFFFF; //Sign bit zero, all other bits 1
//b is now equal to 2,147,483,647
b = ~b; //All bits toggled.
//The sign bit is now 1, and all other bits 0
//b is now equal to -2,147,483,648
```

Bitwise Comparison Operators

The bitwise comparison operators permit you to compare two numbers based on their binary representations. The three bitwise comparison operators are

Operator	Performs
I	bitwise OR
&	bitwise AND
^	bitwise XOR

Using the bitwise OR (I), a bit in the result will be 1 if at least one of the bits in the corresponding position of both operands is 1. For example, consider the operands 1 and 3, whose binary representations are 0001 and 0011, respectively. The resulting binary value is 0011:

```
0001 | 0011 = 0011
```

The bitwise AND operator (&) produces a value in which the resulting bit is 1 if and only if both bits in the corresponding positions of the two operands are 1. Consequently, 1 & 3 is equal to 1:

```
0001 & 0011 = 0001
```

The bitwise XOR operator (^) sets a bit in the result to a 1 only if the bits in the same position of the two operands are different. Consequently, 1 ^ 3 is equal to 2:

```
0001 ^ 0011 = 0010
```

This is demonstrated in the following code segment, which again uses hexadecimal notation:

```
int a = 0x00000001;
int b = 0x00000003;
int k;
k = a | b; //k = 3
k = a & b; //k= 1
k = a ^ b; //k = 2;
```

Integer Comparison Operators

You use the integer comparison operators to compare two integers. The result of the comparison is always a boolean value.

There are six integer comparison operators, shown in Table A-4.

These comparison operators act the same as the corresponding operators available in almost every programming language, but for clarity, the following code segment demonstrates their use:

```
int a = 5;
int b = 4;
boolean c,
c = a < b; //c = false
c = a > b; //c = true
c = a >= b; //c = true
c = a <= b; //c = false
c = a == b; //c = false
c = a != b; //c = true
```

The Integer Conditional Operator

The integer conditional operator requires three operands. The first and second operands are separated by the ? character, and the second and third

A

Integer
Comparison
Operators
Table A-4.

Operator	Comparison
>	greater than
<	less than
==	equal to
>=	greater than or equal to
<=	less than or equal to
!=	not equal to

are separated by the : character. Consequently, you often see this operator referred to by the ?: symbol.

The first argument in a ?: statement must be a boolean expression. The second and third operands are integers. (Floating point, reference, and boolean versions of this operator also exist, however). If the boolean operand evaluates to a logical true, the ?: expression evaluates to the value of the second operand. If the boolean operand evaluates to a logical false, the expression evaluates to the third operand.

This is demonstrated in the following code segment:

```
int a = 10;
int b = 20;
int k;
k = true ? a : b;   //k = 10
k = false ? a : b;  //k = 20
```

The various expressions are evaluated strictly from left to right, permitting complex expressions to be evaluated. For example, consider the following code segment:

```
int a = 10;
int b = 20;
int k;
k = a == b ? a + 1 : b - 1;   //k = 19
k = a*4 == b*2 ? a + 1 : b - 1;  //k = 11
```

Integer Cast Operators

Any numeric expression can be cast to another numeric type using the cast operators. There is one cast operator for each numeric type. To cast an expression, precede the expression to be cast with the type the expression it is being cast to, enclosed in parentheses. For example, to assign a value of type int to a variable of type byte, precede the byte expression with the keyword **int**, enclosed in parentheses.

This is demonstrated in the following code segment. Here, the assignment of the integer value stored in the variable *a* to the variable *b* would normally generate a compiler warning. However, by casting the variable *a* to the type byte, the warning is avoided. It should be noted, however, that this operation may produce unexpected results if the value in the variable *a* exceeds the range of the primitive type byte.

```
byte b;
int a = 1;
b = (byte)a;
```

The Integer String Concatenation Operator

Any time a string and a nonstring value are combined in an expression using the string concatenation operator (+), the result is a new *String* object. The value of that object is the original string plus either the string "null" (if the non-string object is a reference type whose value is null), or a string representation of the expression. If the expression is a primitive type, the string value will be the string representation of the value. If the expression is a non-null reference type, the string will be the original string value plus the value returned by the reference type's *toString()* method.

Floating Point Operators

Java provides a set of operators for use with floating point types. The same five categories of operators available for integer types are available for floating point types, though the specific operators in a particular category are sometimes different. The floating point operator categories are numeric operators, comparison operators, the conditional operator, cast operators, and the string concatenation operator.

As you might imagine, many of the floating point operators work in a fashion similar to their integer counterparts. In fact, the conditional operator, cast operators, and the string concatenation operator all work for floating point types the same way as was previously described for integer types. Consequently, a discussion of those operators will not be repeated here. In fact, differences exist between the integer and floating point operators in the categories numeric operators and comparison operators. These two operator categories are described in the following sections.

Floating Point Numeric Operators

The floating point numeric operators are used to change the sign of an integer, perform floating point arithmetic, and increment or decrement floating point numbers. The floating point numeric operators are listed in Table A-5. Note that Java does not support bit shifting or bitwise operations on floating point types.

Each of these sets of operators works in a manner comparable to their integer counterparts, and therefore, it is not necessary to go into each operator in detail.

A

Type	Operators
sign changing	-, +
floating point arithmetic	+, -, /, *
increment	+
decrement	--

The primary difference between these operators and their integer counterparts is the type resulting from the operation. Sign changing, arithmetic, and increment and decrement operators operating on floating point types produce floating point results. These same operations on integers, by comparison, produce integer results.

Floating Point Comparison Operators

As it does with integer types, Java provides six comparison operators. These are greater than (>), less than (<), equal to (==), greater than or equal to (>=), less than or equal to (<=), and not equal to (!=).

As far as comparison operators go, there are a few anomalies when floating point numbers are involved. For example, -0 is equivalent to +0. Furthermore, NaN is not really a number, and so no two NaN values are equivalent. Specifically, whenever one of the operands is a NaN value, the == operator always produces a logical false, even if both operands are NaN. In addition, when at least one operand is NaN, the != operator always returns false.

The following code segment demonstrates the use of the floating point comparison operations:

```
double a = 1.234;
double b = 2.345;
boolean c;
c = a < b; //c is equal to true
c = a > b; //c is equal to false
a = -0.0;
b = 0.0;
c = a == b; //c is equal to true
a = java.lang.Double.NEGATIVE_INFINITY;
b = java.lang.Double.POSITIVE_INFINITY;
c = java.lang.Double.NaN == (a/b); //c is equal to false
```

The Floating Point Conditional Operator

The floating point conditional operator works just like the integer conditional operator. See the earlier section "The Integer Conditional Operator."

Floating Point Cast Operators

Floating point cast operators work just like integer cast operators. See the earlier section "Integer Cast Operators."

The Floating Point String Concatenation Operator

The floating point string concatenation operator works just like the integer string concatenation operator. See the earlier section "The Integer String Concatenation Operator."

Boolean Operators

Conditions—that is, expressions that evaluate to a logical true or false—play a critical role in the control of execution. Specifically, control structures such as **for**, **while**, **do**, and **if** control their iterative and conditional execution based on the value of boolean expressions. While a condition may consist of a simple boolean expression (for example, a variable containing a boolean value), it may also include one or more simple boolean expressions that are combined using boolean operators to produce the boolean value.

There are six categories of boolean operators. These are comparison operators, the logical complement operator, logical operators, conditional logical operators, the conditional operator, and the string concatenation operator. These are described in the following sections.

Logical Comparison Operators

There are two comparison operators, equals (==) and not equals (!=). The result of either of these operations is a boolean true or false. Both of the comparison operators require two operands of type boolean. If both boolean operators have the same value, the equals operator evaluates to true; otherwise, false. For example:

```
true ==  true; //evaluates to true
false == true; //evaluates to false
```

The not equals operator evaluates to a value of true if one of the operands is true and the other is false. For example:

```
true !=  true; //evaluates to false
false != true; //evaluates to true
```

The Logical Complement Operator

The logical complement operator (!) is a unary operator. The operand must be of type boolean, and the result is the logical opposite. For example:

```
! true;  //evaluates to false
! false; //evaluates to true
```

Logical Operators

The logical operators compare two boolean operands, and the result evaluates to a boolean type. These are three logical operators, OR (|), AND (&), and XOR (^).

The OR operator evaluates to a boolean true if either of the operands is equal to true. Only when both operands are false does it evaluate to false.

The AND operator evaluates to a logical true only if both of the operands evaluate to true. Otherwise, it evaluates to false.

The XOR operator evaluates to true only when exactly one of the operands evaluates to true. If neither of the operands evaluates to true, or both of them evaluate to true, XOR evaluates to a boolean false. In other words, XOR evaluates to true only when the two operands are of opposite values.

The results of these operators are shown in the following examples:

```
true | true; //evaluates to true
true | false; // evaluates to true
false | false; // evaluates to false
true & true; // evaluates to true
true & false; // evaluates to false
false & false; // evaluates to false
true ^ true; // evaluates to false
true ^ false; // evaluates to true
false ^ false; // evaluates to false
```

The Conditional Logical Operators

The conditional logical operators, OR (||) and AND (&&), work similar to the logical operators, but do not guarantee the evaluation of the second operand if the result of the expression can be determined solely on the basis of the value of the first expression. This is known as *short-circuit boolean logic*.

While there are three logical operators, there are only two conditional logical operators OR (||) and AND (&&). This is because the XOR operation always must evaluate both operands in order to evaluate the logical expression.

The conditional OR (||) evaluates to a logical true if the first operand is true, in which case the second operand is not evaluated. This is because the first operand has already determined the value of the expression, and the value of the second operand is irrelevant. If the first operand is false, the second operand is evaluated, and a logical true is returned if the second operand is true; otherwise, a value of false is returned.

The conditional AND (&&) evaluates to false if the first operand is false, since the entire expression must be false regardless of the value of the second operand. If the value of the first operand is true, the second operand is evaluated, in which case the expression is evaluated to a logical true if the second operand is also true.

This is demonstrated in the following example:

```
true || false; //evaluates to true, second operand ignored
true || true; // evaluates to true, second operand ignored
false || true; // evaluates to true, second operand evaluated
false || false; // evaluates to false, second operand evaluated
true && false; //evaluates to false, second operand evaluated
true && true; // evaluates to true, second operand evaluated
false && true; // evaluates to false, second operand ignored
false && false; // evaluates to false, second operand ignored
```

The conditional logical operators can improve performance, since the second operator is not always evaluated. However, the use of conditional operators can have a significant impact on your applications if one or both operands are methods that return boolean expressions. If these methods perform some processing, change the values of variables, or otherwise affect other objects, the use of conditional logical operators may result in a method used as a second operand not being called due to the value of, or the value returned by, the first operand.

While you may want to use conditional logical operators specifically to conditionally execute a method appearing as the second operand, you should do so only after considering the alternatives. In general, producing side effects conditionally based on conditional logical operators tends to obscure your intended results, making the code harder to read and maintain.

The Boolean Conditional Operator

The boolean conditional operator (? :) can be used as a boolean type in the same manner that it can be used as an integer, floating point, and reference type. Like the corresponding operators for the other types, the boolean conditional operator requires a boolean type as the first operand. However, both of the remaining operators are boolean, and the resulting value of the expression is boolean.

The boolean conditional operator is rarely used with simple boolean constants as the second and third operands, since this same effect can be achieved using one boolean constant, or the logical complement operator and a single boolean constant. In most cases, the second and third operands contain expressions including one or more values of any type in addition to operators that evaluate to a boolean type.

The Boolean String Concatenation Operator

Boolean types, like all other types, can be used in conjunction with a *String* object using the string concatenation operator, +. The result is a *String* object where either the value "true" or "false" is concatenated with the original string. This is demonstrated in the following code segment, which assumes that there is a *StatusBar* object named *statusBar*.

```
Boolean tvalue = true;
Boolean fvalue = false;
statusBar.setText("A Boolean type converts to "+bvalue+" or
"+fvalue);
//The status bar displays "A Boolean type converts to true or
false"
```

Reference Operators

Java specifies a number of operators for use with reference types. As you learned earlier in this appendix, reference types may refer to objects, interfaces, or arrays. The reference operators include field access operators, method invocation operators, cast operators, comparison operators, the reference type operator, and the conditional operator.

Reference Field Access Operators

Fields associated with objects can be used in expressions. The value of the expression is based on the type of the field. For example, if the field is declared to be an int, the resulting type of the field is int. On the other hand, if the field is a reference type, the expression is also a reference type.

Field access is provided using the . operator (a period), typically called a dot. This style of notation, therefore, is referred to as *dot notation*. The left side of the expression identifies the class, object, or interface that the field belongs to, and the right hand side defines the field. For example, to refer to a field named **one** associated with the class *MyClass*, you can use

```
MyClass.one;
```

If the reference to the field is made within a method that belongs to the class, the qualifier—that is, the object name and the dot—can be omitted. For example, from within a method associated with the *MyClass* class, the following statement is equivalent to the preceding one:

```
one;
```

A field can be accessed for a class only if it is declared. For more information on field and class declarations, see Chapter 2.

There are two special qualifiers that can be used in field access operations from within an object. One keyword is **this**, and the other is **super**. The object reference **this** refers to the object to which the executing method is attached. Consequently, in most cases, the following two statements are equivalent:

```
one;
this.one;
```

The **super** keyword is used to refer to fields of the current object as defined by its immediate ancestor class—that is, the class from which it inherits.

Reference Method Invocation Operators

Any method, other than one that is declared as void can be used in an expression. The type of the expression is based on the type returned by the method. Otherwise, method invocation is identical to field access as far as reference operations are concerned. Specifically, the dot operator (.) is used to identify the class or interface whose method is being referenced. Also, the special reference objects **this** and **super** can be used with method invocation. For example, using **super** allows an object to invoke methods of the immediate ancestor class that would normally have been overridden by methods declared in the class to which the object belongs.

Reference Cast Operators

Cast operations are permitted between an object reference and a type, so long as the object being cast descends from the type it is being cast to, or descends from a class that implements the interface to which it is being cast. In other words, an object can only be cast to its own class, one of its superclasses, or an interface that it or one of its superclasses implements.

While the cast operators for primitive types use special reserved casting operators, reference types are cast using the name of the class to which the object is being cast. For example, an object being referenced by a variable of type *Component* can be cast to the type *Button*, given that the object being pointed to is a *Button* or a *Button* descendant. The following code example demonstrates how a *Component* can be cast as a *Button*. Note, however, that the object being referenced by the component variable is created by the *Button* constructor. Consequently, the cast will work.

```
Component thisObject1 = new Button();
Button b;
b = (Button)thisObject1;
```

As must be obvious, the type of a cast is the type to which the reference was cast. For example, in the preceding example the variable *b* is of the type *Button*, which is possible because *thisObject1* is a *Button* type. Furthermore, only operations that are valid for the type of the cast are acceptable following the cast. For example, if instead of casting *thisObject1* to *Button* it was cast to *Component* (which is possible, but would not really make sense), it would not be possible to reference fields or methods not available in the *Component* class from the variable *b*. For example, after casting the *theObject1* to *Component*, the following statement would generate a compiler error, since the *setLabel()* method is introduced in the *Button* class, and does not exist in the *Component* class.

```
b.setLabel("New label");
```

The Reference Type Operator

The class membership of a reference type is very important in Java, as well as most other object-oriented languages. This is because it is possible to cast a value of one reference type to the type of one of its superclasses. In order to permit your code to test whether such a cast can be undertaken, and at the same time assure that a reference type refers to an instantiated object as opposed to the value **null**, Java includes the **instanceof** reference operator.

The execution of an **instanceof** expression either produces a boolean value or throws an exception. The first operand of **instanceof** must be a reference type. The second operand must be a class name. If the first operand is not **null** (by failing to point to an instantiated object) and it is possible to cast the first operand to the class specified by the second operator, the result of the **instanceof** operation is the logical true. If the first operator is equal to **null**, the result is a logical false. If the first operand is not a descendant of the type specified in the second operator, the statement is illegal and will cause a compile-time error.

The following code demonstrates the use of the **instanceof** operator. Here, **instanceof** evaluates to a boolean true, since the variable *b* points to an instance of the *Component* class (actually, a descendant class of *Component*).

```
Button b = new Button();
Boolean continue = false;
continue = (b instanceof Component);   //continue = true
```

Now consider an alternative situation where the variable *b* is declared as the type *Button*, but may or may not be initialized prior to the execution of the **instanceof** operator. If, through code logic, *b* is assigned an instance of the type *Button*, the expression:

```
continue = (b instanceof Component);
```

assigns the value true to the variable *continue*. If, on the other hand, *b* has not been initialized, meaning that it is equal to null, continue is assigned the value false.

Reference Comparison Operators

It is possible to have two reference types point to the same object. The reference comparison operators are used to identify whether such a situation exists or not. Unlike numeric equality, which returns a logical true if two primitive reference types contain the same values, reference equality requires that the two reference types refer to the same instance of an object.

There are two reference equality operators: equals (==) and not equals (!=). Both result in a boolean expression.

If both the first and the second operand are references to the same object, the == operator returns a logical true; otherwise, false. If the two reference objects refer to two different objects, even if the two objects are identical in every way (for example, they are instances of the same class, and the value of every one of their fields matches), the == operator returns a logical false.

Likewise, if two reference types point to two different objects, regardless of their class membership and field values, a comparison using the not equals operator (!=) evaluates to a logical true; otherwise, it returns false. Consider the following code segment:

```
Button b1 = new Button();
Button b2;
Button b3 = new Button();
Boolean thesame = false;
b2 = b1; //b1 and b2 refer to the same object
thesame = (b1 == b2); //thesame is true
thesame = (b1 != b2); //thesame is false
thesame = (b1 == b3); //thesame is false
thesame = (b1 == b3); //thesame is true
```

The Reference Conditional Operator

Whereas the numeric conditional operator returned a value of a numeric type based on a boolean expression, the reference conditional operator returns an object reference, again based on a boolean expression. The first expression is a condition—that is, a logical true or false. The second and third expressions are reference types. If the boolean expression evaluates to true, the first object (the second operand) is returned. Likewise, if the boolean expression evaluates to a logical false, the second object (the third operand) is returned.

Literals

Literals are explicit representations of data in Java source code. These values are useful when initializing variables, or for use in expressions where an exact and unchanging value is required.

Literals can be used to explicitly reference each of the following types: int, long, float, double, boolean, char, *String*, and null. In those cases when you need to represent another primitive type not listed, you can cast a literal to the type you want. You cannot represent an object using a literal, and therefore there are no literal reference types.

Integer Literals

Integer literals are denoted by a value that consists of only numbers and contains no decimal places. If the number does not begin with a 0, with the exception of the literal value for zero, the number represented is a decimal number (base 10). Long literals are denoted in a style similar to int literals, with the exception that the number terminates with the letter l (lowercase) or L (uppercase). While technically not prohibited, you should really never denote a long literal using the lowercase letter l, since this letter is easily confused with the numeral 1.

In addition to being represented in decimal format, integer literals can also be defined using octal and hexadecimal notation. Octal numbers are represented with a leading zero (0), followed by the number represented by the numerals 0 through 7. Hexadecimal numbers are represented by a leading 0x or 0X, followed by the numerals 1 through 9 and the letters A, a, B, b, C, c, D, d, E, e, F, or f. Octal and hexadecimal literals are assumed to be of the primitive type int, unless they are followed by the letter l or L, in which case they denote a long integer.

The following are examples of literal int and long literals:

```
int a = 1001; //int type
long b = 1001L; //long type
a = 10928795; //int type
a = 053; //int type in octal. Equal to 43 decimal
b = 053L; //long type, expressed in octal
a = 0X002B; //int type in hexadecimal. Equal to 43 decimal
b = 0X002BL; //long type in hexadecimal. Equal to 43 decimal
```

While the char type is an integer type, it is special in that it is designed to hold unicode characters. Unicode characters are similar to ASCII characters in that they are designed to represent symbols, numbers, and characters. The range of the char type, however, is much greater, permitting it to represent characters from nearly all the world's languages. In fact, the first 127 characters of the unicode character set match the ASCII character set, character for character.

Literals of the type char can be represented in one of two ways. One way is to enclose a single character in single quotation marks. The second way is to use a special escape sequence, which is particularly valuable for represented characters that you cannot type from your keyboard. The escape sequence is represented by a backslash followed by a three-digit octal number, or backslash and the letter u followed by a four-digit hexadecimal number. Using the four-digit hexadecimal version permits you to represent the entire 16-bit unicode character set. The escape sequence must be enclosed in single quotation marks.

A

Java also defines a series of special escape sequences, which are used for representing many of the most common ASCII characters that either cannot be entered from a keyboard or would otherwise be ambiguous. Examples of these characters include the TAB character, the line feed, and the backslash character. Table A-6 lists the special escape sequences.

Escape Sequence	Character
\\	Backslash
\'	Single quotation mark
\"	Double quotation mark
\b	Backspace
\f	Form feed
\n	Line feed
\r	Carriage return
\t	Tab
\uFFFF	Unicode escape

Special Escape
Sequences
Table A-6.

The following code segment demonstrates the use of char literals:

```
char c;
c = 'a'; //A lowercase letter a
c = '\\'; //A backslash character
c = 'A'; //An uppercase letter A
c = '\u0041'; // An uppercase letter A in hexadecimal
c = '\u101'; // An uppercase letter A in octal
```

Floating Point Literals

Floating point literals are denoted by a numeric value that includes at least one decimal place. Specifically, the literal 1 is an int value, while the value 1.0 is a floating point value. Unless otherwise specified, all floating point literals are of the type double. Floating point literals must begin with either a sign, a numeral, or the decimal operator (.). If the initial character is not a sign or decimal operator, the remaining digits may be any decimal numeral or the decimal operator. One, and only one, decimal operator must appear in a floating point literal.

Floating point literals of the type float must be denoted by following the least significant decimal with the letter f or F. For clarity, you may also denote literals of the type double by following the least significant digit with the letter d or D.

Floating point literals may also be expressed in *exponential notation*, sometimes called *scientific notation*. Exponential notation specifies a floating point number using two parts, the *mantissa* and the *exponent*. The mantissa is a floating point number with one significant digit and some number of decimals. The number of decimal places in the mantissa is limited by the type of the floating point number. The second part is called the exponent, and it denotes the power of 10 to which the mantissa will be raised. The mantissa and the exponent are separated by either the letter e or E. If the exponent is a positive number, it indicates how many positions the decimal point of the mantissa should be shifted to the right; if the exponent is a negative number, it specifies how many decimal places the decimal point should be shifted to the left.

Consider the following numbers:

```
double a = 1.2345E+3; //a equals 1234.5
a = 1.2345E-3; //a equals .0012345
```

Exponential notation is typically used to approximate very large or very small numbers. Because all of the significant decimal places are rarely specified when exponential notation is used, their use typically results in a loss of precision.

String Literals

String literals are represented by a sequence of printable characters enclosed in double quotation marks. A single string literal can be formed by concatenating two or more string literals using the concatenation (+) operator. The string literal may include printable characters, escape sequences using octal or hexadecimal numbers, or any of the escape sequences listed in Table A-6. Escape sequences, when used, must be enclosed in double quotation marks. If they are embedded within a string literal—that is, they appear within a double-quoted sequence of characters—this requirement is satisfied.

The following code segment contains some examples of string literals:

```
String s;
s = "This is a string"; //This is a string
s = "This string includes a \" character";
// This string includes a " character
s = "The letter \u0041"; // The letter A
s = "\u0041"; //A
```

A

Boolean Literals

There are two boolean literals: true and false. Unlike some other languages, Java does not permit you to represent a boolean literal using integer values, such as 0 and -1. However, it is possible, though illogical, to compare two primitive type literals for use as a boolean value using the logical comparison operator (==).

Null Constant

There is no null literal. There is, however, a null constant (**null**) that can be used to explicitly denote the value **null**.

Assignment

Assignment is the process by which the value of an expression is assigned to a variable. The variable being assigned appears on the left side of the assignment operator, and the expression appears on the right. If the expression requires evaluation, this evaluation is performed prior to the assignment. Note that the postfix increment and decrement operators result in assignment prior to incrementing or decrementing the variable used in the expression.

There are two classes of assignment: *simple* and *complex*.

Simple Assignment Operator

The simple assignment operator (=) evaluates the expression on the right-hand side of the operator and assigns it to the variable (or field) on the left-hand side of the operator. If the expression and the variable are not assignment compatible, the expression may need to be cast to an appropriate type prior to assignment. If the variable and expression are not assignment compatible, and the expression cannot be cast to a compatible type, a compiler error results.

Simple assignment can take place as part of a variable declaration. For example, the following variable declaration declares an int variable, and assigns the value 0 to it.

```
int a = 0;
```

Simple assignment can also take place any time after the variable is declared. For example, consider the following statement:

```
Button okButton;
//one or more statements here
okButton = new Button();
```

In this simple assignment, a variable of the reference type *Button* is declared. Later, a new button is created and it is assigned to the variable.

Complex Assignment Operators

In complex assignment, the variable that appears on the left-hand side of the complex assignment operator participates in the expression that is assigned to it. There are 11 complex assignment operators. These are +=, -=, *=, /=, %=, <<=, >>=, >>>=, |=, &=, and ^=.

These operators perform the following three steps:

1. The expression on the right-hand side of the operator is evaluated.
2. The operation, denoted by the first character of the assignment symbol, is carried out using the variable on the right-hand side of the operator as the first operand, and the evaluated expression as the second operand.
3. The result of the evaluation in Step 2 is assigned to the variable.

Consider the following code segment, which demonstrates this effect:

```
int a = 5;
int h = 3;
a += b; //a is now equal to 8
```

Following the preceding steps, the variable *b* is first evaluated. It is a simple expression, and it evaluates to the integer 3. The second step is to perform the operation defined by the first symbol of the assignment statement, using the variable on the left-hand side of the operator as the first operand and the evaluated expression as the second. In this case, this produces the following expression: *a* + *b*. This expression evaluates to 8. The third step is to assign the result of this evaluation to the variable on the left-hand side of the operator. This assignment is equivalent to the following statement:

```
a = 8.
```

Consider the following example:

```
int a = 5;
int b = 3;
a -= b; //a is now equal to 2
a *= b; //a is now equal to 6
a <<= b; //a is now equal to 48
```

A

Whether a particular complex assignment operator can be used depends on the types of the operands. Specifically, the operands must be compatible with the operation denoted by the first symbol in the complex assignment operator. For example, the += operator can only be performed on types where the + operator is valid, such as integer, floating point, and String types. Likewise, the operator >>>= is only valid with integer types, since this is the only type that allows unsigned right bit-shifting. In most cases, assignment operators are not used with reference types, since the various operators (-, %, >>, and so forth) are not valid with reference types.

There is one exception to the prohibition of reference types in complex assignment operations. Specifically, the += operator is permitted when the left-hand operand is a String object and the right-hand operator is of any other type (even a reference type). In these instances, the + operation is concatenation, and the right-hand operand is automatically converted to a String using the appropriate *toString()* method.

Order of Evaluation

When all else is equal, Java evaluates expressions in a strictly left-to-right order. Certain operators, however, do have precedence over others, meaning that some operations are performed before others. When an expression contains operators that have the same precedence, the left-to-right processing holds. When an expression contains two operators and one has a higher precedence than the other one, the operation with the higher precedence is performed first, even if the lower-precedence operator appears to its left.

The highest order of precedence is provided by parentheses. Specifically, any expression contained within parentheses will be evaluated first, prior to the resulting expression being used in conjunction with any other operator.

It should also be noted that when an expression is an operand of a more complex expression, all operands of the expression are evaluated prior to the evaluation of the containing expression. The one exception to this is the condition operators (||, &&, and ?:).

The following contains the order of precedence for Java operators; all operators at the same level have equal precedence:

( )
++, --, + (unary), - (unary), ~, !, (cast)
*, /, %
+, -
<<, >>, >>>
<, >, <=, >=
==, !=

&
|
&&
||
? :
+=, -=, *=, /=, %=, <<=, >>=, >>>=, |=, &=, ^=

The next appendix, Appendix B, introduces Java keywords, and describes
how to use comments and control structures. If you are new to the Java
language, or are interested in a brief review, you should read Appendix B
before you return to the other chapters in this book.

A

APPENDIX B

Java Keywords, Control Structures, and Comments

Keywords are reserved words that have special meaning to the Java compiler. They form the foundation of the Java language. Control structures are keywords that permit you to specify the order of execution of your Java statements. This appendix provides you with an introduction to Java keywords in general, and then discusses the use of some of the keywords that you are likely to use most often.

In particular, the Java control structures are discussed in detail. Finally, using comments in Java source code is described.

As in the preceding appendix, the material presented here is of particular importance if you have little or no previous Java experience, or if you are looking for a quick refresher. If you are interested in these subjects in greater detail than found here, consult one of the excellent texts on the Java language, or review the Java Language Specification, which can be accessed using the JBuilder Help system.

Overview of Java Keywords

Java is very similar to the C++ programming language in a number of ways. First, both languages contain relatively few keywords. Second, Java was designed to be familiar to C++ programmers, and consequently the Java keywords bear a strong similarity to those found in the C++ language.

Table B-1 contains a list of the keywords used in Java.

Note that the list in Table B-1 contains a number keywords that, if used in your code, will either be ignored, or will generate a compiler error. These keywords are **byvalue**, **cast**, **const**, **future**, **generic**, **goto**, **inner**, **operator**, **outer**, **rest**, and **var**. They are not currently used by Java, but

abstract	boolean	break	byte
byvalue	case	cast	catch
char	class	const	continue
default	do	double	else
extends	final	finally	float
for	future	generic	goto
if	implements	import	inner
instanceof	int	interface	long
native	new	operator	outer
package	private	protected	public
rest	return	short	static
super	switch	synchronized	this
throw	throws	transient	try
var	void	volatile	while

Keywords
Used in Java
Table B-1.

are included as reserved words in order to provide you with better error detection during compile time.

Many of these keywords are introduced throughout this book. There is, however, a category of keywords that is essential for controlling the execution of your code. These keywords are collectively referred to as *control structures*. Because the use of control structures is so basic, this appendix provides you with an introduction to this important category of keywords.

Control Structures

There are two general types of control structures, *branching* control structures and *looping* (or iterative) control structures. In Java, the **if**, **switch**, and **try** statements are branching control structures, while the **for**, **while**, and **do** statements are looping control structures.

Some of these control structures support the keywords **break** and **continue**. These keywords can be used either with or without labels. In the discussion of the control structures that follows, the use of **break** and **continue** is assumed to be unlabeled. The use of *labeled* **break** and **continue** statements is discussed later in this appendix.

Branching Control Structures

Java supports three types of branching control structures: **if**, **switch**, and **try**. Branching control structures permit you to conditionally execute Java statements. That is, Java statements that you enter may or may not be executed during runtime, based on the value of a boolean expression, referred to as a condition.

The if Statement

You use the **if** statement to conditionally execute a statement. The **if** statement has the following syntax:

```
if  (condition) statement;
```

If the condition evaluates to true, the statement is executed. If the condition evaluates to false, the statement is skipped. The following is an example of an **if** statement:

```
if (counter <= 0) counter = 0;
```

B

If you want to execute two or more statements conditionally, enclose them in curly braces. For example:

```
if (buttonvar == null) {
  buttonvar = new Button();
  buttonvar.setLabel("Close");
}
```

Using an else Statement with if

The **if** statement can also include an **else** clause. When it does, the **if** statement has the following syntax:

```
if (condition) statement;
else statement;
```

If the condition evaluates to true, the statement following the condition is executed. If the condition evaluates to false, the statement following the **else** keyword is executed. If you want to conditionally execute more than one statement in either the **if** or the **else** part, enclose the multiple statements within curly braces.

The following statement demonstrates the use of an **if...else** control structure, where each part has multiple statements:

```
if (a < 10) {
  doSomething();
  doAnotherThing();
}
else {
  statementNotTrue();
  moreToDo();
}
```

Nesting if Statements

It is possible to nest one **if** statement within another. While this is an important technique, permitting you to execute one **if** statement only when the preceding **if** statement's condition evaluates to true, confusion can arise when one of the two **if** statements includes an **else** statement, but both do not. The reason for the confusion is that it is sometimes difficult to determine to which **if** part a particular **else** part belongs. If the **if** statements are nested more than two levels, and some but not all include **else** statements, the problem is compounded.

Java resolves this issue by associating an **else** part with the closest **if** statement to which it can possibly belong. Therefore, in the following **if** statement, the **else** part belongs to the inner **if** statement:

```
if (a == b)
  if (a > c)
    doSomething();
  else
    doSomethingElse();
```

In this code segment, the method *doSomethingElse()* is executed if *a* is not equal to *b*, and *a* is equal to or less than *c*. If you wanted to associate the **else** part with the outer statement in the preceding code segment, you can do so by enclosing the inner **if** statement in curly braces. The braces denote a complete block, and the **else** can therefore not belong to the inner **if**. The following demonstrates this effect:

```
if (a == b) {
  if ( a < c )
      doSomething();
  }
else
  doSomethingElse();
```

In this case, the method *doSomethingElse()* is executed when *a* is not equal to *c*.

The switch Statement

The **switch** statement permits you to execute one or more statements based on the value of an expression. The **switch** statement has the following syntax:

```
switch (expression) {
  case constant_expression1 : one or more statements;
  //one or more additional case statements
}
```

When Java executes a **switch** statement, it compares the value of the switch expression with the constant expressions associated with each of the **case** statements, beginning with the first **case** statement. If a **case** statement is found whose corresponding value matches that of the switch condition, the statements associated with that **case** statement are executed. If there are one or more **case** statements following the one that produced a match, statements associated with the remaining **case** statements are also executed.

B

The type of the switch expression must be one of the following: byte, char, int, or short. The value of the constant expressions must be assignment compatible with the type of the switch expression. The constant expressions can either be literals or final variables, or operations performed on one or more literals and/or final variables, so long as those operators evaluate to a primitive type that is assignment compatible with the type of the switch expression.

The following example demonstrates the use of the **switch** statement:

```
String numberToWord(int k) {
    String s = "None";
    switch (k) {
      case 1: s = "one"; break;
      case 2: s = "two"; break;
      case 3: s = "three"; break;
      case 4: s = "four"; break;
      case 5: s = "five"; break;
      case 6: s = "six"; break;
      case 7: s = "seven"; break;
      case 8: s = "eight"; break;
      case 9: s = "nine"; break;
      case 0: s = "zero";  break;
    }
    return s;
  }
```

Note the use of the **break** statement. This statement prevents the **switch** statement from processing the additional **case** statements once a match is found. By comparison, if you used the following **switch** statement:

```
String numberToWord(int k) {
    String s = "None";
    switch (k) {
      case 1: s = "one";
      case 2: s = "two";
      case 3: s = "three";
      case 4: s = "four";
      case 5: s = "five";
      case 6: s = "six";
      case 7: s = "seven";
      case 8: s = "eight";
      case 9: s = "nine";
      case 0: s = "zero";
    }
    return s;
  }
```

any call to this method in which a single-digit integer is passed in the actual parameter will return the *String* "zero." This occurs because once the match is found, the statements associated with the remaining **case** statements are also executed. The last one of these:

```
s = "zero";
```

defines the return value.

Using a default Statement

So long as the **break** keyword appears after each **case** statement, no statements will be executed within the **switch** if none of the **case** statements matches the switch expression exactly. However, if you include a **default** statement in your **switch**, you can define one or more statements that will be executed even when none of the constant expressions matches the switch expression.

The following is an example of a **switch** statement that employs a **default** clause:

```
String numberToWord(int k) {
    String s = "None";
    switch (k) {
      case 1: s = "one"; break;
      case 2: s = "two"; break;
      case 3: s = "three"; break;
      case 4: s = "four"; break;
       case 5: s = "five"; break;
      case 6: s = "six"; break;
      case 7: s = "seven"; break;
      case 8: s = "eight"; break;
      case 9: s = "nine"; break;
      case 0: s = "zero";  break;
      default: s = "Not a single, positive digit";
    }
    return s;
  }
```

In this situation, the *numberToWord()* method returns a *String* with the value "Not a single digit" if *k* is either a negative number or a number greater than 9. It is important to note two characteristics about this code sample. First, if the individual **case** statements did not include the **break** keyword, *numberToWord()* would always return "Not a single, positive digit." Also, the **default** clause should appear as the last statement within the **switch** statement, and therefore does not require a **break** statement. To put this another way, including a **break** statement as the last statement in a

B

default clause would have no influence on the **switch** statement, since the **switch** statement terminates immediately following the **default** clause anyway.

The try Statement

Unlike the **if** and **switch** branching control structures, which are used to control the flow of code logic based on the value of an expression, the **try** statement controls program flow in response to thrown exceptions. An exception is an error that occurs at runtime. It is either generated by the Java Virtual Machine (VM) in response to an unexpected condition or it is generated by your code as a result of executing a **throw** statement.

A **try** statement includes a single **try** block, zero, one or more **catch** blocks, and an optional **finally** block. Following the **try** block, there must be at least one **catch** block, or a single **finally** block. The following is the syntax of this version of the **try** statement:

```
try {
//one or more statements
}
//If a finally block is present, the following
//catch block is optional
catch (ThrowableClass variable) {
//one or more statements
}
//one or more additional catch blocks may appear here
//If no catch blocks are present, the following finally block
//is required. Otherwise, it is optional.
finally {
}
```

There are two distinct purposes for a **try** control structure. The first is to handle one or more types of runtime errors that might occur within the **try** block. This purpose is served by the **catch** blocks. The second purpose is to specify code that is guaranteed to be executed, despite an exception thrown from within the **try** block. Each of these uses of the **try** statement is described in the following sections. But first, it makes sense to introduce what happens if a runtime error occurs outside of a **try** statement.

Understanding Exceptions

An exception occurs for one of two reasons. First, an exception occurs when a runtime error is encountered by the Java VM. In this case, an instance of an exception object is instantiated. (An exception object is any object descending from *java.lang.Throwable*.) Exceptions generated from runtime errors are called *unchecked exceptions,* since it is not possible for the compiler to determine—that is, check—that your code will handle the exception. This is true simply because a runtime error can occur in almost any part of your program, for a multitude of reasons.

Exception classes that descend from *RuntimeException* and *Error* classes are unchecked exceptions. *RuntimeException* classes are thrown by the Java VM when an unexpected condition is encountered during normal execution of your code. Examples include an illegal cast operation, inappropriate use of a null pointer, and referencing an out of bounds array element. *Error* exception classes signal critical problems that typically cannot be handled by your application. Examples of these types of problems include an out of memory error, stack overflow, or a failure in the Java VM.

Second, an exception occurs when a method explicitly throws an object that descends from the class *Throwable.* A throwable object is thrown using the **throw** keyword. The purpose of throwing an exception explicitly in code is to note an unacceptable condition, such as an invalid state or an unacceptable user interaction.

Thrown exceptions are referred to as *checked exceptions* for two reasons. First, the compiler will confirm at compile time that the method includes code that might **throw** an exception of the thrown type or a superclass of the thrown type. (A method never needs to declare unchecked exceptions.) Second, the compiler requires the code that calls such a method to include this call within a **try** … **catch** statement, and provide an appropriate **catch** block to catch the exception.

When an exception is thrown, whether it is a checked or unchecked exception, execution will attempt to immediately branch to the first **catch** statement in the enclosing **try** block whose associated exception class matches the class of the thrown exception, or whose associated exception is a superclass of the thrown exception. If the exception does not occur within a **try** block, or if the **try** block in which the exceptions were thrown does not contain a matching **catch** block, execution of the method or constructor immediately terminates and control returns to the invoker of the method, where this process is repeated. The result is that the method call chain is unwound until a matching **catch** block is found. If no matching **catch** block can be found, the thread containing the thrown exception is terminated.

If a matching **catch** block is found, the **catch** block is executed, and then execution of the method containing the **try** statement that ultimately caught the exception is continued normally. There is one situation under which normal execution does not proceed. That is when a new exception

B

occurs within the **catch** block. In this instance, Java attempts to branch to the first matching **catch** block outside the current **try** statement.

The try ... catch Statement

When writing your code, you might be able to anticipate certain types of errors that identify conditions that your code can respond to, and even sometimes correct. In these instances, you should catch the exception and handle it. You catch a thrown exception by including the statement or statements that might throw the exception within a **try** block, and then create an associated **catch** block that takes some action. A **catch** block is always identified with a particular class of exception.

Recall that a **try** statement may include one or more **catch** blocks. When an exception occurs within a **try** block, Java will test the class of the exception against the declared class of each **catch** block, beginning with the first **catch** block. If the exception class matches the class associated with a **catch** block, or descends from the class associated with a **catch** block, that **catch** block, and only that **catch** block, is executed. Unlike the **switch** control structure, there is no fall through of **catch** blocks, and so **break** statements are not necessary within **catch** blocks. In other words, unlike the **case** statements in a **switch**, once one **catch** block has been executed, no more **catch** blocks can be executed within the same **try**...**catch**, making a **break** statement unnecessary.

Consider the following code segment:

```
try {
  doSomething()
  doAnotherThing()
  doOneMoreThing()
}
catch (BadDateException ex){
  statusBar.setText("Error: "+ex);
}
catch (RuntimeException ex){
  statusBar.setText("Runtime error: "+ex);
}
catch (Exception ex){
    statusBar.setText("General exception: "+ex);
  }
```

In order for this code to be valid, it would be necessary to declare a new class named *BadDateException* that extends *Exception* (or one of its descendant classes). Furthermore, the methods *doSomething()*, *doAnotherThing()*, and *doOneMoreThing()* would need to be declared to throw an instance of *BadDateException*, or a class that descends from *BadDateException*, as well as

Exception. (It is never necessary for a method to declare that it throws either *RuntimeException* or *Error* objects.) If an exception is thrown by one of the three methods in the **try** block, execution will immediately attempt to branch to the **catch** blocks. If an exception of the type *BadDateException* was thrown, or one that descends from *BadDateException*, the first **catch** block would be executed. If a runtime exception occurred that did not descend from *Error*, the second **catch** block would be executed.

Finally, any exception descending from *Exception* would result in the third **catch** block being executed. You should note that the **catch** blocks that appear earlier in the list of **catch** blocks should be associated with more specific exceptions, and those appearing later should be associated with more general exceptions. If you failed to do this—for example, if you placed the **catch** block associated with the *Exception* class first—the block associated with *BadDateException* would never be executed. Such a placement would render the *BadDateException* block *unreachable.* If the compiler determines that a statement is unreachable, it generates a compiler warning.

If an exception descending from *Error*, such as the exception *OutOfMemoryError*, occurred, none of the **catch** blocks would execute, and control would branch to the next outer **try** block. Because your code should not attempt to handler *Error* exceptions, an *Error* exception would likely cause your application to terminate abnormally.

The try ...finally Statement

The use of a **finally** block permits you to define one or more statements that are guaranteed to be executed, whether or not an exception occurs within the **try** clause. Recall that when an exception occurs, an unhandled exception causes control to leave the currently executing method. When this happens, the remaining code in your method does not get executed. However, if you include a **finally** clause, the statement within it will be executed, even if an exception not handled by one of the **catch** blocks occurs within the **try** block.

There are three circumstances under which a **finally** block is executed. When no statements within the **try** block generate an exception, the **finally** block is executed before execution continues onto the remaining statements in the method or constructor. If an exception does occur within the **try** block, what happens next depends on whether the exception is handled by a **catch** block or not. If the exception is handled by a **catch** block, the **catch** block first executes, and then the **finally** block executes. Execution then continues on to the remaining statements in the method.

If an exception is generated within the **try** block, and no **catch** blocks in the **try** statement catch the exception, the **finally** block is first executed,

B

and then execution branches to the next outer **catch** block that catches the exception. Also, if an exception thrown from within a **try** statement is caught by a **catch** block, but statements within the **catch** block throw an exception, execution of that **catch** block immediately terminates, and the **finally** clause will be executed before execution branches to the next outer **catch** block that matches the exception thrown from within the **catch** block. Likewise, if an exception is thrown from within the **finally** clause, execution of the **finally** block immediately terminates, and control branches to the next outer **catch** block that matches the exception thrown from the **finally** block.

The following code segment demonstrates the use of a **finally** block:

```
try {
  doSomething()
  doAnotherThing()
  doOneMoreThing()
}
catch (BadDateException ex){
  statusBar.setText("Error: "+ex);
}
catch (Exception ex){
    statusBar.setText("General exception: "+ex);
  }
finally{
  queryDataSet1.close();
}
```

This example assumes that there is a *QueryDataSet* named *queryDataSet*, and that it might be open. In order to assure that the query is closed before execution continues (whether or not an exception is thrown by the statements in the **try** block), the *close()* method of the *QueryDataSet* is executed within the **finally** block.

Looping Control Structures

You use looping control structures to repeat one or more statements zero, one, or more times. There are three looping control structures in Java: **for**, **while**, and **do**. The number of times that a loop repeats is controlled by a boolean expression.

One major difference between looping control structures and branching control structures is their use of the **continue** keyword. The execution of looping control structures can be controlled by **continue**, while branching control structures cannot. The keyword **break** can also be used with looping control structures, but this usage is not limited to them. The use of both of these keywords is described separately for each looping control structure.

The following sections describe the use of the looping control structures.

The for Loop

You use the **for** loop to repeat a statement zero, one, or more times. If you want to repeat a series of statements, follow the **for** statement with a block. The statements in the block will then be executed zero, one, or more times.

In its simplest form, the **for** keyword is followed by the statement that will be executed repeatedly. The following is the syntax of this simplest form:

```
for (;;) statement
```

In reality, the simplest form would always be followed by a statement block, since the only single statement that would not produce an infinite loop would be the **break** statement (or a method that throws an exception), which would make the loop completely pointless. The following code segment demonstrates the simplest form of the **for** loop, followed by a statement block:

```
int a = 0;
for (;;){
  ++a;
  if (a > 10) break;
}
```

This loop repeats 11 times. On the 11th execution, the **break** statement causes the loop to terminate and execution to continue with the first statement that follows the statement block.

In this example, the variable *a* is initialized in its declaration. This is unnecessary, however, since the syntax of the **for** loop provides for the initialization of a variable, often referred to as the *control variable* (since its value *controls* the execution of the loop). The following is the syntax of a **for** loop with a control variable:

```
for (initializer;;) statement
```

The following **for** loop performs essentially the same operation as the preceding example:

```
int a;
for (a = 1;;){
  ++a;
```

B

```
 if (a > 10) break;
}
```

It is also possible to both declare and initialize a variable in the **for** statement. For example, the preceding code could have included this statement:

```
for (int a = 1;;){
  ++a;
  if (a > 10) break;
}
```

When you declare and initialize a control variable in the initializer part of the **for** statement, the scope of the control variable is limited to the **for** statement block only. Any attempt to use this variable outside of the **for** statement block produces a compiler error.

As you can see in the preceding example, the **if** statement prevented the loop from executing forever by executing the **break** statement when the looping variable exceeded 10. Instead of performing this operation within the **for** statement block, it can be made part of the **for** statement itself. Specifically, the syntax of the **for** loop permits you to declare a condition—that is, a boolean expression—which, when it evaluates to false, causes the automatic termination of the loop. The following is the syntax of this version of the **for** loop:

```
for (initializer; condition;) statement
```

When you use this version of the **for** loop, the variable is initialized when the loop is first entered and the condition is evaluated. If the condition evaluates to false, the **for** statement block is never executed. If the condition evaluates to true, the **for** statement block is executed once, at which time the condition is evaluated again. If it is still equal to true, the statement block is executed again. This sequence repeats until the condition evaluates to false or the statement block executes the **break** keyword, at which point the loop terminates and control branches to the first statement that follows the **for** statement block.

The following demonstrates this version of the **for** loop:

```
for (int a = 1;a<10;){
   ++a;
}
```

Unlike the previous example, this loop executes only 10 times, rather than 11. The reason for this is that when the expression $a < 10$ evaluates to false, the loop immediately terminates. By comparison, the previous loop executed an 11th time, during which it executed the **break** statement.

The final version of the **for** statement includes an *incrementor* in its declaration. The following is the syntax of this version of **for**:

```
for (initializer; condition; incrementor) statement
```

When a **for** loop using this syntax is executed, the initializer is executed when the loop is first entered. If the condition evaluates to a logical true, the **for** statement block is executed. After executing the **for** statement block, the incrementor is executed, the condition is evaluated, and if it evaluates to true, the process is repeated.

The following code demonstrates essentially the same loop as in the previous code examples. This one, however, has no statements in its **for** statement block, since none are needed to produce the effect of the preceding loop. At this point, it becomes clear that this is a ridiculous **for** loop. To be meaningful, at least one statement would need to appear in the **for** statement block:

```
for (int a =1;a<10;++a){
}
```

While these examples have demonstrated **for** loops that increment the control variable, it is just as easy to set up loops in which the control variable decrements. This is done by including a decrementing statement in the incrementor part of the **for** statement. For example, the following loop will execute ten times. When it is done, the value of the variable *a* will be 1:

```
for (a =10;a != 1;--a){
}
```

Also, although all preceding examples show the control variable incrementing or decrementing by a value of 1, it is possible to increment or decrement in other values. For example, if the incrementor included the statement:

```
a += 10
```

the control variable would increment by a value of 10 after each execution of the **for** statement block. For example, the following code segment includes a loop that will execute nine times. When it is through executing, the value of the control variable will be 100.

B

```
int a;
for (a =10;a < 100;a += 10){
}
```

As shown in a code example earlier in this section, the **break** keyword can appear within the **for** statement block. If an unlabeled **break** keyword is executed, the **for** statement is immediately terminated. This termination causes execution to branch to the first statement that follows the **for** statement block without the condition being evaluated again, nor the incrementor being executed again.

A **for** statement block may also include the **continue** keyword. When an unlabeled **continue** is executed, the remaining statements in the **for** statement block are skipped, and execution immediately returns to the **for** statement. Here, the condition is evaluated. If it evaluates to true, the incrementor is executed and the **for** statement block is executed again. If the condition evaluates to false, the **for** loop is terminated and execution branches to the first statement following the **for** statement block.

NOTE: The use of labeled **break** and labeled **continue** statements is covered later in this chapter.

The while Loop

A **while** loop, like the **for** loop, is used to execute a statement or a statement block zero, one, or more times. Unlike the **for** loop, however, the **while** loop does not provide for a control variable. Instead, it is merely the value of a boolean expression that controls whether the **while** statement is executed or not. The following is the syntax of the **while** statement:

```
while (condition) statement
```

Although it is possible to follow a **while** statement with a single statement, most uses of **while** are followed by a statement block. The following code segment includes a **while** loop that executes nine times. Like the preceding code examples, this example uses a simple **while** statement for demonstration purposes only.

```
int a = 1;
while (a < 10) {
  ++a;
}
```

When the **while** loop is executed, the condition is evaluated first. If it initially evaluates to false, the **while** statement block is not executed and execution branches to the first statement following the **while** statement block. If the condition evaluates to true, the **while** statement block is executed, after which control returns to the top of the loop, where the condition is evaluated again. The **while** loop will continue executing the **while** statement block until the condition evaluates to false, at which time execution branches to the first statement following the **while** statement block. If the condition never evaluates to false, and no exception is thrown within the **while** statement block and no **break** statement is executed within the **while** statement block, the **while** loop will execute indefinitely.

Like the **for** loop, a **while** loop can include **break** and **continue** statements. If an unlabeled **break** statement is executed, execution of the **while** loop terminates immediately, the condition is not evaluated, and execution branches to the first statement following the **while** statement block. By comparison, if an unlabeled **continue** statement is executed, the remaining statements in the **while** statement block are skipped and control returns to the top of the loop, where the condition is evaluated. If the condition evaluates to true, the **while** statement block is executed. If it evaluates to false, the **while** statement immediately terminates and execution branches to the first statement following the **while** statement block.

The do Loop

The **do** loop is almost exactly like the **while** loop, with one important distinction. A **do** loop always executes at least one time. By comparison, a **while** loop may not execute at all. The reason that a **do** loop always executes at least once is that the condition that controls execution is evaluated following the execution of the **do** statement block.

The following is the syntax of the **do** loop:

```
do statement while (condition)
```

Like both the **for** and **while** loops, a **do** loop almost always includes more than one statement. Consequently, a statement block generally appears following the **do** keyword.

When a **do** statement is executed, the statement block following the **do** keyword is executed. Then, the condition following the **while** keyword is evaluated. If the condition evaluates to true, control returns to the top of the loop and the **do** statement block is executed again. If the statement evaluates to false, the **do** loop terminates and control continues to the first statement that follows the condition.

B

The following code example demonstrates a simple use of the **do** statement:

```
int a = 1;
do {
   ++a;
} while (a < 10)
```

Like the other two looping control structures, the **do** statement may include the **break** and **continue** keywords. If an unlabeled **break** statement is executed, execution of the **do** loop terminates immediately, the condition is not evaluated, and execution branches to the first statement following the condition. If an unlabeled **continue** statement is executed, control immediately branches to the condition, bypassing any remaining statements in the **do** statement block. The condition is then evaluated. If the condition evaluates to true, control returns to the top of the loop, where the **do** statement block is executed again. If it evaluates to false, the **do** statement immediately terminates and execution branches to the first statement following the condition.

Using Labeled Statements

Labeled **break** and **continue** statements permit you to break or continue a loop. Unlike the unlabeled versions of these statements, however, a labeled **break** or **continue** does not necessarily apply to the nearest—that is, the innermost—loop. On the contrary, a labeled **break** or **continue** permits you to break or continue to a statement in which the current loop is nested. As a result, labeled **break** and **continue** statements provide you with a high degree of control over the flow of your code.

In order to use a labeled **break** or **continue**, you must supply a label for the statement to which you want to break or continue. The label is created by preceding the statement with an identifier followed by a colon. The identifier may be any combination of letters or numbers, but must begin with a letter and cannot contain spaces.

The following sections describe the use of labeled **break** and labeled **continue** statements.

Using a Labeled break Statement

A **break** statement always causes the immediate termination of a loop, normally causing execution to branch to the first statement following the loop. When a labeled **break** statement is used, the loop also terminates immediately, but execution branches to the first statement that follows the labeled statement. This labeled statement may be an outer loop, one that completely encloses the loop in which the labeled **break** statement appears, or it may be a statement block in which the loop is contained. Consequently, the labeled **break** permits your code to skip not only the remaining statements within the inner loop, but statements immediately following the inner loop as well. There is no limit to the number of levels in which a labeled **break** statement can be nested.

The following code segments demonstrates the basic use of the labeled **break**:

```
int i = 0
label1: {
  doSomething()
  while ( i < 100) {
    update()
    ++I;
    if (! doContinue()) break lable1;
  }
  processResults()
}
continueWork()
```

This example shows a statement block labeled **label1**. Within this block are three statements: a method call, a **while** statement, and another method call. Based on a boolean value returned by a method named *doContinue()*, a labeled **break** statement is conditionally executed. If this **break** statement is executed, control immediately branches to the statement that follows the labeled block, which is the method named *continueWork()* in this example. By comparison, if an unlabeled **break** statement appeared instead, execution would have branched only to the statement that immediately follows the **while** statement, which is the call to the *processResults()* method in this code example.

Although this preceding example demonstrated the use of a labeled **break** to break out of a labeled statement block, it is also quite useful with nested loops. For example, in the following example, the labeled **break** statement permits control to immediately branch out of three loops, if necessary:

```
labeledFor: for (;;;) {
  for (int i = 1;;) {
    for (int j = 1;;) {
      processValues(i,j);
      if ( stopProcessing()) break labeledFor;
    }
    prepareNexti();
  }
```

B

```
    prepareNextOuterLoop();

}
doMoreWork();
```

If at any time the method *stopProcessing()* returns a logical true, the labeled **break** causes the immediate termination of three loops, with execution branching to the method called *doMoreWork()*. Without labeled **break** statements, this same program logic would have required that the outer loop contain a **try** … **catch** statement, and that the second outermost loop be located in a called method, and that the innermost loop be located in another method. Within the innermost method, an exception could be thrown, causing a return to the **catch** clause of the outermost loop, which could then execute an unlabeled **break**. The use of such a technique, however, would have produced code that would be more time-consuming to write, as well as more difficult to maintain.

There is one situation where a labeled **break** statement does not immediately branch to the statement following the labeled statement, and that is when the **break** statement appears within a **try** statement that has an associated **finally** block. In that case, executing the labeled **break** statement results in the **finally** block being executed first, before execution continues to the first statement that follows the labeled statement.

Using a Labeled continue Statement

Unlike the labeled **break**, which can be used to break to the end of any statement, the labeled **continue** is only for use with labeled looping control structures. That is, from within a loop nested within another labeled loop, the labeled **continue** statement can be used to immediately evaluate the condition of the outer loop, and if it evaluates to true, continue executing from the top of the labeled loop without executing either the remaining statements in the inner loop or remaining statements within the outer loop. There is no limit to the number of levels that a labeled **continue** statement can be nested.

The following code demonstrates the use of a labeled **continue** statement:

```
topLoop: while ( stuffToProcess() ) {
  beginWork();
  while ( notDone() ) {
    doSomething();
    if ( ! stillNotDone() )  continue topLoop;
    doMoreStuff();
  }
  prepareForNext();
```

```
}
allDone();
```

This demonstration code includes two loops, with one **while** loop nested within another. If the labeled **continue** statement is executed within the inner loop, execution immediately returns to the top of the outer **while** loop, skipping the calls to the *doMoreStuff()* and *prepareForNext()* methods.

As with the labeled **break** statement, if the labeled **continue** statement is executed within a **try** statement that includes a **finally** clause, the **finally** clause is executed immediately before the **continue** is performed.

Comments

Comments are statements within your Java source code that are not compiled by the compiler. Instead, they are used to document what your code is supposed to do, how it does it, and any other information that is pertinent. Judicious use of comments can greatly improve the readability of your code, as well as improve debugging and code maintenance.

There are three types of comments in Java: single-line comments, multiline comments, and documentation comments. In all cases, the JBuilder Editor is capable of displaying comments using a font color, type, and style that differs from executable code, permitting you to quickly distinguish comments from executable statements. By default, comments appear in a blue, italic font. These settings can be changed from the Colors page of the Environment Options dialog. To display this dialog, select Tools|IDE Options.

Single-Line Comments

A single-line comment is indicated by two slashes (//). The compiler ignores every character from the beginning of the comment to the end of the current line. Single-line comments are generally used when only a short description is necessary. If a single-line comment appears on the same line as code, any code to the left of the // characters is still compiled.

Because single-line comments can coexist on the same line as code, they are particularly important for entering brief phrases or descriptions concerning the accompanying statement. They are also useful for temporarily removing one or more lines while testing and debugging your Java programs. The use of single-line comments in code is demonstrated in the next section.

B

Multiline Comments

A multiline comment begins with the /* character pair, and is concluded by the */ character pair. The compiler ignores everything between these matching pairs, with the exception of the */ characters, which the compiler recognizes as the end of the comment.

Multiline comments are ideal for providing an extended description of a class or a code segment that follows. They are also useful for temporarily disabling two or more lines of code.

You cannot embed one multiline comment within another. If you attempted to do so, the compiler would interpret the closing */ of the inner comment as the terminator of the outer comment. This would most likely cause a compiler error when the compiler tries to compile the remaining part of the outer comment. Single-line comments can be embedded within a multiline comment. However, since the compiler ignores all characters within a multiline comment, with the exception of the comment terminator, the single-line comment is treated as though it were part of the multiline comment.

The following method demonstrates the use of both single-line and multiline comments:

```
/* uniqueRandomIntegers populates an array with integers
 from 1 to the size of the array, without replacement.
*/
public void uniqueRandomIntegers(int [] d){
  int n;  //use to hold the random number
  int j = 1;  //Counter variable
  Random rn = new Random(); /*initialize the random number
                            *generator
  * This statement requires the java.util package
  * appears in an import statement within this package */
  //initialize the array with -1
  for (int i = 0; i < d.length; i++) {
    d[i] = -1;
  } //for
  //for each element in the array
  for(int i = 0; i < d.length; i++) {
    while (true) { //This loop must include a break
      //Generate a random integer from 1 to array length
      n = (int)(rn.nextFloat() * (float)d.length);
      /* If the element of the array associated with the
       * generated integer has not been assigned a non-zero
       * number yet, assign that element the value of j. */
      if (d[n] == -1) {
        d[n] = j;
```

```
        //increment j
        ++j;
        break; //Exit the while (true) loop
      } // if
    } // while (true)
  } // for
} // uniqueRandomIntegers()
```

Documentation Comments

Java specifies special comment identifiers that can be used to extract the associated comments for documentation purposes. The compiler used to produce this documentation is called *JavaDoc*, and it produces HTML (HyperText Markup Language) files that provide an efficient and effective way to describe the features of a class.

Documentation comments begin with the characters /**, and terminate with the characters */. Within the comment delimiters, you can include simple text, HTML tags, as well as special JavaDoc tags. Documentation comments are multiline comments.

The placement of documentation comments is critical to their correct interpretation by JavaDoc. If you use them, documentation comments should appear immediately preceding the declaration of a class or an interface. If you also want to clarify the various field, method, and constructor declarations, you can place documentation comments prior to them within your source code as well.

By convention, the first line of a documentation comment should be a phrase or sentence that describes the role of the declaration. This description is terminated by a period followed by a space. The text that follows this initial description can include one or more of the following:

♦ Additional descriptive text that explains, clarifies, or expands on the initial description.

♦ Additional text enhanced using HTML tags. These tags can define various styles, including bullet points <B>, line items <LI>, emphasis, <EM>, strong <STRONG>, italics <I>, or any other tags that help improve the readability of the comments. Note, however, that the header tabs <H1>, <H2>, and so on, should be avoided, as these are used by JavaDoc in the resulting HTML file, and their use may reduce the readability of the comments.

♦ One or more lines using special @ tags. These documentation comment tags have special meaning to JavaDoc and are described in the following sections.

B

♦ Following the first line of a documentation comment, each line may be preceded by a spaces, tabs, or the * character. These characters are ignored unless the * character is used in the */ pair, indicating the end of the documentation comment.

The @version Tag

Use the @version tag to identify the version of the class or interface. This optional tag is particularly useful when you anticipate releasing different versions of your classes or interfaces over time, and can lead to easy identification between versions.

The @author Tag

Like the @version tag, the @author tag is an optional tag that can be used to identify the one or more authors of a class or interface. A single @author tag can be followed by one or more author names, or multiple authors can each be identified with individual @author tags.

The @see Tag

Use the @see tag for a class, interface, constructor, method, or variable to identify related resources that might be of use to the user of the documentation. The @see tag can include the name of a related package or class, a specific method or field in a class or interface, or even a URL (Uniform Resource Locator).

To use an @see tag with a class package, simply follow the @see tag with the class name. If the class is in a package you have imported, it is not necessary to include the package name. The following are examples of @see tags that reference classes. In the following example, the java.lang package must be imported in order to reference the *Float* class:

```
@see java.awt.Button
@see Float      //assuming that the java.lang package has been imported
```

In order to specify a particular method or field within a class, you follow the class name with a # sign, followed by the name of the variable or method. If you are referring to an overloaded method, you must include the parameter list so that JavaDoc can accurately identify to which of the methods of the same name you are referring. (An overloaded method is one in which two or more methods within the same class have the same name. This is only valid if they can be distinguished by their parameter lists.)

The @exception Tag

Use the @exception tag when documenting a method or constructor that is declared to throw an exception. The @exception tag is followed by the class of the exception, followed by a description of the reasons why the method or constructor would throw that exception. The exception name may be a fully qualified name, but it does not have to be. Since a given method or constructor may throw a number of different types of exceptions, a given method or constructor may have two or more @exception tags. Each @exception tag may describe only one exception.

The @returns Tag

You use the @returns tag to document class or interface methods that return a value (other than null). Follow the @returns tag with a description of the value returned by the method.

The @param Tag

The @param tag is used to document the parameters of methods and constructors. Each @param tag should be followed by the name or the parameter, followed by a brief description. In most cases, you should include one @param tag for each parameter of a method or constructor, and list them in the same order that the parameters appear in the method parameter list.

The @deprecated Tag

The @deprecated tag is the one tag that affects the compilation of your code. This tag identifies a method or instance variable that should be considered obsolete. When the compiler sees that you have used a method or instance variable that is identified by the @deprecated tag, it displays a warning message.

The @deprecated tag is intended to permit you to compile code designed for earlier versions of Java, while gently reminding you that the current version offers alternative statements that are preferable. Normally, you do not add the @deprecated tag yourself to code, unless you are updating an object you created for an earlier version of Java to a new version.

NOTE: The JBCL documentation was produced using an enhanced version of JavaDoc called JBDoc, created by Borland for JBuilder. JBDoc allows documentation for properties and has other extensions not present in JavaDoc. The use of JBDoc is currently undocumented. Also, JavaDoc cannot be invoked from within JBuilder. Instead, you invoke JavaDoc by running it from the JBUILDER\JAVA\BIN directory installed by JBuilder.

B

APPENDIX C

About the CD-ROM

The CD-ROM that accompanies this book contains a number of files. The two most relevant of these are the JBuilder Professional Publisher's Edition and the code samples from this book. Installing the sample files is described later in this appendix.

If you already have JBuilder Professional installed, do not install the JBuilder Professional Publisher's Edition—you already have everything you need to follow the examples in this book. If you do not own a copy of JBuilder, you should install the JBuilder Professional Publisher's Edition from this book's CD-ROM. This is a fully functional copy of JBuilder Professional. However, it is designed for limited use, and will expire 90 days after you install it. Please read the JBuilder Professional Publisher's Edition license that is displayed when you install this software for more details.

To install the JBuilder Professional Publisher's Edition, insert the CD-ROM into your CD drive, and run the SETUP.EXE file found in SETUP\JBUILDER. Then, follow the instructions to install JBuilder.

For additional information on installing the software from the CD-ROM, read the README.TXT file on the root directory of the CD-ROM using your favorite text file viewer (such as NOTEPAD.EXE).

Installing the Sample Files

This book provides you with an opportunity to create many different JBuilder projects. These projects are intended to give you hands-on experience with the various topics that are discussed. If at all possible, you will want to follow the steps given to create these demonstration projects from scratch.

In case you do not have the opportunity to enter these projects manually, we have included the source code for most of the projects described in the book on the CD-ROM that accompanies this book. The only projects that are absent are those that were created in Chapter 1 and Chapter 2. These projects were intended to give you an opportunity to work with the IDE (Integrated Development Environment), and consequently the completed projects were of little consequence.

If you find that you want to use the source code on the CD-ROM, it is necessary for you to run the provided self-extracting file. Furthermore, you need to observe the following guidelines:

◆ Each of these projects appears in a separate subdirectory. Since some files among projects share identical file names (Frame1.java, for example), it is critical that you maintain these projects in separate directories. The installation program automatically creates these separate subdirectories and stores the appropriate files in them.

◆ At a minimum, these projects should be stored under a directory that appears in your default source path. If you have installed JBuilder in the default directory, and have not modified JBuilder's default source path, this will be the directory c:\JBuilder\myprojects.

The root directory of the CD-ROM contains a file named JBE_CODE.EXE. This is a self-extracting file. By default, it will attempt to create the various project directories in c:\JBuilder\myprojects\osborne\jbecd. If your default source path is set to a value other than c:\JBuilder\myprojects, the installation routine will give you an opportunity to change the directory into which the obsorne\jbecd directories are extracted.

Use the following steps to extract the source files:

1. Execute the filename JBE_CODE.EXE from the CD-ROM. To do this you can double-click this filename from within the Windows Explorer. Alternatively, you move to the root directory of your CD-ROM, and enter the following command line at the DOS prompt:

   ```
   JBE_CODE.EXE
   ```

2. When you run JBE_CODE.EXE, the following screen will be displayed:

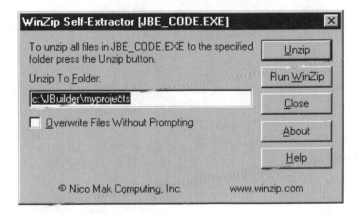

3. If you installed JBuilder into its default directory (c:\JBuilder), leave the Unzip To Folder field set to c:\JBuilder\myprojects. If you installed JBuilder in some other directory, enter the full drive and path to JBuilder's myprojects directory in the Unzip To Folder field. Alternatively, you can enter any directory that you have included in the default source path.

4. Click the Unzip button to unzip the source files into the specified directory.

The self-extracting program will extract the various projects into their corresponding subdirectories. Any required subdirectories that do not already exist will be created for you.

The JBuilder Essentials Web Site

We have established a Web site on the Internet were you can get information about *JBuilder Essentials*. Here you will find Web pages that describe this book's table of contents, where you can order the book, additional code examples, and updated information that corrects any important errors in this book that are identified after this book goes to press.

The general web site for *JBuilder Essentials* is http://idt.net/~jdsi/ jbuilderessentials.html. The general Web site includes a link to the *JBuilder Essentials* Errata. The Errata contains a list of corrections for this book. You should refer to this page if you think you have encountered an error in this book in its code examples. If you believe that you found an unreported error, the Errata page includes an e-mail link, permitting you to report the possible problem. We regret that we will be unable to provide JBuilder technical support via these pages.

Index

F

J

M

Q

To redeem this offer, mail this original coupon (no photocopies, please) along with payment and shipping information to:

Borland International, Inc.
Order Processing
P.O. Box 660005
Scotts Valley, CA 95067-0005

Or call 1-800-932-9994, offer code 1495.

Name _____

Address _____

City _____

State/Province _____ Zip/Postal Code _____

Phone (_____) _____ Fax (_____) _____

Select one:

❏ JBuilder Standard for Windows 95 & Windows NT	CD-ROM	$99.95
❏ JBuilder Professional for Windows 95 & Windows NT (Reg. $799)	CD-ROM	$249.95
❏ JBuilder Client/Server Suite for Windows 95 & Windows NT (Reg. $2,499)	CD-ROM	$1,999.00

Method of payment:

❏ Check enclosed (Make checks payable to Borland International, Inc.)

❏ VISA   ❏ MasterCard   ❏ American Express

Card number: __ __ __ __ - __ __ __ __ - __ __ __ __ - __ __ __ __

Expiration date: __ __ / __ __

Subtotal $ _____

State sales tax* $ _____

Freight ($10.00 per item) $ _____

Total order $ _____

Offer Code 1495

Offer expires October 31, 1998.

This offer good in the U.S.A. and Canada only. International customers, please contact your local Borland office for the offer in your country. Corporate Headquarters: 100 Borland Way, Scotts Valley, California 95066-3249, (408) 431-1000. Internet: http://www.borland.com Offices in Australia (61-2-9248-0900), Canada (905-477-4344), France (33-1-55-23-55-00), Germany (49-6103-979280), Hong Kong (852-2572-3238), Japan (81-3-5350-9380), Latin American Headquarters in U.S.A. (408-431-1126), Mexico (525-543-1413), The Netherlands (+31 [0] 20-503-5100), Taiwan (886-2-718-6627), and United Kingdom (1-[0800] 973139)

Borland International
TRIAL EDITION SOFTWARE
License Statement

YOUR USE OF THE TRIAL EDITION SOFTWARE DISTRIBUTED WITH THIS
LICENSE IS SUBJECT TO ALL OF THE TERMS AND CONDITIONS OF THIS
LICENSE STATEMENT. IF YOU DO NOT AGREE TO ALL OF THE TERMS
AND CONDITIONS OF THIS STATEMENT, DO NOT USE THE SOFTWARE.

1. This Software is protected by copyright law and international copyright
   treaty. Therefore, you must treat this Software just like a book, except
   that you may copy it onto a computer to be used and you may make
   archive copies of the Software for the sole purpose of backing up our
   Software and protecting your investment from loss. Your use of this
   software is limited to evaluation and trial use purposes only.

FURTHER, THIS SOFTWARE CONTAINS A TIME-OUT FEATURE THAT
DISABLES ITS OPERATION AFTER A CERTAIN PERIOD OF TIME. A TEXT
FILE DELIVERED WITH THE SOFTWARE WILL STATE THE TIME PERIOD
AND/OR SPECIFIC DATE ("EVALUATION PERIOD") ON WHICH THE
SOFTWARE WILL EXPIRE. Though Borland does not offer technical support
for the Software, we welcome your feedback.

If the Software is a Borland development tool, you can write and compile
applications for your own personal use on the computer on which you have
installed the Software, but you do not have a right to distribute or otherwise share
those applications or any files of the Software which may be required to support
those applications. APPLICATIONS THAT YOU CREATE MAY REQUIRE THE
SOFTWARE IN ORDER TO RUN. UPON EXPIRATION OF THE EVALUATION
PERIOD, THOSE APPLICATIONS WILL NO LONGER RUN. You should
therefore take precautions to avoid any loss of data that might result.

2. BORLAND MAKES NO REPRESENTATIONS ABOUT THE SUITABILITY
   OF THIS SOFTWARE OR ABOUT ANY CONTENT OR INFORMATION
   MADE ACCESSIBLE BY THE SOFTWARE, FOR ANY PURPOSE. THE
   SOFTWARE IS PROVIDED 'AS IS' WITHOUT EXPRESS OR IMPLIED
   WARRANTIES, INCLUDING WARRANTIES OF MERCHANTABILITY
   AND FITNESS FOR A PARTICULAR PURPOSE OR NONINFRINGEMENT.
   THIS SOFTWARE IS PROVIDED GRATUITOUSLY AND, ACCORDINGLY,
   BORLAND SHALL NOT BE LIABLE UNDER ANY THEORY FOR ANY
   DAMAGES SUFFERED BY YOU OR ANY USER OF THE SOFTWARE.
   BORLAND WILL NOT SUPPORT THIS SOFTWARE AND IS UNDER NO
   OBLIGATION TO ISSUE UPDATES TO THIS SOFTWARE.

3. While Borland intends to distribute (or may have already distributed) a commercial release of the Software, Borland reserves the right at any time to not release a commercial release of the Software or, if released, to alter prices, features, specifications, capabilities, functions, licensing terms, release dates, general availability or other characteristics of the commercial release.

4. Title, ownership rights, and intellectual property rights in and to the Software shall remain in Borland and/or its suppliers. You agree to abide by the copyright law and all other applicable laws of the United States including, but not limited to, export control laws. You acknowledge that the Software in source code form remains a confidential trade secret of Borland and/or its suppliers and therefore you agree not to modify the Software or attempt to decipher, decompile, disassemble or reverse engineer the Software, except to the extent applicable laws specifically prohibit such restriction.

5. Upon expiration of the Evaluation Period, you agree to destroy or erase the Software, and to not re-install a new copy of the Software. This statement shall be governed by and construed in accordance with the laws of the State of California and, as to matters affecting copyrights, trademarks and patents, by U.S. federal law. This statement sets forth the entire agreement between you and Borland.

6. Use, duplication or disclosure by the Government is subject to restrictions set forth in subparagraphs (a) through (d) of the Commercial Computer-Restricted Rights clause at FAR 52.227-19 when applicable, or in subparagraph (c) (1) (ii) of the Rights in Technical Data and Computer Software clause at DFARS 252.227-7013, and in similar clauses in the NASA AR Supplement. Contractor/manufacturer is Borland International, Inc., 100 Borland Way, Scotts Valley, CA 95066.

7. You may not download or otherwise export or reexport the Software or any underlying information or technology except in full compliance with all United States and other applicable laws and regulations. In particular, but without limitation, none of the Software or underlying information or technology may be downloaded or otherwise exported or reexported (i) into (or to a national or resident of) Cuba, Haiti, Iraq, Libya, Yugoslavia, North Korea, Iran, or Syria or (ii) to anyone on the US Treasury Department's list of Specially Designated Nationals or the US Commerce Department's Table of Deny Orders. By downloading the Software, you are agreeing to the foregoing and you are representing and warranting that you are not located in, under control of, or a national or resident of any such country or on any such list.

8. BORLAND OR ITS SUPPLIERS SHALL NOT BE LIABLE FOR (a) INCIDENTAL, CONSEQUENTIAL, SPECIAL OR INDIRECT DAMAGES OF ANY SORT, WHETHER ARISING IN TORT, CONTRACT OR OTHERWISE, EVEN IF BORLAND HAS BEEN INFORMED OF THE POSSIBILITY OF SUCH DAMAGES, OR (b) FOR ANY CLAIM BY ANY OTHER PARTY. THIS LIMITATION OF LIABILITY SHALL NOT APPLY TO LIABILITY FOR DEATH OR PERSONAL INJURY TO THE EXTENT APPLICABLE LAW PROHIBITS SUCH LIMITATION. FURTHERMORE, SOME STATES DO NOT ALLOW THE EXCLUSION OR LIMITATION OF INCIDENTAL OR CONSEQUENTIAL DAMAGES, SO THIS LIMITATION AND EXCLUSION MAY NOT APPLY TO YOU.

9. HIGH RISK ACTIVITIES. The Software is not fault-tolerant and is not designed, manufactured or intended for use or resale as on-line control equipment in hazardous environments requiring fail-safe performance, such as in the operation of nuclear facilities, aircraft navigation or communication systems, air traffic control, direct life support machines, or weapons systems, in which the failure of the Software could lead directly to death, personal injury, or severe physical or environmental damage ("High Risk Activities"). Borland and its suppliers specifically disclaim any express or implied warranty of fitness for High Risk Activities.

BORLAND-AUTHORIZED BOOK PUBLISHER
LICENSE STATEMENT AND LIMITED WARRANTY FOR BORLAND
PRODUCTS

IMPORTANT–READ CAREFULLY

This license statement and limited warranty constitutes a legal agreement ("License Agreement") for the software product ("Software") identified above (including any software, media, and accompanying on-line or printed documentation supplied by Borland) between you (either as an individual or a single entity), the Book Publisher from whom you received the Software ("Publisher"), and Borland International, Inc. ("Borland").

BY INSTALLING, COPYING, OR OTHERWISE USING THE SOFTWARE, YOU AGREE TO BE BOUND BY ALL OF THE TERMS AND CONDITIONS OF THE LICENSE AGREEMENT. If you are the original purchaser of the Software and you do not agree with the terms and conditions of the License Agreement, promptly return the unused Software to the place from which you obtained it for a full refund.

Upon your acceptance of the terms and conditions of the License Agreement, Borland grants you the right to use the Software solely for educational purposes, in the manner provided below. No rights are granted for deploying or distributing applications created with the Software.

This Software is owned by Borland or its suppliers and is protected by copyright law and international copyright treaty. Therefore, you must treat this Software like any other copyrighted material (e.g., a book), except that you may either make one copy of the Software solely for backup or archival purposes or transfer the Software to a single hard disk provided you keep the original solely for backup or archival purposes.

You may transfer the Software and documentation on a permanent basis provided you retain no copies and the recipient agrees to the terms of the License Agreement. Except as provided in the License Agreement, you may not transfer, rent, lease, lend, copy, modify, translate, sublicense, time-share or electronically transmit or receive the Software, media or documentation. You acknowledge that the Software in source code form remains a confidential trade secret of Borland and/or its suppliers and therefore you agree not to modify the Software or attempt to reverse engineer, decompile, or disassemble the Software, except and only to the extent that such activity is expressly permitted by applicable law notwithstanding this limitation.

Though Borland does not offer technical support for the Software, we welcome your feedback.

This Software is subject to U.S. Commerce Department export restrictions, and is intended for use in the country into which Borland sold it (or in the EEC, if sold into the EEC).

LIMITED WARRANTY

The Publisher warrants that the Software media will be free from defects in materials and workmanship for a period of ninety (90) days from the date of receipt. Any implied warranties on the Software are limited to ninety (90) days. Some states/jurisdictions do not allow limitations on duration of an implied warranty, so the above limitation may not apply to you.

The Publisher's, Borland's, and the Publisher's or Borland's suppliers' entire liability and your exclusive remedy shall be, at the Publisher's or Borland's option, either (a) return of the price paid, or (b) repair or replacement of the Software that does not meet the Limited Warranty and which is returned to the Publisher with a copy of your receipt. This Limited Warranty is void if failure of the Software has resulted from accident, abuse, or misapplication. Any replacement Software will be warranted for the remainder of the original warranty period or thirty (30) days, whichever is longer. **Outside the United States, neither these remedies nor any product support services offered are available without proof of purchase from an authorized non-U.S. source.**

TO THE MAXIMUM EXTENT PERMITTED BY APPLICABLE LAW, THE PUBLISHER, BORLAND, AND THE PUBLISHER'S OR BORLAND'S SUPPLIERS DISCLAIM ALL OTHER WARRANTIES AND CONDITIONS, EITHER EXPRESS OR IMPLIED, INCLUDING, BUT NOT LIMITED TO, IMPLIED WARRANTIES OF MERCHANTABILITY, FITNESS FOR A PARTICULAR PURPOSE, TITLE, AND NON-INFRINGEMENT, WITH REGARD TO THE SOFTWARE, AND THE PROVISION OF OR FAILURE TO PROVIDE SUPPORT SERVICES. THIS LIMITED WARRANTY GIVES YOU SPECIFIC LEGAL RIGHTS. YOU MAY HAVE OTHERS, WHICH VARY FROM STATE/JURISDICTION TO STATE/JURISDICTION.

LIMITATION OF LIABILITY

TO THE MAXIMUM EXTENT PERMITTED BY APPLICABLE LAW, IN NO EVENT SHALL THE PUBLISHER, BORLAND, OR THE PUBLISHER'S OR BORLAND'S SUPPLIERS BE LIABLE FOR ANY SPECIAL, INCIDENTAL, INDIRECT, OR CONSEQUENTIAL DAMAGES WHATSOEVER (INCLUDING, WITHOUT LIMITATION, DAMAGES FOR LOSS OF BUSINESS PROFITS, BUSINESS INTERRUPTION, LOSS OF BUSINESS INFORMATION, OR ANY OTHER PECUNIARY LOSS) ARISING OUT OF THE USE OF OR INABILITY TO USE THE SOFTWARE PRODUCT OR THE PROVISION OF OR FAILURE TO PROVIDE SUPPORT SERVICES, EVEN IF BORLAND HAS BEEN ADVISED OF THE POSSIBILITY OF SUCH DAMAGES. IN ANY CASE, BORLAND'S ENTIRE

LIABILITY UNDER ANY PROVISION OF THIS LICENSE AGREEMENT SHALL BE LIMITED TO THE GREATER OF THE AMOUNT ACTUALLY PAID BY YOU FOR THE SOFTWARE PRODUCT OR U.S. $25; PROVIDED, HOWEVER, IF YOU HAVE ENTERED INTO A BORLAND SUPPORT SERVICES AGREEMENT, BORLAND'S ENTIRE LIABILITY REGARDING SUPPORT SERVICES SHALL BE GOVERNED BY THE TERMS OF THAT AGREEMENT. BECAUSE SOME STATES AND JURISDICTIONS DO NOT ALLOW THE EXCLUSION OR LIMITATION OF LIABILITY, THE ABOVE LIMITATION MAY NOT APPLY TO YOU.

HIGH RISK ACTIVITIES

The Software is not fault-tolerant and is not designed, manufactured or intended for use or resale as on-line control equipment in hazardous environments requiring fail-safe performance, such as in the operation of nuclear facilities, aircraft navigation or communication systems, air traffic control, direct life support machines, or weapons systems, in which the failure of the Software could lead directly to death, personal injury, or severe physical or environmental damage ("High Risk Activities"). The Publisher, Borland, and their suppliers specifically disclaim any express or implied warranty of fitness for High Risk Activities.

U.S. GOVERNMENT RESTRICTED RIGHTS

The Software and documentation are provided with RESTRICTED RIGHTS. Use, duplication, or disclosure by the Government is subject to restrictions as set forth in subparagraphs (c)(1)(ii) of the Rights in Technical Data and Computer Software clause at DFARS 252.227-7013 or subparagraphs (c)(1) and (2) of the Commercial Computer Software-Restricted Rights at 48 CFR 52.227-19, as applicable.

GENERAL PROVISIONS

This License Agreement may only be modified in writing signed by you and an authorized officer of Borland. If any provision of this License Agreement is found void or unenforceable, the remainder will remain valid and enforceable according to its terms. If any remedy provided is determined to have failed for its essential purpose, all limitations of liability and exclusions of damages set forth in the Limited Warranty shall remain in effect.

This License Agreement shall be construed, interpreted and governed by the laws of the State of California, U.S.A. This License Agreement gives you specific legal rights; you may have others which vary from state to state and from country to country. Borland reserves all rights not specifically granted in this License Agreement.

8/28/97 6:20:56 PM